Innovation Management

Strategies, Concepts and Tools for Growth and Profit

Innovation Management

Strategies, Concepts and Tools for Growth and Profit

Shlomo Maital | D.V.R. Seshadri

PUBLISHERS & DISTRIBUTORS (P) LTD

7/22, Ansari Road, Darya Ganj, New Delhi
Tel.: +91-11-4077 5252, 2327 3880
E-mail: orders@atlanticbooks.com
Web: www.atlanticbooks.com

Published by Atlantic Publishers & Distributors (P) Ltd 2024

Previously Published by SAGE Publications in 2007

Printed & bound in India by Atlantic Print Services

For Sharona,
Wife, friend, co-author, supporter for 38 years.
For our children and their spouses
Temira and Eli; Ronen and Iris; Yochai; Noam.
For our grandchildren
Tal, Aharon, Maya, Romema, Tuvya, Shoshana, Agam, Tzefanya.
For my country, Israel
For managers everywhere,
who serve their workers, their customers and their shareholders
with energy, integrity and truth.

Shlomo Maital

To the Universal Cosmic Spirit that guides our every breath and thought.
To my Gurus, who have bestowed their torrential flood of blessings and grace, unasked.
To my uncle, Mr D.S. Sastry, who taught me fortitude and resilience by his life.
To my parents, who have made me what I am and guided me at critical junctures in my formative years through their wisdom and sacrifice.
To Prema, my wife of 25 years and my angel daughters, Divya and Nitya who have given me the meaning to persevere and through their acceptance of me as I am, let me pursue my dreams without fetters, and made life's journey celebration and fun.
To my good friends P. Muralidhar and Srinivas Prakhya, who epitomize the attitude of service and were ever ready to help through their sage counsel and unconditional support.
To the many colleagues and managers from various companies with whom I had the opportunity to work and learn over the years.
To my country India, of which I am proud to be a citizen, with a prayer that every one who can make a difference may manifest the values that the nation stands for and help it to rise to its full potential.

D.V.R. Seshadri

Contents

List of Tables

List of Figures

List of Examples and Mini Case Studies

List of Action-Learning Exercises

Preface: Ec, Tec, Exec

Once, there were three tribes. They were known as the Ec, the Tec and the Exec. The Ec were the economists. The Tec were the technologists, or engineers. The Exec were the executives, or managers.

The Ec foretold the future. They were always very dismal about future prospects, but fortunately were almost always wrong.

Some of the Ec set the rules about when the Tec and Exec should open the Strongbox of Capital and use the wealth inside it. It was their rules that said whether the Exec and Tec were doing well or badly.

The Ec were fond of using terms like 'network externalities' and 'weighted average cost of capital' and 'Pareto-efficient resource allocation'. Many of the Exec and Tec found these terms rather mysterious.

The Tec built the future. They used the Strongbox to engage in a very expensive but vital process known as Innovation, which sometimes (though not often) created things that their own and other tribes wanted and needed.

The Exec usually told the Ec and the Tec what to do. They called this Strategy.

The three tribes had common origins, as their names showed. But over time, they came to speak different languages. And they grew distant and unfriendly.

The Tec and the Exec did not like the Ec at all, because they rarely understood what the Ec were saying, even though they sensed it was very important and potentially useful.

The Ec and the Tec did not like the Exec much, because they both felt everyone would be better off if the Exec just left them alone.

The Exec and the Ec were not very fond of the Tec, because they claimed the Tec were much too fond of playing with toys.

An uneasy truce prevailed.

One day, something surprising happened.

'We are tired of being disliked by everyone,' the Ec said. 'We would like to be liked. So we have decided to teach you, the Exec and Tec, our language and our logic. It's actually pretty simple. You'll see—you'll like it.'

The Tec and the Exec were sceptical, but said they would give it a try.

And the results were amazing.

When they had learnt to speak 'Ec', the Tec still played with toys, but the result was wonderful new things that everybody wanted and needed, because the Tec now understood, using the Ec's language and logic, that this was what Innovation was really for. And they were very happy.

The Exec loved the Tec, because by working with the Tec, using the Ec language, they became incredibly prosperous. Their Strategy was simple, focused and got results.

And everyone loved the Ec, because it was their language, tools and ideas that made it all possible.

One day an Exec, aided by a new and rapidly growing sub-tribe known as Em'nay, proposed a merger. Ec, Tec and Exec joined to form one tribe.

We now all speak the same tongue, they said. We will work together to achieve our common goals. Everyone will be better off.

And they did—and they were.

Acknowledgements

First and foremost, special thanks to my friend, colleague and co-author D.V.R. Seshadri. One could not ask for a better collaborator.

For 20 summers I taught in the MIT Sloan School of Management's Management of Technology M.Sc. programme. I owe an enormous debt to MIT, to over 1,000 brilliant engineers from 40 countries whom I taught over the years, and from whom I learned nearly all that I know. Some of the case studies at the end of each chapter in this book were written by them. I am also grateful to MBA students in France, Chile, India and Singapore, on whom the material in this book was tested.

As management professor at Technion-Israel Institute of Technology, Haifa, Israel, and head of its MBA programme, I had the privilege of teaching several generations of creative Israeli engineers, many of whom went on to start their own companies. I greatly value their continued friendship.

I was fortunate to be present when the idea of establishing the TIM-Technion Institute of Management was first broached, in 1987, and am proud to be its Academic Director, serving under our Chair Lester Thurow and CEO Yoram Yahav, both of whom are peerless mentors.

Since 1967, I have lived and worked in Israel. This dynamic little country, younger than me, has given deep meaning to my life and work, a priceless gift. My wife Sharona joined me in the adventure of emigrating to Israel. Wife, friend, mother, colleague, co-author, conversant and, always, partner in adventure, she has been with me through thick and thin; I cannot imagine life without her.

As a citizen of a small, dynamic country, I found the huge dynamic nation, India, fascinating. For me, it is especially meaningful that our book will first be published in this country, and I hope it will contribute to the well-being of India's people.

Our thanks go to our publisher, Sage India, and especially to editor Leela Kirloskar, who quickly grasped the concept of our book and invested immense energy in getting it into print.

To the Creator of the Universe, I offer thanks for the shower of blessings. He has rained down upon me and my family, and commit myself to persistent efforts to do good deeds for others.

Shlomo Maital
Haifa, Israel

My chance meeting with Shlomo Maital at an international conference in Singapore a few years ago sowed the seeds of a great and enduring relationship, one result of which is this book. His intensity and passion in all that he does and his relentless quest for perfection never cease to amaze me. I am grateful to God for giving me a true friend in him.

The Indian Institute of Management, Bangalore, has provided me with a great atmosphere in which to pursue my work and dreams with a high degree of freedom, and I am grateful to the Directors and Deans of the institute for this. My faculty colleagues have helped in many ways and encouraged me while I was establishing myself in my academic career at the institute after my many years in industry. They are too many to name individually and I wish to convey my deep sense of gratitude to each one of them. I would specifically like to thank Professor Mithilesh Jha for believing in me and making my second career as an academic possible, when I badly needed that break. Professor Srinivas Prakhya, my neighbour in the office, gave me free access to his room for ideas, which he generously provided at all times. Many faculty colleagues at IIM Bangalore reposed their faith in me when I was a greenhorn academic over six years ago, and mentored me in my academic career. They are too numerous to name individually, but to each of them I extend my sincere gratitude. In my evolution as an academic I have drawn great inspiration, encouragement and support from Professor James A. Narus of Wake Forest University, and Professor James C. Anderson of the Kellogg School of Management, Northwestern University, both in the USA—they held my hand when I was a toddler in academics.

To my many teachers at various great institutions where I had the opportunity to study, who opened my eyes with their gift of knowledge and infused in me rigour of thought, a strong set of values and the habit of perseverance, I offer my sincerest gratitude. Professors Arabinda Tripathy and P.R. Shukla of the Indian Institute of Management, Ahmedabad—my friends, philosophers and guides over the years—have been gracious in allowing me to partake of their wisdom years after I formally left the institute as their student.

I am grateful to the late B.V. Gopaulakrishna, my first boss at my first job with Madras Refineries Limited, who made a crucial difference in moulding my attitude to work and life, and to the company's then Chairman and Managing Director, V.R. Deenadayalu, who believed in me and gave me so many opportunities. Tata Steel opened its doors to me, so I could study the magic that is unfolding there, and for this I am grateful to its Managing Director B. Muthuraman and his colleagues. Achal Raghavan, formerly Executive Vice President of Ingersoll-Rand India, was always ready to share his vast insights on many occasions. Managers of many other companies have shared their perspectives. Many other managers and participants of various training programmes conducted by me over the years have contributed in helping me to evolve into what I am today. All these experiences with industry have resulted in some of the case studies in this book, and more importantly inculcated in me a strong desire to facilitate the building of bridges between academics and practice.

The Institute for Study of Business Markets (ISBM) India, an affiliate of ISBM USA, has been generous with financial support for making this book possible. Leela Kirloskar of Response Books (Sage India) was a great help; we could not have asked for a better publisher. Her speed and perfection showed us wanting at many times, which prompted Shlomo to comment, 'Move aside, Einstein and your light-speed. We now have Leela-speed.' P. Muralidhar, my friend of 45 years, chipped in by taking care of many of my academic responsibilities during my long days working on this project. Shobitha Hegde and T.A. Krishnamurthy, research assistants, have been a tremendous support. What could we have done without them? Many friends and well-wishers have stood by me over the years. My family has been very indulgent about my wayward ways, including long absences from what was their right to time with me, reconciling instead to what can best described as 'psychic communion'. To all of them and many more whom I have not named here in person, a hearty 'Thank You!'

D.V.R. Seshadri
Bangalore, India

Part I
Strategies and concepts for innovation

Marketplace success → strategy + marketing + production + finance + idea

Chapter 1
The innovation imperative: *Why* innovate?

If you know exactly what you are going to do—What is the point of doing it?

—*Pablo Picasso*[1]

The good-to-great companies at their best followed a simple mantra: 'anything that does not fit with our Hedgehog concept [single simple organizing principle], we will not do. If it doesn't fit, we don't do it. Period.'

—Jim Collins, *Good to Great*[2]

LEARNING OBJECTIVES After you read this chapter, you should understand:

- **The difference between invention, innovation and innovation management**
- **What innovation management is**
- **Why the ability to innovate and innovation management are vital core competencies for every manager**
- **Why innovation should pervade the organization's entire value chain, both direct and indirect**
- **The three reasons why innovation is crucial in order for organizations to survive and thrive**
- **How innovation energizes managers and workers, raises growth and profit, and helps companies survive**

1.1 INTRODUCTION

The ability to innovate is a vital core competency—one that you, as leader, entrepreneur or manager *must* possess, in order to build growing, profitable businesses. At the same time, *managing* innovation is one of the most *difficult* processes that you will guide and shape. It is this combination of high risk and high return, mission-critical importance and Everest-size challenge that makes innovation and innovation management so challenging.

One of the many paradoxes that have innovation at their core is the clash between Pablo Picasso and Jim Collins—the need for free, unfettered creativity, together with the need for focused, systematic discipline—and the overriding imperative to make these two qualities not only co-exist but fall in love and marry. Great organizations score 10 out of 10 on both culture of discipline and creativity. Yet these two dimensions are like wolf and lamb.

The Bible says, 'The wolf and the lamb shall lie down together. "But … they won't get much sleep," commented humorist Woody Allen. Neither will managers trying to reconcile creativity and internal discipline. Judging by Collins' data, few managers fully succeed.

Case study: Pablo Picasso: Creativity and discipline

Picasso is a paradigm of sustained creativity and discipline, without parallel.

He created his first work of art in 1901 and his last in 1973, in the month he died. His life was a 72-year-long stream of pathbreaking ideas. He worked with oil, watercolour, pastels, charcoal, pencil and ink, and he sculpted. A retrospective exhibition of his sculptures at the Pompidou Center in Paris revealed that he never stopped innovating, even at age 90. Yet his real secret was *discipline*. Picasso worked in his studio nearly every single day. He worked incessantly, through the Spanish Civil War and two World Wars and through much turbulence in his personal life. Nobody told Picasso he *had* to work so hard. After he became famous and wealthy, he truly did not need to work. But he did, because he was passionate about art and loved to create, because he loved the *act* of creation, not just its material fruits.

Did Picasso create value? By the market test, he did. His 1905 painting *Garçon a la pipe* (*Boy with Pipe*) was sold at auction in May 2004 for $101 million—a new all-time record for a painting.

Source: Wikipedia (wikipedia.org)

1.2 A KEY FALLACY

Of the many fallacies that surround innovation, perhaps the most damaging is one widely shared by many managers and organizations: 'Innovation is solely what happens in the Research and Development (R&D) centre.' It follows from this that responsibility for innovation lies primarily with the Vice-President (R&D).

Organizations where innovation resides *solely* among R&D engineers are often boring, bureaucratic places to work and rarely sustain growth and profit. *Innovation ought to be a process that pervades every single part of the organization's value chain, as oxygen pervades our atmosphere.* It should drive behaviour throughout the organisation, from R&D to the assembly line, through the customer service centre and down to the mailroom and warehouse.

In your organization, can you imagine a warehouse worker calling up the CEO and saying, boss, why do we *need* a parts warehouse anyway? and explaining how much money could be saved by just-in-time parts deliveries, like the company down the block? And a CEO who will take the call and listen? If you cannot, your innovative culture needs some serious renovation.

DEFINITIONS

Successful *innovation* occurs when an *invention*, related to a product, service or process in some part of the organization's *value chain*, is joined with a *business design*, which in turn is implemented with discipline and skill through *innovation management*.

- **Invention: The creation of novel services, products and production techniques.**
- **Innovation: 'The practical refinement and development of an original invention into a usable technique or product;' or, a process in which creativity is applied to every facet of an organization's value chain, from beginning to end, to develop new and better ways of creating value for customers.**
- **Innovation management: The process of creating and implementing a business design surrounding a creative idea, with the goal of transforming an invention into an innovation, and ultimately to achieving sustained competitive advantage, leading to growth and profit, in the marketplace (see Figure 1.1).**
- **Value chain: The series of related actions, processes and steps required to bring the finished product or service to the ultimate consumer; for example, for the PC industry: product design, acquisition of components, assembly, testing, shipping, customer service and maintenance. An organisation has an *internal value chain* comprising the processes the organisation employs to get its product to market; the industry has a more comprehensive *industry value chain*, that shows all the various processes and products that create value for the ultimate customer.**
- **Business design: An integrated system showing how to create an internal value chain—finance, produce, market, deliver, advertise and service a product or service innovation—and then implement and manage that system, down the value chain, in order to delight the customer.**

The ultimate goal of innovation is *sustained* competitive advantage. Sustained competitive advantage necessarily requires sustained innovation. To bring an innovation to market, companies conceive an invention and create

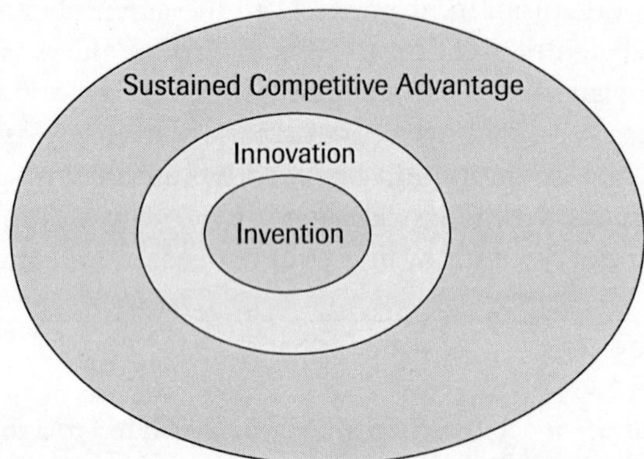

Inventions become innovations when they are refined in a manner that brings them successfully to market. Innovations create sustained competitive advantage when they are implemented in a manner that creates and sustains significant added value for customers above that created by competitors.

Figure 1.1
From invention through innovation to sustained competitive advantage

a 'value chain' around it. Consider some of the key links in a typical direct, or operational, chain of value that brings winning products and services to the consumer: R&D, production, supply chain management, quality assurance, customer service. And in the indirect or supporting value chain: human resource management, finance, strategy, marketing, sales.

To build profitable, in-demand products from appealing new ideas, it is necessary to *manage* the innovative process—that is, wrap an innovative business design or model (how to finance, produce, market, deliver, advertise and service) around a product or service innovation, and then manage that process, down the value chain to the ultimate consumer (see Chapter 5 for a discussion of business models).

Often, innovative products are encased in conventional business models that do not fit the product innovation itself. For example, bringing the MP3 player iPod to market as a stand-alone product would have failed. Instead, the iPod innovation of Apple was part of a large ecosystem or business design that included 99-cent music downloads. Without that key element in the business design, the demand for the iPod would have been substantially smaller.

This is why we argue that *in the term 'innovation management', the noun 'management' is as important as, or more important than, the adjective 'innovation'*. Frequently entrepreneurs break the rules, ask insightful questions, and come up with phenomenal inventive ideas, but fail to ask the three key questions:

- How will I build a business around this idea?
- How will I make money?
- How will I sustain growth and profit?

Lest the reader fears we are preaching unbridled greed let us explain the issue: in our experience, few successful entrepreneurs are driven mainly by greed or by the desire to become extremely wealthy. The ones who are, usually fail. However, unless their organizations achieve sustained growth and profit, they will not survive, the innovations they bring to society will shrivel and disappear, and the jobs that come with them will evaporate. Money is to organizations what oxygen is to living cells. It sustains life. That is how innovators tend to regard money—it enables them to continue inventing and innovating; without it, innovation would grind to a halt.

'Successful strategy is 10 per cent *formulation* and 90 per cent *implementation*,' a senior manager from the information management and storage firm EMC[2] told us. Surely this lesson was learned the hard way from the key management discipline of competitive strategy. Michael Porter's powerful 1980 book *Competitive Strategy* created a new management discipline with the same name.[3] Business schools rushed to develop core compulsory courses in strategy. Companies hurried to appoint Vice-Presidents in charge of strategy. It took a long time for organizations to realize that the key to successful competitive strategy was not the strategy itself *but how that strategy was implemented and managed*.

Harvard Business School professor Robert Kaplan claims companies need a VP (Strategy Implementation). The same principle applies to innovation: '10 per cent innovation; 90 per cent innovation management.' Unfortunately, the reverse proportion holds true in many organizations.

Why are innovation and innovation management so vital? We believe there are *three key reasons* to innovate:

1. Energize your people
2. Build growth and profit
3. Survive

We will now explain each reason more fully.

1.3 INNOVATION TO ENERGIZE

One of the most important answers to the question, *why* innovate? is this: *To energize your existing people and to attract great new ones.* If your organization's competitive advantage is driven by its great people—and in today's global world, nearly all successful organizations fit that description—then it must be innovative, because great people love to think up, develop and implement new ideas. Organizations that do not innovate quickly lose their innovative people. They migrate to organizations that *do* welcome and encourage such people and allow their talents full expression.

> In 2003, 73 per cent of CEOs indicated that they thought of leaving their job. In 2000, the proportion was only 54 per cent. Stress? Pressure? Uncertainty? Certainly, but also boredom and lack of challenge. We believe a far lower proportion of CEOs consider quitting dynamic, innovative, creative organizations.
>
> Warren Buffet, the 75-year-old legendary head of the $133 billion holding company Berkshire Hathaway, 13th on the US Fortune 500 list in 2005, was once asked when he planned to retire.
>
> 'Two years after my death,' he replied. 'Plans I put in place will last for two years after I am gone.' Does Buffet love what he is doing? There is no question. He is a constant innovator and original thinker.[4]

Change society

'We innovate,' notes an IBM report, 'when a new thought, technology, business model or service actually changes society.'[5] Innovation changes the organization and this change can be initiated *anywhere* in an organization, even at the lowest levels.

Ideas can sprout anywhere and everywhere, but the question is: *Does senior management listen?* If no one with the power to implement listens seriously, who will bother to express those ideas? If new ideas are shot down as soon as they are born, a second idea will rarely follow the first. But if every new idea gets a serious hearing no matter who proposes it, one day just such an idea may transform your organization and brighten its future. Global giant IBM is a prime example.

Case study: IBM global services

Today International Business Machines (IBM) is America's 10th largest company (by sales). About half of IBM's total revenue of $91.1 billion (2005) comes from a business unit that did not exist a decade ago, called

Case study continued

Case study continued

Global Services. This division helps companies develop e-business 'on demand', by integrating software and hardware systems. As told by strategy guru Gary Hamel, the story of its birth is instructive. It began early in 1994, with IBM deep in crisis. A junior IBM employee, a programmer named David Grossman, one of some 250,000 IBMers, had a vision. Based at Cornell University, Grossman used a supercomputer to download the Mosaic Web browser (forerunner of Netscape) and quickly envisioned the Next Big Thing: Web-based business. He became determined to get IBM out in front of it, even though IBM at the time still focused on hardware and mainframes. He conveyed his vision to manager John Patrick. They formed a team. Grossman led the technology team, Patrick supplied the business design. They wrote a nine-page manifesto titled 'Get Connected', showing six ways IBM could leverage the Web. New IBM CEO Lou Gerstner championed the idea. And IBM built a powerful, profitable and fast-growing new business, without which its future would have been bleak.

Source: Based on Gary Hamel, 'Waking Up IBM', *Harvard Business Review*, July–August 2000, and Jay Galbraith, *Designing the Customer-centric Organization: A Guide to Strategy, Structure, and Process* (San Franscisco: Jossey-Bass, 2005).

One lesson the IBM Global Services case teaches us is this: Despite common belief, innovation is not necessarily technological. 'Most people, when they think innovation, immediately think technology,' notes the chief strategist for Sony Corp., 'when indeed innovation can be anything. It can be a marketing innovation, a financing model, it could be the way you run your life.'[6] IBM already had the technology it needed to build its e-business model; what it needed was a business design and organizational structure to leverage that technology in order to build growth and profit. Web technology would have been worthless to IBM without a business design to accompany it.

For example, we once worked with accountants from a global electronics company on a new way to finance consumer purchases of electronic devices. This was as much an innovation as the devices themselves: without it, selling those innovations would have been much more difficult.

Successful innovations are often a portfolio of new ideas, with some of them focused on the *product* and some focused on the *value chain* supporting the product innovation. That is why a pervasive spirit of innovation is so necessary and so valuable.

Case study: Motorola–Competing with Japan

A pioneer in pagers, Motorola found, like many companies, in the 1980s, that superior Japanese efficiency in manufacturing pagers, and their lower prices, would drive Motorola out of this business entirely, unless rapid remedical action was taken. Motorola innovated. It came up with custom-tailored pagers: customers could design their own pager specifications. Each customized pager sold for $200, twice the price of the standard 'commodity' pagers. The key innovation here was in the business design or value chain. Orders were transmitted by fax to Motorola headquarters, sent by computer to the factory in Boynton Beach, Florida, where sophisticated robots produced each unique pager, then shipped by FedEx to the customer, all in a matter of days.

Source: From B. Joseph Pine, *Mass Customization: The New Frontier in Business Competition* (Boston, MA: Harvard Business School Press, 1992).

Innovation is like skydiving—fun, scary and risky. The risk can only be managed and minimized by disciplined organization. The levels of innovation risk should parallel the Three Bears' porridge: not too hot, not too cold. When risk is optimized, people are energized, successes emerge and growth and profit result. When companies avoid risk altogether, they perish. The greatest risk is to attempt to avoid risk altogether.

Case study: Bizet's *Carmen*

Sometimes innovation exacts a heavy personal toll; the fruits of victory can come too late to benefit the innovator, or perhaps never, at all. Perhaps the best-loved opera ever composed, Georges Bizet's *Carmen* is just such a tale.

Carmen premiered at the Paris Opera Comique on 3 March 1875. At the time there were rigid rules for composing operas. There were grand operas (Wagner was the paradigm) with larger-than-life tragic themes, and comic operas, featuring lighter-than-air love stories, large choirs and no social themes.

Bizet, a virtuoso pianist and aspiring composer, decided to innovate—to break the rules. His *Carmen* debuted at the Comic Opera, but had a tragic theme. The first act was more or less conventional and the audience applauded. But after that, it was all downhill. Both the audience

Case study continued

Case study continued

and the critics severely panned it after the tragic Acts 2 and 3. Bizet died, apparently broken-hearted, a few months later.

That same year *Carmen* was performed 46 times. Its popularity grew steadily until it attained its unchallenged position as one of a handful of truly great operas. Bizet did not live to enjoy the fruits of his successful innovation. Did he regret composing his revolutionary opera? We cannot know for certain.

Innovators like Georges Bizet often reconcile two conflicting metaphors: that of the 'internal compass' and the 'radar'.

- 'Internal compass' is an inner voice that drives creative energies. Writers sometimes talk about simply putting down on paper what an inner voice tells them. It is oblivious to, and independent of, external signals.
- Radar is a highly sensitive device that collects signals from people and uses those signals to generate innovations people want, need and enjoy.

Innovators need both compass and radar—neither works alone. Bizet sensed what opera-goers love. He generated a new form of opera, ignoring the existing conventions and constraints. But he listened to his internal compass. He was both 'in the box' (of opera lovers' needs and wants) and 'out of the box' (of existing forms, rules and conventions).

Action learning

Envisioning Your 'Photograph of the Future'.

Picture yourself as Georges Bizet in 1874. You can compose a safe conventional opera—comic or grand—and achieve acclaim. Or you can take risk and innovate by combining those two genres in a creative, novel way.

Suppose you are a short-term clairvoyant. You *know* your innovative opera *Carmen* will be panned and booed. You do *not* know how it will be regarded 50 years from now. Would you compose it anyway? Is the personal sacrifice worth the ultimate result? Would your internal passion for innovation sustain you through the hard times that you know will come? Be brutally honest with yourself.

Suppose now you are a long-term clairvoyant—you *know* Carmen will ultimately become perhaps the most popular, best-loved opera of all. Would you still compose it knowing that it will face certain vilification?

What role do you think vision plays in driving innovation?

Are you having fun?

The world's leading industrial design company is called IDEO. Based in San Francisco and run by legendary Stanford professor David Kelley and his brother Tom, IDEO has come up with hundreds of winning ideas.

IDEO has on its staff anthropologists, psychologists, MBAs and engineers. They have a secret weapon: they have fun. They love to come to work. They throw rubber darts at one another. Hung high on the ceiling above their workplace is the wing of a DC-3. Why? Because someone thought it would be neat.

Creating an energized workplace, which workers enjoy being in because they have fun is a highly serious winning strategy. Great innovators are those who sometimes do and say outlandish things. Workplaces where this is frowned on throw a wet blanket on creativity.

Not everyone agrees. We know of a leading global high-tech company that, as a startup in the 1970s, was a fun place to work. As competition heated up and as the company became increasingly global, a stern message went out from the CEO and top management: 'It is a competitive jungle out there. The fun is over. We are at war. Let's get serious. Cut out the horseplay and nonsense.'

We understand the reasons underlying this message, but strongly doubt the company became more competitive as a result. The opposite is the case: the company lost creative people who were stifled by its new approach.

Case study: Basketball–Win games by having fun

Few basketball fans have ever heard of the Grinnell College Pioneers, a basketball team in Divison III of the NCAA (United States National College Athletics Association). Yet it is hugely successful.

- They are the highest-scoring team in the NCAA, averaging 128.9 points a game, with 100 field goal attempts a game, including 63 three-pointers.
- They have won the Midwest Conference championship three times in the past seven years.

Case study continued

Case study continued

Their 'recipe' is simple: have fun. Here is their 'business design'. Grinnell has three complete teams of five players. The coach, David Arsenault, puts a whole new team in after 35 seconds (the length of the shot clock), or at every whistle or dead ball. The players love it—they 'run and gun' at a furious pace. The crowd loves it because the pace is very fast and scores are high. The team once scored 149 points ... and lost, to Illinois College, who scored 157!

'This is the best time I ever had playing basketball!' says Paul Nordlund, one of the players. 'There's great camaraderie because everyone plays and plays about equal time ... here I can run and gun. It's great!'

Arsenault has essentially built a radically new 'business model' for college basketball. When he got the job 15 years ago, the Grinnell basketball team had won four games in the previous three seasons combined. It is not surprising. Grinnell has only 1,400 students and the college, in a small Iowa town, is ranked as one of America's top academic institutions. Arsenault had brainy players whose individual ability was far below the average in the league.

So, how do you win games? By building a system based more on teamwork than on individual ability. Teamwork means everyone plays, about a third of each game. 'Because everyone plays, not just the stars, we're more of a team than other teams,' says Steve Wood. Wood averages 28 points a game, even though he only plays a third of the 40-minute game on average. Grinnell players press all the time, all over the court, double- and triple-teaming the opposing player with the ball. They have fun—and they excel. Those two qualities are closely linked.

Action learning

Fun and Energy

In your organization, are managers and workers having fun? Do they enjoy coming to work? Are they energized as a result? Or do they drag in as if they were attending their favourite aunt's funeral? Do *you* wake up and look forward to coming to work with enthusiasm, on most days?

Think about how you can put some fun into your workplace. Innovation is often a workplace equivalent of Grinnell College's 'three team, run-and-gun' model. Can you become the business world's equivalent of Grinnell?

If you are not passionate and enthusiastic about what you do for a living, can you remedy this in your current workplace? If not, find something else to do that does generate passion and energy.

1.4 INNOVATE FOR GROWTH AND PROFIT

There is a second, powerful and practical answer to the question, *why innovate?* It is to achieve high, sustained growth and profitability.

It is an empirical fact that companies that excel at innovation are also far more profitable than companies that do not (see Table 1.1). Boston Consulting Group asked nearly a thousand senior executives to rank companies by their innovativeness. The top 20 companies almost always lead their respective industries in return on equity, total return to investors and profit margins. The link between successful innovation and profit is almost a tautology (a self-evident truth). By definition, innovative products that achieve marketplace success generally command higher prices and higher profit margins than competing products. It is also a near-tautology that successful innovation demands high-level innovation management.

Innovation is one of the best ways to build market share. And, in turn, market share is directly related to Return on Investment. Market share exceeding 40 per cent is, on average, associated with pre-tax return on investment exceeding 20 per cent (see Figure 11.3 on page 341).

If successful innovation is the key to profitability, *why then do some organizations fail miserably at it*? We believe the reason is this: global organizations follow a three-step procedure to attain growth and profit. Those three key steps embody an internal contradiction. They are:

1. Innovate
2. Deploy and scale up
3. Adapt locally

There are built-in tradeoffs between innovation and scale, and between scale and local adaptation and customization. These trade-offs are difficult enough to be described as paradoxes.

Innovation comes from empowered individuals and teams who break rules. To exploit their creativity, organizations need to deploy—produce, market, distribute, sell, service—them worldwide. Increasingly, this applies to small start up companies as well. Organizations that deploy globally from day one will have a competitive advantage over those that defer going global. This brings economies of scale (cost savings). But size may destroy innovation;

Table 1.1
The top 20 innovating companies in the world and their growth and profitability (for global firms)

Company	*% of executives who chose this company*	*Profitability measures*
1. Apple	24.8	201.4% total return to investors (TRI) in 2004, highest for any firm its size
2. 3M	11.8	28.8% return on shareholders' equity (RoE), 2nd highest in its industry
3. Microsoft	8.5	23% annual TRI (1994–2004), $8.2 b profit in 2004, highest in its industry
4. General Electric	8.5	$16.6 b profit in 2004, 3rd highest in Fortune 500 (F500); 18% annual TRI, 1994–2004
5. Sony	5.9	–
6. Dell	5.6	52% TRI 1994–2004, 2nd highest in Fortune 500 list; 47% RoE in 2004 (16th highest in Fortune 500 companies)
7. IBM	5.3	$8.4 b in profit in 2004, $147 b market value (#10 in F500), 19% TRI 1994–2004
8. Google	5.2	Sales more than doubled in 2004 to $3.2 b while profits nearly tripled
9. Procter & Gamble	4.2	$6.5 b profits in 2004, 38% RoE
10. Nokia	4.2	–
11. Virgin	4.0	–
12. Samsung	3.9	–
13. Wal-Mart	3.2	Leads world in revenues ($288 b), 5th highest market value ($222 b)
14. Toyota	3.0	–
15. EBay	2.9	80% TRI in 2004, #1 in industry, 24% net margin, #1 in industry
16. Intel	2.7	$7.5 b profit (up 33%), #1 in its industry, and 19% RoE, #2 in its industry
17. Amazon	2.7	$588 m in profits, up 1,588% in 2004 (second-biggest rise in its industry)
18. IDEO	2.2	–
19. Starbucks	2.1	36% RoE in 2004, highest in its industry, 34% TRI in 2004, highest in its industry
20. BMW	1.7	–

Source: Data from *Business Week*, 15 August 2005, based on a poll of 940 senior executives in 68 countries by Boston Consulting Group; profitability data are from the Fortune 500 (*Fortune*, 18 April 2005).

creative persons tend to feel lost in large organizations, especially when 'scale' implies bureaucracy, discipline, and 'following the rules'.

'How can we *be* big, and *feel* small?' a senior Intel executive once asked us. Some of the ways to do this will be discussed in Chapters 2 and 4.

Another paradox, or internal contradiction, pertains to 'scale and adapt'. Cost savings derive from selling standard products everywhere, enabling long production runs and learning-curve savings. As a result, there is continual pressure to make products standard. But local markets often differ widely in culture, preferences and tastes. Adapting products for each market can be essential for market success but fatal for costs and profit margins.

Sometimes, powerful branding and marketing can overcome local taste differences. Philadelphia brand cream cheese is sold all over Europe, in the same flavour, taste and package even though tastes for cheese differ widely between countries. More often, however, local adaptation is essential. Even Coca-Cola subtly calibrates the sweetness of Coke across different countries.

In Israel, the Magnum ice-cream bar was introduced—but it flopped. Only when managers realized that Israelis prefer milk chocolate—while the existing Magnum had a dark chocolate covering—did they adjust the product and attain huge success with it. 'Adapt' was a vital next-step, after 'Deploy'.

Excess standardization ruins the product. Some believe General Motors over-standardized its cars, so that all the once-powerful car brands became homogenized look-alikes. But Toyota, now challenging General Motors for the title of global sales leader, once overly adapted, proliferating options to the extent that costs soared.

Case study: Vicks Vaporub: Think local, act global

'Think global, act local' (deploy globally, adapt locally) has become a cliché. But, notes a former Procter & Gamble top manager, Gurcharan Das, the reverse is also true; 'International managers must also think local and then apply their local insights on a global scale ... re-employing communicable ideas in new geographies ....' One of Das' innovations was to introduce Vicks Vaporub in India in small 5 gram tins. Priced at 10 cents each, it was cheaper to buy four of them than the larger 19 gram tin. 'The trade thought we were crazy,' notes Das. But it was a wise local adaptive innovation. Working-class people bought the small tin. Middle-class consumers bought the larger one. Each segment remained loyal to the tin size that suited it. The same strategy was successful for shampoo. Tiny one-dose sachets sold well to those who could not buy a whole bottle. Even package size can sometimes be a major profitable innovation.

Source: From Gurcharan Das, 'Local memoirs of a global manager', *Harvard Business Review*, March–April 1993.

Risk

Discerning readers may be asking themselves this question: for every successful innovation story, like those above, there must be many failures. It is certainly true that innovation is risky. But when the nature of the risk is analysed carefully, it can be reduced significantly. Here is how this might be approached.

Statisticians argue that there are two types of errors. Type I error (rejecting a true hypothesis, equivalent in the courts to convicting an innocent person whose 'hypothesis' is, 'I didn't do it!') and Type II error (accepting a false hypothesis, equivalent to acquitting a criminal who falsely says, 'I didn't do it!').

Both errors exist in innovation. You can reject good, high-potential ideas (Type I error), and you can accept and implement terrible ideas (Type II error). Great innovators not only choose and implement good ideas, *but they are very good at rejecting terrible ones.* It is remarkable how many terrible ideas are brought to the marketplace, at high cost, only to find certain failure. This happens when managers fail to face the brutal facts.

Case studies: What were they thinking?

Marketing expert Robert McMath has 80,000 new products in his New Products Showcase and Learning Centre in Ithaca, New York. There are a lot more 'fizzlers' (failures) than 'sizzlers' (successes), he notes. New products succeed, he observes, when 'just about everything that needs to go right does go right'. He claims *you are a success as a new product developer if you abandon ideas destined to fail.* Among the new products that flopped and were certain to flop in advance:

- Gillette's 'For Oily Hair Only' shampoo (who wants to admit they have oily hair?). ('Break the rules'—later, other shampoos did create special products for dry, brittle, oily hair, but more subtly.)
- Frito-Lay Lemonade: While millions love salty Frito-Lay snacks that make you thirsty, who would buy a product with the same name that purports to *quench* thirst? Another major flop.

Source: From Robert M. McMath and Thom Forbes, *What Were They Thinking? Marketing Lessons You Can Learn from Products that Flopped* (New York: Three Rivers Press, 1998).

In the justice system, most people find Type I errors (convicting the innocent) horrifying, more than Type II (freeing the guilty). In innovation,

Type I errors (rejecting good ideas) happens all the time. We know of strong businesses established by picking through the junk piles of other companies and bringing to market ideas they rejected. If you know of such a junk pile, you may find exceptionally powerful innovations in it. In a sense, the patent system is just such a junk pile. There are millions of patents registered by the United States Patent Office alone, and millions more in Europe and Asia. An overwhelming proportion of patents are never used or implemented. Wise innovators are good at searching for existing patents before they begin reinventing the wheel.

In innovation, Type II errors are generally very costly. Courage to kill projects doomed to fail is often rare, if only because of the sunk-cost fallacy ('we've already spent $× million, let's spend a bit more and get this project done'). As McMath observes, successful innovation often relies more heavily on deciding which innovations *not* to implement, than the ones to be implemented. Wrong decisions waste not only money but, more importantly, *time.* You often get one chance to capture a window of market opportunity. Waste it, and the window closes, sometimes forever. We have personally seen many innovative projects, in which the engineers charged with carrying them out know with near-certainty, long before the projects are completed, that they will fail, but do not communicate this knowledge to (or are not heard by) senior decision-makers. Money and crucial time-to-market are both lost.

Make your innovative ideas leap high hurdles. Why waste years struggling uphill with a bad idea, when you might be having fun implementing a great one?

Innovation as hurdle jumping

One way to understand why innovation management is so vital, and so very difficult, is through a metaphor: The 110 metres hurdle event in the Olympics. There are key success factors common to both sprint hurdles and innovation management.

Suppose you are an Olympic hurdler. Olympic hurdle sprint races for men are run over a distance of 110 metres. Hurdles are 42 inches high and there are 10 of them. Suppose you have trained for years and are an expert at the hurdle-leaping technique. You know that to win, you must leap over all 10 hurdles successfully; knocking over a hurdle is allowed but slows your pace considerably. Suppose the probability of leaping over a hurdle is quite high, 80 per cent, or eight times out of 10. *What are the odds you will leap over all 10 hurdles?*

The answer is 0.8 multiplied by itself 10 times,

$$(0.8)^{10} = 0.107$$

or just over 10 per cent. In nearly nine races out of 10, you will hit at least one hurdle and probably lose (though admittedly, some Olympic hurdlers, and some hugely successful innovators, have knocked over one or even two hurdles and still won, by superhuman effort).

Why is hurdling a metaphor for innovation management? Because, like Olympic hurdlers, innovators must leap a series of high barriers successfully; failing at any one means failing in general. They must develop a good idea, find resources, hire a good team, produce the product, market it, distribute it, sell it, advertise it, package it, service it. Failure at any step will cause the innovation to fail. They have to get every step right. This is a key reason why innovation management is so crucial. *Success at the ideation stage is far from a guarantee that the product will find success in general; the idea is only the first hurdle, and often the easiest.*

As McMath observes, there are four million parts in a Boeing 777 airliner. Every single part has to be precision-made and assembled properly for the airliner to fly well and safely. Successful innovations are not unlike the 777. Every part in the business design has to fit and has to work. One missing part can cause even worthy innovations to crash and burn.

1.5 INNOVATE FOR SURVIVAL

The third key reason for innovating is simply survival. Today's global marketplace is fiercely competitive. *Organizations that fail to bring to market innovative products that create value for their customers will quickly find that their competitors have done so, and that their own existence is in danger.* There is no better way to describe this than in terms of Darwin's theory of evolution driven by survival of the fittest. Organisms best adapted to their environments, and best able to *change* in response to changes in that environment, are most likely to survive.

Today, innovation is an adaptive competence that is necessary for survival in global markets. Those organizations that lack innovation will simply not last in the long run.

Figure 11.5, on page 349, portrays the dilemma that companies face once they start innovating. As once-innovative products become mature, their growth slackens and they reach market saturation. This is the point in time when profits from these products are highest, because huge investments in

R&D, launch, advertising, marketing and branding have been completed and scale economies are the biggest. At this time products are most vulnerable to attacks by other innovators.

Wise companies attack *their own mature products* by introducing new, better ones. Intel was famous for introducing next-generation microprocessor, the '486', even while the old one, the '386', was making large profits, in order to pre-empt its competitors' products. Knowing how to balance mature and innovative products in a company's portfolio, and knowing how and when to kill profitable but aging products, are among the most valuable leadership skills that managers possess. At the same time, skill in keeping mature products alive is also valuable. Procter & Gamble still makes money from a brand of soap, Ivory, that is now over 120 years old. Because it is a respected and recognized brand, advertising and marketing costs are negligible. By maintaining its core brand identity for over a century, Procter & Gamble has kept a cash cow alive far beyond a product's average life-expectancy; yet, at the same time, P&G is one of the world's great innovators.

Case study: Intel

Intel's profits plummeted from $198 million in 1984 to less than $2 million in 1985. The reason: fierce Japanese competition, and commoditization in Intel's key product memory chips. Intel President Andrew Grove, together with CEO Gordon Moore, decided to shut down the entire memory chip business. They did this by doing what Harvard Kennedy School of Government scholar Ron Heifetz calls 'getting on the balcony'(stepping outside a subjective perspective). If we got kicked out and the board brought in a new CEO, Grove asked Moore, what would he do? Get out of memories, said Moore. Why not walk out the door, come back, and do it ourselves? asked Grove. Grove said that at the time he had a hard time getting those words out. 'Face the brutal facts' is a key skill of great companies, notes Jim Collins—easy to say, very hard to do—and a crucial component of innovation. Intel fired 8,000 people in 1986 and lost $180 million, but by innovation management, transitioned successfully to microprocessors and as a direct result became no. 49 in the Fortune 500 (2005 list), with $38.86 billion in sales, $8.7 billion in net income and 99,000 employees.

Source: Intel's decision to abandon memory chips is recounted in R. Tedlow, 'Lessons in Leadership—The Education of Andy Grove', *Fortune*, 28 November 2005 (also on Fortune.com).

1.6 SUMMARY AND CONCLUSION

There can be little doubt that competition in global markets in virtually every product, service, industry and market segment is fierce, and in the coming decade will grow even fiercer. In order not only to *endure* but to *prevail*, global organizations will find that bringing products to market that are Bobbsey Twins relative to existing products is a strategy doomed to failure. *Only innovative differentiated products that create substantial additional value, relative to what customers can buy already, can succeed.*

To achieve this, organizations will need skills, competence and excellence in innovation management. In the Darwinian world of global markets, the companies able to innovate and manage innovation will be the survivors who will be significantly better than their competitors. They will understand that winning innovation is a set of Russian 'Babushka' dolls, and that the 'idea', the innermost doll, is of no value unless wrapped in successive and successful 'dolls'—marketing, sales, service, strategy, production, etc., that together comprise a powerful, compelling business design.

In business schools and executive education programmes, courses on innovation and new product development have been increasing in proliferation. Courses on innovation *management* are rather scarce. It is our hope that this book on innovation management will support its becoming a core discipline in business schools everywhere, just as strategy management is now a core course in virtually every graduate management degree programme.

1.7 THE STRUCTURE OF THIS BOOK

Part One of this book comprises four chapters (1 to 4), which focus on innovation, creativity and supply answers to the four questions: why innovate, how to innovate, what to innovate, and who innovates. Part Two comprises ten chapters (5 to 14), each providing a key management tool to guide the manager in implementing innovative ideas by building and managing a winning business model.

The proportion, four chapters to 10, reflects our view that *managing* innovation is as important as, or more important than, the initial creative idea.

In the next chapter we explore the question, *what* to innovate? In the process we examine proven tools that enable innovators to create successful, profitable innovations that find marketplace success.

CASE STUDY 1.1

Tata Steel

The story of Tata Steel from the difficult days in the early 1990s, when the company, used to a protected environment, was suddenly exposed to global competition consequent to the liberalization of the Indian economy, to the present time marketplace is that of a company that has focused relentlessly on price, value and costs to gain astounding success. The company closed the year 2004–05 with a record profit of Rs 34.74 billion (about $800 million). A series of initiatives launched by the company over the last 15 years culminated in these stellar results.

The great visionary Jamsetji Nusserwanji Tata (J.N. Tata) founded Tata Steel in 1907. It is one of the crown jewels of the Tata group, which has businesses spanning automobiles, steel, chemicals, information technology, communication, power generation, consumer products, hotels and much more. The company started production of pig iron from its blast furnace in 1911. Since then it has added various manufacturing facilities. These facilities together constitute a totally integrated steel manufacturing complex, including raw materials mining and processing, sinter making, coke making, iron making, steel making, steel rolling, and a host of other manufacturing facilities and services.

Economic policies in post-Independent India (1947–91) held back Tata Steel from blossoming into a global corporation at the cutting edge of technology. Protectionism and government-controlled prices curbed the industry's competitive spirit. When liberalization finally came in the early 1990s, the company was ill-prepared to face the emerging business situation that was increasingly characterized by market-determined prices, lower import tariffs, intense competition, and the move from a seller's market to a buyer's market. This period also coincided with a change in leadership at Tata Steel when Mr Ratan Tata (J.N. Tata's great-grandson) took over as the Chairman of the company and Dr Irani took over as the Managing Director.

After decades of operating in a protected environment, there was considerable complacency in the rank-and-file of the company, as was the case with most companies in the country during the pre-liberalization era. The range and magnitude of problems that confronted the company by the early 1990s included global competition, product quality issues, poor compliance in meeting delivery commitments, an outdated plant and an oversized workforce of more than 80,000. The company took concerted

Case study 1.1 continued

Case study 1.1 continued

action over the next 15 years, focused on the three levers, price, cost and value, as the following discussion demonstrates.

Phase I: Embarking on the reinvention journey

When the management decided to reinvent the company in 1992, it began by initiating a series of concerted actions. Many of them sought to leverage the existing strengths of the company, which did not require large cash outflows.

- Intense inward focus on the part of top management to improve its performance without getting distracted.
- Harnessing new and better sources of raw materials, many of which the company had access to through captive sources (these had not been a focus of attention in the pre-liberalization era).
- Innovativeness in using blue dust, which is an iron-rich ore. It is a by-product of iron-ore mining operations and is as fine as talcum powder. Historically, the ore was mined and the blue dust was left undisturbed. The management decided to explore the possibility of using the blue dust as raw material for its sinter plant. This change resulted in uniform mining operations.
- Process innovation in the sinter plant through benchmarking with the best in the world to improve productivity.
- New coke-making technology: Process innovation through the 'stamp charging technology' developed in-house through painstaking laboratory tests and pilot plant trials over a 10-year period. This facilitated use of cheaper Indian coking coal that has higher ash content compared to imported coal. This was risky in that if the experiment failed, it would have resulted in a big setback to the company. The trials were however successful and all the coke ovens were eventually redone using this new method. The new technology reduced to a large extent the use of costly imported coal for producing coke needed for steel making. This gave the company significant sustainable cost advantage because Indian coal is relatively low cost and the company has an unlimited supply of medium-coking coal.
- Blast furnace optimization.
- Reducing energy costs through process innovation.
- Addressing overstaffing, reducing headcount of employees from 80,000 to 40,000 in a humane way, over a 10-year period, without any trade union-related problems.
- Modernization of facilities.

Case study 1.1 continued

Case study 1.1 continued

- Creation and spread of a new performance culture in the organization.

Phase-II: The quest for business excellence

Tata Steel's journey to international competitiveness had much to do with the personal commitment and change-oriented leadership of its top management, with an intense focus on the 3Cs: change (mutate and improve furiously), cost (ruthless cutting of wasteful expenditure) and customers (strive relentlessly to build relationships and influence consumption). All this was anchored in the Tata Steel code of conduct, which provides a strong, ethical value base and moral compass for each employee in the company.

The top management's checklist for driving change in the company included the following:

- Lead the change process and take personal ownership—the responsibility for this cannot be delegated.
- Be a role model and the first to change—personal involvement and investment of time is the key to success.
- Create endless opportunities for two-way communication within the company.
- Create a sense of urgency (not panic)—embrace change even when it does not appear necessary.
- Set up a small hand-picked group to drive change in the organization—train and empower them.
- Set Key Result Areas (KRAs) carefully—include the top management in it.

Quality and cost at the centre-stage

The journey towards excellence has been facilitated by implementing the Tata Business Excellence Model (TBEM). TBEM has been adopted from the Malcolm Baldridge business excellence model. It covers almost every aspect of a corporation including: visionary leadership, focus on the future, focus on results, organizational agility, customer-driven excellence, valuing employees and partners, management by fact, managing innovation, systems perspective and public responsibility. The progress of Tata Steel on the journey of business excellence can be seen from its steadily increasing scores on the JRDQV assessment: 587, 616 and 643 (on a scale of 1,000) during 1999, 2000 and 2001 respectively.

Case study 1.1 continued

Case study 1.1 continued

Over the last three years the company has consistently achieved scores in excess of 700, which is considered excellent by world standards.

Changing mindsets and ensuring accountability at all levels

The willingness of the top management to create total transparency and subject its own performance to discipline and the scrutiny of the entire organization, helped greatly in bringing about a mental transformation in the workforce. The company relies heavily on the balanced scorecard, a performance management and strategy deployment method developed by Harvard Professor, Robert Kaplan and consultant David Norton, to break down strategy into its component elements and track performance across the organization starting from the Managing Director. It defines KRAs for the top managers, which are then cascaded down, using the Balanced Scorecard tool for strategy translation, communication and implementation. In this manner, strategic alignment across the organization is achieved.

Challenge of being internationally competitive

With all the steps discussed above, a lot of progress was made in putting Tata Steel back on track and positioning it strongly to face the emerging competition in India. The plants were modernized with significant investments (more than Rs 100 billion over a 10-year period). The company implemented several initiatives towards quality enhancement. Product delivery was reasonably streamlined. However, the emerging global steel scenario during the late 1990s was a cause for concern for the top management. The forces at play during the turn of the century (late 1990s and early 2000) clearly indicated that the steel industry was indeed in dire straits. There was severe pressure on world steel prices. The world steel industry's cyclical nature had been irrelevant during the pre-liberalization era. This scenario underwent a sea-change post-liberalization. To survive in a globalized world, the company realized that its manufacturing costs had to be globally competitive. Thus, by 1998 operational improvement became the top priority of the company. Since quality had been largely addressed through the various business excellence initiatives, the spotlight now shifted to reducing manufacturing costs and maximizing output from the plants.

In response to these strategic forces impacting the company, a variety of initiatives such as Total Operational Performance (TOP) to ruthlessly drive down costs and improve productivity of the plants by taking on

Case study 1.1 continued

Case study 1.1 continued

stretch targets and tapping into the innovative potential of all the employees, Total Productive Maintenance (TPM), Knowledge Management (KM), Operations Research and Decision Support Systems (OR & DSS), and Six Sigma were launched. These were integrated through an umbrella programme, ASPIRE (ASPirational Improvement to Retain Excellence). The idea was to drive cost reduction in operations and effect drastic improvement in productivity. Some of these initiatives also laid a strong foundation for a culture of innovation in the organization.

Phase-III: Relentless focus on the customer

Having ensured that its operations were world-class and that its costs were amongst the lowest in the world, Tata Steel then turned its energies towards the customer. It first undertook an intense process of product and customer rationalization to weed out unprofitable products and customers. It was clear that the old way of selling was no longer relevant. Hitherto, the focus of the sales force comprising CAMs (Customer Account Managers) to the company's business market customers was on meeting the targets. The sales were largely based on offering low prices, ensuring timely deliveries and leveraging the Tata name. The company did not focus much on retail markets in the past.

The old paradigm of doing business suddenly appeared to have lost its relevance in the changed environment. In the past lowest price was the basis for obtaining an order. This was further reinforced by the customer's aggressive approach of treating steel as a commodity product. Thus supplier–customer relationships, far from being co-operative, were largely transactional. The steel industry, in general, historically operated on a 'one-size-fits-all' approach. The top management realized that all this had to change, and if it could drive the change in the industry, Tata Steel would emerge as a leader.

In mid-2001, the company was restructured along the profit centre concept as against the earlier functional organization structure, with a view to making it more responsive to the needs of the marketplace. Two distinct profit centres, viz., flat products and long products were created, each headed by a Vice-President (VP), who was responsible for both manufacturing and sales. A key challenge was how the salesforce, which was essentially the same set of people from yesteryears, could be energized to take up the new challenges. It was not uncommon for the customers to squeeze Tata Steel on price, frequently demanding a 3–5 per cent drop in price each year. With the resulting suspicion on the part

Case study 1.1 continued

Case study 1.1 continued

of both the company and its customers, it was clear that neither was gaining from the relationship. Customers clearly began to have many options. The company became acutely aware that it needed to find ways to come out of the commodity trap.

The company found answers to these issues through its now celebrated Customer Value Management (CVM) initiative for business markets and Retail Value Management (RVM) for its retail markets. CVM and RVM have redefined the way steel is marketed and sold in the country and have been seminal initiatives that have placed the company firmly on a trajectory of profitable growth. These were relentlessly driven by the top management, and in a span of about four years the entire sales and marketing was brought on par with the best practices of the top steel plants anywhere in the world. CVM has emerged as an important vehicle for customer retention in business markets. Through CVM, Tata Steel, under increasing pressure from relentless competitive forces, sought to retain and increase the share of business from profitable existing customers. In this way, it hoped to find a way out of downward spiralling price pressures. Tata Steel has redefined steel retailing in the country through its RVM initiative lunched in 2002. It has brought order and discipline into the hitherto disorganized retail steel business. These initiatives have helped the company to increase the value delivered to its customers while seeking a better price for the higher value delivered and a greater share of the customer's wallet.

Results

Tata Steel had taken significant strides to address the challenges that confronted it consequent to the changed economic policies of the country during most of the 1990s. It had put in place rigorous systems to ensure that operational costs were examined through a structured process and ruthlessly reduced. It had implemented mechanisms for productivity enhancement and monitoring equipment to ensure maximum uptimes and efficiencies. The top management found ways to ensure that the enthusiasm of the employees involved in implementing these initiatives was sustained. Appropriate reward and recognition mechanisms were put in place to ensure the development of true meritocracy in the company.

CVM has resulted in the company focusing on a few profitable companies with which it chose to do business and deliver extraordinary value to them. This has helped the company to come out of the intense

Case study 1.1 continued

Case study 1.1 continued

price pressures of commoditization in its business markets. It has resulted in increasing the share of wallet that the company enjoys with its chosen customers. This is especially true of customers in the automobile, white goods, and construction industries, where the company primarily seeks to do business. RVM has established Tata Steel as the leader in branded steel for retail markets as the company successfully pioneered the concept of branding steel in the country for retail markets.

Looking ahead

According to B. Muthuraman, the company's Managing Director, 'The focus is now on gearing up for growth. We need to get past the 20 million tons per annum capacity and beyond in the next few years, from the 5 million tons per annum plant we were a few years ago. We will doubtless have to face even stiffer global competition in the years to come. There is likely to be a huge global over-capacity in steel production worldwide in the next few years putting pressure on prices. At the same time, enormous opportunities are opening up that companies with a winning spirit can harness. The country's most respected entrepreneur started our company with a pioneering spirit a century ago. Our challenge is to sustain that spirit across the organization. To scale newer heights from the stage we have now reached, a managerial attitude alone is not enough. We need an entrepreneurial approach across the organization. We have to find ways of continuing to innovate across all levels in the organization. One of the things we have to guard against is complacency. It is very easy for people in our company to look at what we have achieved since the early 1990s, and believe that "we have climbed the Mount Everest." While we have achieved a lot, how do we continue to press ahead, and ensure that the sense of urgency and purpose is not diluted? How do we continue our forward momentum with ever more acceleration?' The Price-Value-Cost dynamic is clearly a moving target, and no company can afford to rest on its past laurels.

So *why* do you have to innovate? It is clear from the Tata Steel case study that if it had not innovated the way it did over the last 15 years it may have ceased to exist in its current form. Thus, innovation is not a luxury but a necessity for your organization.

Notes

1. From a postcard purchased by Shlomo Maital at the Picasso Museum in Antibes, France.

2. James Collins, *Good to Great: Why Some Companies Make the Leap … and Others Don't* (New York: HarperCollins, 2001). The book discusses at length the clash between the 'culture of discipline' and 'creativity'.
3. Harvard Business School professor Michael E. Porter's book *Competitive Strategy: Techniques for Analyzing Industries and Competitors* (New York: The Free Press, 1980) sold over a million copies, went into 60 printings, and was translated into 19 languages.
4. Burton Marsteller, *Forrester Magazine*, Issue 1 (2005), p. 37.
5. *Global Innovation Outlook: 2004* (Armonk, NY: IBM, 2004), p. 3.
6. Quoted in *Global Innovation Outlook: 2004*, p. 3.

Chapter 2
The innovation portfolio: *What* to innovate

Even in these daunting times, one person with a good idea can still change the world.
—Adam Cohen, *International Herald Tribune*[1]

LEARNING OBJECTIVES After you read this chapter, you should understand:

- **How and why vision drives innovation**
- **How to differentiate between a good innovative idea and a bad one**
- **What a unique value proposition is and how to define it for your product;**
- **How demographics, technology, generational change, economic downturns, tastes, legislation and customers can inspire innovation**
- **What are the various 'feelings' and 'needs' and how to determine the feelings and needs your product satisfies;**
- **The difference between 'brands' and 'lovemarks'**
- **Why experiences are a fruitful area for innovation**
- **How to distinguish between incremental, standard and radical innovations**
- **How to optimize a portfolio of low-risk and high-risk innovations**

2.1 INTRODUCTION

The business of innovation pervades the daily business of life. When implemented and managed with skill, innovation enriches and enhances our lives immeasurably. This is the ultimate goal of innovation and it drives the vision of most great innovators, as this chapter shows.

The first chapter focused on '*why* innovate?', this chapter focuses on *what* to innovate—ways to determine which novel products, services and processes will achieve marketplace success for growth and profit. It is important to link this chapter's 'what?' with the previous chapter's 'why?'. A study by Kim and Mauborgne of the business launches of 108 companies[2] found the following:

- The vast majority of launches, six out of every seven, were in what the authors call 'red oceans' (incremental improvements within existing industries). They accounted for 62 per cent of total launch revenues, but generated only 38 per cent of total launch profits.

- A small minority of launches, only one in seven, were in what the authors term 'blue oceans' (industries *not* in existence today); they accounted for 38 per cent of revenues but 62 per cent of launch profits. Note that these figures include launch failures that bring no revenue and only losses, which are much higher, of course, in 'blue' than in 'red'. Nowhere is the link between risk and return sharper than in innovation.

In cricket, batsmen score an over-the-fence 'six' infrequently. To win the test match, or achieve a century (100 runs), you need many singles, 'twos', 'threes' and 'fours' as well. In baseball, the top hitter hits over-the-fence home runs at most once every 12 at-bats (Boston Red Sox's Manny Ramirez). To win the game, you need singles and doubles as well. This is equally true of innovation.

Start ups and entrepreneurs strive for 'home run' innovations, because they cannot otherwise defeat powerful incumbents. Existing companies seek an optimal balance between sixes, fours, threes, twos and singles, while knowing when to 'swing for the fences' (invest massive effort in finding a truly radical innovation). Determining what to innovate will thus differ for different firms depending on their age, resources, size, industry and capabilities.

2.2 VISION, PORTFOLIOS AND FEELINGS

There are three core messages in this chapter, related to vision, innovation portfolios and subjective feelings and needs:

1. *Vision, not greed, drives successful innovation.* A powerful visionary 'photograph of the future' is vital to create and sustain the energy needed for profit-driven innovation and to guide the blueprints for implementing it.
2. *Innovation is fundamentally different for entrepreneurial startup companies than it is for established organizations.* Startups need to focus on offerings sharply different from those already available and which create and sustain measurably and perceptibly higher value than that provided to customers by existing products. Established organizations need to optimize their innovation portfolio, balancing mature products with *incrementally* new and *radically* new ones.

Each organization will have a different optimal innovation portfolio, depending on market conditions, competitors, resources and technology and that portfolio will change, sometimes rapidly, over time. Startup companies will have to transform themselves and their innovation portfolios more than once, as they evolve from small to medium and then to large established global players.

3. *Successful innovations create powerful feelings and emotions, and satisfy well-defined needs.* The more clearly you define the feelings your innovations arouse and the needs that they satisfy, the more likely it is that your innovations will succeed. A winning innovation is driven by skill in connecting with and responding to customers' needs and feelings.

The leading online auction company, eBay, helps illustrate these three principles. Driven by a simple, yet powerful vision, eBay has successfully transformed itself from a start up to an established company in the past decade, retaining its innovative energy while adapting constantly to its complex environment, meeting competitive challenges and customer needs. In the process, the company has changed many peoples' lives. It proves that while good innovators improve our lives, great ones fundamentally change how we lead our lives—how we work, spend, save, consume, travel, and enjoy leisure.

Case study: eBay–From ponytails to suits

As the world's largest online auction company, eBay shows that a person with a good idea can indeed change the world. In 2005, it had $4.6 billion in revenues, with profits (before taxes, interest, depreciation and amortization) of $1.82 billion, or a 32 per cent operating margin. The company employs 2,500 people.

While almost everyone has heard of eBay, few know the name, Omidyar. If one day an Innovators' Hall of Fame is built, eBay founder Pierre Omidyar will doubtless have a place of honour in it. The market value of eBay stock is $56.6 billion, as of 5 February 2006, making Omidyar one of the world's richest people; he personally owns 202 million shares, currently worth over $8.2 billion.

Who is this innovator and what can we learn from him?

Omidyar was born in 1967 in Paris to French–Iranian parents and moved to the US when he was six. At the age of 24, in 1991, he launched a start up, one of whose by-products was software for online commerce. The company, eShop, was sold to Microsoft in 1996, making Omidyar a millionaire before he was 30.

Case study continued

Case study continued

But he was only getting started.

Omidyar's vision is 'a global marketplace, driven by free, open supply and demand, enabled by the Internet, where every human being everywhere can be both seller and buyer, producer and consumer, of anything.'

In global markets, you can sell anything, anywhere, to anyone, at any time—eBay makes this possible.

'I sat down, frankly, over Labor Day weekend 1995, and I just whipped up some [software] code,' recounts Omidyar. 'By Monday afternoon I had the site up.'

Like all radical innovations, there were powerful naysayers who claimed, 'strangers won't trade online with strangers', and 'people will cheat (take the money and not deliver the goods).' But Omidyar, who wore Birkenstock sandals and had a ponytail, says only 30 sellers out of a million fail to deliver on their online promises.

The initial stock issue of eBay was in 1998. Omidyar wanted to auction the shares (as Google did in 2005), but Wall Street underwriters said no!

Some 724,000 Americans make either primary or secondary income from selling on eBay. It is global, not American; over 170,000 people in 12 European countries make money selling on eBay, and 50 million Europeans (one in every six) buy from or browse the site. Since its inception, eBay has sold over 45 million items; 250,000 items are added daily, and there are 50 million registered users. Today, the value of something is often measured by what it can bring on eBay.

The metaphorical shift of eBay from ponytails to suits came as a result of a crisis. The 'ponytail' company neglected its technology and had no backup. On 10 July 1999, the eBay site crashed and was down for nearly a full day. That led to large investments, more systematic management and conceptual 'suits'—though founder Omidyar still drives a battered VW convertible.

How does eBay connect with feelings? A key eBay principle from the start has been to treat small and big customers in precisely the same way—with direct email access to Omidyar himself. The Feedback Forum has buyers and sellers rating each other after a transaction; the ratings are compiled and placed after users' names. The result: a business that is huge but that was purposely built to feel small and intimate.

Today eBay faces major challenges from Google and Microsoft, both now adding online shopping to their search engines. The response, led by its CEO Meg Whitman, has been continual innovation.

Case study continued

Case study continued

But eBay's future success is by no means assured. Successful innovation management generates profits that attract competitors in droves. That is why innovation and innovativeness must be sustained over time. One way to ensure this is by asking the right questions.

Sources: Some information on eBay is available online at http://www.internet-story.com./ebay.htm and on the CNN Money Website at http://cnnmoney.com. Another source is Paul Meller, 'Europe's Entrepreneurial Spirit is Alive and Well—On eBay', *International Herald Tribune*, 2 February 2006, p . 14.

2.3 WHAT IS THE (RIGHT) QUESTION?

That is *not* the right question.
—former Intel CEO and Chair Andy Grove[3]

Former Intel CEO Andy Grove was famous for rebuking his managers for not asking the right questions. If you do not ask the correct question, Grove noted, then by definition, the answers will be irrelevant; knowing the questions is more important than knowing the answers.

What, then, is the key question regarding *what* to innovate?

It is this: *How can innovators tell the difference between a winning business idea and a disastrous one?*

Much is at stake when innovators select ideas for implementation. Many radically new ideas seem at first sight to be ridiculous; that is why great innovators insist on never rejecting any idea at once. And many ideas that sound wonderful at first hearing turn out to be disasters. Can one tell the difference?

In economics, Gresham's Law says that bad money drives out good (i.e., fake gold coins stay in circulation, real gold coins are withdrawn and hoarded). The same is true of innovation. Bad ideas drive out good ones, because they capture scarce resources and time. How then can innovators avoid wasting time and money on doomed ideas? What are the hallmarks of a winning innovation? A good place to start is with 'vision', expressed as a Unique Value Proposition.

DEFINITION

Unique Value Proposition (UVP): A short sentence stating how your product or service creates substantial added value for customers in ways that competitors do not.

Consider the following 12-word 'Unique Value Proposition' (see Chapter 12, for further discussion):

Uninterrupted mobile phone service everywhere in the world, any time, any place.

This was the value proposition of Motorola's Iridium. It sounds sure-fire. But it failed; the added value (above conventional cell phones) did not justify the $3,000 price. (The high price was driven by the enormous cost of building and launching dozens of low-orbit satellites.) In addition, the Iridium phones were heavy, clumsy and did not work well. Could Motorola have known in advance that the idea was a loser? If so, how?

Here is a key question to ask about your innovative idea, suggested by management educators W. Chan Kim and Renee Mauborgne, that can help discriminate between winning and losing ideas:

How does your idea change your customers' or clients' lives?

It seems obvious, but ideas driven by demand—needs and wants—based on real evidence and data are far more likely to succeed than those driven by supply—fascination with virtuoso technological skill and gadgetry. Ideas 'pulled' by demand and the market are far more likely to succeed than ideas 'pushed' by technology and inventors. An idea that, when implemented, delights customers will tend to be a winner. Iridium flunks the test: it aimed at improving people's ability to communicate, but did not fundamentally *change* it because people already had cell phones (even though they might not work in Antarctica or Timbuktu—but how many people need to call home from Antarctica?).[4]

Every winning idea has a powerful Unique Value Proposition; *if you cannot frame one, your innovation is in trouble.* In our experience, innovators (especially those founding companies) err with wishy-wishy UVPs. In their book *Built to Last*, authors Jim Collins and Jerry I. Porras define what they call BHAGs (Big Hairy Audacious Goals), such as NASA's 'a man on the moon by the end of the '60s' or General Electric's 'become #1 or #2 in every market we serve'.[5] A BHAG gets powerful momentum from a strong UVP. And it should directly address, and connect with, human wants, needs and feelings.

One must keep in mind, however, that many pressing needs are not consciously recognized or verbalized by customers. Truly innovative ideas are often initially rejected by customers precisely because they are different, strange and unfamiliar. *Great innovators anticipate needs long before they are articulated.* The following case study provides an example.

Case study: Checkpoint: Anticipating a real need

The Israeli global software company, Checkpoint was born in a stuffy Tel Aviv apartment in July 1993. Three software-engineer friends wrote a business plan for Firewall-1, an Internet security product designed to protect networks from hackers and invaders.

The World Wide Web had been launched only two years earlier, in 1991, but already showed signs of phenomenal growth. Based on their experience in military intelligence, the three engineers knew that there would eventually be a demand for 'firewall' security for internal company networks, even though few companies used such networks at the time and there was no demonstrable market demand. The three innovators sensed that with Web users growing by 50 per cent yearly, and with security issues inevitably arising from it, the ultimate market would soon be huge. The friends created a software solution for an embryonic need that market research most likely could not have shown or revealed. They perceived that need because they themselves needed the product they were launching. In 2004, Checkpoint, a market leader, had sales of nearly $600 million, and net profit of about half that, or $300 million.

Source: Based on Harvard Business School case study 9-298-071, 'NSK Software Technologies Inc.' (1998), by Jeffrey Anapolsky.

Very often, new product ideas arise from inventors who themselves feel a need for the product they ultimately invent. Legend has it that Omidyar built the eBay Website after his fiancée said she was having problems finding other PEZ candy dispenser collectors with whom to trade (a nice story, though it is now said to be untrue). 3M's very successful product, the ubiquitous 'Post-it®' likewise emanated from the personal need of Art Fry, 3M's legendary innovator, while there was no immediate need for the product from customers. Intuition and introspection, then, are good tools for finding new product ideas. If you yourself really need the product you innovate—chances are, others do too.

2.4 IDENTIFYING FEELINGS AND NEEDS

After defining how your innovation alters peoples' lives, the next logical question is: What specific aspects of people's *lives* are improved by your innovation, what specific *feelings* are generated and which *needs* are met?

A comprehensive list of 'feelings when your needs are satisfied' is given in Table 2.1. The categories of feelings are: affectionate, confident, engaged, inspired, excited, exhilarated, grateful, hopeful, joyful, peaceful, refreshed. Table 2.2 provides a list of the needs themselves. The categories of needs are: connection, honesty, play, peace, physical well-being, meaning and autonomy.

Table 2.1
List of feelings when your needs are satisfied

AFFECTIONATE	EXCITED	JOYFUL
compassionate	amazed	amused
friendly	animated	delighted
loving	ardent	glad
open hearted	aroused	happy
sympathetic	astonished	jubilant
tender	dazzled	pleased
warm	eager	tickled
CONFIDENT	energetic	PEACEFUL
empowered	enthusiastic	calm
open	giddy	clear headed
proud	invigorated	comfortable
safe	lively	centred
secure	passionate	content
ENGAGED	surprised	equanimous
absorbed	vibrant	fulfilled
alert	EXHILARATED	mellow
curious	blissful	quiet
engrossed	ecstatic	relaxed
enchanted	elated	relieved
entranced	enthralled	satisfied
fascinated	exuberant	serene
interested	radiant	still
intrigued	rapturous	tranquil
involved	thrilled	trusting
spellbound	GRATEFUL	REFRESHED
stimulated	appreciative	enlivened
INSPIRED	moved	rejuvenated
amazed	thankful	renewed
awed	touched	rested
wonder	HOPEFUL	restored
	expectant	revived
	encouraged	
	optimistic	

Source: Center for Nonviolent Communication, http://www.cnvc.org, 2005; used with permission.

Table 2.2
List of needs

CONNECTION	HONESTY	MEANING
acceptance	authenticity	awareness
affection	integrity	celebration of life
appreciation	presence	challenge
belonging	PLAY	clarity
cooperation	joy	competence
communication	humour	consciousness
closeness	PEACE	contribution
community	beauty	creativity
companionship	communion	discovery
compassion	ease	efficacy
consideration	equality	effectiveness
consistency	harmony	growth
empathy	inspiration	hope
inclusion	order	learning
intimacy	PHYSICAL WELL-BEING	mourning
love	air	participation
mutuality	food	purpose
nurturing	movement/exercise	self-expression
respect/self-respect	rest/sleep	stimulation
safety	sexual expression	to matter
security	safety	understanding
stability	shelter	AUTONOMY
support	touch	choice
to know and be known	water	freedom
to see and be seen		independence
to understand and be understood		space
trust		spontaneity
warmth		

Source: Center for Nonviolent Communication, http://www.cnvc.org, 2005; used with permission.

In the 21st century, people are starved of emotion and feeling because many modern technologies limit or reduce face-to-face human interaction. Increasingly, then, products that meet this basic human need by creating emotional bonds between product and buyer become successful innovations. 'Prices,' Princeton University Professor William Baumol once said, 'are relationships among people, expressed as relationships among things.' Innovations, too, ultimately are relationships among people, but are expressed as relationships between people and things. It is a forlorn commentary on modern life that emotional attachments to things have come to fill the void left by a lack of attachment to people.

Former Swiss psychiatrist Clotaire Rapaille who now lives in America and works with Fortune 100 companies says his mission is to 'decode' basic emotions that cause people to buy things. 'People have unspoken needs,' he says, 'they're not even aware of those needs.' Rapaille counsels, 'Don't say, buy my product because it's 10 per cent cheaper. You don't buy loyalty with percentages. It is not a question of numbers; it is the first reptilian (basic, primal, emotional) reaction.' He advised car firms that despite findings from focus groups and from what customers *said* they *wanted*, what buyers *really* wanted in SUVs (sport utility vehicles) was not 4 × 4 off-road capability, but size, muscle, control, dominance.[6]

Make them bigger, Rapaille advised. Give them tinted windows. And it worked. At the deepest level of successful innovations you will find a clear emotion or feeling the product supplies; you will find an almost audible 'click' between the feelings the innovation arouses and the feelings people most value. This is true not only of consumer goods but to some extent of capital goods as well.

This emotional aspect is in part the basis for the 'solutions' approach to innovation, which claims that what buyers want is not a product but a solution for their problems, generating calm, relaxed and serene feelings and meeting the need for safety, security, stability and support. Customers ultimately want an experience, not a product.

2.5 INNOVATING EXPERIENCES, BATTLING COMMODITIZATION

Many global CEOs lose sleep wondering how to get customers all over the world to *like* their product enough to buy it. But in today's competitive markets, the real question is: *how do you get customers to love your product?*

In his book, *The Experience Economy* (with Joseph Gilmore), strategist B. Joseph Pine describes a product 'ladder'.[7] At the bottom are commodities, standardized undifferentiated products where competition is based solely on cost and price; next, goods, which are differentiated, often through branding; then, services, and then, transformational experiences—*services offering a memorable and delightful experience that we love and remember them.* Some examples; a trip to Disney World for children, a flight on the Concord, a weekend at a superb resort, or highly-user-friendly software.

DEFINITIONS

- **Transformation: The individual is the offering.**
- **Experiences: The encounter is the offering.**
- **Services: The process is the offering.**
- **Goods: The product is the offering.**
- **Commodities: The material is the offering.**

The higher your product is in the commodity-to-transformation ladder, the higher your profit margins and the stronger your customer loyalty. Truly wonderful experiences are the uppermost rung on the ladder. Pine calls them transformations. For example, after a day at Disney World, one of our children said with a huge smile, 'Mom, Dad, that was the best day of my life!'. Such experiences are so powerful, they can change our lives. Companies that provide superior customer service, for instance, make sure that every touch-point they have with customers comprises a positive, memorable experience of this kind. *Innovation should aim as high as possible on the Experience Economy ladder.*

In today's global markets, there are powerful, inexorable forces that drive innovative products down the ladder to quickly become low-margin commodities. Inevitably, as innovative products 'click' with buyers, they are imitated and become standardized and commoditized. The only effective 'pushback' is to follow up with continual innovation, remaining as high as possible, as long as possible, on the Pine 'ladder'. Great managers find ways to push their products up the ladder and resist this commoditization. Experiences and transformations create an emotional bond with customers—the basis of enduring customer loyalty and powerful global brands. For innovators, the eternal question is, '*How can our products be kept from sliding down the ladder, becoming commoditized, and how can we push them up the ladder by shaping them into memorable customer experiences?*'

2.6 TECHNOLOGY AND PSYCHOLOGY

The story of radio and television exemplifies how technology and intuitive psychology interact to satisfy unarticulated needs and create memorable experiences when in the hands of master visionary innovators like David Sarnoff.

Case study: Radio and TV: David Sarnoff as visionary and innovator

Two of the most powerful innovations of the 20th century are radio and television. Both were pioneered by one man—David Sarnoff. Sarnoff immigrated to America from Uzlian, Russia with his parents at age nine.

Radio

Sarnoff was a Marconi telegraph operator atop a tall department store in Manhattan when on 14 April 1912, he picked up the message, 'S.S. Titanic sinking fast.' He rapidly relayed the news to the world. Sarnoff proposed to his company, Marconi, a vision for a 'radio music box' at a time when radio was largely used in shipping and by amateur Morse code enthusiasts. 'Bring music into the house by wireless,' was Sarnoff's vision—a radio in every home (reminiscent of Bill Gates' vision, 'a computer in every home'). The idea was ridiculed. But in 1919 General Electric formed Radio Corporation of America (RCA) to absorb Marconi's assets in the US. Sarnoff and his imagination were among those assets. Sarnoff conceived an ecosystem business model for his radio innovation, comprising *content* (music, news, sports), a *radio music box* (RCA's Radiola, priced at a steep $75, or $750 in today's dollars), and a *national network* of stations. In 1921, Sarnoff arranged for a ballyhooed prize fight between Georges Carpentier and Jack Dempsey to be broadcast on the radio, a memorable experience and watershed marketing event. In 1926, Sarnoff became general manager of RCA's subsidiary, National Broadcasting Corp. (NBC). And the profits rolled in.

Television

Sarnoff saw at once the amazing potential in inventor Vladimir Zworykin's 1923 'iconoscope' (precursor to television). In 1928, Sarnoff set up an experimental TV station, and launched the first commercial telecast from WNBT in 1941. 'Now we add sight to sound,' he said simply.

Today *the average US family watches TV for more than 50 hours a week*—more than they spend sleeping or working. Television certainly passes the hurdle of a life-changing innovation.

Source: From Marcy Carsey and Tom Werner, 'David Sarnoff', *Time*, 'Special issue: Builders and Titans of the 20th Century', 7 December 1998, p. 88.

Action learning

People's Feelings and Needs

1. Study the list of feelings people experience when their needs are satisfied (Table 2.1). In your opinion are there any gaps? Can you prioritize those feelings based on your own subjective views—which are most important to you?
2. Do the same for the list of people's needs in Table 2.2; prioritize them for yourself. For television and radio:
   (a) Which feelings do you think Sarnoff's radio innovation aroused initially when radio was born? When television was born?
   (b) Which needs do you think radio and television met?
   (c) Would market research, focus groups or panels have identified those needs in advance? Why/why not?
   (d) What feelings are aroused, and which needs are met, by radio and television today?
3. For your new product idea: what feelings does your new product, service or process idea inspire? Why? How? Which needs does it meet? For the market you are targeting, are these feelings and needs very important?

2.7 INNOVATION, FEELINGS, NEEDS: CREATING EMOTIONAL APPEAL

How can an innovator transform a product or service into an experience with strong emotional appeal? Kevin Roberts, worldwide CEO of Saatchi & Saatchi, a global advertising company, has some answers.[8] Born in Lancashire, Roberts left school at age 16. He worked with the inventor of the mini-skirt, Mary Quant, worked in marketing with Gillette, Procter & Gamble, Pepsi, and then joined Saatchi & Saatchi. Roberts coined the term 'lovemarks' (products that arouse deep emotional ties), and explains how to tell the difference between an ordinary branded product and a 'lovemark' (Table 2.3).

Table 2.3
The difference between a brand and a lovemark

Brand	*Lovemark*
Information	Relationship
Recognized by consumers	Loved by people
Generic	Personal
Presents a narrative	Creates a love story
The promise of quality	The touch of sensuality
Symbolic	Iconic
Defined	Infused
Statement	Story
Defined attributes	Wrapped in a mystery
Values	Spirit
Advertising agency	Ideas company
Professional	Passionately creative

Source: Kevin Roberts, *Lovemarks: The Future Beyond Brands* (New York: Powerhouse Books, 2005).

Roberts' message is best stated in his own words:

> People are trying to get emotion into every brand promise. Wal-Mart has gone from being trusted to being loved. Procter & Gamble, the world's biggest branded company, seeks to improve the lives of consumers, through creating 'brands they love'. Once brands were admired, trusted, respected, now ... they have to *be loved*. The people are voting and they are voting emotionally. *They want to buy things they have an emotional connection with.* McDonalds campaign is: 'I'm loving it'. Not hamburgers. Love, loving, feelings. Harley-Davidson does not sell motorcycles, but rather the experience of a rebel lifestyle. They say '*What we sell is the ability for a 43-year-old accountant to dress in black leather, ride through small towns and have people be afraid of him.*' You want *mystery*. You want to connect past, present, future. You want to connect with the icon .... Cut emotion loose and let it rip. Emotion is an unlimited resource with unlimited power. By streaming the power of emotion, *design can be an extraordinary force for good.*[9]

The invention of transformational experiences is a fruitful area for innovation. In modern economies, services comprise 75 per cent or more of gross domestic product. Some services, like haircuts, are low level and commodity-like. But some are high-price and high-margin. And by definition, innovation in creating experiences is almost entirely about emotions and feelings. With the right ambience, style and panache, even haircuts can become a profitable, transforming experience and a highly profitable business. Big industries have

Action learning

Name Your Lovemarks

Examine Table 2.3 (brands vs lovemarks).

- Name three products with which you feel a strong emotional bond, based on nostalgia, love, affection or admiration. (An example: [1] our old Isuzu Trooper jeep, which has a nickname and a personality, and bonds our family together through off-road outings; [2] our bread machine, whose fresh-bread smells delightful at six in the morning; [3] my Hersey Special running shoes, which have taken me for many hundreds of kilometres without injury or pain and will see me through a marathon.)
- Try to define precisely what it is that generates your emotional response to those products.
- How can you introduce emotion to your own, or to your organization's innovative products or services?

been built by innovators able to transform commodities into experiences. Starbucks is an example.

Case study: Starbucks: Coffee at $5 a cup

Entrepreneur Howard Schultz had a vision: to alter how and where every American has their breakfast coffee—cappuccino at Starbucks rather than instant coffee at home—by transforming coffee from a 50-cent commodity into a $5 experience. It succeeded. Today Starbucks (the name Starbucks comes from a character in the Herman Melville novel *Moby Dick*) is a large global chain of coffee shops, with 5,715 company-operated outlets worldwide: 4,666 of them in the United States and 1,049 in other countries and US territories, together with 3,956 joint-venture and licensed outlets, 2,222 of them in the United States and 1,734 in other countries. By creating ambience and stressing the international 'coffee culture', Starbucks is able to charge high prices for its coffee, while delighting customers (the average Starbucks client visits Starbucks 18 times a month, almost daily on workdays) thereby realizing Schultz's vision. Starbucks continues to innovate, providing WiFi (wireless computing) hot spots and lately, music downloads. In 2005 Starbucks had $6.4 billion in revenues, $495 million in net profit, and in the period 1995–2005 paid its shareholders an average annual return of 27.6 per cent.

2.8 SEARCHING FOR INNOVATION OPPORTUNITIES: FIND A PERFECT STORM

Where should innovators search for new opportunities and ideas?

A simple answer is: Wherever there is significant change (in tastes, preferences, technology, market structure or regulation). We once heard a renowned marine biologist speak about a powerful storm on the seacoast. She noted that by stirring up the sea bottom, storms create new opportunities for many organisms. Things that live in the sea love storms, she said. So do innovators, we believe. Innovators look for perfect storms. They constantly track social trends and find opportunities where others find only crises or problems. Here are some examples:

Aging

With birth rates plummeting, the age pyramid of countries in both West and East is growing older and shallower. This will create a new demand for a wide variety of products tailored for older people—in housing, electronics, vehicles, furniture, clothing, medical treatment and medicines.

Technology

Contrary to prevailing opinion, new technologies often *do* trumpet their birth long in advance. The difficult part is not forecasting technology but translating new technology into innovative businesses. The Internet is an example.

Case study: Internet—1969 to present

The Internet was born in 1969, when a computer engineering firm BBN (Bolt, Baranek & Newman) built ARPANET (Advanced Research Agency Projects Network), to link computers far apart on behalf of the US Defense Department for four US universities. BBN then developed an electronic mail software programme, in 1972, in the second stage. In the third stage, in 1991, a European Research Laboratory CERN (Conseil Européen pour la Recherche Nucléaire) released the software code written by a CERN physicist, Tim Berners-Lee, to help researchers exchange information. The World Wide Web (WWW) was born. Finally the WWW consortium adopted a new standard for defining and naming data, known as Extensible Markup Language (XML). The Internet, as we know it today, took 37 years to reach its current state. Yet, it continues to surprise many managers—like those in the embattled music industry.

Source: John Hagel III, *Out of the Box* (Boston, MA: Harvard Business School Press, 2002), p. 20.

Case study: Music

In 2004, more blank CDs were sold than ones with recorded music. This is evidence that the music industry, once large, growing and profitable, has been almost destroyed by Internet music downloads, some of them illegal. Yet the Internet, as shown above, has existed (at least in primordial forms) since 1969. Why did music industry executives choose to fight this technology, futilely, in the courts, rather than join it and innovate to harness it? Those who did—Apple's iTunes, for instance, with 99 cent download per tune—reaped large rewards, but they were among the exceptions.

Generational changes

Often, there are large differences in tastes, values and habits between generations, e.g., between baby-boomers, born in 1947–61 and baby-busters, born after 1961. As one generation ages, and is replaced by another that grows into a high-spending age, business opportunities arise as core generation values change. For example, Charles Schwab's discount brokerage was ridiculed but it turned out to appeal strongly to baby-boomers.

Economic downturns

While many businesses shudder at the thought of recession, others profit. Downturns make buyers price-sensitive and create opportunities for new lower-priced products that provide strong value for money.

Tastes and preferences

Consumer tastes may change rapidly, especially in the face of 'tipping point' phenomena, where markets seem to change almost overnight and a critical mass of initial buyers quickly pulls others into the circle. The food industry now faces such a change: consumers who once wanted foods that did not damage their health now seek foods that *actively* reinforce and build good health. Subway is an example.

Legislation

Changes in government regulation create superior opportunities for innovation. Chapter 10 relates how entrepreneurs anticipated the 1978 US PURPA (Public Utilities Regulatory Policy Act) that encouraged co-generation of electricity and launched Cogentrix, a company that supplied co-generation plants. By anticipating the legislation, they gained a decisive competitive edge on competitors who only reacted to the legislation after it was passed.

Case Study: Subway

Subway is a chain of fast-food restaurants specializing in 'subs' (submarine sandwiches); it leaped on the health trend with its 'Jared' campaign, built around 425-pound college student Jared Fogel, who lost many pounds by living on a Subway turkey sub for lunch and a Veggie Delite for dinner for a whole year. Subway offered '7 under 6' (a powerful memorable and simple UVP, meaning '7 subs under 6 grams of fat'). In December 2001, Subway's 13,247 shops surpassed the number of McDonald's outlets in the US, though McDonald's revenues are still eight times higher.

Source: From Rita Gunther McGrath and Ian C. McMillan, *Marketbusters* (Boston, MA: Harvard Business School Press, 2005), p. 159.

Another example is generic medicines.

Case study: Innovation through legislation

Teva Pharmaceutical Co., headquartered in Israel, is one of the world's largest generic medicine companies. (Generic medicines are drugs that contain the same active chemical ingredients as patented 'branded' products and are 'bioequivalent' in their effects; they come to the market when patents expire.) Teva CEO Eli Hurvitz spotted an opportunity when the Hatch-Waxman Act was passed by the US Congress in 1984, encouraging generic drugs as a way to cut the soaring cost of medicines for consumers. Teva quickly aligned its competencies with the generic business model and in two decades became the world's largest supplier at a time when for years other drug companies scorned the low margins inherent in the generic business.

Source: As related to the first author by Tera's Eli Hurvitz.

Customers

MIT Professor Eric von Hippel has shown that a great many successful innovations come from companies' major customers (whom he calls 'lead users'). When a customer steps up and says, 'If you make X, I will gladly buy 500 of it,' there is a *double* dividend—the idea itself and potential buyers. According to von Hippel's research, 77 per cent of innovations in scientific instruments are developed by users as are 67 per cent of innovations in semi-conductor and printed circuit board process. However, he notes, customers do not always come forward with their new ideas; 'users ... may keep [innovations] hidden behind their factory walls as a trade secret', as a source of competitive advantage and profit. Stronger and closer contacts with their customers will help businesses discover their customers' valuable innovations.[10]

Contracting, declining industries

Great innovators pick a declining industry no one finds attractive and revive it with novel ideas. Southwest Airlines is said to have paid the highest enduring total return to investors of any company. Southwest is in an industry plagued by enormous, persisting losses, but itself has been consistently profitable, through its innovative point-to-point, efficient no-frills business model. Fire-eater (literally) Guy Laliberté, CEO of Canada's Cirque du Soleil, entered the rapidly-disappearing circus industry and reinvented it, creating startling productions seen by 40 million people in 90 cities worldwide. By creating an entirely new experience, Cirque du Soleil drew new customers, delighted them—and charges prices many times higher than conventional circuses. In declining markets, innovative products revive growth and profit by drawing customers who previously scorned the old product.

2.9 PROCESS INNOVATION

One of the most underexploited innovation opportunities lies in the business processes that firms use. Excellence in process innovation—small incremental improvements that cumulatively generated unsurpassed efficiency—led Japan to global pre-eminence in manufacturing in the 1980s. Part II, Chapter 5 relates how IBM saved billions by radically re-engineering its supply chain management. Process innovation often involves many small incremental improvements, each of which is insignificant but together, leads to enormous productivity gains and cost reductions. This type of innovation requires participation of every worker and demands great persistence and patience. It is driven by a strong culture of continuous improvement that is shared by a company's entire work force.

Innovation itself, of course, is a key business process; so are the processes of cost management and operations management. Major cost reduction is a type of innovation that can impact the lives of billions of people; e.g., bringing cheap cellular phones to poor developing countries with little or no fixed-line infrastructure or the $100 laptop.

Case study: The $100 laptop computer

MIT Professor Nicholas Negroponte, founder of the MIT Media Laboratory, is the driving force behind the $100 laptop computer aimed at bringing durable, affordable laptops to students in poor countries. It uses free open-source software (Linux) rather than the more costly Windows. For obvious reasons Negroponte faces fierce opposition from Microsoft. In general, innovations that bring order-of-magnitude cost reductions threaten incumbents who may have large resources and use them vigorously to defend their business designs.

Source: From John Markoff, 'Battle to Bring Cheap PCs to the Masses', *New York Times*, 30 January 2006.

Here are two examples of how companies use value-creation and cost-reduction innovation in very different ways to build growth and profit.

Case study: Rubbermaid vs Wal-Mart; 3M vs Best Buy

Rubbermaid vs Wal-Mart

Fortune magazine conducts an annual survey that chooses America's most admired companies. In 1994, Rubbermaid was high on the list. Rubbermaid won its laurels in part for its value-creation innovation, launching new products almost daily. Its *forte* was value creation through continual innovation.

A decade later, in 2004, Rubbermaid was replaced in the list by Wal-Mart. Wal-Mart, too, is an innovator, but its invention was its cost-reduction business model, built on 'everyday low prices' (see case study 'Wal-Mart' in Chapter 8). With growing inequality in the distribution of income in the US, low-income groups seeking value and low prices grew proportionately rapidly. Wal-Mart's 'low-price' UVP won their hearts. Wal-Mart's low prices, are driven by low costs, powered in part by large-scale imports from China. If Wal-Mart were a country, it would be the world's sixth-largest importer from China. Wal-Mart's huge Global Processing Center in Shen Zhen, China, deals with some 6,000 different suppliers. Many of Wal-Mart's imports arrive in containers at Long Beach Port, near Los Angeles—$36 billion worth a year. Wal-Mart's core competency is the use of information technology to manage its store inventories and supply chain.

Case study continued

Case study continued

3M vs Best Buy

3M's legendary President, and later Board Chairman, William L. McKnight built a culture that put employees in direct contact with customer problems and encouraged initiative and innovation. His philosophy was to listen to anyone who proposed an original idea and to let him or her 'run' with that idea through what he called 'experimental doodling'. '... It's essential that we have many people with initiative if we are to continue to grow,' he said. Today 3M has a 15 per cent rule, requiring technical and scientific employees to invest about a sixth of their time to pursue ideas that are not related to their official job assignments. Along with its spirit of innovation, 3M is fiercely profit-focused—every innovation must pass the 3M trial-by-fire: 'Will it make 3M (profit) margins?'

Best Buy, a chain of retail consumer electronics stores, fourth largest in the specialty-retail industry in the US, defines innovation focus as 'continuous innovation in operations and service, to cater to the changing tastes of consumers'. Its process innovation begins with a consumer need, identified by an individual, who forms a team that then presents its ideas to senior management. Best Buy had sales of $25 billion in 2004, up 10 percent from 2003, net profit of $705 million and 100,000 employees.

Source: The account of 3M's William Mcknight is from *Managing Creativity & Innovation* (Boston, MA: Harvard Business School Press, 2003), p. 109; also from personal communication with MBA student Nimesh Bhandari.

2.10 INNOVATION PORTFOLIOS FOR ESTABLISHED ORGANIZATIONS

Financial advisors recommend a portfolio approach to asset management by dividing investments among different types of assets (stocks, bonds, foreign exchange). By diversifying, investors can reduce risk without reducing their returns.

A similar approach applies to innovation. While entrepreneurs generally focus on a single core innovation, established organizations work on balancing and optimizing a spectrum of innovations, from incremental to radical.

One way to classify innovations is by their impact on product features. This approach, known as 'feature driven innovation', will be explained in detail in the next chapter. Meanwhile, here are some basic definitions:

DEFINITIONS

Product Attribute: A characteristic or feature of a product, comprising an essential element of how the product satisfies wants and needs and capable of being quantified and compared.

Incremental Innovation: An innovation in which a new version of an existing product is created, by improving or altering some of its existing attributes. Example: a corporate jet, say, Gulfstream IV. A reconfigured improved Gulfstream V may have better range, speed, payload, climb and cabin room.

Standard Innovation: One additional attribute is added to the product that did not exist before. Example: the addition of a CD-ROM read-only drive to PCs.

Radical: Several significant new attributes are created which did not before exist, thus creating, essentially, a new product. Example: a handheld computer (e.g., Palm Pilot).

Source: The definitions of incremental, standard and radical innovations are from S. Maital and H. Grupp, *Managing New Product Development and Innovation: A Microeconomic Toolbox* (Cheltenham, UK: Edward Elgar, 2000), Chapter 1.

Table 2.4 shows three different 'innovation portfolio' strategies for a large company, depending on the proportion of resources invested in radical (high risk) innovation compared with incremental (low risk) innovation.

Table 2.4
Innovation portfolio strategy: Fraction of innovation resources and time invested in each type of innovation

	Low risk	*Moderate risk*	*High risk*
Incremental	70%	50%	25%
Standard	20%	30%	15%
Radical	10%	20%	50%

Each organization needs to optimize its own innovation portfolio, taking into account the fact that a 'low risk' strategy focused on incremental innovation is highly vulnerable to a radical innovation strategy by a competitor. Paradoxically, in innovation, low risk policies may ultimately incur the highest risk of all, as the fierce battle between Nokia and Samsung illustrates.

2.11 PIONEERS, MIGRATORS, SETTLERS

The notion of managing and optimizing an innovation portfolio is a widespread concept in innovation management. There are many different typologies

Case study: Nokia vs Samsung

For years, Nokia followed a winning strategy of incremental innovation, improving the performance and design of its cell phones by 5 per cent yearly to remain ahead of its competition. The strategy worked—until Samsung came on the scene with large resources and several radical innovations in cellphone design and performance. According to market research firm Gartner, in 2004 'sales of mobile phones jumped sharply to record-setting levels during the first quarter, but longtime leader Nokia saw its share of the market fall to the lowest level in five years', falling from 34.6 percent in 2003 to 28.9 per cent in the first quarter of 2004. Nokia's share price fell precipitously as a result. A Gartner expert explained that Nokia's market share dropped because other phone makers [like Samsung] were more aggressive in rolling out more feature-laden phones.

Source: Based on a report by Keith Regan in *E-Commerce Times,* 9 June 2004.

of innovations. For instance, Vijay Govindarajan distinguishes between *continuous process improvement* (countless small investments in incremental process innovations), *process revolutions* (improvements in existing business processes, but in major leaps); *product or service innovations* (creative new ideas that do not alter established business models) and *strategic innovations* (innovations in process or product that involve new, unproven business models).[11]

A more colorful typology is that of Chan and Mauborgne, who use a *How They Won the West* metaphor to describe a growth portfolio consisting of 'settlers' (mature cash cow products), 'migrators' (products once pioneers, now becoming settlers), and 'pioneers' (innovative new products in their markets). Innovators, say the authors, should 'wisely balance between profitable growth and cash flow at a given point in time'. This may involve a major shift toward 'pioneers'—which often encounters resistance from a coalition of interests, including shareholders (who seek short-term gain), employees (threatened by rapid change), and senior managers (who may lack the energy, leadership and competencies that 'pioneering' requires). Only strong leadership, a key component of successful innovation, can overcome such resistance.

Jeffrey Immelt, General Electric CEO who succeeded legendary CEO Jack Welch in September 2001, is an example. Under Welch, GE focused on operational excellence, using such tools as 'Six Sigma' (a system for eliminating errors and slip-ups). Under Immelt, GE is focusing on innovation. 'The biggest challenge is continuing to drive consistent growth in a world that is more volatile and has less economic growth,' Immelt told *Business Week*.[12] Innovation is the tool he chose to achieve this goal.

2.12 CONCLUSION

It is sometimes believed that in innovation, the most challenging and difficult task is coming up with new ideas. In our experience, this is not the case. When people are empowered, inspired by vision, provided ample time and resources and an appropriate environment, ideas proliferate like wild flowers in springtime. The main challenge lies not in ideation—producing ideas—but in winnowing wheat kernels from chaff, good ones from bad, and then in matching innovative business designs to innovative ideas for products and services.

Bringing innovative products to market is risky. But refraining from doing so is even riskier. Remember this wise business advice from poet Robert Frost:

Two roads diverged in a wood, and I—
I took the one less traveled by,
And that has made all the difference.

CASE STUDY 2.1

Ingersoll-Rand (India) Ltd.*

Sanjay Mehta, sales executive of Ingersoll-Rand (India) Ltd., Mumbai was excited to receive the first order for a Rs 9.3 million (about $200,000) centrifugal compressor from Deccan Textiles—an account that was historically the stronghold of a competitor. The very next day, he gatecrashed into the office of Mr Anand Ranganathan, Executive Vice President—Air Compressors, at Ahmedabad: 'Boss! I have clinched this order of our dreams!' The grim expression on Anand's face after he had finished reading the customer's order got Sanjay worried.

Anand paused for a moment and then replied in a calm voice, 'As impressive as this deal looks on the surface, I wish you had not taken the order.' 'I don't understand, Boss! I thought you would be very impressed

* Names of people, figures, client company name, etc., have been disguised to preserve confidentiality of the company's information.

Case study 2.1 continued

Case study 2.1 continued

with this!', exclaimed Sanjay, clearly disappointed. 'At this price, this sale will earn us only a 2–3 per cent profit. I see no sense in offering a world class high value product at such a heavily discounted price!', was Anand's terse response. 'Well then, if we cannot afford to offer our compressor for Rs 9.3 million, our competitors will be more than happy to offer theirs at a price 10 per cent lower than this price. Anyway, I am too shaken up now, and need to compose myself first before hearing from you on what you want me to do on this order', said Sanjay raising his voice. Without wasting another minute, he walked out of Anand's office in a huff.

With a turnover of over $9 billion, Ingersoll-Rand worldwide has a truly diversified product portfolio that includes construction equipment, refrigeration equipment, temperature-control equipment for the transport industry, security and safety equipment and air and gas compressors. Ingersoll-Rand (India) Ltd. (IRL) set up its first manufacturing plant in India in 1965 at Naroda, Gujarat to manufacture reciprocating compressors, and in 1978 IRL commissioned its second production unit at Bangalore to manufacture various construction equipment. With an annual turnover of Rs 4,062 million (2001–02) and an employee strength of about 1,000, IRL delivered an annual growth rate of 7.69 per cent in revenues and 5.62 per cent in profits after tax for the year 2002. There are a variety of compressors manufactured by the company, and in each of these product categories, competition is intense from both domestic and foreign suppliers.

After Sanjay stomped out of Anand's office, Anand decided to convene an emergency meeting of his senior colleagues to discuss the issue at hand. The meeting was held later that day.

At the emergency meeting, the sales and marketing people were appalled that rather than celebrating the event for the big order received, the room seemed filled with gloom. According to the Finance Controller, 'Offering this product at a price as low as Rs 9.3 million would mean undervaluing the product. Besides, we will end up losing money, should we sell it at such a low price, since there are a lot of hidden costs involved in the implementation, over which we do not have too much control. Our present business model of selling such sophisticated equipment by competing on price simply does not make sense!'

On completion of the emergency meeting, Anand created a 'fact-finding' team that included Sanjay and two others. The reason he constituted this fact-finding team was to get a better understanding of the challenges being faced by Deccan Textiles. He asked the three members of this team to report back their findings to him within a week.

Case study 2.1 continued

Case study 2.1 continued

'Should IRL continue to bleed, doing business this way?' Anand asked himself, at the end of a long and eventful day, after his team of senior managers left on conclusion of the emergency meeting. 'If we carry on doing business in this manner, we will come under enormous bottom-line pressures. Also, we will end up growing the company at about the same rate as the growth of the economy.'

Anand recollected some of the concerns expressed by Simon McDonald, President, Industrial Technologies group at IR, USA, during a recently held meeting in the global headquarters in USA only a few weeks earlier. 'There is much more potential for air compressors in the Indian market', Simon had said confidently to Anand. 'You guys in IRL are not capitalizing on this opportunity. Something is missing somewhere. You have the right kind of people, the required technological skills, the market seems to be there, but your growth has not been anywhere near the "aha" that I have been hoping for!' Anand came away from this meeting with a clear directive that he had to grow the domestic air compressor business at a faster clip. In parting, Simon advised Anand that the way forward was for IRL to 'do something very different.' Anand was too seasoned a manager to ask Simon if he knew what that 'something very different' should be!

The fact-finding promptly came back in a week with their report of the ground realities prevailing at Deccan Textiles. The findings are summarized as follows:

- Sales and marketing function at Deccan Textiles was under enormous pressure to increase the company's domestic and international market shares.
- The company's falling turnovers and profits figures over the last three years has had the Managing Director (MD) of Deccan Textiles worried.
- In his drive to cut costs and minimize waste in the company, the MD has given the Vice President (Manufacturing) a clear mandate to reduce cost of production in the three divisions, viz., textiles, cotton yarn and denim.
- Known to be shrewd extractors of price concessions and service support from vendors, the purchase department has over the years created a lot of negative feelings amongst its vendors.
- Over the past three years the utilities manager of Deccan Textiles had encountered numerous problems with many of the equipment (for instance, exhaust fans, transformers, motors, etc.) purchased by

Case study 2.1 continued

Case study 2.1 continued

the company. He felt that this was due to the mercenary policies adopted by the company in its price negotiations with the suppliers.

- The maintenance head had his own bag of woes to recount to the IRL team. He highlighted the sudden breakdown of critical equipment such as compressors used to supply compressed air to the process plants as one of his biggest problem areas. He attributed this to poor quality of equipment purchased.
- In trying to follow the instructions of the MD, the VP (Finance) was all set to ensure that the company ramped up its profitability 'anyhow.' His approach to contain costs and enhance profits would clearly be through time-tested methods: steep reduction in overheads, variable costs as well as sales and marketing expenses and controlling investments in R&D.

All the soul-searching that followed the receipt of the report on Deccan Textiles from the fact-finding team led to a change in the business model. Rather than simply focusing on pushing compressors to customers, the involuntary crisis that resulted from bagging the Deccan Textiles order forced Anand and his team to re-examine the value they were actually providing their customers. Intense discussions within the team resulted in the realization that they were in the business of helping their customers like Deccan Textiles to actually succeed in their respective marketplaces.

Over the next several months, this realization resulted in the company exiting from the 'never-ending battle of commoditization' that was taking place even in the markets for sophisticated compressors and the resulting price wars. Instead, IRL decided to focus on providing solutions to its customers through its 'solutionizing initiative'. However, this was not without its challenges. The company found that moving into solutionizing threw up many new challenges relating to the people, processes, customers and financial aspects of doing the business.

After about three years of sustained effort, the company succeeded in fully implementing its new business model, based on providing effective solutions to the customer, rather than 'hard sell' a compressor as a 'product' as they had done in the past. This led to considerable improvement in the company's market performance, including revenue and profitability growth. In the case of Ingersoll-Rand, the innovative change in business model encompassed their entire way of doing business, and resulted in a totally different business model vis-à-vis the traditional business model that they had followed for decades and that their competitors continued to follow. The results of IRL's Air Solutions Division (the new name for the Air Compressor Division, to reflect

Case study 2.1 continued

Case study 2.1 continued

change in the business model) in terms of indicators of performance relating to the financial, customer, internal business processes and employees, have been excellent.

So *what* do you have to innovate in your organization? The IRL case study shows that when pushed against the wall, it had to innovate the entire business model, thereby leading to a change in nearly all aspects of its 'goint to market strategy.' There is a powerful lesson in it for your own organization—constantly look for vulnerabilities in your business model and get your funnel of innovation flowing!

Notes

1. This quote is taken from Adam Cohen's account of how eBay was founded: 'Pierre Omidyar's Perfect Store', *International Herald Tribune*, 8 September 2005, p. 7.
2. W. Chan Kim and Renee Mauborgne, *Blue Ocean Strategy* (Boston, MA: Harvard Business School Press, 2005), p. 7.
3. Quote from Richard S. Tedlow, 'The education of Andy Grove', *Fortune*, 12 December 2005, p. 34.
4. W. Chan Kim and Renee Mauborgne, 'Knowing a Winning Business Idea When You See One', *Harvard Business Review*, September–October 2000, pp. 129–37.
5. Jim Collins and Jerry I. Porras, *Built to Last: Successful Habits of Visionary Companies* (New York: HarperCollins, 1994).
6. Material on Clotaire Rapaille is drawn from the video, 'The Persuaders' in the PBS *Frontline* series (Boston, 2005).
7. B. Joseph Pine and James H. Gilmore, *The Experience Economy: Work is Theatre and Every Business a Stage* (Boston, MA: Harvard Business School Press, 1999). See also their article, 'Beyond Goods and Services: Staging Experiences and Guiding Transformations', *Strategy & Leadership*, May–June 1997.
8. See Kevin Roberts, *Lovemarks: The Future Beyond Brands* (New York: Powerhouse Books, 2005).
9. A rough transcription from an interview by Peter Day on the BBC World Service's *Global Business*.
10. Eric von Hippel, *The Sources of Innovation* (London: Oxford University Press, 1988).
11. For innovation typologies, see Vijay Govindarajan and Chris Trimble, 'Not All Innovations Are Equal', *Harvard Business School Working Knowledge*, 5 December 2005; and Kim and Mauborgne, *Blue Ocean Strategy*, p. 98.
12. 'Best Managers of 2004', *Business Week* online, 10 January 2005.

Chapter 3
The innovation voices: *How* to innovate

Thirty thousand new consumer products are launched each year...over 90 per cent of them fail...after marketing professionals have spent massive amounts of money trying to understand what their customers want.
—Clayton Christensen, *Scott Cook and Taddy Hall*[1]

LEARNING OBJECTIVES After you read this chapter, you should understand:

- **Why innovation processes work best when they are structured, organized and disciplined**
- **Why in-the-box thinking leads to out-of-the-box creativity**
- **What the four innovation 'voices' are**
- **How to use the five arithmetic creativity templates**
- **What product profiles are, how to build them, and how to use them for innovation**
- **How to use empathic design**
- **How and why customers can be great innovators**
- **How to adapt one of the five innovative-process templates to your organization**
- **What the inspiration/perspiration 'eutectic point' is**
- **What the six myths about creativity are and why they are false**
- **How to listen to your inner voice (intuition) when innovating**

3.1 INTRODUCTION

The first two chapters explored *why* and *what* to innovate. This chapter examines *how*. It defines each of four innovation 'voices' as a source of inspiration and methodology for result-oriented innovation for growth and profit: products' voices, customers' voices, organizations' voices, and our own inner (intuitive) voices. We offer tools and techniques for listening to each of the voices and for extracting maximum innovation value and information from them. The sole objective is to find ways to significantly improve the daunting nine-to-one odds against success facing innovators.

The core message of this chapter is: *Effective, applied creativity, the foundation of innovation, is structured, disciplined and systematic. Great innovators have a system.*

Research overwhelmingly supports this. Paradoxically, it has been found that 'out-of-the-box' thinking is best done *inside* the box, where 'box' represents the real *constraints* in which innovators must operate—technological, psychological, business, financial, human. The main reason is that *all* innovation is constrained in some manner. It is unwise to discard or ignore the 'box' (constraints); better, rather, to know where to *position* the box, i.e., to know which constraints must be accepted and which can be ignored.

3.2 THINKING 'INSIDE THE BOX'

The phrase 'think outside the box' is at least 30 years old. Its origins lie in a famous puzzle (Figure 3.1). To solve the puzzle, connect nine dots, arranged in a square grid, by drawing four straight lines *without your pen leaving paper.* The only solution to this puzzle is one where some of the lines extend *beyond the border of the box* (Figure 3.1).

Our own mind tends to limit our pen within the imaginary box formed by the nine dots. This box may be imaginary, but such imaginary boxes are at times more confining than iron cages.

The puzzle illustrates the principle that innovators need to discard self-imposed constraints, such as the assumption that the lines must remain

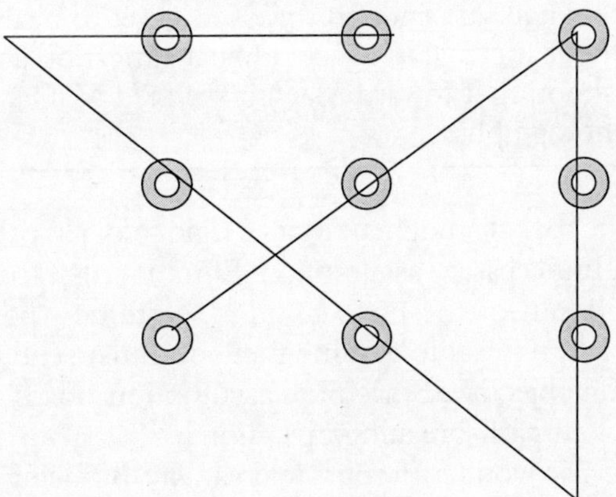

Join the dots with four connected straight lines without your pen leaving the paper.

Figure 3.1
'Out-of-the-box'

within the box, to create novelty. But the true secret of creativity and innovation lies in thinking *inside* the box, because in business and management, boxes (constraints) *always* exist. The question is, *which of the constraints are truly constraining and which are not and can be ignored*. The small box formed by the nine dots is not a real constraint. But the need to draw four connected straight lines *is*.

Here are two examples of outside-the-box inside-the-box thinking, from outer space and from inner space.

Case study: Going to Mars by changing the box

Years ago, engineers and scientists at America's NASA (National Aeronautical and Space Administration) were dealt a severe blow. The problematic 'box' was the maximum weight constraint. Because of problems with their launch rocket, the Mars Explorer spacecraft they had spent years designing was found to be too heavy. The rocket lacked thrust. Even after paring down its weight to the bare minimum, the rocket could not get it to Mars. It looked like the mission would have to be cancelled, a waste of years of work. The 'box' had changed—and threatened the idea itself.

One creative engineer refused to give up. He solved the problem with creative thinking that was both inside the box (the available rocket thrust) and outside the box (the trajectory).

The Mars explorer was not launched toward Mars. At this innovator's suggestion, it was launched in the opposite direction toward nearby Venus! The rocket had just enough thrust to get it to nearby Venus. As it circled Venus, the planet's gravity acted like a slingshot, accelerating the spacecraft and shooting it toward Mars. It reached Mars and sent back thousands of photographs.

Was aiming the rocket straight at Mars a rigid 'box', like the rocket thrust? In fact it was an unnecessary assumption. Eliminating it led to an innovative 'in-the-box' (and 'out-of-the-box') solution. Note how powerful *hidden* assumptions are. It is natural to assume that you must send the rocket in the direction of your objective. Smashing 'assumption boxes' is a proven tool for coming up with path-breaking inventions.

Yet 'boxes' are also wonderful spurs to creativity. By facing up to constraints on time, money, space, weight and technology, innovators dream up amazingly ingenious solutions. Ignoring real 'boxes' generates ideas that at best are scrapped, and, at worst, swallow resources futilely before failing. Yielding to unreal boxes leads to more-of-the-same ideas. Great innovators know which constraints can be discarded.

Case study: Curing ulcers–In the body, in and out of the box

In the early 1980s two Australian scientists, J. Robin Warren and Barry J. Marshall, decided to prove it was a *bacterium* that caused stomach ulcers, not stress. Their wild notion faced several constraints—vested interests in the prevailing wisdom, including drug companies, ulcer surgeons, and psychiatrists and psychologists who treated stress; and science—doctors had been taught for years that no microbes could grow in the stomach's corrosive gastric juices. Warren, a pathologist, had seen *Helicobacter* bacteria in stomach biopsies as early as 1979. 'Once I started looking for them, they were obvious,' he said, 'but convincing other people was another matter.' A librarian found that doctors had described the bacteria in published papers as early as the late 19th century, but their findings had been ignored. Warren and Marshall were ridiculed by their peers. In desperation, Dr Marshall performed a famous self-experiment—he swallowed a culture of the bacteria, got an ulcer, documented it and was cured with an antibiotic—now the standard cure. Warren and Marshall won the 2005 Nobel Prize for medicine.

A former medical school dean, Dr Samuel Hellman, commented how doctors 'often fall in love with a hypothesis.... Medicine's peer-review system ... tends to adhere to things that are consistent with prevailing beliefs and models.' So do unsuccessful innovators, he might have added.

Source: From Lawrence K. Altman, MD, 'Nobel Came after Years of Battling the System', *New York Times*, 11 October 2005.

Warren and Marshall worked *inside* the box of medical science, but *out of the box* of rigid mindsets and prevailing assumptions. And they *listened*—to their 'product' (ulcers), their patients, their organizations and their own inner voices.

3.3 THE FOUR VOICES

Innovators, it is said, are inspiring speakers. They lead by communicating their unique innovative vision to their people, teams and organizations.

This is sometimes true. But what is *always* true, we believe, is that innovators are outstanding *listeners*. Their ears are literally to the ground.

Geologists tell us the earth rests on continent-sized tectonic plates that drift on a sea of hot liquid rock. The plates move a few inches a year, slower than the rate at which fingernails grow. Though very slow, their movements are inexorable. In places where plates meet and collide, such as where the

Indian plate encounters the Eurasian plate, earthquakes occur, like the recent tragic one in Kashmir.

Innovators live on the business equivalent of tectonic plates. To succeed, they need the human equivalent of a geologist's seismograph, a highly sensitive one, to listen to underlying trends, some of them initially faint but potentially powerful.

As an aspiring innovator, *to whom* should you listen, and *how*? How can you construct your own sensitive, internal seismograph?

There are four different voices you must listen to regularly:

- The voice of your own *products* and those of your competitors;
- your *customers'* voices;
- the voice of your *organization*;
- and, not least, your own *inner voice*.

Here, in turn, is how each voice can lead you to profitable innovation. We begin our discussion with a case study, Lego, which exemplifies how an embattled Danish family business survives by listening, in its own way, to each of the four voices.

Case study: Lego: Big company, little bricks

Lego is an example of a great innovator that has struggled for profit. The name Lego comes from two Danish words, *leg godt*, meaning, 'play well'. Lego is the Danish family-owned company that makes the famous Lego 'automatic binding bricks' first patented in 1958. The secret: tiny tubes that ensure the bricks lock together firmly, with machine tolerances as small as 0.002 metre.

Lego is a great serial innovator and, by sales, is the world's fourth-largest toymaker. After the initial Lego brick invention, Lego innovated Lego Technic (advanced Lego bricks), Minifigures, Lego Technic computer control (with MIT Media Lab), LEGOLand theme parks, Lego Mindstorms (the intelligent Lego brick, integrated with robot technology), Lego retail stores, Clikits (a new design for girls), and Bionicle (combines construction toys and action themes).

For the first Lego toys, carpenter Ole Kirk Christiansen listened to his *inner voice*. His son, Godtfred Kirk Christiansen, pioneered interlocking Lego bricks, in part, by listening to the *product* itself. The grandson of the founder, Kjeld Kirk Kristiansen, retired as CEO in 2004; his skill lay in listening to Lego's *customers*. Today's Lego managers, when upgrading a

Case study continued

Case study continued

Lego robit kit, Mindstorm, listen to their customers in interesting and novel ways (recounted below), and listen to the Lego *organization*, adapting its innovation system to its culture, history and personality.[2]

Despite these successful innovations, for Lego it is an uphill battle. Increasingly children prefer computer video games. Lego is squeezed at the high end of the market by these games and by cheap Asia-made imitations at the low end. As a result, Lego has lost money in three of the past five years, despite its innovations, cost-cutting and restructuring. Yet had it not been for innovations like Mindstorm, Lego would have disappeared long ago. In competitive industries like Lego's, sometimes survival is an even bigger achievement than achieving growth and profit in less Darwinian industries.

We begin our discussion of the four 'voices' with the product itself.

3.4 VOICE OF THE PRODUCT

Listen to the voice of your product. It will tell you how to change and improve it, sometimes radically, if you just listen to it carefully.

But how? Here are two related approaches, 'innovation templates' and 'product profiles'. Both provide a systematic, structured approach to a process known as ideation (the process of developing novel ideas) that is widely (and wrongly) believed to require an unstructured, almost chaotic approach.

The innovation template method is based on the thinking of a Russian inventor and scientist Genrich S. Altschuller, who studied thousands of creative ideas and identified the patterns that created them. Some of his early thinking on the subject was done while he was a prisoner in Stalin's *gulag*, jailed for criticizing the Soviet establishment's dismal lack of innovation. TRIZ (Theory for Inventive Problem Solving), a method widely used by engineers all over the world, is based on Altschuller's ideas.

TRIZ, a Russian acronym for *Teoriya Resheniya Izobretatelskikh Zadatch*, meaning 'Theory for Inventive Problem Solving', is a method for generating innovative ideas and solutions for problem-solving. TRIZ expands approaches developed in systems engineering and provides tools and systemic methods for use in problem formulation, system analysis, failure analysis, and patterns of system evolution (both 'as-is' and 'could be'). In sharp contrast to techniques such as brainstorming, based mainly on random idea generation, TRIZ aims to create a systematic, algorithmic approach to the invention of new systems and the refinement of old ones.

A particularly powerful version of Altschuller's algorithm was developed by a group led by Hebrew University Professor Jacob Goldenberg, and is today applied to its global concerns by a Tel Aviv-based company, Systematic Inventive Thinking (SIT). 'Don't listen solely to the voice of your customer,' cautions Goldenberg. Customers are creatures of habit and become habituated to overcoming deficiencies inherent in the products and services they buy, to the point where they may be unaware of those deficiencies and unable to articulate them. 'Listen to your product,' Goldenberg advises. Analyze your products' features.[3]

The SIT approach uses five patterns, or templates, to guide innovation based on those features. Here is our own, simplified version of the templates, which we trust does not distort or devalue the original SIT version; we recommend that readers read and study the full version.[4]

If you can apply one of these four basic arithmetic operations to your product's voice, we argue, then you can achieve winning innovations:

1. Subtraction

Most innovators begin with addition—by adding features on to an existing product. Why not *subtract*? Most products today are excessively complicated (for instance, the 'programmable' VCR that nobody can programme), because many innovators assume wrongly that innovative product improvement *invariably involves more and better features*. Philips, aided by SIT, came up with a winning sleek design for its DVD player, with a single button for control, by applying subtraction single-mindedly. Precisely because it is counter-intuitive, subtraction often generates powerful new innovations.

2. Addition

A conventional approach is to add features to an existing product. Examine the product, observe carefully how customers use it (see later, voice of the customer: empathic design), and look for features that strengthen the product's unique value. For instance, Cirque du Soleil added to the conventional features available at Ringling Bros/Barnum and Bailey circus—artistic music and dance, and a refined viewing environment.

A different approach to addition involves combining two or more product features, to make one feature perform two different functions. For instance, designers of the early Volkswagen Beetle used air pressure from the spare tyre in the front trunk to power the windshield wipers. This form of addition is often effective for cost reduction as it was for VW.

Finally, author Daniel Pink notes that 'the most powerful ideas come from simply combining two existing ideas nobody else ever thought to unite.'[5] For instance, Reese's Peanut Butter Cups that combine peanut butter and chocolate. (See the case study on Viewmax in Chapter 5—Do Hyun Kim combined TV and VCR for LG Electronics.)

3. Division

Divide your product into its component parts (physically, or by function). Look at the parts, then reconfigure them in unanticipated ways, to create unforeseen benefits. An Israeli household rug company took a standard rug, divided it into four 'ruglets', and created an innovative product—a rug that could be assembled in unique ways, or used as four separate small rugs, or two smaller rugs. Sony engineers separated a tape recorder's record/play heads from its speakers (with earphones), to make it smaller, and a new product, the Walkman, resulted (but not before the engineers were ridiculed for creating a tape recorder that could not record).

4. Multiplication

Once you have an innovation, can you multiply it, to create a whole product line, benefiting from scale and scope? This is known as a platform strategy. (See Chapter 10 for a discussion of 'platform leadership'—using multiplication to create a range of many products out of one innovative design.) There are more than 200 different versions of the Walkman, making this innovation a veritable industry in itself. Apple, too, has used multiplication to create many varieties of iPod.

A design principle cliché says: 'form follows function'. The SIT innovators invert this, saying 'function follows form'—listen to the product, study its form, and derive new functions from it.

There is a fifth SIT template that does not fit easily into the four arithmetic operations, which we may call *transformation* (in fact, also a mathematical operation, but in matrix algebra). You transform a product by giving an existing feature an entirely new role. Here is a case study.

Case study: 'Eat your fork, Johnny!'

A startup company we studied invented remarkable technology for producing *edible* straws—straws stiff enough to drink through, yet made of tasty food-like matter that could be eaten. The technology was patented. The same material could produce edible plates and cutlery (forks, knives and spoons). The 'cutlery' product had the following key features: functionality, hardness, elasticity, weight, price, appearance, storability, and shelf life. The 'snack' product had the following features:

Case study continued

Case study continued

taste, texture, colour, sweetness, appearance, aftertaste, and natural food content. The standard cutlery features were transformed, to take on 'snack' features. But the company had difficulty defining whether it would sell the product mainly as an edible cutlery, or as a cutlery-like snack novelty. The product did not reach the market.

Action learning

Applying the Five Mathematical Operators

Take your organization's product, or any product you like and buy. Study it carefully; examine its functionality. Then, apply one or more of the five mathematical operators listed above (subtract, add, divide, multiply, transform) to create an innovation. Begin with subtraction.

3.5 PROFILE YOUR PRODUCT FOR PROFIT AND GROWTH

No one in the history of the world ever bought a car. Or, for that matter, a TV, VCR, house, toaster, computer or stereo. It *is* true that the 6 billion inhabitants of the world, in 225 countries, buy about 16–18 million vehicles every year. Overall, they buy some $45 trillion worth of cars, TVs, VCRs, houses, toasters, computers, stereos and much more (accounting for bulk of the world GDP) each year.

But what are they *really* buying? They are buying the pleasure-giving, problem-solving and want-satisfying *properties*, or characteristics, of goods and services. Ultimately, people buy what products do for them.

Define 'features' as 'what products do for people' in order to satisfy their wants and needs. People buy goods and services because they have features they want. By identifying, measuring and benchmarking product features, and by systematically examining which existing features should be improved and which new features should be added, the often chaotic process of innovation and new product development can be systematized to attain greater profitability and faster growth. This is the essence of our feature-driven innovation approach.

This approach has originated and evolved largely independently in four different disciplines: economics, marketing, competitive strategy and management of technology and innovation. Perhaps the most compelling version is that of Kim and Mauborgne, whose 'value innovation' and 'blue oceans' tools have been used successfully by many innovators.

Here is how to listen to your product's voice, profile your product and generate winning innovation. In many ways, this tool, variously known as feature-driven innovation, or value innovation, is similar to the Altschuller 'innovation template' approach. It is implemented in four steps.

1. Choose the fundamental characteristics or attributes that capture how the product, process or service creates value for customers. These attributes usually number between five and 12 (even for complex products, the main value-creating features usually do not exceed a dozen), and must be measurable, even if the measures are at times subjective.
2. Measure those attributes and do the same for comparable competing products. Choose your benchmark carefully; sometimes, the competition for software is a pencil (see the case study on Quicken later).
3. Graph, aggregate, and otherwise analyse, the product's strengths and weaknesses, across all attributes.
4. Use the resulting 'product profile' or 'value curve' as a tool for innovation, by asking:

    - Can I create an innovative product by eliminating some features, perhaps using the savings and resources to strengthen others?
    - Can I create an innovative product by adding one or more completely new features? (Table 3.1).

Table 3.1
Profile your product

There are four ways to innovate, based on product features. You can:

p

Raise existing feature or features above industry standard

o

f

Introduce totally new feature or features

Lower feature below industry standard to reduce cost and price

Eliminate feature low in value to reduce cost and price

Here are two examples of how product profiles can generate successful innovations: detergent and wine.

Case study: Wheel detergent

After losing market share, the Indian detergent company HLL (Hindustan Lever Limited) launched a new detergent known as 'Wheel'. It did this by creating a new 'product profile' (Figure 3.2), which included features not present in existing detergents. 'Wheel' targeted the villages (there are a million of them in India) with door-to-door sales, tailored the product to those who previously did not use detergent, created a formula suitable for hand-washing in rivers, eschewed expensive national media advertising and instead used local fairs and vans. The result: substantially higher return on HLL's capital.

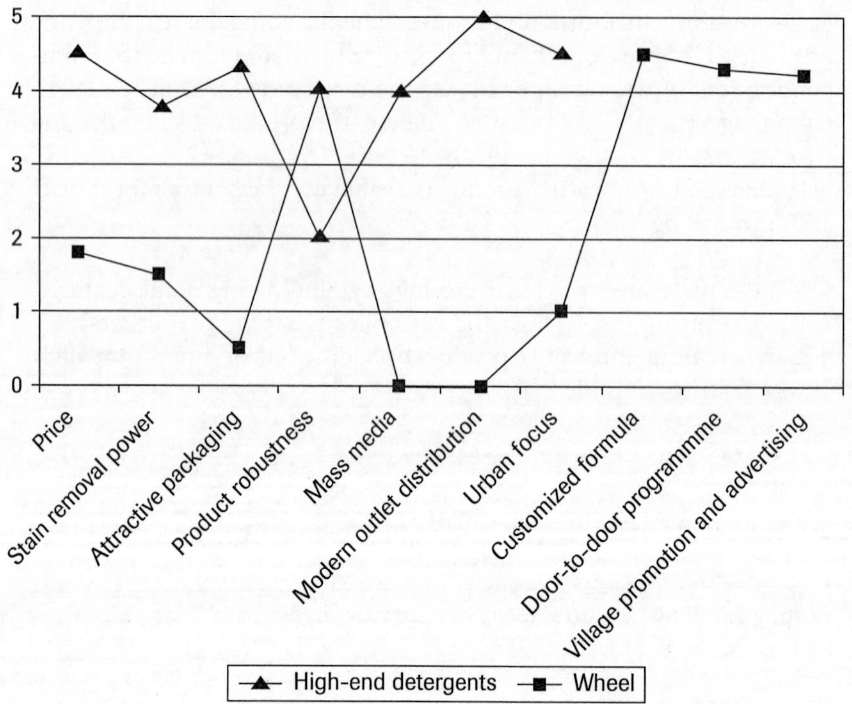

Figure 3.2
Wheel strategy

Source: Value Innovation for the Bottom of the Pyramid: profitability pursuing superior value and low cost in emerging markets (really) by Bernardo Sichel, Director of Consulting, Decision Sciences International (www.thinkdsi.com).

Case study: Yellow Tail wine

In the late 1990s, a small family-owned Australian winery, Casella, entered the US wine market which is characterized by 60,000 new wine labels yearly, intense competition, and consolidation (eight top companies controlling most of the volume). Traditionally, wine appealed to knowledgeable connoisseurs. But Casella's innovation, 'Yellow Tail', took a new approach, appealing to those who normally did not drink wine. New features were added to conventional ones (Figure 3.3): easy drinking, easy selection and above all, 'fun'. Only two Yellow Tail wines were made: one red, one white. The wine had a soft, sweet and fruity taste. The logo on the bottle was a kangaroo. Yellow Tail quickly became the number one imported wine in the US and the fastest-growing wine in US and Australian history. The key: Yellow Tail's recognition that only one Americana in four drank wine, that the potential market among non-wine-drinkers was far bigger than among those who already drank wine and the key to this market, in turn, was a new product profile.

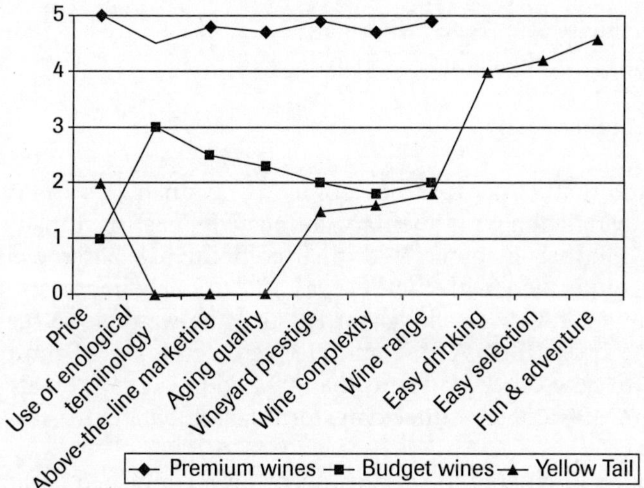

Figure 3.3
Yellow Tail strategy
Source: See Figure 3.2.

An advantage of the 'product profile' approach to innovation is that it is *visual*. We believe modern innovation tools should generate visual images. Only when senior managers can convey their vision and direction clearly will that vision be implemented; to this end, there is no substitute for a sharp, striking and memorable graphic portrayal of that vision.

Here are two additional examples of feature-based innovation in action, Palm pilot, and 'Centrino', Intel's innovative microprocessor.

Case study: Palm pilot

Jeff Hawkins developed an idea for a consumer-focused handheld computer while he was Vice President (Research) at GRiD systems, a manufacturer of pen-based computing devices. He founded Palm Computing to develop a new generation of PDAs (Personal Digital Assistants), in January 1992, with backing from GriD's parent Tandy Corp. A joint venture with Tandy was formed in 1992, with Casio brought in as a manufacturing partner. Two products were produced, Tandy's Zoomer and Casio's Z-7000. Similar to Apple's Newton, both flopped.

Palm then adopted a feature-based approach. They surveyed their Zoomer customers and found that customers' purchase decisions were driven by four product features:

- Connectivity
- Size, shape and weight
- Data entry
- Performance

They found that 92 per cent of Zoomer owners had PCs and of those half were buying Palm's rudimentary connectivity pack that made it possible to link their Zoomers with their computers. It became clear to them that 'connectivity with the PC' was an extremely important feature.

As a leading software developer for PDAs, Palm was able to see what products Motorola, IBM, AT&T and HP were developing. Palm became convinced that the other platforms 'had missed in each of the areas customers most wanted: connectivity, form factor, data entry and performance'.

Jeff Hawkins originated the core concept for a connected organizer as an accessory to the PC, making *connectivity* a central driver of the design. The Pilot 1,000 and Pilot 5,000 were announced in January 1996. The results were 'astounding'—at a price of $299 all-in-all, they 'reinvigorated the market for handheld computing devices'. The company shocked everyone in the industry, as everyone had assumed that Palm was only developing software applications.

Source: From 'Palm Computing—The Pilot Organizer', Harvard Business School Case Study #9-599-040, prepared by Rajesh Atluru, Keven Wasserstein, guided by Professor Thomas J. Kosnik.

Case study: Centrino

According to Stephen H. Wildstrom, a *Business Week* columnist writing in the year 2000, Intel has turned laptop computers into 'speed demons', matching the performance of desktop PCs. The problem is, the fastest micro-processors drain batteries quickly, he noted. A laptop with a 650 MHz processor gives about 2½ hours of battery life. Intel has put resources and energy into boosting speed, because faster processors cost more and have higher profit margins, and the product feature 'speed' has become the core of Intel's Unique Value Proposition.

But there is a feature-based trade-off between speed and battery life. Is innovation that boosts speed rather than seeks longer battery life what buyers really want? Wildstrom claimed that he would be happy if some of the engineering genius that goes into producing faster machines at the expense of battery life 'went into making slower notebooks that run longer'. However, he noted, 'speed sells'.

As Wildstrom was writing those words, teams of Intel engineers were developing precisely what he asked for—a powerful microprocessor called Centrino that provided longer battery life, to support wireless computing—'Unwire your World', became Intel's new marketing slogan. Intel's new unique value proposition shifted from speed to mobility. Laptop computers, now selling more units than desktops, themselves voiced the need for this innovation.

Source: The article that anticipated the Centrino microprocessor is 'Laptops Catch Up to Desktops' by Stephen H. Wildstrom, *Business Week*, 7 February 2000, p. 8.

Action learning

Rating a Product You are Familiar with

Choose a mass-market product with which you are familiar and which you purchase regularly. Identify five to 10 key features for this product. Rate each feature relative to the leading competitor. Draw a product profile. What strategic conclusions can you draw for this product? Does the product profile generate ideas for innovations for you?

3.6 VOICE OF THE CUSTOMER

> The great gift of human beings is that we have the gift of empathy.
>
> —Meryl Streep[6]

After listening to the voice of our product, we now look for ways to listen to the voice of our customers. But how can innovators effectively listen to their customers, when their customers are unable to clearly articulate or communicate their true needs?

Anthropologists claim that two-thirds of all communication is non-verbal, done by body language, gestures, facial expressions and other ways of 'speaking'. It follows, then, that innovators must learn to become amateur anthropologists, who 'listen' to their customers by closely watching them.

But how?

A proven approach by Dorothy Leonard and Jeffrey Rayport is known as empathic design: watching customers use products and services in real-world settings, in the course of everyday routines.[7] 'Empathy' is a feeling of concern and understanding for another's situation or feelings, or 'climbing into another's mind to experience the world from that person's perspective'.[8] It differs from *sympathy*, sharing the feelings or interests of another, because with empathy, you do not *share*, you actually *feel* what others feel. 'Sometimes,' note Leonard and Rayport, 'customers are so accustomed to current conditions that they don't think to ask for a new solution.' By empathizing with how customers *overcome* difficulties inherent in 'current conditions', new product ideas emerge in droves.

According to Leonard and Rayport, empathic design follows the following four stages:

1. Observe
2. Capture data
3. Reflect and analyse
4. Brainstorm for solutions.

They are illustrated the case studys, Quicken.

Case study: Intuit: *Quicken* your sales, 'follow me home'

1. Observe

Intuit is the leading producer of book-keeping software. In 1984, in Palo Alto, California, near Intuit's hometown of Menlo Park, Intuit founder and president Scott Cook observes several well-dressed women, members of Palo Alto junior league, sitting at keyboards trying to use computers to write cheques. Cook watches. Empathizes. And learns.

2. Capture data

Intuit developed a version of empathic design known as 'Follow Me Home', in which Intuit managers closely observe customers as they buy Quicken, open the cellophane wrap, load it on their computers and begin to use it. They never intervene, even when tempted, but observe, take notes and sometimes videotape.

3. Reflect and analyse

A year earlier, in 1983 Cook had an epiphany. Realizing that more and more consumers and small businesses were buying PCs, he saw that software that would write cheques and keep financial statements should be a hit product, because software could automate dull, humdrum book-keeping tasks. The problem was: There were already dozens of such products on the market. Cook had to find a way to compete. He asked a group of women from the Palo Alto Junior League to sit in front of computers and operate Quicken. Some had never touched a computer in their life.

'People couldn't be bothered learning a complex programme', he found. There was a big market: but the product had to be cheap, fast, hassle free, easy to use. Cook benchmarked Quicken not against other software but against the leading competitor, the pencil. The first conclusion: Quicken had to be very cheap, priced at between $20 and $50, because pencils sell for a dollar a dozen. By matching the pencil's ease-of-use (making Quick exceedingly simple to load and run), and adding other features that pencils lack (speed, accuracy), Quicken's product profile dominated that of the pencil. It lacked a large number of optional features that competing software had—but people did not find those options important. As a result of another empathetic insight, Intuit observed that buyers of Quicken were not using it to manage their cheque books—they were managing their small businesses with it!

Case study continued

Case study continued

4. Solutions

Knowing how customers were really using Quicken enabled Intuit to adapt and sell to, in a focused way, a market it had not been aware of previously: small businesses.

Quicken became the #1 product in its area, and was in fact so successful that a $1.5 billion acquisition offer from Microsoft to acquire Intuit was vetoed by the US Justice Department on anti-trust grounds.

Source: John Case, 'Customer Service: The Last Word', *Inc.*, April 1991.

Product profiles are always seen *relative* to those of competitors and require choice of a benchmark against which the product is compared. Picking the right product is essential. The story of Quicken illustrates this point well. Entrepreneur Scott Cook wisely benchmarked his software NOT against other leading personal financial software packages—but against his real competitor: the pencil! The result was to focus Intuit's creative energies on making Quicken as simple and user-friendly as humanly possible, resulting in a winning product.

Democratizing Innovation: One of the most powerful models of innovation involves using lead users, or key customers, as full-blown partners in the process of new product design starting with ideation. Here is how Lego implemented this idea successfully, with the upgrade for its Mindstorm product.

Case study: Lego's Mindstorms: When your customers innovate

'In Billund, Denmark (Lego's manufacturing centre), not only is the customer right, he's also a candidate for the R&D team', notes a journalist in *Wired* magazine. How is this done?

Lego's innovative Mindstorms, which combines Lego bricks with programmable robots, debuted in 1998 and with no advertising became Lego's all-time bestseller. It sold 80,000 units in its first three months, and 1 million units in all. But six years later it needed an update. Lego lost $238 million in fiscal 2003.

In September 2004 Lego executives felt the Mindstorms innovation team needed a fresh perspective. Lego decided 'to outsource its innovation to a panel of citizen developers', known as a Mindstorms User

Case study continued

Case study continued

Panel (MUP). Such panels often serve as 'beta' sites (testers of prototypes and working models). But Lego's MUP was different. It would actually design and invent. Four members were chosen, from a short list of 20. They received no pay and even paid their own airfare! They met with Soren Lund, head of Mindstorms, in Washington DC, to hammer out the final details of the upgrade, known as NXT. Why are you doing this? Lund asked them. Because, they said, they were playing a vital role in shaping a product they loved. According to Wired magazine, 'opening the (innovation) process engenders goodwill and creates a buzz among the zealots, a critical asset for products (like Mindstorm) that rely on word-of-mouth evangelism'. If NXT is a hit, the 'democratized' innovation process may be extended to the full range of Lego products.

Product Opportunity Gaps: A useful approach for listening to the voice of the customer is what authors Jonathan Cagan and Craig M. Vogel call POG—product opportunity gaps.[9] But how does an innovator identify such trends? The authors recommend using SET: social, economic and technological factors that create new trends and generate POGs.

DEFINITIONS

- **POG, product–opportunity gap: The gap between what is currently on the market and the possibility for new or significantly improved products that result from emerging trends.**
- **SET: The changes in social, economic and technological factors that produce new trends and create POGs.**

Case study: The Good Grips peeler

Cagan and Vogel describe a vegetable peeler; its designer's wife had arthritis and had trouble gripping existing peelers. The POG was the opportunity to design kitchen utensils that were easy to hold in the hand as well as being aesthetic (so the user would not be labelled as 'handicapped'). The designer used SET as follows:

- Social: Increased awareness about the needs of the physically challenged; growing numbers of older people; more food preparation in the home.

Case study continued

Case study continued

- Economic: High disposable income among seniors; more spending on house wares; children buy aids for aging parents.
- Technology: New molding techniques, new application of Neoprene.

A revolutionary grip for the peeler was designed, that was comfortable, convenient and aesthetic. Ultimately, the company launching the new peeler made the New handle a part of every one of its products held in the hand.

3.7 VOICE OF THE ORGANIZATION

Every organization, small or large, needs an innovation *system*—a method for creating, developing, designing, planning, producing and marketing innovative products, services and processes. It is important to stress that *there is no one-size-fits-all innovation system* that matches every organization's needs, personality, culture and values.

We interviewed key players in organizations with proven track records in innovation, from widely differing industries and walks of life. We then identified five different models, or templates, for organizing inspiration and perspiration.

The great dictator

In this model, a single person controls the entire innovative process, from idea selection through implementation, production, marketing and distribution. The single leader/manager/arbitrator provides integration and a broad market perspective, knitting together conflicting forces within the young organization. What most characterizes Great Dictators is big-picture thinking—the ability to perceive how the whole is composed of its parts, without becoming lost in details. Successful Great Dictators are good at systems thinking—they see all parts of the business system and from the outset work to knit them together into a powerful single unit, which they personally lead.

This was the model employed with huge success—at least for a time—by Thomas Edison, in bringing electricity to homes and businesses around the world. As Edison's biographer notes: 'One consistent sign of Edison's genius ... was his inclination to think globally long before achieving success locally. "All parts of the *system* must be constructed with reference to all other parts," he wrote of the electric light endeavor, as he viewed it, "since in one sense all the parts form one machine."'

Edison was a Great Dictator. He led the efforts at invention. He found the right material for the light bulb's filament. He built the business model. He did the public relations work and raised the funds. And he built the organization that electrified America.

Great Dictators rarely know when to exit gracefully from the stage. Later in his life, a victim of 'founder's disease' and deaf, Edison became alienated from his company and the disciplined bottom-line management ethic he had instilled. He was forcibly removed by the managers of the company he founded. All too often, Great Dictators end their career in ignominy, as they fail to change and adapt to the times. This is one of the key flaws of this model.

Separation of forces

We found this model in a leading Israeli advertising agency. The basic principle: Separate the idea *creators* from the idea *choosers* and idea *implementers*. Here, the creative department focuses on the *inspiration* (ideas) while another department concentrates on the *perspiration* (implementation). Management must help choose the ideas and continuously mediate the often fierce built-in conflict between the two. In high-tech companies, this model is sometimes implemented by having separate R&D (or engineering) and marketing functions.

As one of the founders of the Israeli ad agency told us:

> You must have complete freedom in coming up with ideas. Otherwise: you'll get 'more of the same'. There are lots of great creative ideas. *You have to choose among them*. Often, the wrong ones are chosen for implementation. The American adman Bill Bernbach (of the legendary ad agency Doyle Dane Bernbach) often said: the essence of creativity lies in *choosing* ideas—there are endless ideas out there, the problem is to pick the right one!

The Israeli adman continued:

> The creative department (note: creative people are highly paid—higher than other parts of ad agencies) comes up with ideas. The campaign is presented to the implementation department. Ideas are often broad. A sketch of a film is presented. This then goes to the CEO and comptroller—they have authority to authorize the campaign. Once authorized, the media

department chooses the media. The final film is an end product. A budget could be $2 million for a campaign; a costly film for TV could run for only 15 or 30 sec.

On the set itself: the creative people have the last word! This was once not the case—we learned that often, during the past 15 years, key ideas were changed, and got lost. So the creative people, and implementers, each have to OK the final result.

What we learned from a major global ad company, who invested in us, is this: After the whole process ends, and the film has been made: the CEO must give his final OK. And he may say NO! This is costly, but has happened. This is very important—killing projects before they are launched. There are other milestones, but this final one is a key one. The CEO may cancel a campaign even when it is finished and this could cost hundreds of thousands of dollars. And this has happened more than once.

To sum up the four principles of Separation of Forces:

1. Separate the creative process from the implementation process.
2. Final authority for implementing the creative idea lies with the CEO.
3. Authority for deciding on *how* the creative idea is put into practice should rest with the creative people who invented it.
4. Creative people must be educated in working under constraints (time, money, etc.). Constraints ('in-the-box thinking') can be an aid to successful innovation rather than a hindrance.

This train runs on time

We found this model at the Philips Design Studio in Singapore. In this approach, discipline becomes a strategic asset throughout the innovation process, including the ideation/creativity stage. Singapore-based innovation must take into account the cultural values within which innovation occurs: Singapore's highly disciplined regulated society and economy.

Case study: Game port

In Philips Singapore, innovation is like a train; it stops at well-defined stations, at defined points in time according to a very clear and precise timetable. The innovation cycle lasts about a year. Weeks 1 through 26 are

Case study continued

Case study continued

driven by innovation. Then there is a kind of 'handoff' with weeks 27 through 52 being driven by product planners and marketing; marketing is involved right from week 27. Here is how the method was used to develop a successful variant of a mini-stereo system.

The kick-off event is the New Paradigm workshop in week 3. Preparation for this workshop begins at the start of week 1. Francis Chu explains the process:

> The New Paradigm workshop aims to trigger ideas. We provide rich context as personal experience to facilitate idea generation. Sometimes when designing, we forget about what people's homes look like, how the set will be competing with others on the shop floor. For example we took time to check out IKEA and illustrate how the product looks on their furniture's shelves. I took photos of shelves—and shared them with the team as an additional input to trigger ideas.
>
> Over 100 different ideas were generated by the participating teams who then reported them in the plenary session. Ideas for implementation were then chosen, based on analysis of their costs and benefits.
>
> After the workshop, further development of the chosen ideas is done in innovation teams. For example: a team of five persons is assembled, including an innovation manager, a designer, and one each from the areas of software, mechanical, and electrical. The final decision always rests with the commercial person.
>
> During week 16, a Product and Development Workshop is held, to move the ideas forward .... We've found it useful to observe users experiencing the product—try it, play with it ... then we observe how they use it. Sometimes we videotape them. This can inspire new thinking, which can improve the concept. This is *not* like many focus group studies or statistical research. This method provides instant feedback to the team. *The innovation team itself facilitates it, not an agency.* The loop is: see the product used → change it → see again how it is used.
>
> A midyear update workshop is held during week 26. This is to check user feasibility and technical specifications. This is the stage at which marketers, and product planners, become dominant, and begin to pilot the project toward the market.

Case study continued

Case study continued

Soon after, during week 30, a Long Term Product Planning workshop is held, at which the 'architecture' of the product for the coming 18 months is defined. The innovation team meets with the planner and a product Road Map for the next 18 months is constructed. At this stage the planner communicates the new product idea to various geographical regions and asks for feedback on the product and on its price. Often a product profile is constructed, comparing the product with its competition, feature by feature. This is followed in week 44 by the High Design Process workshop. In many innovation systems, the product designer joins only at this stage, after the product specifications are clearly defined. But in the Philips system, the product designers participate in the process from the outset, right from preparations for the week 3 New Paradigm workshop.

According to Philips' Corporate Market Intelligence group, 'The FWC577 (one of the game port mini systems developed using the above method) was doing very well in the US between August–October 2003. It is the best-selling Philips Mini/Micro product in the period with 2.3 million units sold.'

Elders of the tribe

We encountered this model during interviews with senior military officers. According to it, creative individuals (often younger members of the organization, but not always) spark ideas, which are then very carefully examined, explored and tested by experienced senior officers, 'elders of the tribe', who bring long years of field experience to their analysis. This template creates what some see as a 'schizophrenic' organization. It focuses on day-to-day discipline, emphasizing safety and risk-minimization, and including compliance, hierarchy, procedures. At the same time the organization admires and promotes risk-takers *who challenge all of the above*. This is the most emotionally demanding template for reconciling the conflicting values, *because members of the organization have to struggle with the double-message all the time.* The elders of the tribe are often examples of people who were promoted because they broke some laws, took risks and succeeded. These elders are then placed in charge of maintaining discipline—and of encouraging creativity. It is they who show the adaptive leadership that makes this difficult system work.

Head in the clouds, feet on the ground

In this model, creative groups brainstorm and float sometimes utterly outrageous ideas, with their 'heads in the clouds'. Then, as this process exhausts itself, at a signal, the group shifts gears and changes focus. The focus in stage two becomes one of 'feet on the ground', checking for feasibility: testing the business design and viability of the idea, its potential and its technical feasibility. Often academic research is conducted this way in technological areas: researchers frequently switch modes between ideation and evaluation, and every new piece of work is judged both by the originality of the idea and by its practical feasibility. In this way, organizations retain creativity but ensure that operational discipline is also invited to the table.

Case Study: PC-based ultrasound cardiology

An Israeli startup came up with an idea to build a device for ultrasound cardiologic diagnosis based on the PC ('head in the clouds'). The idea was rather 'wild' because at the time (1998) the PC was far from having the processing capacity needed for the idea to be feasible. However creative R&D engineers felt that through Moore's Law (computing power doubles every 18 months) this constraint would be eliminated when the product reached the market in 2–3 years.

In late 1998, GE Medical bought the company. GE Medical had earlier rejected the idea of PC based ultrasound for cardiology. But they agreed to let the acquired start-up's team pursue the 'head in the clouds' idea. Once a prototype was created, GE's feet-on-the-ground management system, based on what is known as 'Six Sigma', took over, and guided the innovation process through to ultimate marketing, sales and servicing. The startup founders themselves say they were unlikely to have attained market success without GE—while GE Medical may not have had the bold head-in-the-clouds creativity of the startup. This is why feet-on-the-ground companies often seek head-in-the-clouds ideas by making acquisitions of startup companies.

Each of the five templates we have described contains a high-level challenge for those who manage them, and 'sinks' that absorb large amounts of energy. For example: the divide and conquer approach in 'separation of forces' creates rivalry among members of different teams which management must deal with all the time. The 'elders of the tribe' model involves a kind of organizational split personality that creates continual tension and potential instability.

Each organization needs to define its own innovation system, according to its culture, history, values and personality. The better the fit, the more productive and profitable the innovation is likely to be. No organization is exempt from this voice—each must look inward and outward, examine its culture, structure, strategy and resources, study best practices and, based on this inventory and needs assessment, build an approach for bonding discipline and creativity that is most suited to it.

Action learning

Defining Your Organization's Innovation System

Define your organization's innovation system. Which of the five organizational innovation templates resembles most closely the system your organization uses? Which of the other templates could your organization learn from, and adapt, to improve its innovative effectiveness?

3.8 INSPIRATION, PERSPIRATION

One of the key determinants of an organization's innovation system is the search for balance between 'inspiration' (free open creativity) and 'perspiration' (systematic disciplined management). In the two-dimensional space of creativity and discipline, there is a 'eutectic point' uniquely suitable for each organization.

DEFINITION

Eutectic point: The term is used in metallurgy to describe the alloy of two component materials with a precise 'eutectic' proportion of each. When a non-eutectic alloy freezes, one component of the alloy crystallizes at one temperature and the other at a different temperature. With a eutectic alloy, the mixture freezes as one at a single temperature. It must be aggressively sought and, once attained, determinedly maintained.

In his book *Good to Great,* author Jim Collins shows that of the thousands of organizations he and his team studied, only 11 attained true greatness (measured by order-of-magnitude superiority in returns to shareholders over a sustained period), and all 11 succeeded in achieving a high degree of discipline and 'culture of creativity' simultaneously. The optimal balance between creativity and discipline may change over time, varying with the particular stage of the innovation project—early, middle or late.

Figure 3.4 shows an example of how the optimal 'eutectic' point in creativity-discipline balance, changes with discipline proportionately increasing. The term 'chaotic creativity' should be regarded with caution; many of the superior models for the process of ideation are in fact highly disciplined and systematic.

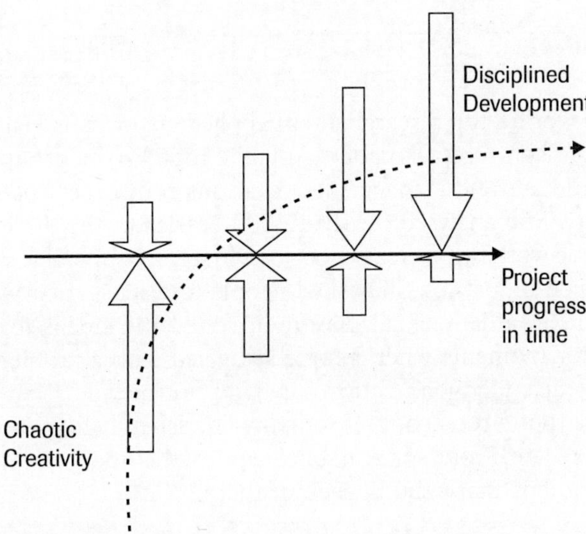

During an innovation project, the optimal balance between open 'ideation' or creativity and disciplined development varies, with 'discipline' growing in importance as the project progresses. Each stage of the innovation project will have its own 'eutectic' or optimal balance, just as metal alloys have a 'eutectic point' that differs according to the properties desired.

Figure 3.4
Creativity vs discipline
Source: David Perlmutter, VP (Mobile Processing Group), Intel Corp.

The innovation systems of organizations are dynamic. As organizations grow, they may need to shed old systems, like snakes shed their skins, and embrace new ones, *even when such systems have proved enormously successful in the past.* Implementing change under perceived success is a major challenge. As they mature, many organizations focus on operational discipline and cost reduction. In today's competitive global marketplace, this is vital. Yet no organization can grow and thrive solely by optimizing efficiency and slashing costs. The discipline that cost reduction entails should not be allowed to strangle creativity. Cost reduction and value creation must become allies, not warring enemies.

The innovation system of each organization must be constantly defined, examined, dissected and where needed, altered. Where no such system exists, one must be developed. Innovation must not be left to random forces or serendipity.

3.9 HOW TO FOSTER CREATIVITY IN ORGANIZATIONS

One of the world's top researchers on applied creativity is Harvard Business School Professor Teresa Amabile. Amabile mobilized a group of Ph.D and graduate students and managers from various companies and collected data on creativity. She analysed nearly 12,000 entries in the diaries maintained by 238 people working on creative projects in the consumer products, chemical and high-tech industries. She asked people to discuss their work and work environment in a daily email. She then coded the emails for creativity, by searching for moments when people struggled with a problem or came up with a new idea. Her goal: 'Study creativity "in the wild"!'

What she found runs counter to many cherished beliefs about how to innovate. Here are Professor Amabile's six myths about creativity, and the research findings that debunk each of them.[10]

1. Creativity comes from only from creative types

Untrue. 'The fact is, almost all of the research ... shows that *anyone* with normal intelligence is capable of doing some degree of creative work.' Creativity depends on experience, talent, an ability to think in new ways and the capacity to push through uncreative dry spells. You *can* teach people to be creative. It has been proven. Motivate people, empower them, *listen* patiently to their ideas. But you need to really listen and defer judgement. Kill an idea too fast, twice or three times, and the person offering ideas will never offer another.

2. Money is a creativity motivator

False. Amabile asked her subjects, *to what extent were you motivated today by monetary rewards?* We do not think about our paycheque on a day-to-day basis, they said; this is not what it is about. The real problem with bonuses and pay-for-performance innovation is that it tends to make people risk-averse. Avoid this. You want people to be willing to take some chances without worrying about how it will affect their pay. And remember the basic principle of psychology: an intrinsically-motivated person—someone driven to innovate simply because it is fun and fulfilling—will respond badly when rewarded, because the 'extrinsic' motivation tends to destroy the intrinsic.

3. Time pressure spurs creativity

Generally, untrue. Amabile's 12,000 days of work time showed the opposite. People were least creative when fighting the clock. A sense of urgency in business is of course vital. But extreme time pressure is usually counter-productive. Under time pressure, reflection is suspended; routine and habit rule, in order to boost speed. People are most creative when they are under zero pressure and are given adequate idle 'do nothing time' to ponder. We find that among managers, lack of such idle time is one of their most vexing problems. Make such time for yourself and your workers.

4. Fear generates breakthroughs

Again, the opposite is true. People are most creative when they are experiencing feelings of joy, happiness, fulfilment, and satisfaction. They are least creative when they are unhappy, pressured, stressed, and depressed. Do not use fear as a motivator. It is ineffective.

Case study: Serious? or IDEO?

We are told that in its early days, a large high-tech organization was a fun place to work, and as a result, was a fountain of individual creativity. When competition stiffened, senior management told their engineers: it's a jungle out there. Get serious. Get competitive. This may have been a mistake. A workplace that lacks playfulness may drive creative people to leave. In contrast, perhaps the world's greatest design organization, IDEO, is a place where fun, jokes and laughter are encouraged.

Founded by Stanford design professor Dave Kelley, along with his brother Tom, IDEO stresses its unique combination of free-wheeling eccentricities (for instance, the IDEO designers' request to mount a DC-3 wing on the ceiling) with disciplined, organized design process and rapid prototyping. IDEO designers, it is said, postpone studying for their advanced degrees, simply because they are having too much fun.

5. Competition beats collaboration in creativity

No. Creativity is at its best when people cooperate and work together in teams. High performance teamwork is a hallmark of highly creative organizations. You get more innovation when you lead individuals and teams together to explore diverse points of view, synergies, and complementary skills.

6. Lean, mean, streamlined organizations are creative

Amabile studied a large global electronics firm during a severe downsizing that took 18 months. Every single measure of creativity and innovation suffered. Make sure your short-run cost reduction programme does not kill the key strategic resource, creativity and innovation, that you need to ensure long-run survival. It has happened more than once. Harvard Professor Robert Kaplan and Management Consultant David Norton developed the Balanced Scorecard, which is a management tool that if implemented properly, seeks to ensure that such compromise between short term financial objectives of the company and its long-term ability to innovate and compete does not happen.[11]

Professor Amabile summarizes:

> My 30 years of research and these 12,000 journal entries suggest that when people are doing work that they love and they're allowed to deeply engage in it—and when the work itself is valued and recognized—then creativity will flourish. Even in tough times.

3.10 LISTENING TO YOUR INNER VOICE

The fourth voice—and in some ways the most important one—is the inner voice of our intuition.

In his book *Blink: The Power of Thinking Without Thinking*, author Malcolm Gladwell provides evidence that our snap judgements and first impressions can be educated and controlled and often produce results far better than those from systematic decisions based on encyclopaedic data.[12]

Each of us has what psychologists call an 'adaptive unconscious'. This is the part of our brain that works like the Fire Department—alert while we sleep, always on guard, processing information and sending us warnings. Great innovators know when and how to listen to it. Mediocre ones rarely do.

Gladwell's book contains a wealth of evidence based on interviews with researchers in favour of such intuitive thinking. He describes intuitive decision-making as 'thin-slice decisions'—the ability to deduce, like Sherlock Holmes, a major conclusion from tiny fragments of evidence, just as forensic experts track a criminal from a few molecules of DNA. Often, he shows, we make far *worse* decisions by collecting more and more data.

The inner voice is not about snap judgements. It is about how the unconscious part of our mind knows things the conscious brain does not—and how innovators consult with, and listen to, it.

Action learning

Do You *Listen to* Your *Inner Voice?*

1. List on a piece of paper the last three important decisions you made.
2. For each, state whether your 'gut feeling' played a role—and if it did, how important a role? Did your 'gut feeling' match what the data told you, or did it contradict them?
3. State whether each decision turned out to be right, wrong, or in-between.

In general: What do you do, when your 'gut feeling' goes directly against expert opinion and data?

Case study: Blink and the Aeron chair (Herman Miller)

An industrial designer named Bill Stumpf designed a radically new office chair for furniture maker Herman Miller. He called it the Aeron. Stumpf made the most ergonomically correct chair ever conceived. The seat pan and the back of the Aeron chair move independently, the best technique to ensure no undue stress is placed on the back. The arms are fully adjustable. There is support for the shoulders—the top of the chair was wider than the bottom. It had a wire frame and looked weird.

The chair was tested for comfort. It scored 4.75 on a scale of 10. 'Chair of Death,' joked Herman Miller managers. Everyone thought it was a monstrosity. After changes, the comfort score rose to 8. But when people were asked if they liked how it looked, it scored below zero. So they put together a focus group of facility managers and ergonomic experts. They all said it would never sell to corporate clients. Dump it, they said.

Aeron project manager Bill Dowell had a hunch and sent the innovative chair design into production. The chair attracted attention from the cutting edge of the design community. It won awards. In Silicon Valley it became a cult object. It was cool. It appeared in films and on TV. By the end of the 1990s, Herman Miller realized that it had on its hands the best-selling chair in the history of the company. What seemed ugly had become beautiful—and had changed forever the rules of the design game for office chairs.

Case study: New Coke

In the mid-1980s Pepsi was gaining ground on Coke. Worried Coke executives ran extensive market research tests. In blind head-to-head taste tests, 57 per cent preferred Pepsi to Coke. Coke had twice as many vending machines, more shelf space, and double the advertising budget—and was losing to Pepsi! Why? 'You have to begin asking about taste,' said Coke managers. Thus was born New Coke—lighter and sweeter than Old Coke. In blind tests with hundreds of thousands of consumers all over North America, New Coke beat Pepsi by 6–8 percentage points. New Coke was launched. It was a disaster. There were protests all over the country. CEO Roberto Goizueta revived Classic Coke. What happened? Sip tests ('take one sip') were misleading. One sip is different from drinking a six-pack. Sweetness becomes cloying when a litre of sweet stuff is consumed. Home-use tests give better information ('take it home, drink it, tell us how you like it'). Goizueta may have ignored his intuition. It nearly cost him his job. He kept it because he insisted on launching a new product, Diet Coke, even though it failed every taste test. Why? His inner voice told him there was a market need, and it was right. Diet Coke became one of the hottest new product launches ever.

3.11 CONCLUSION

This chapter opened with a quote that cited depressing statistics. Even with extensive market research, the data show, your innovative products will fail more than nine times out of 10. Out of 30,000 new product launches in the United States, fewer than 3,000 achieve growth and profit.

How can innovators improve their chances for success? Become great *listeners*, we argue. Develop skill in listening to the four innovation voices. Make each of these voices an integral part of your own unique innovation system. Learn how to amplify their signals when they are especially quiet. Learn how to mediate when the voices send conflicting messages. Recall that the high probability of failing in innovation is simply an average. It includes many innovators who do not use best-practice methods. By listening closely to your products, your customers, your organization and your own inner voice, you can achieve consistent innovation success far above the one-in-ten average.

CASE STUDY 3.1

Tata Motors Ltd.

For the last several decades, Tata Motors has manufactured the heavy vehicles around which 'body-builders' build trucks and buses. Over the last about 15 years, the company has made forays into passenger cars. Their first cars were large, in the station wagon range, for which the company leveraged its knowledge in building heavy vehicles (some of these models were the Estate, Safari and Sumo). Using this experience, the company subsequently got into the manufacture of traditional passenger cars, with its Indica and Indigo models.

These were the company's first fully Indian, 'true' passenger cars, competing with other passenger cars built by the big players on the Indian market such as Maruti and Hyundai. The car was christened the Indica and its larger variant, the Indigo. It was built on the dream and passion of the company's chairman, Ratan Tata. Many industry observers felt that Tata Motors could never succeed in this effort, as making passenger cars was a very much more complex task than making truck and bus platforms. Nearly all successful car manufacturers in India were either foreign companies or had a strong foreign collaboration.

Given this backdrop, the launch of the passenger car by Tata Motors created a lot of hype in the market, and customer bookings were brisk. However, there was a lot of teething troubles, including quality issues, and competitors—including many multinational car manufacturers—went into overdrive to suggest that Tata Motors would never be able to recover from this debacle. This period, in the early 2000s, was really a testing time for the company. Many industry analysts predicted that the company and the Tata group itself was finished with this ill-fated project.

However, Ratan Tata continued to believe in his dream. He gave his all to set the project back on track, addressed all the issues that plagued the car, and invested a whopping Rs 17 billion (about $400 million) to create what has now become a winner in the Indian auto industry. The success of this turnaround effectively silenced Mr Tata's critics. The Indica V2 version of the re-launched car has been a success in the Indian marketplace, and also has gained considerable momentum in the export market. It was clearly a do or die situation as far as the company was concerned, and its response proves the adage: 'when the going gets tough, the tough get going.'

Case study 3.1 continued

Case study 3.1 continued

Soon after pulling off the impossible in the Indica/Indigo car project, Ratan Tata announced another impossible project: that his company would deliver by 2007–08 the one lakh-rupee (Rs 100,000) car, equivalent to $2,300. There is no car at this price range available anywhere in the world. With India's billion-plus population and the similar population of China together accounting for a third of the world's population, Mr Tata felt that these markets could explode with opportunity for his company if they could make this car a success. This move also fits well with the exhortation of strategy guru C.K. Prahlad, that the next frontier for companies to tap is the 'bottom of the pyramid'. The project was derided as a non-starter by nay-sayers and rivals in the industry. Typically, large auto companies make their profits on the higher-end cars, where margins are better. In India, the cheapest car sells for upwards of Rs 250,000 (over $6,000)! If Tata Motors had to sell its 'people's car' for Rs 100,000, it would have to restrict the cost of manufacturing the car to less than Rs 70,000 (about $1,600), to provide margins for the company and the distributors.

While the path ahead on how to make the 'people's car' a reality may not be very clear, the company is pushing ahead on this 'project impossible', fuelled by the Ratan Tata's vision, and by the success that the company had tasted with the Indica/Indigo in the Indian market, despite having taken on big and established players such as Hyundai, Ford, Suzuki and others. However, this new project defies all conventional thinking of car manufacturers anywhere in the world. If this ambitious project must see the light of the day, it will require innovation in nearly all aspects of car-making and at every step along the way. While the project is currently a closely guarded company secret for obvious reasons, the general perception is that the company is making steady progress. This car will not be a stripped-down version of any existing car (low-end Indian cars, selling at $6,000 apiece, are already stripped-down!) but would be a 'ground-breaking experience' for the company, according to Ratan Tata. It will seat four or five passengers, be safe and adhere to stringent emission norms. What is known from company statements is that it will not have the finish of normal cars, and it will also not be capable of going at very high speeds. However, it will not be a scooter or three-wheeler converted into a car. It will have a rear engine and will be gearless. It will be a 'compact' car.

While much of the technology and know-how for the car will be in-house, in areas where the company presently does not have know-how Tata Motors is partnering with other industry leaders who are willing to

Case study 3.1 continued

Case study 3.1 continued

rise to the challenge. These partners will also have to innovate in the design, development and manufacture of their respective modules/ components. The partners include Delphi for electronic engine management, and the Italian design company IDEA for styling, Exide for technologically advanced small car batteries, and another foreign company for continuous variable transmission technology to provide for gearless driving.

The Indian market for two wheelers is the largest in the world, over 10 million vehicles per year, while the car market is about a tenth of that size. What Tata Motors' 'people's car' will do is to get potential two-wheeler buyers to purchase its car instead, thereby opening the floodgates to a huge market. The company hopes that these large numbers will enable economies of scale to kick in, making it attractive for various partners to design and develop inexpensive components that will go into the car. Mr Tata is also keen that his company should not waste resources on reinventing the wheel, and if there is some know-how that is tried and tested and readily available elsewhere, the company will go out and source it through innovative partnering. Thus, a consortium of companies will actually have to innovate to deliver on his promise. He is also banking on the innovative engineering and manufacturing skills in the country to make his car a reality.

To contain costs, it has been reported that the company is toying with implementing innovative ways of assembling the car. One option that has been quoted in the press is that the company would give prospective customers the entire car in a 'kit' form, which they would take to one of the thousands of authorized assembly mechanics who would be trained for the task. These authorized assembly mechanics would in turn assemble and test the car and get the car ready for the customer to drive home in! Now if this is not innovation, what is? Whether or not the company actually ends up doing this is less important than the fact that the team involved in building the car is constantly thinking of new and innovative ideas to make the 'mission impossible' people's car project a reality.

The key learning from the Tata Motors story is that when an impossible target has been set, innovation must take place across the entire value chain. There are no holy cows that cannot be questioned. 'Mission impossible' will soon be a mission reality for Tata Motors. So, how do you innovate? Well, get everyone in your organization to think innovatively, and do whatever it takes to get the innovation engine in the organization into 'cruise' mode.

Notes

1. From Clayton Christensen, Scott Cook and Taddy Hall, 'Marketing Malpractice: The Cause and the Cure', *Harvard Business Review*, December 2005.
2. The story of how Lego used its fans to upgrade its Mindstorms robot kit is from Brendan I. Korner, 'Geeks in Toyland', *Wired*, 2 February 2006. See also Eric von Hippel, *Democratizing Innovation* (Cambridge, MA: MIT Press, 2005).
3. The 'innovation template' approach is described in Jacob Goldenberg and David Mazursky, *Creativity in Product Innovation* (New York: Cambridge University Press, 2005); and in Jacob Goldenberg, Roni Horowitz, Amnon Levav and David Mazursky, 'Finding Your Innovation Sweet Spot', *Harvard Business Review*, March 2003.
4. Francis Chu, Avinoam Kolodny, Shlomo Maital and David Perlmutter, 'The Innovation Paradox: Reconciling Creativity & Discipline: How Winning Organizations Combine Inspiration With Perspiration', paper presented to the IEMC (IEEE International Engineering Management Conference) annual conference, Singapore, 2004.
5. Daniel H. Pink, *A Whole New Mind: Why Right-Brainers Will Rule the Future* (New York: Riverhead Books, 2005), p. 133.
6. Quoted in Daniel H. Pink, op. cit., p. 167.
7. Dorothy Leonard and Jeffrey Rayport, 'Sparking Innovation through Empathic Design', *Harvard Business Review*, November–December 1997.
8. Pink, op. cit., p. 153.
9. Jonathan Cagan and Craig M. Vogel, *Creating Breakthrough Products: Innovation from Product Planning to Program Approval* (Upper Saddle River, NJ: Prentice-Hall, 2002).
10. Reported in *Fast Company*, December 2004.
11. Robert S. Kaplan and David P. Norton, *The Balanced Scorecard: Translating Strategy into Action* (Boston, MA: Harvard Business School Press, 1996).
12. Malcolm Gladwell, *Blink: The Power of Thinking without Thinking* (Boston, MA: Little Brown, 2005).

Chapter 4

The innovative mind: *Who* innovates

> You need three things to be an original thinker. 1. a tremendous amount of information. 2. be willing to pull the ideas, because you're interested. 3. ability to get rid of the trash ... you cannot think only of good ideas ... you must be able to throw out the junk immediately.
>
> —Mihaly Csikszentmihalyi[1]

> Many psychologists view creativity as some kind of innate ability. I, on the contrary, view it largely as a decision. People are creative largely by dint of their decision to go their own way. They make decisions that others lack the will or even the courage to make ....
>
> —Robert Sternberg[2]

LEARNING OBJECTIVES After you read this chapter, you should understand:

- **Why innovators operate on three levels (individual, team, organization)**
- **Whether you *want* to be an innovator**
- **The role of *vision* and independent thinking in individual innovation**
- **How innovative clusters (like Silicon Valley) form**
- **How to exercise your creativity 'muscles'**
- **What factors characterize successful global innovation teams**
- **How to use 'catchball' for team innovation**
- **What the eight 'realms' of innovation are and how your organization ranks in each**
- **What 'skunk works' are**
- **Who America's most innovative organizations are in 2006 and why**

4.1 INTRODUCTION

In the first three chapters, we looked *outward*, toward innovative best practices by individuals and companies, to answer the questions: why innovate? what to innovate? and how to innovate? In this, the concluding chapter of Part I of this book, we ask our readers to look *inward*, deep inside yourselves. We ask you to question whether you have the *desire* to achieve excellence in inovativeness and whether you, your team and your organization have the necessary *core competencies*.

'We may travel to the moon,' Charles de Gaulle once remarked, 'but that is not far at all; the greatest distance we have to travel lies within us.' To assist you in this journey, we will provide a number of diagnostic tools; as a result, this chapter has plenty of action-learning exercises.

Before beginning this journey into yourselves, we ask you to prepare to be brutally honest. 'Face the brutal facts' is a key factor for success in organizations, according to author Jim Collins, and it is equally vital for success in individuals.

4.2 THREE LEVELS OF INNOVATION

There are three levels of innovation. The first is the innovative *individual*. Many ideas are born in the brains of creative individuals. The second is the innovative *team*; most serious innovative work in developing ideas is done in small and large groups. And the third is the innovative *organization*, which provides the setting, vision, goals and resources for innovative ideas—to deploy, produce and market them.

In this chapter, we provide some answers to the questions, who are innovative individuals, teams and organizations? How do they function? And, what are their personalities and nature? We explore each of these three levels in turn, moving outward from the individual at the core to the team and finally to the organization.

Heroes, it is said, are made, not born. The overriding question this chapter addresses is 'nature or nurture?'—are creative persons 'made', by circumstance, desire and learning, or are they 'born'? Can *anyone* learn to be creative or does creativity come from our DNA?

The prevailing view is that creativity is innate. We differ. Along with Robert Sternberg, one of our generation's leading psychologists, we believe that creativity and innovation are the result of decisions. We believe that anyone can innovate successfully, and that creativity is largely an acquired, learned skill, not an inherited one.

The starting point for all innovation is the question: Do I truly *want* to innovate? Not everyone wants to engage in the creative act, fraught with risk, difficulty, ridicule and often, dismal failure. Innovation requires both the *desire* to innovate (motivation) and the *ability* to carry out the intention. Motivation is a necessary (though far from sufficient) condition for success.

4.3 THE INDIVIDUAL INNOVATOR

This section explores the question: *who* is suited for creative endeavours?

Motivation

We begin with an action-learning exercise that addresses the key question of motivation and desire—do you really *want* to innovate? Above everything else, innovators *want* to create new ideas and are willing to invest the effort, and undergo the rejection and ridicule that this entails.

Action learning

Eight Jobs—Pick One

There are many different tasks people do in their work; innovation is only one. Here is a classification of eight types of work.[3]

1. *Application of Technology:* Use technology and engineering to solve business problems
2. *Quantitative Analysis:* Use mathematical and financial analysis to solve problems
3. *Theory Development & Conceptual Thinking:* Take an academic, conceptual approach to business problems
4. *Creative Production:* Generate innovative business ideas
5. *Counselling and Mentoring:* Help others in their careers, develop personal relationships in the workplace
6. *Managing People:* Achieve business goals by working with, and directing, people
7. *Enterprise Control:* Having ultimate strategy and decision-making authority
8. *Influence Through Language and Ideas:* Exercise influence through skilful use of persuasion

Now:

1. Write each of the eight tasks on a slip of paper.
2. Arrange the slips on the table in front of you. For each of the eight types of work, picture a concrete task and a flesh-and-blood person doing it (preferably, yourself).

3. Then, *arrange the slips in order of their desirability for you*—which of them would you love to do, and which would you avoid at all cost? Which of them make you leap out of bed in the morning, eager to tackle them, and which makes you want to place the pillow over your head and smash the alarm clock? Allow ties.

Where does 'creative production' rank—honestly? If it ranks low, then you may be highly creative but simply prefer to do other things.

In his research, psychologist David McLelland found a strong link between success and what he calls 'n-achievement', the motivation for high achievement. This is certainly true of innovation.

Defy the crowd

According to psychologist Robert Sternberg, 'creative people ... are ones who are willing to defy the crowd ... they make decisions that others lack the will or even the courage to make, daring to define problems in ways different from those in which their colleagues define them.' The case study of Chuck House and HP (Hewlett-Packard) illustrates this principle—in this case, among the 'crowd' House defied was the company co-founder and CEO.

Case study: 'Get that thing out of here!'

Twenty-six-year-old Chuck House, an engineer, had been with Hewlett-Packard for just a few years, but had already tasted failure. House observed that people were buying HP oscilloscopes—a piece of electronic test equipment that creates a visible graph of a signal, as, for instance, a wavy line—and using them as monitors (see case study in Chapter 3,
'When your customers innovate'). This pointed the way to a big new market, he thought. At the time, HP had new technology that could electronically focus a cathode ray, achieving higher resolution without the huge tube that at times stretched a full 4 feet behind the screen. House and his superiors built a display using the electronic lens that was faster, smaller, used less power and was brighter. But when they tried building such displays for the FAA (Federal Aviation

Case study continued

Case study continued

Administration) air controllers who guided air traffic, they failed; with the HP prototype, the FAA controllers could not read the tiny code numbers that identified each plane. The resolution was not quite high enough for that purpose.

Many might have given up. But House, against his superiors' wishes, went to war. He loaded a large prototype monitor into his Volkswagen (tearing out the front passenger seat to do so), and set out to do some one-on-one market research, violating HP's sacred principle that you *never* show prototypes to customers. He went to 40 potential customers (mainly computer manufacturers) and came back fired up, believing oscilloscopes could become displays.

At the annual review of the division in which House worked, however, HP founders William Hewlett and David Packard saw House's monitor and heard the marketing people describe the dismal reaction they had gotten from oscilloscope customers. David Packard ordered House's project aborted. 'Next year I don't want to see that project in the lab,' he said. Chuck's response, later, was: 'If we put it into production, Packard won't find it in the lab.'

A year later, Packard returned to the project. The monitor was on the market. And it achieved glory. When America launched the first manned rocket to the moon on 20 July 1969, NASA scientists watched it through HP's innovative high-resolution monitor, using a new type of cathode ray tube. It also found use in a medical monitor used in the first heart transplant and quickly came to be used in almost half of HP's instruments. House won an HP 'Medal of Defiance'. His product soon reached $10 million in annual sales with no redesign and made high profit margins.

The key success factors? A creative, defiant individual; a strong team; a champion; House's one-on-one market research with users; House's perseverance—and rank insubordination; *defying the crowd*; a sponsor in the form of House's manager; and an organization culture that tolerated such insubordination.

Source: Gifford Pinchot III, *Intrapreneuring* (New York: Harper, 1985), pp. 23–30.

This case confirms a theory of creativity by Sternberg, who borrows a saying from legendary investor Bernard Baruch (1870–1965). Baruch's recipe for accumulating wealth: 'Buy (assets) low, sell high.' According to Sternberg, creative persons 'buy low'—they propose theories that are 'cheap' because no-one will accept them, then slowly or quickly persuade their peers; and 'sell high'—see their innovations meet high demand and high value; then go on to do the same process yet again.

Many creative entrepreneurs, like Chuck House and Steve Jobs, achieve serial innovative successes, by repeatedly buying low and selling high. HP's Chuck House went on to develop more innovations. Steve Jobs built Apple, left, built NeXT (computers), returned to rebuild Apple as CEO (for a salary of $1 a year), innovated iPod, and then founded Pixar Animation Studios, which sold to Walt Disney for $7.4 billion in 2006.

What is the secret of these serial innovators? One key element is 'vision'—they all have a powerful vision that drives them forward in the face of seemingly insurmountable obstacles.

Vision

Innovators are visionaries. The reason is simple. To sustain the high energy and dogged determination needed to succeed, to push the idea through to the marketplace, a powerful vision is vital (see Chapter 5, 'The Power of Vision').

Vision, according to Jim Collins and Jerry Porras, is an 'envisioned future', or a *photograph of the future*. It is feasible, yet bold and audacious; it challenges people to stretch and it excites and energizes them. Their colourful term for vision, BHAG (Big Hairy Audacious Goal), has become part of business language. It excites the emotions, not just the powers of reason.[4]

Vision is concrete, identifying what needs to be done and what should *not* be done. Such a vision transformed an entire country, Ireland, from poverty to wealth and growth, despite enormous obstacles.

Case study: Ireland

For two centuries, Ireland was poor. Its young people finished high school and hopped onto the next ship to find work abroad. As a result, there are estimated to be 70 million ethnic Irish abroad, with only 4 million Irish in Ireland itself.

Today Ireland is wealthier than Britain, with per capita GDP of $47,000, low unemployment, $75 billion total in inward foreign direct

Case study continued

Case study continued

investment, and strong economic growth. How did this happen? In 1987 Charles Haughey, head of the Fianna Fail party, enunciated a bold vision:

> We will win for Ireland, its people and its regions, the best in international innovation and investment so as to contribute to the continued transformation of Ireland to a world-leading society which is rich in creativity, learning and personal and social well being. We will work in partnerships with other organizations to enhance the best of Irish capabilities and talents and match them to the best of global investment. We will carry out our vision with integrity, professional excellence and responsiveness to all with whom we work or are in contact.

Ireland's IDA (Industrial Development Agency), fuelled by this vision, has largely implemented it, through innovative policies (especially, a 10–12 per cent corporate tax rate) that brought the world's leading global companies to build plants in Ireland.

Source: IDA (Industrial Development Agency), Ireland.

Excellence, passion, resources

Vision, as Jim Collins explains, occurs at the intersection of three circles—*passion* (something the innovator truly and deeply cares about), *excellence* (a skill or realm where the innovator and team feel they are or can become the very best), and *resources* (the time, money and people needed to implement the vision). All great innovations have a vision at their core. And all great innovators are capable of envisioning the future boldly to inspire those around them.

If you err in your vision, err on the side of boldness. A watery, dull vision is no vision at all. From our experience of working with product-development teams in both startup and established technology-intensive companies, 'visions' such as: 'Raise our market share by 5 points' or 'achieve a 15 per cent operating margin' are very common, but are not true visions. They do not inspire. The response to a vision should be a 'Wow!', or its equivalent. If you fail to draw a 'wow'—reformulate.

Case study: Global construction equipment firm

We worked with an India-based R&D team, that is, part of a global firm that makes construction equipment. The team worked on two new pieces of road-building equipment. Their initial 'vision' was to achieve market success and profitability. We indicated that this was not a true vision and would not energize the team to invest the long hours needed to complete the project fast and successfully. After discussion, a new vision was shaped: Creating equipment that would help link 700 million Indian villagers with the rest of India, enabling them to share in India's growth and progress by facilitating road-building. This vision excited the team and helped contribute to the innovative designs that ultimately reached the market.

Case study: Google

Two Stanford Ph.D candidates named Larry Page and Sergey Brin set up shop in a garage in 1998. Their vision: *Use the Internet to make nearly all information accessible to everyone all the time.* (Note: 'all' and 'everyone' are powerful, inclusive, energizing words.) How? By creating a search engine algorithm that was fast and far-reaching. In 2005 Google made $1.5 billion in net profit on $6.1 billion in sales (mostly advertising), with a 67 per cent gross margin. As of 22 February 2006, its market value was $108.3 billion (making it the world's largest media company), and its stock price had risen from its initial price of $85 to as high as $475. Google's three-word credo is: 'Don't be evil,' though few know precisely what those words really mean. Brin and Page brought in a veteran manager, Eric Schmidt, Google's CEO today; the three provide a good balance of vision, discipline and managerial skill.

Source: www.moneycentral.com, and Adi Ignatius, 'In Search of the Real Google', *Time*, 20 February 2006, pp. 28–28.

Independent-minded

Innovators and entrepreneurs are independent thinkers. We often ask students, how many of you intend to become entrepreneurs? Those who respond favorably often come from homes where fathers or brothers are independent businesspersons rather than wage earners and serve as role models. For example, the 'father of the spreadsheet', Dan Bricklin, inventor of Visicalc, relates that his father headed a family printing business in Philadelphia, Bricklin Press, founded by Dan's grandfather. Afternoons spent at the printing plant, Bricklin relates, prepared him for trials faced in his own business.[5] FedEx founder Frederick Smith's father, too, was a rather flamboyant businessman.

A study by MIT Professor Edward Roberts of startup firms in the Greater Boston area[6] reveals the following:

- 'Entrepreneurs tend strongly to come from families in which the father was self-employed.'
- Fifty-nine per cent of technical entrepreneurs had fathers who were either professionals or managers.
- There is no 'first-born effect' (oldest children show no special tendency to become entrepreneurs).
- Some 10–25 per cent of each sub-sample of new high-technology firms are formed by someone born outside of the United States (Greece, Sweden, etc.).
- Regarding age, Roberts finds that the median age at time of company founding is 35–38 years.
- Entrepreneurs, before launching their companies, tend to work in *development*, not in *research*, and had an average of 10 years of work experience.
- And finally, many entrepreneurs had work experience with a 'key technology source organization', i.e., large technology-intensive laboratory or company, where knowledge and skills were acquired. Ken Olson, founder of Digital Equipment Corp., worked for years in MIT's Lincoln Laboratories, for instance. The latter factor explains the 'cluster effect'—entrepreneurs tend to cluster in geographical areas, such as Bangalore, India; Route 128 in Greater Boston, and Silicon Valley.

Creativity loves company

Apparently innovation, and innovators, love company. Innovation tends to occur in geographical clusters, because innovators often like to remain in the area where they studied science or engineering: Boston/Route 128 (MIT), Palo Alto/Silicon Valley (Stanford), Bangalore, Chennai (Indian Institute of Technology), Cambridge, UK (Cambridge University), Research Triangle (Duke, North Carolina) and so on. For instance, shortly after India gained its independence on 15 August 1947, Prime Minister Jawaharlal Nehru announced that India would build five (later seven) Indian Institutes of Technology (IIT), to rival the best such institutes abroad. Today many of

India's high-tech companies are driven by IIT graduates, who built their companies not far from the campuses where they studied, for example, Bangalore, home to the Indian Institute of Science, now a key information technology hub in India.

Case study: Silicon Valley

Silicon Valley is an 80 km stretch of former apricot and walnut orchards radiating outward from Stanford University, between the San Francisco Bay on the east, Santa Cruz Mountains in the west, and the Coast Range to the southeast. (Silicon, of course, is the wafer on which semiconductors are constructed.) It has become synonymous with fever-pitch technology-based entrepreneurship generating rapidly growing companies, funded by dynamic venture capital.

The 1990s saw Silicon Valley virtually explode with startup activity. Between 1990 and 1997, 7,500 high-tech companies were formed. Brilliant research at Stanford University and the University of California at Berkeley graduated entrepreneurs who approached angel investors and venture capitalists.

Stanford University was founded in 1891 by California Governor Leland Stanford in memory of his son. In the 1920s, Stanford recruited one of its graduates, Frederick Terman, a stellar electrical engineering professor at MIT. Terman encouraged his students to start businesses near the university, to keep graduates from migrating to the East Coast in search of jobs. Two of his students were William Hewlett and David Packard. Hewlett, a graduate student, had designed and built an audio oscillator. Terman saw market potential in it and persuaded Packard, who worked for GE on the East Coast, to return home and join Hewlett. In 1937, in a small garage in Palo Alto, Hewlett and Packard began to produce their audio oscillator commercially. It was used in 1939 in Walt Disney's pioneering film *Fantasia*. Hewlett-Packard (now known as HP), based in Palo Alto, is America's 11th-largest firm, with $79.9 billion in annual sales in 2004, $3.5 billion in profits and a market value of $59 billion.

In 1955, William Shockley (inventor of the transistor at Bell Labs) brought a team of brilliant young scholars to the Stanford area to found Shockley Transistor. Some of his team disagreed with his choice of germanium as an optimal semiconducting material, preferring silicon. Members of that team, including Gordon Moore and Robert Noyce, started their own company, known as Fairchild, and began to mass produce a device able to integrate large numbers of electrical

Case study continued

Case study continued

on-off switching functions, etched onto a silicon chip, and known as an 'integrated circuit'. That company formed the basis of many famous start ups: Intel, AMD and National Semiconductors. These companies were the core of a semiconductor industry that led to the name 'Silicon Valley'. Intel, based in Santa Clara, California, is now the world's largest producer of semiconductors, with annual sales of $34.2 billion in 2004, a net profit of $7.5 billion, a market value of about $145 billion, and employing some 80,000 employees worldwide.

While Silicon Valley pioneered semiconductors, Japan quickly became far better at producing them. In 1984, Intel senior managers Andy Grove and Gordon Moore decided to stop producing memory chips entirely. Silicon Valley's days of prosperity seemed to be over. But like the Phoenix, Silicon Valley reinvented itself and rose from its own ashes. The resurrection was based on the PC—the personal computer.

In March 1975, a group of students formed a club, the Homebrew Computer Club, in Menlo Park to experiment with home computers. Among them was Steve Wozniak. He built a computer with an inexpensive microprocessor that he bought at a computer show and built a machine around it. Later, his friend Steve Jobs joined him to form Apple Computer Co. in 1976. On 1 April 1976, they released the Apple I. Apple II in 1977 was a big success. In August 1981, IBM introduced its own PC. An enormous industry resulted—one that caused Silicon Valley to boom.

Source: Some material from Timothy J. Sturgeon, 'How Silicon Valley Came to Be', in Martin Kenney, ed., *Understanding Silicon Valley: The Anatomy of an Entrepreneurial Region* (Stanford, CA: Stanford University Press, 2000).

4.4 CREATIVITY MUSCLES

One of the most complete theories of creativity is that of social psychologist Mihaly Csikszentmihalyi, who between 1990 and 1995 intensively interviewed 91 'exceptional individuals' in art, literature and science.[7] He calls his theory of creativity 'flow'. 'Creativity does not happen inside people's heads,' he observes, 'but in the *interaction* between a person's thoughts and a socio-cultural context. It is a systemic rather than an individual phenomenon.' The system within which creativity occurs, Csikszentmihalyi calls the 'domain'.

DEFINITIONS[8]

- **Domain: The existing set of rules, procedures, conventions and accepted wisdom.**
- **Creativity: Any act, idea or product that changes an existing domain, or that transforms an existing domain into a new one.**
- **A creative person: Someone whose thoughts or actions change a domain or establish a new one.**
- **Gatekeepers: Those who decide whether a new idea or product should be included in the 'domain'.**

In order for creativity to succeed, the innovation must be accepted by the 'gatekeepers'. (For instance, in academic research the gatekeepers include those who edit and review research for scholarly journals.) This implies that creative people must first understand the domain within which they work and find ways to persuade those in the domain to accept their novel ideas. Most breakthroughs, Csikszentmihalyi notes, 'are based on linking information that usually is not thought of as related.' In creativity, 'integration—across domains and within domains—is the norm rather than the exception.'

The nine main characteristics of extraordinarily creative people mentioned repeatedly in his interviews were:

1. Clear goals at every step
2. Immediate feedback (both given and sought)
3. Balance between the level of difficulty of a task and the skill required to accomplish it
4. Action and awareness are merged
5. All distractions are ignored
6. There is no fear of failure
7. Self-consciousness disappears
8. The sense of time disappears
9. The creative activity is autolectic (an end in itself)

Can you practise creativity? Csikszentmihalyi recommends 'creativity muscle exercises'.

Action learning

Creativity Exercises

1. Try to be surprised by something every day.
2. Try to surprise someone every day.
3. Write down what surprised you, and how you surprised another.

4. When anything interests you, pursue it, no matter what.
5. Relearn how to enjoy curiosity. To do this: increase the complexity in the things you do well, make plenty of time for reflection and relaxation, wake up with specific goals to look forward to, shape your own physical space and do far more of the things you love doing and far less of what you hate.

When we teach innovation, we consistently urge our students to stretch their creativity muscles during the course by consciously abandoning habits, because habit is the sworn enemy of creativity. Eat different foods, listen to different music (try opera, if you generally listen to rock), rise earlier or later, come to class using a different mode of transportation than usual. By smashing conventions in one area of your life, you may find that the effect continues into other areas as well.

Applied creativity in action: Kilby and Walton

Jack Kilby was a man who, perhaps more than any other, changed our world. He invented the integrated circuit while working for Texas Instruments (TI). He definitely qualifies for the title of 'extraordinarily creative'. Here is his story, and that of Sam Walton, founder of Wal-Mart, whose creativity expressed itself not in technology but in an innovative business model that also changed our lives. Both regularly exercised their creativity muscles—and changed the world as a result.

Case study: Jack who?

Integrated circuits are the building blocks for every appliance we love and use today, including personal computers.

How did Kilby dream up and produce his invention? During a TI plant shutdown, engineers went on vacation. But Jack went to work. Using borrowed and improvised equipment he built the first integrated circuit, half the size of a paper clip, on a piece of germanium. It was Kilby's idea that made it possible to shrink a huge mainframe computer down to the size of a palm. Kilby's first integrated circuit contained one lonely transistor. Today's microprocessors hold more than 100 million

Case study continued

Case study continued

transistors. Kilby won the Nobel Prize for Physics in 2000. Six months after Kilby's prototype, Intel co-founder Robert Noyce came up with a similar idea independently. The two were friends and shared the credit.

What was the secret of Kilby's breakthrough? In order to miniaturize, Kilby needed to get rid of the massive wires needed to connect the transistor to the devices it served. *Let the chip itself be the connector*, Kilby thought. 'The following circuit elements could be made on a single slice (of germanium or silicon): resistors, capacitor, distributed capacitor, transistor,' he wrote in a notebook in 1958. The wires were an unnecessary 'box', or constraint. Forty-seven years later—our world is utterly changed as a result of Kilby's insight.

Case study: Sam Walton: A little anarchy

The founder of Wal-Mart, Sam Walton, attributed his success to his 'constant tinkering':

> I never could leave well enough alone, and, in fact, I think my constant fiddling and meddling with the status quo may have been one of my biggest contributions ... I have always been driven *to buck the system*, to innovate, to take things beyond where they've been ... I have always been a maverick who enjoys shaking things up and creating a little anarchy.

Creative people like Walton enlist the principles of Charles Darwin, innovator of the theory of evolution. They try many 'market experiments', observe the results, quickly end the many experiments that fail, and rapidly leverage the few that succeed. Walton tried lowering prices, found it worked like magic—and built a powerful business model on 'everyday low prices'. Innovative companies regularly try such 'market experiments', because ultimately only the marketplace and consumer are the final arbiters of whether an innovation truly meets needs.

Source: Jeffrey A. Krames, *What the Best CEOs Know* (New York: McGraw-Hill, 2003), pp. 206–13.

Kaleidoscope thinking

Great innovators see the world differently from others. Federal Express (FedEx) founder Frederick Smith calls this 'kaleidoscope thinking', a term coined by Harvard Business School professor Rosabeth Moss Kanter. In 2005 FedEx had $29.4 billion in revenues, $1.4 billion in net income and ranks 70th among the US Fortune 500 companies. In 2006 FedEx is the second-most admired company in America (after GE), and fourth most-admired in the world. Here is how Smith founded FedEx in 1973.

Case study: Frederick Smith and FedEx–'It's only money'

Smith, born in 1944, served two tours of duty as a Marine in Vietnam. His father was an independent businessman. While at Yale, Smith wrote an economics paper proposing the concept that ultimately became Federal Express. His professor was unimpressed. Smith does not recall his grade, but remarks that he got a 'gentleman's C' on all his courses. Federal Express aircraft—named that, because Smith hoped, in vain, to get a contract from the US Federal Reserve system flying checks among banks—first flew in March 1973, after Smith raised $42 million from investors, bankers and family members. Smith faced huge difficulties; FedEx was a network, and its value could not be proven before huge sums were invested in creating it. But, explained Smith, 'what we were really talking about was money, not life and death issues', a valuable perspective he acquired in Vietnam.

His insight was that in the age of computers, there would be enormous demand for overnight package delivery—a demand that only a company that used both planes and trucks could meet. No such company existed. Starting one would be risky and expensive. But Smith used 'kaleidoscope thinking'. He looked at IBM, and realized it would need a logistics system that 'provided parts and pieces wherever its computers were located, whenever it was needed'. He invented a new, unique value proposition: 'We would be the transportation system that an organization like IBM needed,' he thought. Others saw the computer business, Smith saw the transportation and logistics network that it would vitally need to run. Today, FedEx is a vital part of the value chain created by, say, a company like Dell Computers; direct sale of computers to customers requires an efficient, worldwide network to deliver them quickly.

Source: Gretchen Morgenson, *Forbes Great Minds of Business* (New York: John Wiley & Sons, 1997), pp. 35–72.

Penicillin? Or mould?

Nobel Laureate (for medicine) Hans Selye, pioneer of modern trauma theory, tells of his days as a research assistant. He noted a Petri dish covered in mould and threw it out in disgust. Much later, Donald Fleming saw precisely the same thing—but noticed how the mould destroyed bacteria, and, curious as to why this happened, went on to discover the uses of penicillin. Fleming thus developed the first antibiotic, and saved hundreds of thousands of lives as a result during World War II. Innovators see things differently than others, often with extraordinarily beneficial results!

Stubborn, dogged persistence

Innovators are doggedly, stubbornly persistent. They do not give up easily, or at all—those who do never see their ideas implemented. Illinois-born Abraham Lincoln, elected the 16th American president in 1860, is not generally regarded as an innovator, yet his career typifies the persistence needed to succeed, in the face of repeated failure.

Case study: Lincoln as loser

The list of Lincoln's defeats is long. He failed in business in 1831 and had a mental breakdown in 1836. He then lost at least eight elections, among them, for state legislature (1832), Speaker (1836), Elector (1840), Congress (1843 and 1848), for the Senate (1855 and 1858), Vice-President (1856) ... but ultimately won the great prize, when he was elected President of the United States in 1860. One must believe that like great entrepreneurs, his character was forged in the fires of adversity and defeat, strengthening him to lead his nation in the desperate Civil War, 1861–64.

4.5 INNOVATIVE TEAMS

> It may be that the future HP hero will not be limited to the engineer with the new idea for a circuit, but will also include the person who can make groupsof people separated by product type and geography work together successfully.
>
> —the late Lew Platt, *former president & CEO, HP*

Increasingly, innovation occurs within teams. MIT Professor Edward Roberts found that the likelihood of a technology-driven start up succeeding increases dramatically if there are two or three founders rather than just one. Apple was founded by Steve Wozniak and Steve Jobs; Google, by Sergey Brin and Larry Page; Intel, by Robert Noyce and Gordon Moore. The reason team-based innovation succeeds more often is clear. Teams outperform individuals. Successful innovation management requires a broad range of skills: technological, human, business, administrative. There are few individuals who alone embrace *all* the needed skills. An ideal start-up team includes a technology expert, a manager, and a sales and marketing expert.

Whom should you invite to join your team? This exercise may help.

Action learning

Whom Would You Take to Mars?

This exercise was developed by Jim Collins and Jerry Porras, and appears in their book *Built to Last.* The objective: identify people who share your core values and vision:

> Imagine you've been asked to recreate the very best attributes of your organization on another planet, but you only have seats on the rocket ship for five to seven people. Whom would you send? They are the people who likely have a gut-level understanding of your core values, have the highest level of credibility with their peers, and the highest level of competence.[9]

What *is* a team? Jon R. Katzenbach and Douglas K. Smith note that the term 'team' is used loosely. Many teams are simply loose 'working groups'. While working groups discuss and *delegate*, teams do real work *together*, they note. Working groups have individual measures of output, while teams measure their *collective* output. Successful teams do some or all of the following: they select their members for skills and potential, not for personality; establish urgency, set demanding performance goals and offer clear direction; set clear rules of behaviour; challenge the group regularly with new facts and information; spend time together; and exploit feedback, reward and recognition.[10]

Action learning

The Wisdom of Teams

There is a saying, 'Two heads are better than one.' Four heads are even better than two. Here is proof.

1. On a slip of paper, estimate the height of former star NBA Chicago Bulls basketball player Michael Jordan (in inches, or in centimetres).
2. Now gather a group of 4–5 friends. Ask each to do the same.
3. Calculate the average of the 4–5 estimates. Normally, the average estimate of the group will be closer to the true answer than any single estimate.

For the actual height of Michael Jordan, see the endnotes to this chapter.[11]

Catchball

One method for managing innovation in teams, developed in Japan, is known as 'catchball'. Like the metaphor of tossing and catching a ball, a team member creates an idea 'ball' and tosses it to a collaborator. The person catching it takes responsibility for understanding the idea and for finding a way to improve it. He or she then tosses it back to the group, where it is again caught and improved. Through the cycle of improvement, the process of tossing and catching builds commitment and 'buy-in'. Catchball emulates the Socratic dialogue approach described by Plato; team members engage in a dialogue by means of serially improving a core idea.[12]

Action learning

Catchball

Form a team. Ask someone to suggest a new-product idea. Then implement catchball—have him or her toss the idea to another team member, and so on. Keep a log or diary, and list the details of the idea as it is transformed in the process. Are there any breakthroughs? Does the idea progress, get better, or get worse? Do team members work with less energy when the idea does not originate with them? Does the final idea resemble its original formulation? Is it overly complex, with unnecessary features added on? Do team members realize that 'subtraction', and not only 'addition', can produce an improvement?

4.6 HOW TO BUILD A GLOBAL TEAM

Vijay Govindarajan and Anil Gupta studied 70 global business teams to determine why they succeed or fail.[13] Most such teams, they found, failed. Among the key factors that senior executives listed for success were (in order of importance): trust among team members, overcoming communication barriers, aligning individual members' goals, ensuring the team has the needed skills, and obtaining clarity for team objectives. Their prescription:

1. Define the team's 'charter' or mission clearly and make sure it is well understood by all members.
2. Choose team members with care; encourage diversity in skills, perspective, and personality, but do not allow the diversity to fragment the team's efforts.
3. Keep team size manageable—make the 'core team' no more than 10; while the extended team can be larger. Choose the team leader with care and be sure there is a team 'champion' (senior manager within the organization).
4. Manage the team well—foster trust, use frequent face-to-face meetings, rotate meeting locations, link rewards to performance and build decisions on data.

Case study: HP medical products group (MPG): Viridia

During the 1990s, HP's Medical Products Group generated roughly $1.3 billion in annual revenues, creating some 400 new products sold throughout the world. Lew Platt founded and for years headed the division (he later became HP CEO). MPG used cross-functional teams, defined as 'teams that perform unique, uncertain tasks to create new and non-routine products or services.' The cross-functional approach was employed to roll out the Viridia Patient Care System—'a family of patient-monitoring and information management systems designed to help caregivers balance clinical and business objectives in healthcare

Case study continued

Case study continued

settings'. Viridia required teams able to develop and deliver the various components, including diagnostic workstations, remote computer and communications links, and the healthcare telemetry system. Six teams were set up, with some 200 members in all. A special training programme was set up to foster speed, efficiency, leadership and group decision-making. During product development, efforts were made to keep all six teams in close touch with one another ('teamwork among teams'). All 200 team members met face-to-face twice, once in Massachusetts and once in Germany—an expense that would deter many companies. There were also weekly videoconference calls. Teams were not only cross-functional, they were also cross-divisional, cutting across division lines, thereby ensuring that HP divisions, too, would cooperate and collaborate. Thomas Legate, in recounting this experience, notes: 'Organizations should limit ... bureaucracy and rules ... and create a fluid, entrepreneurial culture.'

Source: See Thomas Legate, 'How Hewlett-Packard Used Cross-Function Teams to Deliver Healthcare Industry Solutions', *Journal of Organizational Excellence*, Autumn 2001, pp. 29–40.

4.7 THE INNOVATIVE ORGANIZATION

Innovative individuals and teams can be successful and productive, even if the organizations within which they work are bureaucratic, conservative and risk-averse—but their life is much harder.

How innovative is your organization? How well does it nurture and encourage innovative individuals and teams? How can it be made more innovative? We begin this section with a diagnostic tool that helps answer this question.

Action learning

How Innovative is Your *Organization?*

Here are eight questions designed to diagnose strengths and weaknesses in innovation within organizations or business units. For each, rate the factor on a scale of 1 to 10, where 10 is the score of the organization that excels in this factor. Then, draw a graph, or profile, of your organization's eight innovation characteristics. What actions must be undertaken *tomorrow*? (Note: the 'organization' could be the business school or university at which you are currently studying.)

How competent is your organization in:

1. *Defining goals*: Clearly defining its innovative objective.
2. *Generating ideas*: Coming up with new, original ideas for products, services and processes.
3. *Choosing among ideas*: Selection of the best idea from among many for implementation.
4. *Implementing ideas*: Managing the implementation of a chosen idea through to the marketplace.
5. *Choosing creative people*: Selecting and hiring people who are motivated to innovate, and who are good at it.
6. *Managing the creative process*: Managing the process through which ideas are created, chosen, organized into implementation projects, and administered, up to a prototype and market testing.
7. *Conflict resolution*: Skill in resolving conflicts that arise among individuals and teams, in new product development.
8. *Fostering a creative culture*: Creating a culture that empowers creative individuals and teams, motivates them and implements their ideas.

All these eight attributes of innovativeness are important. But perhaps the last, fostering a creative culture, is most important, because innovation cannot flower if the soil (i.e., culture) within which it is planted is acid and hostile. As companies merge in order to attain global scale, they find that their very size discourages innovation, while, paradoxically, they increasingly *need* innovation to develop new products susceptible to global scale and deployment. An innovation culture can offset this.

There are two approaches to fostering innovation within large organizations. One is the so-called 'skunk works' approach; a second is 'intrapreneurship'. Skunk works create an isolated 'island' of entrepreneurial, innovative culture; 'intrapreneurship' spreads that Island culture to the whole organization.

Skunk works create a kind of 'playground', populated by eccentric, individualistic, creative people; give them tools, time and isolation from daily corporate pressures, challenge them with difficult, unsolved (and ostensibly unsolvable) problems, then leave them alone, and come back in six months to harvest the solutions. In this approach, the polluting impact of corporate bureaucracy is kept at bay, almost like creating a 'clean room' in a semiconductor factory that filters out even the tiniest of impure particles.

A second, and opposite, solution is 'intrapreneurship'—entrepreneurial innovation *inside* a large organization, rather than in a small start-up company. In this approach, the entire organization is structured to foster and support maverick entrepreneurs who spring up and work within the system as an integral part of it. Here are two case studies that illustrate each approach.

Case study: Lockheed Skunk Works

In the American comic strip Li'l Abner, created by Al Capp, the *skonk works* (sic) was an (illegal) alcohol still, where its operators tossed shoes and dead skunks into the vat. Lockheed's version, officially known as the Advanced Development Programs unit, was set up downwind of a smelly plastics factory in Burbank, California, during World War II. (In 1989 it moved to Palmdale, California, where it exists today.) Its legendary head Kelly Johnson gave it the name Skunk Works when an engineer came to work wearing a gas mask. Later, the skunk logo and name Skunk Works became official Lockheed trademarks. Among the remarkable inventions of this creative unit were the P-38 Lightning fighter, the spy planes U-2 and SR-71 Blackbird, the F-35 Joint Strike Fighter and the X-27. Lockheed's Skunk Works is credited with inventing the design principle known as KISS (Keep It Simple, Stupid). Skunk Works has become an engineering term for secret (or 'black') projects.

Source: Ben Rich and Leo Janos, *Skunk Works* (Boston, MA: Little, Brown & Company, 1996).

Case study: Entrepreneurship within organizations: Art Fry, Post-It notes

The ubiquitous yellow Post-It notes invented by 3M's Art Fry are perhaps the most widely known and cited example of innovativeness and intrapreneurship. Yet the story is still worth telling. Fry noticed that, as a member of a church choir, the paper markers he used to mark places in the hymnal tended to fall out; he felt he needed a marker that would stick to the page yet not damage it. He made one, using an adhesive (a glue that did not really glue) developed at 3M, and circulated it in the hope someone would find a use for it. Fry was told 3M could not manufacture the product, so overnight he developed a crude machine that could.

Case study continued

Case study continued

Then, 3M Marketing said its research revealed no market for it and a four-city campaign failed, because potential customers 'did not understand what they were being asked to buy'. But Art's manager became a supporter and champion. Boise, Idaho, was chosen for a market test, and Post-It's were placed everywhere for people to try. Sales were huge, and regional, national and international success quickly followed.

Source: Pinchot, op. cit., pp. 137–42.

Which approach works best: skunk works or intrapreneurship? It depends on the nature of your organization.

Here are eight questions, based on a questionnaire designed by Gifford Pinchot, that test your organization's 'intrapreneurship readiness'. If the answers are mainly 'no', either change your organization culture, or persuade your CEO to set up a protected skunk works where the organizational culture cannot destroy creativity.

Action learning

Intrapreneur-Free Zone?

For your organization, answer these questions. If the answers are mainly 'no', it may be an 'intrapreneur-free zone'.

1. Does your organization encourage, or even permit, self-appointed intrapreneurs?
2. Are there stories told about such people?
3. Can people quickly and informally access resources to try new ideas?
4. Are people encouraged to try many small experimental products and businesses, even beyond the product lines that now exist?
5. Does your organization tolerate failure and accept risk?
6. Does it stick with an idea long enough to give it a true and fair test?
7. Is it easy to form cross-functional autonomous teams?
8. Do intrapreneurs hit walls because people defend their turf, at the expense of new ideas?

4.8 CONCLUSION

Each year, *Fortune* magazine surveys thousands of senior managers and board members, to determine the 'most admired companies'. The respondents rank companies in eight dimensions. The first (and perhaps most important) is 'innovation'. Here are, in order, America's most admired companies for innovation for 2006:

1. Apple Computer
2. Google
3. UnitedHealth Group
4. Procter & Gamble
5. Walt Disney
6. FedEx
7. Genentech
8. Nike
9. Advanced Micro Devices (AMD)
10. Target

Each of these firms is innovative in a unique way. There is, however, a common denominator. Each has found a compelling answer to four questions: why innovate? what to innovate? how to innovate? and, who innovates? For AMD, a producer of microprocessors and competitor of chip giant Intel, the focus is on designing new, innovative chips that meet and anticipate market needs. Against the global scale and efficiency of Intel, only innovation can help AMD survive and prevail. Procter & Gamble's innovativeness focuses on brand management, an expertise this company has developed over seven decades. Nike's innovation is in its winning designs. Target's, in a business model that competes with the compelling low-price economies-of-scale business design of Wal-Mart. Genentech, a biotech firm, innovates in new processes for drug discovery.

These companies all share another common skill. Having answered the four questions (Why? What? How? Who?), and having identified innovative business ideas that create unique value, they are now expert in the next two crucial stages. After 'innovate' comes 'deploy' (usually globally), and 'adapt'. Facility in innovation requires operational efficiency (deploy widely) and customer intimacy (adapt to local markets and segments) in order to achieve growth and profit.

In Part II of this book, 'Tools for Profit and Growth', we offer 10 chapters, and 10 tools, that show how to manage innovation by deploying and adapting innovative ideas, through estimating and managing costs (Chapters 5–11), understanding consumer demand (Chapter 12), managing risk (Chapter 13) and balancing competition and cooperation (Chapter 14).

We urge readers to use the four chapters in Part I of this book to develop an innovative business idea. When you have one, apply the 10 tools in Part II of this book in order to build an innovative business design well aligned with this idea, to generate growth and profit. Combining the strategies and concepts of innovation with the tools of innovation management gives innovators the best chance of building competitive, growing and profitable brands, product lines and businesses.

CASE STUDY 4.1

Reinventing Project Management at Tata Steel

Implementation of the cold rolling mill (CRM)

In March 1996, R.P. Singh joined the senior management of Tata Steel, Jamshedpur, with a brief to focus on new projects. He had earlier worked in projects at Bokaro Steel Plant and the Vizag Steel Plant prior to joining Tata Steel. In November 1997, the Tata Steel Board decided to go ahead with the ambitious 'Cold Rolling Mill' (CRM) project, approved at a cost of Rs 18.74 billion (about $400 million) and implementation time of 36 months, which were reasonably aggressive targets, given other similar project implementations worldwide by other steel plants.

R.P. Singh and B. Muthuraman (currently the managing director of the company, but at that time the director responsible for the project) benchmarked worldwide CRM projects and felt it would be great if Tata Steel could create a world record, in terms of both implementation time and cost, in the CRM project. They found that recent implementations worldwide included Baoshan Steel, China (38 months), Siam United Steel, Thailand (37 months), Bethlehem Steel, USA (30½ months) and Posco, South Korea (29 months), which was currently the fastest implementation for a CRM project worldwide. They decided to set themselves a completion time target of 28 months and a project cost of Rs 16 billion for the Tata Steel CRM project; which, if achieved, would set a new world record.

Tata Steel had a 300-strong, well established engineering division, with its own way of implementing projects. Perhaps the innate desire to create a new culture in project implementation was what prompted the top

Case study 4.1 continued

Case study 4.1 continued

management to induct Singh as the project in-charge. In a large organization like Tata Steel, such a senior induction for heading the company's most important project in decades was not likely to be received enthusiastically by the existing project management group.

When Singh made his time and cost targets known to his team of project engineers, contractors and collaborators, many silently wondered whether such an aggressive target was part of the initial enthusiasm of a new entrant. They were certain that in due course Singh would accept ground realities and reset the target to a more realistic timeline and cost estimate. Existing senior managers in good humour cautioned him that the way he was going, it would cost him his future in the company. Singh handpicked a team of 60 engineers with proven track record from different parts of the company and set about his task. He communicated his dream to these 60 engineers and about 300 others, representing various contractors and suppliers, in an open meeting in January 1998. He proposed the brave new target cost and implementation time for the CRM project. He also presented the goals of the CRM project:

- Create a 'world-class cold rolling mill complex at the lowest project cost'.
- Set a world record in implementation time and project cost so that Tata Steel becomes the new benchmark.
- Develop people with a new 'mindset'.
- Develop improved systems with universal applicability, that can be carried over to other Tata Steel projects.
- Make the CRM project an example of change for others.

The reaction from the group ranged from stony silence followed by polite amusement to outrage and outright disagreement. The group was unanimous in its verdict: 'Commissioning in 28 months is impossible!' It was clear to Singh that the culture was not aligned to the vision. Foreign contractors such as Hitachi, Fluor Daniel and others were kinder in their responses but the implicit message was the same. They clearly put forward the question 'Mr. Singh, you are Indian. How can you even think of these outrageous targets for a project being implemented in India?'

Over the next two years, by means of a large number of innovations in project management and by motivating people, Singh and his team actually completed the project in about 26½ months and well within the tight budget of Rs 16 billion. Innovative practices he brought in included

Case study 4.1 continued

Case study 4.1 continued

meticulous hour-to-hour planning, creating winners out of ordinary people, breaking the barriers between contractors and the owner (which is a bane in most projects, leading to a lot of wasted energy) and meticulous monitoring. He also found innovative ways to ensure that everyone involved in the project took complete 'psychological' ownership of the project and drove innovation in his/her areas of responsibility. He demonstrated what is possible by 'leading from the front' and by setting an example for others to emulate.

To achieve the lowest project cost, Singh insisted on:

- Economic design of civil and structural works
- Optimum tender specifications
- Each tender specification being given a target cost value, based on extensive homework by the project team
- Enough competition among the bidders
- Hard negotiation with the bidders
- No additions in scope after order placements
- Any deletions in scope suggested by the bidders being entertained only on merit

Revamp of Blast Furnace F

Soon after the completion of the world record-creating CRM (cold rolling mill) project in 2001, R.P. Singh was given his next challenge: the revamp of Blast Furnace F. The old furnace had out-lived its utility and had to be totally upgraded. Its capacity had to be increased to 1 million tons per annum (tpa) from the current 0.60 million tpa. Foreign companies estimated implementation time and cost for the completion of this project at 210 days and Rs 5 billion ($110 million). These estimates were not acceptable to Singh. Each day that could be reduced in the schedule meant a large addition to the company's top and bottom lines, since the furnace could then begin production sooner. Most foreign consultants, including Paul Wurth, dissuaded Singh from attempting anything more ambitious, stating that lesser estimates would be impractical even in western countries, let alone India.

Singh passionately believed that results could be achieved through the right efforts and hard work. One of the concerns of the project team that Singh was heading was its inability to visualize what the new blast furnace would look like, and the complexities that could arise during the revamp process. Singh thought that a good place to begin shrinking the timelines was through detailed and meticulous planning. He believed

Case study 4.1 continued

Case study 4.1 continued

that planning was the crux of successful project implementation. Another big challenge was to coordinate the work of dozens of world-class contractors to ensure that each performed their role in the given short period of time. There were over 5,000 activities to be completed. The project was scheduled to commence on 6 February 2002. Singh and his team had about a year before the project commencement date to plan out the various activities. Singh wanted to leverage the experience gained in the Blast Furnace F revamp to sharpen the project management skills of the company, so that two other major projects that were to follow, that is, the Blast Furnace G revamp and the expansion of steel-making capacity, could also be successfully completed against challenging cost and time targets.

Singh was certain that a lot of difficult challenges would arise as the project for the revamp of Blast Furnace F unfolded. The fact that the entire work of revamping the 'F' blast furnace had to be done during summer when peak ambient temperatures soared over 45°C, and the fact that adjacent to this furnace, other furnaces would be in operation during the project work, only added to the complexity of the task at hand. For instance, the thickness of the scab in the furnace could only be speculated upon during the planning stage. The actual magnitude of difficulty in removing the scab would be known only when the furnace was opened. Relaying the refractory would have to be done after removal of the scab, and this was a time-consuming job.

The project also had to meet the highest standards of quality and safety, while adhering to the time and cost budgets, since any sloppy work would impact the operation of the furnace once it was re-commissioned.

Once again, through a series of innovations in project management, Singh and his team completed the revamp in a record time of 104 days, against Singh's revised target of 110 days, and the cost was less than half of what the foreign consultants had quoted. He came up with innovative ways of ensuring that each of the 5,000 people who would be working on the project, including Tata Steel engineers, many contractors and a large number of unskilled labour, had a complete picture of the project, and knew their particular role in it and the consequences of delays. He got their commitment for timely completion of the project at target cost, with highest quality while ensuring safety. This project again set a world record for a project of this magnitude.

Having tasted what it means to be a winner, Singh has managed to create a team that is 'addicted to winning', so much so that the next

Case study 4.1 continued

Case study 4.1 continued

project, the revamp of the Blast Furnace G, which was nearly twice as big as Blast Furnace F, was completed in 95 days. Singh has now welded together a team of people who are ready for even bigger challenges as the company embarks on a rapid expansion programme.

Just what keeps Singh at such high levels of energy and passion is captured in his interpretation of one of Patanjali's (a great ancient Indian scholar) many aphorisms from the Patanjali Yoga Sutras: 'When you are inspired by some great purpose, some extraordinary project, all your thoughts break their bands—your mind transcends limitations, your consciousness expands in every direction and you find yourself in a new, great and wonderful world. Dominant forces, faculties, and talents become alive and you discover yourself to be a greater person by far than you ever dreamed.'

So *who* innovates? The case study of R.P. Singh and project management at Tata Steel suggests that if your organization can succeed in unleashing the innovation potential of your entire workforce, as Singh had done of his entire project management team, your organization can achieve the impossible!

CASE STUDY 4.2

Indicorps: Harnessing the Power of Youth through Volunteerism by Creating a Meta-NGO

Indicorps was set up to inspire collective action amongst NRI (non-resident Indian) youth towards engaging productively in the development of India, the country of their origin, roots and identity. Anand Shah, at the age of 28, is the embodiment of exuberance and dynamism, combined with an immense passion for the country. Mahatma Gandhi's words, 'We ourselves must be the change we want to see in the world,' seem to sum up what he and his sisters Sonal Shah and Roopal Shah have set out to do through Indicorps. Indicorps seeks to bring together people with a desire to contribute to society and an ability to visualize where India should be going in the years to come. Through Indicorps, the Sahas hope to unite Indians around the world in a common vision for the nation by effectively engaging them in the development of the country.

Case study 4.2 continued

Case study 4.2 continued

The Shah family migrated to the USA in 1971. Sonal, Roopal and Anand did their elementary education there. All of them had enviable educational and professional careers in the USA, before they decided to start Indicorps. Their upbringing had ingrained in them values such as humility, sacrifice and cooperativeness, which enabled them to do great things together.

In 1988, the entire Shah family took a three-month tour of rural India. Towards the end of the trip the three had resolved that they would someday do something to contribute to the progress of rural India. During the 1990s, Sonal, Roopal and Anand each got the opportunity, separately, to spend a year in India. Each came with a different motive and took back with them a deeper and broader experience of India.

In the late 1990s, Anand journeyed to India to study Indian philosophy. This experience changed Anand's perception of life. He discovered his own potential, which convinced him that he had the capability to satisfy the burning passion inside him to serve the Indian community. A transformed Anand went back to Houston. A couple of months later, he lost a very dear friend of his in a bus accident in South America. This event shattered Anand and roused in him great anger towards God and Fate, raising questions as to why such cruel things had to happen only to good people. This was a defining moment in Anand's life, and made him realize that the same thing could happen to him, that he may not live tomorrow, and therefore that he had to get started *now* with what he really wanted to do, which was to serve the community. The three siblings discussed this dream among themselves and made a firm decision and commitment to fulfil their passion to serve Indians in India. They had no concrete plan about how to go about this. They decided, however, that at any given time, one of the three would work in the USA to help pay for the living expenses of the other two in India. The sisters also decided not to get married as this might deflect them from their goal.

Anand's frequent interactions with the Indian community in America revealed that second-generation Indian-Americans were interested in doing something outside-the-box and wanted to contribute to the development of India, despite the resistance of their parents. It was obvious to Anand that Indian-American youth were enthusiastic about volunteering their services to make India a stronger country, but they had neither the opportunity nor an organization that they could go through. These were usually second-generation Americans with no

Case study 4.2 continued

Case study 4.2 continued

direct contact with India. In many cases their parents, usually first generation immigrants, had left India for greener pastures and, having prospered in America, did not want their children to be concerned with India and her myriad problems. However, what was clear to the younger generation of Indians was that, even in America, they could not run away from their Indian-ness. Anand resolved to set up an organization that would foster a pan-Indian identity to provide Indian youth in America with opportunities to engage meaningfully with India. He felt that an important strength of India was the voice of Indian-Americans, and this was not being meaningfully harnessed.

The initial plan was to provide human capital for the voluntary sector through a fellowship model—inspiring NRI children in America to come as volunteers to India to work on rural development projects in coordination with reputed local NGOs (non-government organizations). In October 2001, Anand put together a network of reputed NGOs, with Indicorps as a 'meta-NGO' that would work with each of them to provide human capital in the form of NRI youth who wanted to volunteer in India. There were several challenges in the voluntary sector in India. Most NGOs had no vision of where they wanted their organization to go or what they wanted to achieve. From time to time, some of the better-known NGOs would get requests from volunteers based overseas (both foreign and NRI) to work with them for a period of time. However, these NGOs did not have the means to judge the capabilities of the overseas volunteers. Anand realized that, apart from providing human capital to the voluntary sector, Indicorps had to work with its partner NGOs to help each one to create an immediate and a long-term vision for itself. It had to provide the NGOs with people with leadership potential and drive to help realize their vision.

As per the fellowship model crafted by the founders of Indicorps, each fellowship year was to begin on 15 August (Indian Independence Day) and end in July the following year. Fellows of the Indicorps programme would spend a year in India working on a grassroots project of their choice. They had to provide for their own airfare to/from India, their health insurance (together costing about $3,000) and all local living expenditure. Indicorps would cover only the costs of the initial month-long orientation and in-country travel costs. Indicorps partner organizations (i.e., the partner NGO) would arrange for living arrangements and materials for the projects. The projects would be suggested by partner organizations and Indicorps would send its fellows

Case study 4.2 continued

Case study 4.2 continued

to help implement them. The first fellowship programme commenced on 15 August 2002, and has been growing from strength to strength ever since.

Indicorps specifically chooses to focus on projects in rural India, because small interventions can go a long way in rural areas. By leaving their comfort zones and placing others' interests before their own, the Indicorps fellows get an opportunity to test their own potential and take a lead by committing themselves to effecting change in the world around them. The guiding philosophy is: 'If you move the youth, you move the nation.' The fellowship experience is expected to fit into a larger vision that each volunteer will carry for his/her life. The Indicorps experience, it is hoped, will kindle in them the desire to contribute something that they perceive as value to the society and world around them, no matter what they choose to do later in life, and to inculcate in them a spirit of service. Indicorps hopes to produce fellows with integrity and passion who will become some of India's most powerful assets and leaders in the future, playing the role of 'ambassadors' for India when they go back to their home countries.

Inspiring a global movement that allows a large number of people who care about India to collectively take responsibility for the country's progress and give back to India through grassroots service is one of Indicorp's key goals. Helping NGOs to create their own voluntary programmes to engage Indians within India to contribute to the development of the country is another key goal. There is a vast training gap in the voluntary sector, a gap that Anand hopes Indicorps will help fill. A broader vision of Indicorps is to bring about an attitudinal shift in Indians within the country and in people of Indian origin in America—unless the attitudes of people change, they feel, India as a whole will not progress to its full potential. Every single person who is 20 or older, whether in India or abroad, should recognize that they have the ability to do something constructive for the country.

Challenges ahead

The voluntary sector in India does not perceive the young vibrant energy present in the organization to be an asset and a primary contributor to its success. Consequently, convincing this sector about the infinite potential of the young fellows of Indicorps in particular and youth in general is a huge challenge. Indicorps also has to contend with the day-to-day bureaucracy at various levels—getting visas issued to its fellows,

Case study 4.2 continued

Case study 4.2 continued

for example. Indian parents abroad resist sending their children on the Indicorps programme for a variety of reasons. On the administration front, Indicorps is supported by only a handful of staff members, most of who are NRI volunteers. Activities of the organization require both NRI and Indian staff. NRI staff are invariably fellows who volunteer to stay back after their fellowship programme and serve Indicorps for a year or two thereafter. Staff is only paid a modest stipend. Attracting NRIs to take on permanent staff roles is not very easy. At the same time, Indicorps incurs huge costs in retraining new people every time.

So *who* innovates? Here we have a stellar example of Anand and his sisters who, as social entrepreneurs, have carved out, through innovation, a great opportunity for their dreams to be translated into reality. And they are having loads of fun doing it too! Having set up an entrepreneurial venture, the fellows and other staff at Indicorps innovate every day of their lives, solving some of the difficult problems in India's hinterland.

Notes

1. Mihaly Csikszentmihalyi, *Creativity: Flow and the Psychology of Discovery and Invention* (New York: HarperCollins, 1996), p. 1.
2. Robert Sternberg, 'Creativity is a Decision', President's Column, *American Psychological Association Monitor*, November 2003.
3. From James Waldroop and Timothy Butler, 'Finding the Job You Should Want', *Fortune*, 2 March 1998.
4. Jim Collins and Jerry Porras, 'Building Your Company's Vision', *Harvard Business Review*, September–October 1996.
5. Dan Bricklin, 'Natural-Born Entrepreneur', *Harvard Business Review*, September 2001.
6. Edward Roberts, *Entrepreneurs in High Technology: Lessons from MIT and Beyond* (New York: Oxford University Press, 1991), Chapter 3.
7. Csikszentmihalyi, op. cit.
8. Ibid., p. 23.
9. Jim Collins and Jerry Porras, *Built to Last*, 2002, Chapter 11, p. 223.
10. Jon R. Katzenbach and Douglas K. Smith, *The Wisdom of Teams: Creating the High-Performance Organization* (Boston, MA: Harvard Business School Press, 1993). Reprinted as 'The Discipline of Teams', *Harvard Business Review*, July–August 2005.
11. Michael Jordan's height is 6 feet 6 inches, 78 inches, or 198 centimetres.
12. Catchball is described in *Managing Creativity and Innovation* (Boston, MA: Harvard Business School Press, 2003), pp. 47–49.
13. Vijay Govindarajan and Anil K. Gupta, 'Building an Effective Global Business Team', *MIT Sloan Management Review*, Summer 2001.

Part II
Tools for profit and growth

Marketplace success → strategy + marketing + production + finance + idea

Chapter 5
Price–cost–value

When you see a successful business, then know that someone once made a courageous decision.

—Peter Drucker

LEARNING OBJECTIVES After you read this chapter, you should understand:

- **How price, cost and value together form an 'ecosystem', or interrelated business model**
- **Why great managers think in terms of feedback systems, rather than linear cause and effect**
- **What customer value is, and what its seven essential elements are**
- **How to benchmark price, cost and value visually against competitors**
- **Why innovativeness in designing business models is no less important than in inventing new products and services**

TOOL

Price–cost–value #1

5.1 INTRODUCTION

If you're an engineer, then you're also a manager. Engineers manage technology—therefore, you cannot escape managing human and financial resources as well.

As you gain experience and seniority, your managerial responsibilities will grow. If you're a manager, but not an engineer, chances are you still manage technology, because in today's competitive global markets, even so-called low tech businesses are high tech—all successful businesses use sophisticated systems to manage their supply chains and design, produce, market and distribute their products and services.

Case study: CEMEX

CEMEX, a leading Mexican cement company, has a low-tech product (ready-mix concrete). But to get the cement to the right place at precisely the right time, when builders need it, CEMEX uses a highly complex technology: global satellite positioning that guides trucks to their destinations and tells dispatchers where each truck is at every moment of the day. Technology is thus no less crucial for CEMEX's business than it is for, say, Intel.

Engineering, management and economics all intersect at a vital juncture—they are each concerned with making effective use of resources. That, in fact, is how economics is commonly defined: as 'the study of the use of scarce resources which have alternate uses.'[1] By 'scarce', economists mean 'more is wanted and needed than is available'.

People, time, money, human energy, fossil fuel energy, machines, all are scarce. Deciding how best to use them is of interest to economists, engineers and managers alike—to the Ec, Tec and Exec. And we believe that the language and logic of economics are powerful aids to engineers and managers in their efforts to innovate and strategize. Teaching you, the reader, how to make effective use of both the language and logic of economics in a clear, focused and interesting manner is the objective of this book.

Management guru Peter Drucker once said that managers have only two functions: to innovate (create and bring to market winning new products and services) and to market (those products). Innovation and marketing together form the core of business strategy. We are convinced that the basic concepts of economics presented in the 10 chapters of Part II of this book can be used effectively to build winning business strategies—to build companies that achieve sustained growth and profit through innovation.

5.2 DO YOU SPEAK EC?

Managers use basic economic concepts every day. Managers and engineers speak 'Ec' all their lives, sometimes unknowingly—like Molére's doctor, who spoke prose all his life without being aware of it. Over many years of teaching engineers and managers, we discovered that in the classroom, at least half of the time we were showing our students how to formally define and apply tools and concepts they already understood intuitively and had used for years. They may not have known what 'marginal opportunity cost' was, but they used the concept well in making trade-off decisions, for example.

Why, then, should engineers and managers invest their scarce time in learning something they already know? The reason is: to become more proficient at using concepts that lie at the core of what managers do daily—make decisions and choices. As Peter Drucker noted, a single bold decision can create an entirely new industry.

Economics as a management discipline is like one of those programmable VCRs that no-one ever programmes. The underlying idea is simple, but applying it successfully in the real world—'Press button A, then buttons B and C, then A again'—can be exceedingly complex. By formally describing the language and logic of economics in a simple, systematic way and giving numerous examples and case studies showing how they are used in management decision-making, we hope readers will become much better at using ideas they have already employed for years, as well as acquiring an understanding of a number of rather new ideas.

One of the most important concepts in science is that of 'the principle of parsimony', or 'Occam's Razor', formulated in the 13th century by William of Occam. It states: 'If two theories work equally well, choose the simplest.' Einstein said it best: 'Make everything as simple as possible—but not simpler.'[2]

This is a powerful idea for managers as well. Simple strategies are easier to understand, easier to communicate and easier to implement, and hence usually work best. We often cite Henry Ford's straightforward definition of capitalism: 'If you want to make a dollar, go ahead and try. If you succeed, you can keep it.' Huge centrally planned countries crumbled when that simple idea was understood and embraced by their people. Winning products often have very clear, simple and terse value statements—like Ford's value statement for capitalism.

5.3 WHAT IS A BUSINESS MODEL?

What is the simplest possible way to define the challenges engineers and managers face in confronting innovation and strategy? Here is an attempt:

DEFINITIONS

A business model is an ecosystem that determines three key variables and how they interact: price, cost and value.

Managers and entrepreneurs seek to build business models that create sustained growth, profitability and competitive advantage and to build wealth for shareholders, value for customers and monetary and non-monetary satisfaction for employees.

Price, cost and value are the three pillars of profit. Winning business models excel in each of these three variables and in the ways they interact.

Economics can provide powerful tools for guiding managers' decisions regarding price, cost and value.

Every time we describe an economic tool or concept, our manager–engineer students unfailingly hold our feet to the fire and insist that we define the term and state the unit of measurement. How then are price, cost and value defined?

Note, first, that price, cost and value are always defined in terms of a single unit of the product or service provided by an organization. Rather than repeat 'unit cost', 'unit value', 'unit price' tediously, we simply refer to cost, value, price.

5.4 DEFINITIONS

Price

Price is some unit of value (comprising, generally, a sum of money) given up by one party in return for something from another party. For the seller, price is the *monetary value charged for the sale of one unit of its products or services.* For the buyer, it is the money given up, along with other indirect or hidden charges. For instance, the cost of maintaining a PC during its lifetime often greatly exceeds the purchase price, just as the lifetime cost of fuel used by a vehicle, or electricity consumed by a refrigerator, exceed their purchase price.

Cost

Cost is the explicit and hidden charge, both monetary and non-monetary, incurred by an organization in producing one unit of the product or service.

Value

Value is 'the perceived worth of the set of benefits received by a customer [from one unit of the product or service] in exchange for the total [price] of an offering, taking into consideration available competitive offerings and prices'.[3] In other words: value is what you get, less what you give.

Action learning

Develop Your Product's 'Value Statement'

Choose a product or service (your own, or one you like). Use the following template, or model, to write the product's 'value statement', by filling in the blanks: For [customer] who has [wants, needs, opportunities], the [product name] is a [product category] that [compelling reason for customer to buy/key benefit to customer]. Unlike [primary substitute or competitive alternative] this product [unique ways it is better and different].

Now, do the same exercise for a product you dislike, identifying reasons not to buy it and ways it is inferior to competitors.

How could you make the poor product into a winning one? Use the price-cost-value tool.

5.5 BUSINESS DESIGN AS ECOSYSTEM

What do we mean when we say a business model is an 'ecosystem'?

An ecology is a system of relations between living organisms and their environment. For instance, plants photosynthesize, that is, take in carbon dioxide and use sunlight and chlorophyll to convert it to oxygen and food, while mammals breathe in oxygen and exhale carbon dioxide—an ecology crucial for human life on our planet, one that global warming endangers.

An economy is a specific kind of ecology: a set of relations among people and their material resources and technology. The words 'ecology' and 'economy' both come from the same Greek root, *oikos*, meaning 'house'. Today's global economy is an enormous, complex 'household' in which over 6 billion people live, work and interact.

Every successful innovation creates a business ecosystem in miniature. Take for instance the Viewmax, a TV–VCR combination first produced by LG Goldstar (now LG Electronics) and awarded the 1987 Consumer Product of the Year Award (see case study 'Viewmax').

Case study: Viewmax: TV+VCR

Value

Buyers got a compact product that took much less space than separate TVs and VCRs—important for students with small dorm rooms, for instance, or retailers who wanted video displays on countertops.

Case study continued

Case study continued

Price

The Viewmax was priced in retail at $499 (the sum of the retail prices of the TV, $259, and the VCR, $239). This gave LG its first $500 consumer product. But the FOB (free on board) price LG charged retailers, $290, was $19 less than the FOB price of one TV and one VCR. By offering retailers higher profit margins, LG gave them an incentive to sell the Viewmax rather than the separate units.

Cost

Because only one tuner was needed for the combined product, the total cost of making the Viewmax was $30 less than that of the separate units. LG was not greedy; it passed on $19 of the cost saving to retailers through lower prices and kept $11 for itself.

The second half of the term 'ecology' comes from the Greek *logos*, meaning 'the study of'. The second half of the term 'economics' is the Greek *nemein*, meaning 'management'. Ecology is a branch of biology that studies the global household, including all species, while economics is a social science that studies mainly the *management* of the human global household.

A business or organization is a special type of ecology. Managers should keep that fact uppermost in their minds, because understanding the complex interactions in an organization and optimizing them are their main task. And achieving that insight requires skill in an especially difficult type of thinking, known as 'systems thinking'.

5.6 SYSTEMS THINKING

The ability to think in terms of systems or ecologies is one of the most valuable competencies a manager can have. Linear thinking says, X will cause Y. Systems thinking says, X will cause Y, and Z, which in turn will affect X ... and so on. A manager who is also a systems thinker is like a champion chess player—she thinks 10 moves ahead, anticipating competitors' responses to a new product and designing good responses to them in turn ... and so on.

Case study: Federal Express

Yale University undergraduate Frederick W. Smith wrote a term paper in 1965 about the need for an airfreight system that could deliver overnight time-sensitive shipments like medicines, computer parts and electronics, delivered by a company that operated both planes and trucks.

His professor gave him a C.

But he got an A from the marketplace when he launched Federal Express in August 1971. Today FedEx carries 2.1 million envelopes and packages every night; 1.3 million of them arrive at huge sorting arenas in Memphis, Tennessee, alone, where swarms of planes stack up at night waiting to land. Scanners, conveyer belts, workers, delivery trucks, satellite dishes, all form a system that generated $29.4 billion in sales in 2005 and employs 215,838 workers. The word 'Federal' came from Smith's goal of getting a contract from the US Federal Reserve System for overnight shipping of thousands of mail bags full of checks. He failed—but the name stuck.

Source: FedEx Website, www.fedex.com. See also David Brooks, 'FedEx and the productivity myth', *New York Times*, 10 April 2004.

5.7 FEEDBACK EFFECTS

Price, cost and value are a set of two interrelated feedback loops (see Figure 5.1). Value affects price, because what you can charge for your product is directly related to the differential value it creates, compared to competing or substitute products. Price, in turn, affects the customers' perception of value, which is always based on the ratio between what they receive and what they give up or pay. Similarly, price affects cost—as prices fall, volume of production increases and with it, costs decline through economies of scale or learning curve effects (see Chapters 10 and 11). In turn, as costs fall, companies can reduce their prices without impairing their profit margins.

These two interlocking feedback loops are central to every business model. Understanding how the entire system works or will work when it is launched is vital. Innovators who bring new products and services to market need to consider carefully the ecology, or business model, defined by price, cost and value. We have found that enormously creative individuals and teams labour tirelessly to innovate product features, but devote minimal time to innovating their invention's business model—usually, with unhappy results. *It is essential*

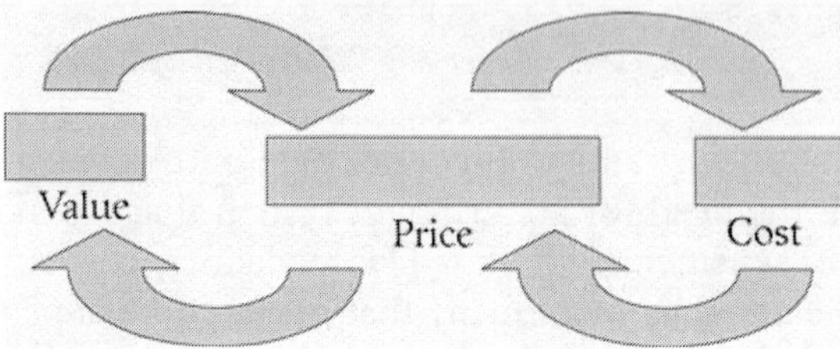

Figure 5.1
The price, cost, value dynamic

to invest the same level of creativity in an innovative product's business model as is invested in the product itself.

In the term 'price–cost–value', the components are listed in ascending order of importance. *Value* is clearly the most important, because if a product or service fails to create value, relative to competing offerings, then its price and cost are irrelevant. *Cost* is next, because unless value can be created at reasonable cost, the result will not be sufficiently profitable to sustain the company or organization, its owners, managers and workers. And *price* is last in importance, because generally, if value creation is high enough, customers will be willing to pay handsomely for the offering.

For profitable, successful products, price is determined by value, not by cost. If you are pricing your products by what it costs to produce them, then chances are you are in a commodity-type business, where your offering is no different from that of competitors. While it is possible to endure and even excel in such markets, companies that build wealth for their shareholders are almost always those that produce high-value products priced by value rather than by cost.

Sometimes customers judge value by price (for instance, when high-priced products are perceived as higher-quality). We have found that a common error made by startup firms is to under-price their product, as they try to gain a foothold in the marketplace. Raising prices later is far harder than lowering them; and for new products, a cheap price is often a signal that the innovator is trying to compete on price rather than value.

Case study: General Motors vs Microsoft

For some 60 years, General Motors was the world's largest industrial corporation (measured by sales). It has lost its first-place position to Wal-Mart, but remains among the world's largest companies, with sales of $193.5 billion in 2004 and 324,000 employees (see table on page 161).

Case study continued

Case study continued

Yet the market value of General Motors shares (the number of outstanding shares multiplied by the price per share on 17 March 2006) was only $11.9 billion, *about 4 per cent of the value of Microsoft shares ($284 billion), even though GM had sales seven times larger than Microsoft*. It is only a slight exaggeration to say that the founder and principal shareholder of Microsoft, Bill Gates, could acquire GM, if he wished (*Forbes* magazine estimates his personal wealth at $57 billion).

Why is this the case?

Microsoft is able to create and sustain value, and charge high prices, creating high profit margins and large profits. GM is in the automobile industry, where there is excess capacity; moreover, GM cars have become commodities, prices are not high, and profit margins are razor-thin. (We will learn later in this book that in fact GM makes much of its profits not from making cars but from its finance arm that lends car buyers money.)

	Microsoft	General Motors
	(2005 figures)	
Market value of shares[a]	$284	$11.9
Sales	$39.8	$192.6
Shareholders' equity[b]	$48.1	$16.7
Net income	$12.3	–$10.6
Employees	61,000	327,000
P/E Price–earnings ration	23	n.a.

Notes: (a) On 17 March 2006. Financial figures are in US$ billion.
(b) Shareholders' equity is the difference between the value of the company's assets and its liabilities (bonds, bank debt, etc.); net income is the company's profit (sales minus costs, including taxes); P/E ratio, or price/earnings ratio, is the price of the company's stock divided by the earnings, or net income, per share.

5.8 TECHNOLOGY, MEET PSYCHOLOGY

The value–price ecology shows why manager–engineers must be experts in both *technology* and *psychology*. Technology drives innovation. Psychology drives the basic understanding of customer wants and needs that underlies innovation. Successful innovation and value-creation integrate technology and psychology. Many high-tech products fail because they attain new heights of sophistication in technology, but provide solutions for wants and needs that in fact do not exist (or that customers do not perceive to exist). Sometimes, in order to sell a new product, expensive and difficult customer education must be undertaken; only then is the need perceived, and the product purchased in large amounts.

We worked with a startup company that produced an amazing robotic lawnmower that could sense obstacles and boundaries and cut the grass all by itself. But the product failed. It did not meet a real need. Many people simply do not mind cutting the grass with a conventional lawnmower, or do not mind it enough to invest their money in a robotic one. The technological virtuosity far outstripped the understanding of grass-cutters' psychology.

Seven fundamental lessons on customer value[4]

1. Perception is reality

It is not what you, as manager or entrepreneur, think is valuable that matters; it is what the customer perceives is valuable that is crucial. And customers never buy a good or service; they buy what the good or service does for them. As the CEO of CEMEX, a large innovative Mexican cement company notes, nobody wants to purchase cement. Rather 'they want to build a house or bridge or road'. Charles Revson, founder of Revlon, said it best: 'In the factories, we make cosmetics. In the department stores we sell hope.'

2. Practise empathy

Understand that you, manager or entrepreneur, are not the customer. Sometimes customers' real reasons for buying are quasi-rational, utterly different from the rational reasons they themselves give. For instance, consumers may *say* they buy sport utility vehicles (SUVs) because they are safer and handle better in tough conditions—but in fact they buy them mainly because in the asphalt jungle, where other drivers are after you, the bigger your vehicle, the likelier you are to crush rather than be crushed. Try hard to read the subtext of customer value.

3. Products too are ecologies

Never forget that products, too, like business designs, are ecologies; they exist in specific frameworks or contexts. Customer value depends on the five Ws and one H: who are the customers, what do they want to do or experience, why are they buying, when and where do they need the product, and how do they intend to use it?

4. Never forget 'emotional value' and 'economic value'

Products are bundles of features, and 'feature value' is an important determinant of value. But it is only *one* factor. Customers buy *emotional value* (the prestige value of wearing a Rolex) and they also buy *economic value* (savings in time, effort and money, relative to the money investment in the product).

5. Price may be only a small part of the customer's costs, because of hidden costs

Mohanbir Sawhney gives as an example the sale of plastic bottles to a pharmaceutical company to replace glass ones. While the plastic bottles themselves are cheaper than glass, the relative savings are in fact much larger, because glass bottles generate hidden costs: breakage, labelling, inventory and shipping (they are heavier). Customers are not always aware of these hidden costs, and sometimes sellers (e.g., of glass bottles) are not eager to educate them.

6. Churchill's Law

Everything (especially value) is relative. Winston Churchill was asked how he felt on turning 80. He replied: 'Fine—when I consider the alternative.' Customers, like Churchill, gauge value by comparing a product with alternatives. Always judge your product's value against the best alternatives. The entrepreneurs who invented Quicken, the leading book-keeping and chequebook software, benchmarked their software's simplicity not against other software, but against the *pencil.*

7. Creating value

'You are always on my mind.' As in the Elvis Presley song, value creation is a mindset that informs and permeates managers' thinking and their business designs. It is such managers that create growing businesses or even whole new industries.

5.9 CREATING VALUE, CUTTING COSTS: FRIENDS OR FOES?

In fiercely competitive global markets, poorly managed companies ultimately shrivel and die. There is no mystery in this. But frequently, *well-managed* companies die too. In general, as Arie de Geus has noted, the average life span for companies is barely a dozen years, far shorter than should be the case.[5] Good companies, not just bad ones, fall sick and die. The question is—why?

Clayton Christensen explains the decline of strong companies by a paradox—they listen *too well* to their customers:

> When the best firms subsequently failed, it was for the same reasons—they listened responsively to their customers and invested aggressively in the technology, products, and manufacturing capabilities that satisfied their customers' next-generation needs. This is one of the innovator's dilemmas: Blindly following the maxim that good managers should keep close to their customers can sometimes be a fatal mistake [because a new technology with poor initially performance, unwanted by customers, can 'blindside' responsive companies and their managers].[6]

We believe there is a fundamental paradox of management that offers a non-technology-based explanation for the rise and fall of corporate well-being, even under seemingly expert management. The paradox is this: two basic management mindsets exist for raising profitability—value-creation (innovation) and cost-reduction.

When well executed, both approaches are powerful. They each reflect 'increasing returns', meaning the more you cut cost or create value, the higher the return. That is why managers who choose one or the other of these two paths continue to march along them—often, until disaster strikes.

- Cost reduction is generally successful in boosting earnings per share, and earns applause from shareholders and boards of directors. But the culture, goals and behaviours engendered by cost reduction are inimical to those required by value-creation. And companies who fail to invest in research and development (R&D) find themselves without new products to compete with those of innovative competitors.
- Value-creation involves innovativeness in building brand value, improving existing products and developing radically new ones. Innovation is often expensive. A single successful pharmaceutical drug now costs $800 million in R&D, testing and evaluation. And there is no guarantee that such investments will turn out to be eventual market successes.

As a result, cost reduction may lead companies to achieve *local* profit maximization, while foregoing the higher *global* profit maximization of value creation. Competitors who do embrace value-creation quickly ascend in market share and shove aside what until very recently was a highly successful company. Like dinosaurs who could not adapt to the sudden drop in global temperatures caused by the dust cloud of a large meteor, cost-cutting firms quickly become extinct when aggressive innovators attack them.

The perpetual tension between cost reduction and value creation increases dramatically during a global economic downturn, such as the 2001–03 global recession, because the need to carefully protect cash reserves and slash costs in the face of falling revenues and profits can easily undermine or destroy the innovative spirit so vital for science-based start ups.

The essence of the paradox is not technology but managerial mindset:

> Short-term profits are extremely sensitive to unit cost reduction, leading managers to adopt organizational attitudes for cutting costs that are inimical to another powerful driver of long-term profits: value creation and innovation. As a result, companies can cost-cut themselves into extinction.

Companies that endure and prevail, through global downturns, are those that can successfully maintain world-class value-creation and cost-reduction capabilities, *in parallel rather than in serial fashion*, within the same organization, while successfully resolving the inevitable tensions and conflicts that arise between operational decisions, strategic plans, and the individuals who make and build them. The tensions are exacerbated significantly, because both value-creation and cost-reduction investments in general are subject to increasing returns—that is, additional dollars of investment bring ever-higher bottom-line returns, reinforcing senior management's tendency to continue with such investments. Exclusive focus on cost-reducing or value-creating strategies can quickly run into discontinuities that can destroy a company or its key products in a very brief period of time. Making creativity and thrift into allies, living under one roof, rather than enemies, is a skill great managers have, and mediocre ones lack.

Case study: Compaq Computer Co.

Compaq zigged and zagged, oscillating between value-creation and cost-reduction strategies, until one day it zigged when it should have zagged, and was absorbed by HP.

Value-creation, 1981–85

The first IBM PC came to market in August 1981. Compaq's portable almost single-handedly created the PC clone market. It weighed a

Case study continued

Case study continued

tonne (20 lb), but it was the first successful PC clone. It was expensive ($5,000), and its buyers loved it. Columbia Data Products just preceded Compaq that year with the first true IBM PC clone, but they didn't survive for long. It was Compaq's quickly gained reputation for quality, and its essentially 100 per cent IBM compatibility (reverse engineered), that created the clone market.

While IBM was busy developing its proprietary MicroChannel-based PS/2 systems, clone vendors ALR and Compaq grabbed control of the ×86 market by introducing the first 386-based PCs, the Access 386 and Deskpro 386, just a couple of months after Intel began shipping the 80386 processor. This marked the end of IBM's dominance of the IBM PC market. Both 386 clone systems maintained backward compatibility with the 286-based PC/AT. Compaq's Deskpro 386 had a further performance innovation in its bus architecture—it split the ×86 external bus into two separate buses: a fast local bus to support memory chips fast enough for a 16 MHz 386, and a slower I/O bus that supported existing expansion cards.

Compaq's value-creation strategy, even as a high-cost producer, brought it rapid growth in sales and profits.

Cost reduction, 1985–90

A dominant design quickly emerged for PCs, and the number of PC clone manufacturers soared. Asian producers in Taiwan were able to make PCs far cheaper than Compaq could in Houston, Texas, especially since the soaring US dollar made American-made products very expensive. Compaq found its very existence in danger.

Almost overnight, Compaq transformed itself from a high-cost into a low-cost producer, by shifting production offshore to Asia, reducing overhead, standardizing computer models and implementing just-in-time. This remarkable feat of management kept Compaq among the market leaders. But as PCs became commodities, profit margins fell sharply. Compaq returned to value-creation.

Value creation, 1990–95

Compaq saw the rise of networking and related equipment, and entered the server market, building highly reliable servers that met customer needs. This value-creation strategy restored Compaq's profit margins, but again only temporarily, as competitors invaded Compaq's server territory and again commoditized the product.

Case study continued

Case study continued

Cost reduction, 1995–

Compaq focused again on cost reduction, battling the falling prices that excess capacity and commoditization had created. In 1998 Compaq acquired DEC—Digital Equipment Corp.

On 4 September 2001, the number-two computer maker HP announced a $25 billion 'merger' with Compaq, then number three in the market—a merger that in effect was a takeover. The head of the merged entity was HP CEO Carly Fiorina.

Compaq to all intents and purposes ceased to exist. It had fallen victim to a *serial* cost-reduction value-creation strategy. In its final attempt to reinvent and transform itself, Compaq had not succeeded, and disappeared.

What follows are three examples of managers who excelled in focusing on one of the price–cost–value variables. The chapter then concludes with a case study of four winning business 'ecologies' in which all three axes of the business 'triangle' combine to build a powerful product platform with enduring profitability.

Cost reduction

Robert W. Moffat Jr has been termed IBM's Clark Kent. While running IBM's Personal Systems business, he overhauled IBM's enormous supply chains—and generated cost savings of $5.6 billion! Some of this cost reduction was due to falling component prices unrelated to anything Moffat did. But the savings his actions generated still totalled $3 billion.[7] He accomplished this by selling three factories, shifting manufacturing to cheaper locations and simplifying product designs. *Moffat knew that on average, 70 per cent of manufacturing costs are determined—set in concrete—at the design stage. Simple, cost-effective designs can save enormous sums.* To cut costs, IBM created an Integrated Supply Chain division, IBM's fourth-largest, with $40 billion in annual spending and 19,000 employees. This is an example of cost-saving that reinforces, rather than replaces, value creation.

Value creation

The founder of Starbucks coffee houses did not seek to create value by offering superior coffee. His vision was broader: to change America's (and later, the world's) lifestyle, by having virtually everyone come in to a Starbucks coffee house for their morning coffee rather than make it at home, because

Starbucks could make it a lot better. The average Starbucks customer visits the company 18 times a month.

Price innovation

At one time, Netscape was the world's favourite Internet browser. The developers of Netscape provided it free of charge. By doing so, they gained enormous visibility, publicity and goodwill. They made their profits through sale of high-margin server software—sales that were often generated by the marketplace's familiarity with the Netscape browser.

Wal-Mart is another example of paradoxically low pricing and strong profits. Wal-Mart makes very little profit in selling things to people (the difference between the price Wal-Mart charges and the price Wal-Mart pays to suppliers is very small). But because Wal-Mart is efficient and sells products almost as soon as they are put on the shelves, and because it *pays* its suppliers only 90 days later, it receives a large interest-free loan from the suppliers, representing 'float' that earns Wal-Mart billions each year when invested.

5.10 THE POWER OF VISION

Innovative products and services begin with a concept of value-creation. Often, underlying this value creation concept is a far-sighted vision, seeking to create an entirely new ecology or system to meet a need that existing and future customers may not even perceive exists.

Entrepreneurs, managers and visionary builders can, through the power of their vision for value creation, build organizations that dominate their field for a century or longer. In every case, a courageous decision was involved. And in each case, the visionaries saw a complete business system, not just a new product or service.

Case study: MIT, Pan Am and RCA

MIT

The Massachusetts Institute of Technology, in Cambridge, Massachusetts, USA, is one of the world's great science and engineering universities. MIT opened its doors to its first 15 students on 20 February 1865. MIT's founder and first president, William Barton Rogers, a famous natural scientist, had a vision. He sought to

Case study continued

Case study continued

create value by creating a new type of educational institution, where students would learn not only how to *acquire* knowledge but also how to *apply* it (a revolutionary idea at that time), that stressed basic research and, above all, *built professional competence by coupling teaching and research with attention to real-world problems*, giving graduates not only the ability to work wisely, effectively and creatively for the betterment of mankind but also the passion for doing so. Rogers chose as MIT's slogan *Mens et manus* ('mind and hand' in Latin), and placed on MIT's crest the figures of a scholar and a craftsman. Now, 141 years later, this vision still drives MIT graduates and faculty to apply new technologies to pressing social problems. As a result, MIT has led the Massachusetts high-tech renaissance along Route 128, generating jobs, income and wealth for the state and the nation.

Pan Am

Pan American Airways founder Juan Trippe, who founded the airline in 1927, had from the outset a vision for making airline travel global and affordable for the masses. In October 1958 the first Pan Am Boeing 707, flying twice as fast and twice as high as the propeller aircraft it replaced, made the first flight from New York to Paris. Trippe persuaded the head of Boeing, Bill Allen, to build an even larger jet, the 747, and made key design suggestions. (Pan Am went bankrupt when Trippe bought too many 747s and failed to adapt his vision to the post-1973 realities of high fuel costs.)

RCA

RCA Chair David Sarnoff had a vision for making radios (in 1915, mainly used in shipping and by Morse code enthusiasts) into a 'household utility', to 'bring music into the house by wireless'. RCA was formed in 1919, when General Electric acquired Marconi. Sarnoff envisioned a complete business design where RCA would create programming (news, sports, music) so that buying the radio music boxes (called Radiolas by RCA) would be worthwhile; he created national broadcasts by linking hundreds of radio stations into a network, known as NBC. He later did the same with television.

Sources: MIT: Rogers' vision is described in the booklet distributed at the 2003 MIT Graduation Ceremonies.
Pan Am: Related by Richard Branson, pioneer entrepreneur of Virgin Airlines, *Time*, 7 December 1998, pp. 135–36.
RCA: *Time*, 7 December 1998, pp. 89–90.

5.11 WHAT BUSINESS AM I IN?

Harvard Business School professor Theodore Levitt, an expert in marketing and long-time editor of the *Harvard Business Review*, once wrote a famous article titled 'Marketing Myopia'. In it, he explained why railroad companies and Hollywood film companies shared a common fate—gallons of red ink and, for some, bankruptcy and extinction.

What did railroad executives and movie magnates both do wrong? Perhaps, Levitt wrote, they failed to ask themselves a key question, one that can never be asked too often or too fervently: *What business am I in?*

Movies and railroads skidded downhill rapidly because the managers who ran them failed to ask, and answer correctly, Levitt's question. Hollywood moguls thought they were in the *movie* business, instead of in the *entertainment* business. Television, a new form of entertainment, and later cable TV and video recorders, nearly buried movies because in the industry of entertainment value, television proved to be an inexpensive and convenient substitute for movies.

Railroad executives complacently assumed that they were in the railroad business. In fact, they were in the business of creating value by transporting people and goods. So were truckers and airlines. Stiff competition from them, with some help from public policy, killed the railroads. Paraphrased loosely, the question 'what business am I in?' breaks down into several sub-questions:

- What are my customers' needs and how are they changing?
- How well does my product meet those needs, compared with its competitors?
- What price can my product command for its need-satisfying value?
- At what cost can I produce that value?

High-value products and services that command premium prices can compensate for excessive costs. But even bare-bones costs will not enable a company to survive, if its products fail to create adequate value for customers in the marketplace.

Oscar Wilde once defined a cynic as 'someone who knows the price of everything and the value of nothing'.[8] His statement has been used to define an 'economist'. But economists, and managers for that matter, are no cynics. They need to know the value of their products, the cost of producing them, and the price those products can command in the marketplace and they need to constantly challenge their perceptions by acquiring new evidence. Good management is a perpetual juggling act in which cost, price and value are kept in an appropriate balance, with a sharp eye focused on trends and change that might in the near and distant future alter that balance, for good or for ill.

5.12 YOU ARE YOUR OWN BEST MARKET RESEARCH

Often, hugely successful companies are built because an entrepreneur creates a product he himself or she herself would like to have or buy but failed to find in the marketplace. Here are two examples.

- Israeli computer engineers Arik Vardi, Amnon Amir, Yair Goldfinger and Sefi Vigiser wanted to engage in email chat in real time with their friends all over the world, but did not know which of them were logged on to their computers. So they created software that gave them this information, and they called it ICQ (I Seek You), started a company known as Mirabilis ('miraculous' in Latin) and offered the world their software for free. Some 12 million people downloaded it. America On-Line bought Mirabilis in 1998 for over $400 million—justifying the name of the little company whose total revenues did not exceed $30,000. Some 300 million people worldwide now use ICQ, based on user ID numbers.[9]
- Ted Leatherman, an American helicopter mechanic, watched Vietnamese teenagers tear down and rebuild Honda motorcycles with virtually their bare hands, on the streets of Saigon in the 1970s. To do this himself, he realized he needed a pocket knife that included basic tools. So he built one in his garage. It was eight years before he sold his first one—it packed 13 tools into a jackknife device—in 1983. Today one in every dozen American men and women owns one. Leatherman Tool Group has sold 35 million pocket tools worldwide.[10]

VISUAL TOOL

Price–cost–value triangle #1

To make effective use of economic tools, managers need to know not only how to *use* them to make wise decisions, but also how to communicate those decisions and how they were reached to others. That is why the most powerful decision tools are ones that lend themselves easily to vivid visual pictures.

The price–cost–value tool lends itself well to this, as a three-dimensional diagram, with price, cost and value on each of three axes, on a scale of 1–10. The price and value axes are measured *from the perspective of the customer*, for competing products. Lowest price scores 9 or 10, highest price, 3 or 4. Highest *perceived* value scores 9 or 10, lowest value scores, say, 5 or 6 (all depending on the customers' perceptions).

The cost axis, of course, is measured from the perspective of the organization: Low cost scores 9 or 10, high cost scores 3 or 5.

An example is given in Figure 5.2 for shaving products: Gillette's Mach 3, compared with the comparable product by Schick (Extreme 3) and an electric razor. This is a highly subjective analysis done by a former student—who, as it happens, worked for Gillette. It may or may not reflect customer thinking. This exercise should begin with the product's value statement. For instance, for Gillette's Mach 3 product:

> For persons who regularly want to remove their bodily hair, Gillette provides superior shaving products that maintain a smooth skin, provide the tightest shave and avoid cuts on a daily basis. Unlike lower cost disposable competitive products, our shavers provide the best possible shave in every price segment.
>
> For men who shave daily, the Mach 3 provides the best shave available today, worldwide. Unlike Schick Extreme and mid range electrical Razors, it leaves no hair beyond the skin surface level and does so without harming the skin or causing pain while shaving.

To be useful, this exercise in benchmarking must be accompanied by serious data collection; benchmarking price is easiest to acquire data on, benchmarking value is hardest, and cost falls in between. The goal is to compare the value statement, as the company wishes it to be, with reality.

The price–cost–value triangle shows Gillette's Mach 3 product as high-value, high-price and relatively high cost. As long as buyers confirm this, Gillette can charge high prices for this product. An erosion of the value differential would quickly change this picture.

Case study: Barbie, Dell, J&J, Edison: Find the common thread

Question: What do the following four things have in common?

1. Mattel's Barbie doll
2. Johnson & Johnson's new 'stent' (device that holds arteries open)
3. Dell computers
4. Edison's light bulb

Case study continued

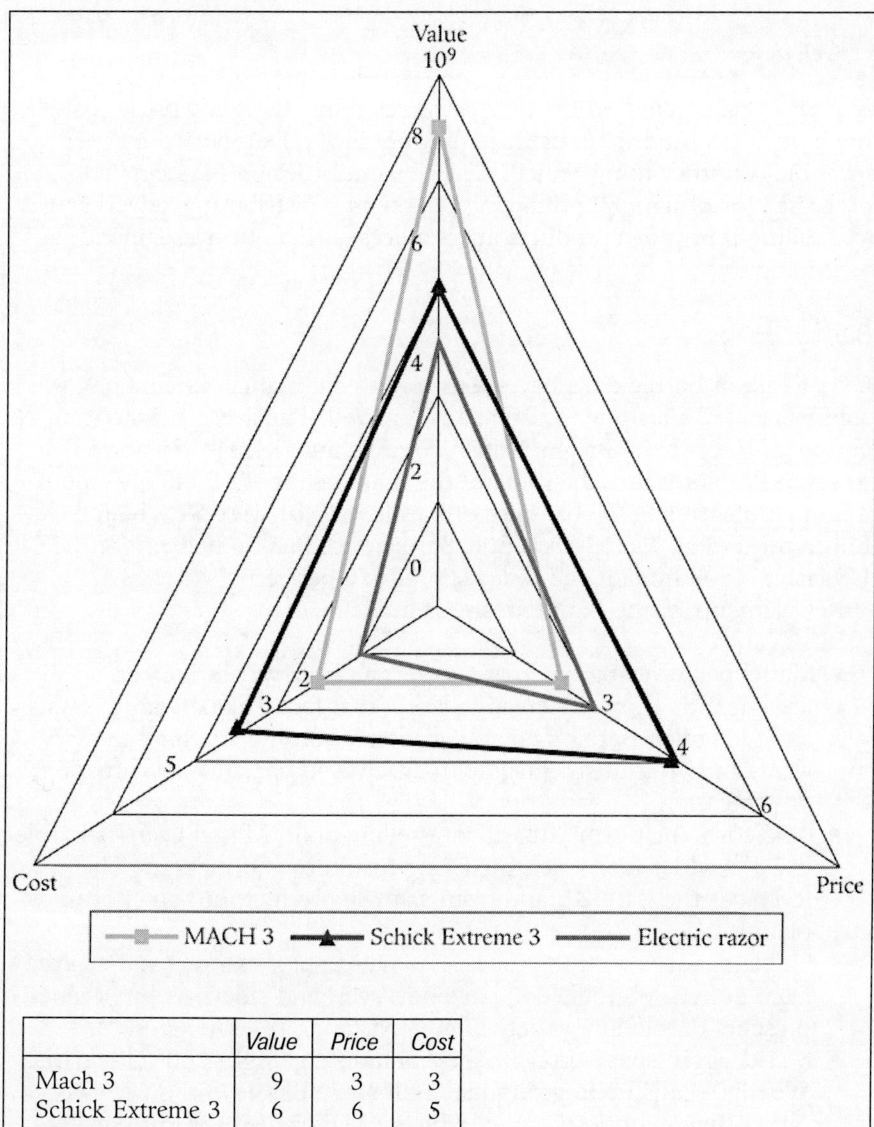

	Value	*Price*	*Cost*
Mach 3	9	3	3
Schick Extreme 3	6	6	5
Electric razor	5	4	2

Figure 5.2
Price–cost–value triangle: Three pillars of profit

Case study continued

Answer: All generated profits by creative, carefully designed price–cost–value business models, sometimes (but not always) supported by technology. Other things equal, clever business design—systematic processes for designing, producing, marketing, distributing, advertising and selling innovative products and services—wins out over superior technology.

Barbie

Over a billion Barbie dolls have been sold to date, since the first one was sold by Mattel, a leading toy company, in 1959. The average American girl owns 10 of them. Italian, British, French and German girls own five to seven Barbies each. The value of the brand alone is $2 billion—more than that of Armani. Global sales of Barbie in 2001 were $1.6 billion, fully a third of all Mattel's revenue. Barbie once had 90 per cent of the US fashion doll market and today still has 70 per cent.

Key elements of the Barbie business model:

- Mattel perceives Barbie not as a doll but 'as a way of life', or 'a lifestyle, not a toy'. By creating a doll that looks like an adult, says Ruth Handler, Barbie's creator, girls can become anything they want, and vicariously imagine themselves in virtually any situation or profession.
- Barbie is a 'platform'. Apart from selling dolls, Mattel licenses Barbie in 30 product categories, including furniture and makeup. This leverages the Barbie brand from a single product into an enormous platform.
- Barbie changes with the times. Her hairdo has changed and evolved from ponytail, bubble cut, page boy, swirl and side-part hip. Mattel presents Barbie in a variety of contexts and professions.
- Mattel aggressively protects their brand's copyright and trademark. When a Danish pop group had a hit song 'Barbie Girl' in 1997, rather than exult in the free publicity Mattel sued for infringement of their rights. (They lost in court.) Even the bright Barbie pink colour is trademarked.
- Barbie is a vehicle for constant creativity and innovation. Barbie is a 'business-school case study in innovation', says a Boston Consulting Group consultant. Each year Mattel designs 150 different Barbie dollars and some 120 different new outfits.

Case study continued

Case study continued

Barbie is plastic, not technology. By understanding the nature of the product and by building the brand based on it, Mattel has built an enormous, enduring cash-cow business design that has dominated its market segment for 45 years, and could continue to do so for another 40.

Dell

Dell Computer Co. had $41 billion in sales in 2003 and earned over $1 billion in profits. Its 27 per cent return on equity (RoE) led the industry. In the decade to 2003, earnings per share grew by over 30 per cent yearly—doubling every two years. Investors who bought Dell stock in 1991 and held it until 2001 earned a 59 per cent annual return on their investment, compared to 16 per cent for the industry as a whole.

The key to Dell's success is the business model designed by Michael Dell, who as a young University of Texas student found he could assemble computers from off-the-shelf parts faster, better and cheaper than Big Blue IBM, and sell them directly to customers (value). The direct-sale model meant he was in close contact with customers daily, could spot market trends, never had large accounts receivable (payment *preceded* delivery), never held inventory, and could customize computers, a feature customers loved (cost). Within 12 years of founding Dell, Michael Dell's company had $12 billion in sales.

Dell sells mass customization (sale of unique products, designed to order, to a mass market), not technology. The key to Dell's ongoing success is its business model and, above all, the skill with which it is implemented. It is no easy task to take an order for a computer, laptop, or server, assemble it, and ship it in three days. It requires great management skill in ensuring that parts and components are on hand precisely when needed. Suppliers, manufacturers, shippers are all integrated into Dell's business model seamlessly.

Flexibility in altering the original winning business design is as important as the business model itself. When Dell discovered, by accident, that customers loved buying customized computers from the Web, Dell quickly built Web pages attached to corporate Websites where employees could buy computers similar to those they used at their offices. Web sales grew rapidly.

Business designs cannot in general be patented or copyrighted. Dell's design is protected by two aspects: skill and practice in managing the

Case study continued

Case study continued

complex model, acquired over 20 years; and transition problems—computer companies that use retailers cannot easily shift to direct sales, because retailers would instantly drop their brand and sales would fall during the transition period.

J&J

A 'stent' is a mesh-like device that holds blocked arteries open. When they work, stents reduce the need for repeated angioplasties (operations that open arteries with a catheter) and for heart bypass surgery. The stent market grew to $3.2 billion in 2003, and $4 billion in 2004, from around $1.6 billion in 2000.

Johnson and Johnson (J&J) pioneered the stent in 1994. The technology was amazing. But the business design that accompanies it was not. J&J made numerous errors.

- The $1,600 price, very high, was set without establishing that medical insurance would cover the cost. Often it did not. When competing devices hit the market at lower prices, J&J quickly lost market share, because they stubbornly refused to cut their price.
- J&J did not perceive how valuable the stent invention was, failed to exploit their lead, and failed to continue to develop new and better stents. They squandered their technology lead.

But J&J learned from past mistakes. The CEO of Cordis, the J&J unit that makes and sells stents, got a second chance. J&J researchers invented a new stent that is drug-coated. Between 20 per cent and 40 per cent of patients with ordinary stents suffer re-blockage of their arteries because scar tissue forms over the stent. J&J scientists found that if they coated the stent with a drug known as Sirolimus, scarring could be greatly reduced.

Learning from the past, J&J has:

- made certain medical insurance would pay for the new stents; Medicare agreed to pay the cost of the drug-coated stent even before it won FDA approval—mainly because the new stent clearly could reduce treatment costs, and frequency of costly heart surgery, thus saving the medical insurers money;

Case study continued

Case study continued

- set the price at $3,000—though double the cost of current devices, this is still cost-effective, because it greatly reduces the need for costly repeat treatments and surgery. In other words, the price passes on considerable savings and value to the customer;
- been aggressive in meeting with hospitals, showing them the powerful cost-benefit appeal of the new stent;
- worked to ensure that new versions of the drug-coated stent are already in the works.

When business designs fail, most companies (especially start ups) do too. Once in a while, companies get a second chance. J&J did, and learned well from past mistakes. Their unique technology has been accompanied by an equally creative business model.

Edison

We noted earlier how Ted Levitt taught managers to ask, 'What business are you in?' as the first step to designing a business model.

Thomas Edison and the companies he set up electrified America. But Edison was not in the business of providing power or light. 'Electricity is not power,' he once remarked. 'It is a method for *transporting* power.' This insight held the key to his business design. It led him to woo Wall Street bankers and financiers (including J.P. Morgan), raise large amounts of capital to build the wires and requisite generating stations, work tirelessly to create public relations and a 'buzz' for electricity, and aggressively patent all aspects, not just the light bulb, of electricity—216 patents in all. He purposely lit up Pearl Street, in downtown Manhattan, near Wall Street, to interest and excite the wealthy barons of New York.

Edison thought in terms of *systems.* He saw electricity as a disruptive technology that would replace (not complement) gas lighting, in contrast to his British rival Joseph W. Swan. He chose carbon for his light-bulb filament, rather than platinum, because he understood that the economics of platinum were unfavourable—costly, possibly unreliable sources of a product that at the time was little needed or used.

Edison had a franchise model, licensing the technology to companies in Europe and South America. He worked hard to build a cadre of talented young engineer-managers to run the Edison companies.

Case study continued

Case study continued

True, Edison was a brilliant tireless inventor who slept very little. But unlike many inventors, he also had an intuitive business sense that led him to construct creative business models even as he was making his new creations—like the phonograph and light bulb. Even when rivals moved ahead of him in technology—as J.W. Swan did, when he demonstrated a carbon-filament light bulb eight months before Edison—Edison's superior business model, built on large resources, won the day.

Sources: Barbie: Based on 'Barbie: Life in Plastic', *Economist*, 19 December 2002.
J&J: Based in part on 'J&J Prognosis Improves', *International Herald Tribune*, 2 January 2003.
Edison: Based on S. Maital, 'Inspiration Joins Perspiration: Thomas Edison as a Dynamo of Applied Creativity', European Case Clearing House Case, 2004.

Action learning

Microsoft's Price–Cost–Value Business Model

What is Microsoft's price–cost–value business model for Windows, that made founder Bill Gates the world's richest individual? How did Microsoft achieve a 69 per cent market share in 2003 for server operating systems, compared with 12.6 per cent for Linux? Does Linux's business model (based on an 'open' system where the software code is available to everyone, free of charge, and where improvements are shared moments after they occur) threaten that of Microsoft?

5.13 CONCLUSION

Great technology is not a *sufficient* condition for business success—as J&J's original stent in 1994 proves. Nor is great technology a *necessary* condition for business success. There is no superior technology or engineering in Barbie or Dell.

But a creative, winning business design *can* be a sufficient condition for business success and profit. And the combination of great technology and a superior business model can prove virtually unbeatable.

Innovative companies should put a major part of their creative efforts and resources into the design of the business model—the value statement, pricing strategy and cost structure—that accompanies their new products and services. Failure to do this is one of the key mistakes that cause many start ups, and long-established firms, to fail. Winning business designs can, like Barbie dolls, dominate their market for decades.

Readers are invited to view 'Pillars of Profit: Segment #1, Price Cost Value' in the accompanying CD.

CASE STUDY 5.1

Viewmax*

Case study discussion topics

1. What was Goldstar's 'brand image' problem?
2. Why didn't Japanese firms, dominant in the TV and VCR markets, not want to develop a TV–VCR combo?
3. What were Viewmax's cost advantages?
4. How did Viewmax create value for customers?
5. How did Goldstar choose to price the Viewmax?
6. Why did Viewmax enjoy relatively high profit margins?

In 1984, the consumer electronics branch of the Korean firm Lucky Goldstar weighed a proposal to develop and market a new product for the US market that would combine in one case a TV and VCR. At that time, Goldstar Co. (GS) had been exporting a large number of TVs and VCRs to the US market. Most models were low-price products, not helpful for the image of the GS brand, and had small profit margins. GS felt selling high-end products in the US market was important to enhance its brand image. However, attaining reasonable market shares in the high-end market for individual products was difficult. Therefore, GS proposed to develop a TV–VCR combined product that would be priced at about $500.

The TV market had two broad segments—large-size models of over 19 inches and small models of under 13 inches. Well-known manufacturers, mostly Japanese and GE/Philips supplied a majority of

* This case study is a summary of the case authored by Do Hyun Kim.

Case study 5.1 continued

Case study 5.1 continued

the large-size models. The small-size models were all produced by Korea, Mexico and China. Japanese makers dominated the VCR market (80 per cent market share). Their outstanding market share in both TVs and VCRs prevented them from developing a TV-VCR combined product. Tables 5.1.1 and 5.1.2 give the global demand for TVs and VCRs, respectively during the late 1980s.

Table 5.1.1
Global demand for TVs in the late 1980s

Size	*Demand (%)*	*Average retail price*
13 inches	5,173 (31.4)	$202
19 inches	6,837 (41.5)	$280
25 inches	4,459 (27.1)	$457

Note: 13 inches include under 13 inches size and 25 inches include over 25 inches size. Figures in brackets are percentages. The demand quantities are in thousands of sets.

Table 5.1.2
Global demand for VCRs in the late 1980s (in '000 # sets)

Grade	*Average retail price*	*Specification*	*Demand (%)*
2HD MO	$249	Mono	9,850 (77)
4HD ST	$369	Stereo	2,558 (20)
HI-FI	$459	S-VHS	384 (3)

Source: EIA Annual Report, 1988.

The major export areas of GS were low-end products like 13 inches/ 19 inches Mono TV and 2HD Mono VCR. The company's sales network comprised principally of discount stores. GS was considering improving the image of its brand, which suffered due to the export of low-end products, while additionally facing a stiff price competition. Further, the company had to shift its sales from low-end products to middle and high-end products because other Asian producers including China were aggressively marketing their low-end products in the US market. Given this situation, GS deliberated the viability of the proposed TV–VCR combo product. Despite negative reactions, the top management at GS set up a task force and proceeded with the development of the new product that was named Viewmax. It turned out that Viewmax was a big hit in the American market and worldwide. It bagged the 'Consumer Electronics Product of the Year' award (1987) in the US.

Case study 5.1 continued

Case study 5.1 continued

Cost and Price Analysis

The Viewmax cost was $30 lower than the combined cost of the individual TV and VCR units. The most important reason for the lower cost was the use of only one tuner. Separate TV and VCR units generally have a tuner each, but when combined into one unit, one tuner serves the purpose for both the TV and VCR. On account of its lower cost ($271 against $301), Viewmax ended up earning twice the net income being earned on separate units. Despite Viewmax's lower cost, the F.O.B. price was set at only $20 lower than the price of the combined units, while the retail price was set at the same level as the combined price of the separate units. Table 5.1.3 provides additional details on cost and pricing.

Table 5.1.3
Cost and pricing for TV, VCR and Viewmax

	19 inches TV	*2HD*	*Total of TV*	*Viewmax*
Retail price	$259	$239	$498	$499
F.O.B. price	$160	$149	$309	$290
Total cost	$156	$145	$301	$271
Net income (unit)	4	4	8	19

Viewmax was a clear winner in the US market as its manufacturing costs were less and it created more value for the customer through simplification and ease of use. It fixed a good price that generated reasonable profits for GS and retailers.

CASE STUDY 5.2

Air Deccan: Revolutionizing the Indian Skies

'Every Indian can fly'

> It hit me like a ton of bricks. This country has a population of a billion, but only 15 million air passengers. Maybe the time is right. If one billion people can fly, and we get a miniscule percent of the market, imagine how big that will be? It's not an impossible dream.
>
> —Captain Gopinath, *The Hindu*, Sunday, 15 August 2004

Case study 5.2 continued

Case study 5.2 continued

> What happens to the urban man with rural roots who wants to visit his native small town? What happens to the working woman who wants to visit her family which lives far away from a metro?
>
> —Captain Gopinath *in an interview with the BBC in August 2004*

A chance visit to USA in 2001 made Captain Gopinath (Gopi, to his friends) realize the world of possibilities that would open up by starting a low-cost airline in India. During this visit, he discovered that a relatively small city, Phoenix in Arizona, USA had over 1,500 flights a day, catering to over 150,000 passengers daily or about 40 million a year. USA, with a quarter of the Indian population, had over 40,000 flights a day! In stark contrast, India, a country with a huge population of over a billion people, had less than 1 per cent as many flights a day. If he could find ways to reduce costs of operating an airline, he could price the cost of air travel considerably lower than the well-established airlines, and entice huge numbers of people who had hitherto never flown, to using his low cost airline by offering them value at a lower price.

Started in 2003, a distinctive strength of Air Deccan vis-à-vis any of the big three airlines in the country (Indian Airlines, Jet and Sahara) is its ability to penetrate into the small towns of India. This untapped market comprised 70 per cent of the Indian population. This case study illustrates how a start-up with a strong value proposition could take on the well-established players in the industry, by 'frame-breaking' innovation. In addition to the usual approaches to cost containment adopted by low-cost airlines worldwide, Air Deccan has implemented several measures that are unique to the Indian context. The entry of Air Deccan has resulted in fierce competition and price wars in the Indian skies, with the net result being that the passenger has benefited significantly.

The 'lean and mean' approach of low-cost airlines across the world

Low-Cost Airlines (LCA) usually operate on a Three-pronged policy of low operational costs, appropriate positioning and no-frills services to harness only those customers who value cheap fares. Low-operating costs are ensured through cost containment in all aspects of the airline's operation such as contracting non-core activities, lower airport fees, shorter time on the ground through quick turnarounds, simple boarding processes, higher percentage of online sales of tickets thus reducing the commission payable to travel agents, larger number of seats on the

Case study 5.2 continued

Case study 5.2 continued

aircraft by optimally utilizing space on the aircraft, elimination of business-class section on the flight to pack more seats and ensuring that the flights run to full capacities. Unlike legacy airlines, low-cost airlines do not use the traditional 'hub and spoke' model. They offer no inter-line arrangements for seamless passenger transition or baggage handling from one airline to another. Positioning would include targeting non-business passengers, passengers travelling on leisure or on personal work, and price-conscious business passengers. It involves aggressive marketing strategies to attract targeted customers. Services provided are very simple with meals and drinks provided for a price. Seats are narrower to increase seating capacity. There are no seat reservations. Benefits such as frequent-flyer programmes are done away with. No assurance of onward connections is made to the passengers unlike in the case of legacy airlines.

Innovations in bringing down project cost

Air Deccan saved significantly on the project cost through several innovative methods:

1. Going in for an inexpensive Internet-based reservation system developed by a Delhi-based startup software company rather than using one of three expensive global reservation systems (e.g., Galileo and Saber) that nearly all airlines and travel agents use.

2. Air Deccan innovatively negotiated with aircraft vendors such as ATR (for the smaller aircraft) and Airbus (for the larger aircraft). Rather than pay the normal six months' lease deposit, which is a very substantial amount, Air Deccan's message to aircraft manufacturers was simple and rather blunt: 'Miss the opportunity to provide aircrafts to Air Deccan (free of lease deposit!), and you will have missed the fastest growing aviation market in the world!' This resulted in the company getting a waiver on the deposit amount.

Innovations to achieve tight operational cost control

1. Most of the tickets sold to passengers are through the Internet. This eliminates commissions to travel agents, ensures that Air Deccan gets the money upfront (no credit policy) and obviates the costs involved in printed tickets.

There is another unintended benefit of this system. The penalty to a passenger for cancellation of an air ticket has been traditionally low the world over. Since the booking of tickets in the legacy airlines is done by

Case study 5.2 continued

Case study 5.2 continued

credit extended by the airline to the travel agent, and vice versa, a passenger may be tempted to hold multiple tickets on different flights for a segment, so that s/he is not deprived of a ticket at a last minute, should s/he desire to travel. For the airline, this can be a nightmare, resulting in some flights being light due to a lot of last-minute cancellations, or conversely, flights going overbooked in which case the airline has to handle and accommodate irate passengers. This is not the case for Air Deccan, where the payment is upfront, and the penalty for cancellation of a ticket is considerable.

2. A lower turnaround time of 15 minutes from landing to take-off of an aircraft ensures that Air Deccan aircraft are air-borne for a much longer time each day. In contrast, legacy airlines have turnaround times of 30 to 50 minutes. This translates into higher frequency of flights, more flying time per day of the aircraft and consequently more passengers flown per day by each aircraft.

3. Through its Internet-based system, Air Deccan can dynamically track load factors and adjust fares online. It just takes one broadcast on the Internet for Air Deccan to announce its fare for a particular flight on a particular day, and this is immediately picked up by passengers who are constantly tracking the company's Website for lower fares. This results in higher load factors on its flights.

4. Air Deccan resorts to extensive outsourcing of non-core activities that helps in its cost-containment strategies.

5. In some of the areas like aircraft overhaul or repair, the company has subscribed to schemes such as 'fly by the hour' offered by specialist third-party agencies that keep spares, etc., and take responsibility for the overhaul and repair activities. Air Deccan only pays a pre-agreed charge, akin to that of an insurance policy. The company, however, keeps its own staff for the routine day-to-day maintenance.

Positioning

Air Deccan's target market segment is the middle class and the lower middle class of the Indian population, market segments that the legacy airlines never considered as their target customers. Captain Gopinath is convinced that Air Deccan can provide an alternative to road or rail transport commuters as well as corporate staff like sales executives. The success of Air Deccan provides a solid endorsement of the value delivered to this target segment.

Case study 5.2 continued

Case study 5.2 continued

Challenges ahead

The key to the success of Air Deccan in the initial years has been the very hands-on approach of the top management of the company with absolutely no dependence/recourse on consultants. Quick implementation of new ideas has been another key strength. A strong ideology 'to democratize air travel' drives the company.

In the future, as the airline scales up its operations, the challenge will be to get enough disciplined people who share the founder's ideology, and who will join the company and stay with it for a long time. Unlike in developed countries, the policies relating to civil aviation in India are archaic. Air travel has for long been seen as a luxury. Consequently, there are a number of airline-baiters among politicians. This results in policy swings with each new government that comes to power. For instance, minor changes in taxation on jet fuel can have a significant impact on profitability. The escalating cost of oil globally is a cause for worry. The Indian air traffic agency is not geared to meet the challenges posed by the steep increase in traffic over the last few years. Limited infrastructure at airports, such as runways, results in planes having to wait in long queues for both landing and take-off. The implications of this for costs and customer satisfaction are obvious. Another issue is whether the system as a whole is geared to take on the new responsibilities all this puts on safety.

Despite these and other challenges, Captain Gopi is optimismtic about the future of his entrepreneurial venture that offers *value* to Air Deccan's targeted customers (who were ignored by the legacy airlines) by making the *price* of air travel affordable for large sections of the Indian population through innovation in containing *cost*s in running the airline.

What innovation can you do in your own organization to harness the power of the Price–Cost–Value equation for competitive advantage?

Notes

1. Lionel Robbins' famous definition of economics is cited by Thomas Sowell, *Basic Economics* (New York: Basic Books, 2003), p. 4, an excellent introduction to general economics for non-economists.
2. The origins of Einstein's quote about simplicity is described in Alice Calaprice, *The Expanded Quotable Einstein* (Princeton, NJ: Princeton University Press, 2000), pp. 314–15.
3. The definition of value is drawn from Kellogg School of Management professor Mohanbir Sawyhney's terse four-page article 'Fundamentals of Customer Value', (p. 4), available on the author's Website, www.crmproject.com.

4. Adapted from Sawhney, op. cit.
5. Data on the life expectancy of companies is from Arie de Geus, *The Living Company* (Bostan, MA: Harvard Business School Press, 1997).
6. Clayton Christensen, *The Innovator's Dilemma* (New York: Harper Business, 2000).
7. Daniel Lyons, 'Back on the Chain Gang', *Forbes Global*, 13 October 2003, p. 40.
8. Oscar Wilde, *Lady Windermere's Fan.*
9. Yuval Dror, 'US Awards ICQ Founders Patent for Instant Messenger Software', *Ha'aretz*, 17 December 2003, p. 6.
10. Andrew Kramer, 'Pocket Multitool Marks 20th Anniversary', *Toronto Star*, 5 July 2003, p. D10.

Chapter 6
Hidden costs, hidden benefits

The cost of a thing is the amount of what I call life, which is required to be exchanged for it, immediately or in the long run.
—Henry D. Thoreau[1]

Cynics know the cost of everything, and the value of nothing.
—*Adapted from an aphorism of Oscar Wilde*[2]

LEARNING OBJECTIVES After you read this chapter, you should understand:

- **The difference between economic and accounting costs**
- **The primary 'hidden cost' and how to measure and manage it**
- **How to apply the concept of economic rent, or economic value added**
- **How to identify and measure hidden benefits, especially brand value**
- **How to reconcile cost-cutting with growth strategies**
- **How to engage in collaborative re-engineering**
- **Why some accounting costs, even large ones, should be utterly ignored in decision-making**

TOOL #2
The hidden costs of lost opportunities, the hidden benefits of intangible assets

6.1 MISSING: $5.76 BILLION

We sometimes use a whiff of melodrama to catch the attention of our students. Pedagogy and show business are not enemies.

'Is your organization cost-conscious? Do you make strenuous efforts to measure your costs, to manage them, and to reduce them as much as you can?' we ask.

The answer is always 'Yes.' We know of very few organizations, except perhaps the New York Yankees baseball team, that have *not* undergone major cost-cutting programmes in recent years.

'We wager,' we say, 'that the *largest single line-item cost for your organization* cannot be found *anywhere* in your financial statements. You are cost-conscious, yet you ignore the largest cost of all.'

The bet is always taken and nearly always won. As the reader will learn later in this chapter, Intel's largest single cost in 2003 came to $5.7 billion—but that number cannot be seen anywhere in its financial reports, despite the fact that Intel meets stringent Securities and Exchange Commission rules and religiously follows Generally Accepted Accounting Principles (GAAP) for true financial reporting.

There is a second part to this bet. We then claim that billions of dollars in accounting costs, carefully listed in financial statements, are *not* true economic costs and not only *can* be ignored but *must*, if the manager is to make wise decisions.

Before we reveal why this is true, we take this opportunity to explain why seven of the 10 chapters of Part II of this book focus on some aspect of cost measurement.

6.2 MEASURE AND MANAGE COSTS

The first author of this book taught microeconomics and macroeconomics in MIT Sloan School of Management's Management of Technology M.Sc. programme for some 20 years. After a decade or so, he contacted his students, mainly engineers who had returned to their organizations, and asked them which of the 30-odd tools in the economic toolbox he had taught them proved most useful and applicable in their day-to-day decision-making. Many economics textbooks stress demand analysis. But the truth is, economists know very little about consumer preferences. The engineers' answers came back loud and clear—top scores went to the tools that helped the former students *analyse, measure and understand costs*: price–cost–value (Chapter 5 of this book), hidden costs (Chapter 6), trade-offs (Chapter 7) cost functions (Chapter 8), economics of scale and scope (Chapter 10) and learning curves (Chapter 11) were highly rated. A few years later, he repeated this survey—and got the same results.[3]

What we learned from our engineer-managers was this: *Economics as a discipline understands costs well, and can provide executives and managers with tools that help measure, manage and reduce them.* According to Bain & Co. research, 'top-performing companies achieve nearly half their total profit improvement directly from cost reduction.' You cannot reduce what you cannot accurately measure. So great importance attaches to some very basic, simple economic ideas that illuminate and elucidate the complex question: What are true costs?

To make good on the wager at the head of this chapter, let us begin with the fundamental economic notion of 'opportunity cost', in order to understand the difference between how accountants and economists define and measure costs.

6.3 ACCOUNTING VS ECONOMIC COSTS

Accountants and economists take different approaches to measuring costs. Each approach is legitimate, each has its own purpose, and it is vital for managers to understand the difference and to know when and why each is valid. For some costs, the two approaches coincide. In other cases, they differ (see Table 6.1).

In this chapter, we will address two important cases: hidden costs that are not regarded as accounting costs, but *are* economic costs (the 'yes' 'no' box [1]), and sunk costs that are *not* economic costs but are treated as accounting costs (the 'no' 'yes' box [2]).

Table 6.1
Accounting costs vs economic costs

	Economic cost?	
Accounting cost?	NO	YES
NO	Both: NO	[1]
YES	[2]	Both: YES

6.4 TWO SETS OF BOOKS?

It is very important to understand that accounting costs and economic costs are designed for different purposes. Accounting costs are part of a system that seeks to accurately report on and reflect the income and expenses of an organization, as a kind of common language that enables investors, shareholders, analysts and others to understand and communicate important facts. Accounting definitions and practices change slowly, just as language changes slowly, because a conservative approach to such change has been found to provide stability and continuity. Once everyone has learned and embraced the accounting 'language', changing it too rapidly would cause confusion and miscommunication. This is the dilemma of accounting—the pace of change in the global economy is rapid, and the language of accounting must change too, yet changing it too radically and swiftly would be harmful. Many managers believe that accountants tend to excessive caution.

Economic costs are concepts designed to help managers make decisions, by accurately measuring trade-offs and alternatives, based on fundamental economic theory. Each of the two approaches is valuable and legitimate in its own context. Each is a 'language', and every language is useful in the appropriate context.

We recommend keeping two 'sets of books'—accounting and economic. When used, for example, to hide income from tax authorities, a second set of books is illegal. But if the economic set of books is used solely for internal decision-making, the practice may not only be legal but highly valuable and may save your organization vast sums of money. Many organizations have such systems in place.

6.5 DEFINITIONS

As usual, we begin with several definitions.

Income (or profit-and-loss, P&L) statement

Used to calculate a company's net income after tax. The basic elements of profit-and-loss accounts begin with sales revenue, and deduct costs to reach the 'bottom line', or net income.

Sales revenue minus cost of goods sold, minus research and development, marketing and general and administrative expenses equals *operating profit*; minus financial expenses equals net income before tax; minus tax equals *net income*.

Balance sheet

Statement showing what an organization *owns*—its assets (cash, machines, inventory, buildings, etc.); what it *owes*—its liabilities (what it owes to banks and suppliers); and the difference between the two, known as 'shareholders' equity', or the net worth, that belongs to the shareholders who own the organization. The balance sheet does balance, because it is always true that a company's *assets* (what it owns) are equal by definition to what it owes (*liabilities*) plus its shareholders' equity (SE). This is similar to calculating your own net worth—take your assets, subtract your debts, and what is left is your net worth, or 'individual equity'. (See Table 6.2 for simplified profit and loss statements and balance sheets for Intel Corp. and British Petroleum.)

Intel is the market leader in manufacturing microprocessors, the devices (Pentium, Centrino) that are the brains of our computers. British Petroleum (BP) is the world's largest oil company, measured by sales revenue, and second-largest company in the world overall, just behind Wal-Mart.

Table 6.2
Profit and loss statements for Intel Corp. and BP ($ billion)

	Intel		*BP*	
	2003	*2002*	*2003*	*2002*
Sales	$30.1	$26.8	$232.6	$178.7
Minus:				
Cost of sales*	–22.6	–22.4	–216.2	–168.5
Equals:				
Operating profit	$7.5	$4.4	$16.4	$10.2
Minus:				
Interest & taxes	–2.1	–1.3	–6.0	–1.3
Equals:				
Net income	$5.4	$3.1	$10.4	$8.9

Source: www.intel.com and www.bp.com.
Note: * Including: raw materials, labour, R&D, general and administrative costs.

Accounting costs
Business expenses that are recognized by the Financial Accounting Standards Board (FASB) in the USA (or other equivalent bodies of other countries) as appropriate and legitimate for inclusion in financial statements made available to shareholders, analysts and the general public. An accounting cost usually, though not always, is something for which the company treasurer or other manager writes a cheque and follows FASB (or equivalent) rules.

Opportunity cost
The value, product or revenue generated by resources, when they are used in their best alternative. In his famous book, *Walden*, Henry D. Thoreau showed in detail how he could live with incredibly few material possessions in a hut he built on Walden Pond. Gaining those possessions, he argued, had a huge opportunity cost—'life', or time that could be spent in doing what he chose to do, rather than what he had to do to earn income and buy material goods.

Economic costs
For a particular resource, such as labour hours, or machine hours, or shareholders' capital, ask: What is its most productive alternate use, or 'opportunity', that generates value? What is the *value* of that alternative use? Call this value 'opportunity cost'. It is what is given up when the resource is used. This is the true economic cost. If a resource has *no* alternative value, its opportunity cost is zero. For example, a machine that has no other use than to clean silicon wafers has no economic opportunity cost when it sits idle. Employing a previously unemployed worker has no opportunity cost,

because the worker produced zero income or output previously. Thinking in terms of valuing alternatives, or opportunities, is a simple, powerful and valuable mindset that successful managers cultivate. Lost opportunities are often hidden costs. Potential new opportunities (even if they fail to materialize) are hidden benefits. Each must be taken into account, if costs are to be managed and measured truly.

6.6 READING THE NUMBERS

A practised eye can learn a great deal about Intel and BP from the financial statements in Table 6.2. First, both Intel and BP were highly successful and profitable in 2003, earning $7.5 billion, and $16.4 billion, in operating income respectively in 2003. Second, both companies have been profitable for many years and the profits have been reinvested in the business, as 'retained earnings'. Retained earnings become a part of shareholders' capital, or 'shareholders' equity'. As a result, their shareholders own far more in assets than they owe in liabilities. Their 'shareholders' equity' totalled $37.8 billion for Intel shareholders at the end of 2003, and $75.9 billion for BP shareholders.

And now, it is time to make good on the wager that began this chapter.

According to Tables 6.2 and 6.3, Intel shareholders could in theory sell off Intel's assets, pay its debts and pocket the difference of $37.8 billion. (Note that Intel has from its birth followed a policy of refraining from borrowing money, choosing instead to finance its growth and investment from its profits, on the grounds that bankers and bondholders do not really understand technology-driven businesses. That is why its debts or 'liabilities' are so small.) Shareholders could then invest this sum elsewhere—say, in Intel's small but aggressive competitor AMD (Advanced Micro Devices) or in a portfolio of semiconductor stocks. They could earn, over time, say, 15 per cent, *at the same risk*. Buying US Treasury bonds would yield, say, 6 per cent—

Table 6.3
Balance sheet for Intel Corp. and BP ($ billion)

	Intel		*BP*	
	2003	*2002*	*2003*	*2002*
Assets	$47.1	$44.2	$177.6	$159.2
Minus:				
Liabilities	−9.3	−8.7	−101.7	−89.8
Equals:				
Shareholders equity	$37.8	$35.5	$75.9	$69.4

Source: www.intel.com and www.bp.com.

but that is not a fair comparison, since such bonds are far less risky than Intel shares, and hence pay far less. (We will say more about risk later.) So the 'opportunity cost' (the return on the best risk-comparable alternate use of shareholders' equity, 'SE') is:

Opportunity Cost of SE for Intel = 0.15 × \$37.8 billion = \$ 5.67 billion

That is, Intel shareholders could earn \$5.67 billion (about \$ 5.7 billion) on their money if they were to invest it elsewhere, at the same level of risk.

The 15 per cent opportunity-cost may strike readers as very high. They should keep in mind that the semiconductor industry is highly uncertain. Boom–bust cycles occur every 2–3 years, competition is fierce and technologies change rapidly—so the return on equity must reflect uncertainty, because return on investment and risk are closely related, and because shareholders expect to be compensated for bearing this risk.

Using a 12 per cent rate for BP, we find that BP shareholders' opportunity cost of capital is 0.12 × \$75.9 billion = \$9.1 billion. We use 12 per cent, rather than 15 per cent as for Intel, because the oil business is somewhat less risky than the semiconductor industry.

6.7 RISK-ADJUSTED OPPORTUNITY COST OF SHAREHOLDERS' EQUITY

Every dollar of invested capital deserves an appropriate rate of return, and that rate of return consists of two components: the basic, or risk-free rate of return (what a dollar of capital can earn on an investment that is essentially free of any risk) plus a 'risk premium', or additional return, reflecting the fact the capital investment is exposed to risks of various sorts, hence the investor may not receive any interest, or indeed may lose the whole amount of the principal.

Rate of return on investment = Risk-free rate of return + Risk premium

The risk premium, in turn, is made up of two parts: (*i*) a measure of the number of units of risk inherent in the investment, multiplied by (*ii*) the premium per unit of risk.

Total risk premium = No. of units of risk × Premium per unit of risk

For instance, suppose a share of Intel stock has been found to have 1.5 units of risk. Suppose also that the premium 1 unit of risk commands in the capital market is 6 per cent. Intel's risk premium, therefore, is 1.5 × 6 = 9 per cent. Add this to the 'basic' risk-free interest rate, and you get a risk-adjusted opportunity cost of capital of 6 + 9 = 15 per cent. Chapter 13 will examine this calculation in greater detail.

6.8 IN SEARCH OF THE BOTTOM-BOTTOM LINE

What all this means, then, is that the 'bottom line' in Intel's and BP's profit-and-loss statements is not *truly* the bottom line. One more line must be added, after deducting the imputed, or calculated, 'opportunity cost of shareholders' capital'. When this deduction is done, we have what is commonly called economic rent, or 'Economic Value Added', a basic concept trademarked by the New York-based consulting company Stern Stewart, which turned it into a powerful consulting tool.[4]

DEFINITION

Economic Value Added is net income after tax, minus the opportunity cost of shareholders' equity (SE).

Economic rent, or Economic Value Added is so called because it is the net value, or wealth, *added* to Intel shareholders by its board of directors, executives, managers and workers. What Table 6.4 shows rather sharply is that even though 2003 was a stellar year for both companies—owing to strong demand for microprocessors and high oil prices—and 2002 was a year of recession, each company essentially managed to attain its opportunity-cost benchmark or hurdle return for capital.

Have we thus made good on the bet with which this chapter began? Neither BP nor Intel records this opportunity cost on its profit-and-loss statement,

Table 6.4
Economic value added for Intel Corp. and BP, 2002, 2003 ($ billion)

	Intel		*BP*	
	2003	*2002*	*2003*	*2002*
Net income	$5.6	$3.1	$10.4	$8.9
Minus:				
Opportunity cost of SE	–5.7	–5.3	–9.1	–8.3
Equals:				
Economic Value Added	–$0.1	–$2.2	–$1.3	–$0.6

Source: BP's global standing is taken from *Fortune's Global 500*, 26 July 2004, p. 163.

nor can they, because it is not a recognized accounting cost. One might ask: Why not change the accounting rules? One reason is that opportunity cost of shareholders' equity is in a sense 'imaginary', answering the question: what *could* Intel and BP shareholders earn, if they were to withdraw their capital and invest it elsewhere at the same risk level? Accountants understandably shun 'what if' questions. They must deal in measured reality.[5] But, economists argue, this 'what if' question is entirely real, because shareholders can and do pull their capital (by selling their shares) when companies under-perform. Contingent events are real, even if only a likelihood or probability is attached to them. In recent years, shareholders, represented by their boards of directors, have been increasingly aggressive and swift in replacing CEOs who do not achieve positive bottom-bottom line profits.

6.9 EXCESSIVELY HIGH HURDLE?

Some managers, especially entrepreneurs in startups, criticize the EVA 'hurdle rate', which can be as high as 20 per cent for risky new ventures, saying that few investments can attain such high profitability. Our response to this is two-fold. First, an appropriate horizon must be chosen. Investments must be given a sufficient window of time to mature and capture value and market share. Second, those who invest in startups use the EVA approach. They know that many startups fail; in order for those who invest in startups to profit and build wealth, the successful start ups will need to be highly profitable. That is why startups, based on innovative ideas, must have the potential for high profitability. Without it, they will fail to justify their existence and to attract investment funds. A key principle of startups is: Raise money when you can, not when you must. But once raised, that money must be directed only into high-potential high-profit uses (see case study 'Borland').

What we are arguing is that Intel's CEO Craig Barrett must make $5.7 billion in 2003 just to preserve shareholders' existing wealth, while BP CEO (Lord) John Browne must make $9.1 billion in net income to achieve the same goal. The Economic Value Added concept may thus strike the reader as a draconian high hurdle for managers. But what we have shown is that *according to the economic definition of costs, successful, profitable companies like Intel and BP—which have piled up large amounts of capital over the years through reinvestment of profits—must be like Olympic hurdlers, leaping over ever-higher 'opportunity-cost' hurdles*. Their managers must leap higher in order to make the growing pool of shareholders' capital generate rent and wealth at high 'hurdle' rates. For them, life is hard. This is one reason why innovation is so crucial. Only innovative products that find high demand can offset the constant pressure of imitators, competition, substitutes and falling prices and profits.

What the Economic Value Added tool says to managers and executives is simply this: *Treat your shareholders' capital with great respect.* It is valuable. It need not remain in your company's pockets. It can migrate elsewhere. So compute its value, and *charge yourself for that value, because that cost is a very real one, even though it is imputed, or estimated, as an 'opportunity cost'.*

Case study: Borland, or 'The lights are going out all over Silicon Valley'

Once there was a brilliant, innovative software company named Borland, founded by a bold entrepreneur named Phillip Kahn. Borland developed and sold the market-leading spreadsheet software known as Quattro. Many people used it and loved it. One day, the company's executives decided that Borland needed a head-office building befitting its market leadership position. Many millions of dollars were invested in this relatively unproductive asset—resources that might better have been employed as innovation investment in R&D, to develop better future versions of Quattro, in order to compete with Microsoft's Excel and Lotus 1-2-3.

This misallocation of resources had disastrous results. Drivers on Silicon Valley's main highway passed Borland's beautiful headquarters building, and watched as the company slid downhill and the lights in the building went out one by one, day by day, until the company was gone. The hidden cost of investing in a building, rather than in more productive innovation assets, suddenly became a very visible one, as the lights went out for Borland, figuratively and literally. A contrast to the Borland story is Nike, a company that conserves its capital and invests it in two key areas: design, or R&D, and marketing, preferring to contract out its manufacturing and permit others to invest capital in fixed assets such as factories.

As a management philosophy, Economic Value Added tells every single manager, executive and employee who uses company capital to charge themselves for that capital a fair opportunity-cost rate, and to measure their success and profitability only after deducting that expense as a true cost. When implemented intelligently, this philosophy creates a new respect for the use of capital, and generates enormously creative ideas about how to conserve it—as the late Roberto Goizueta, former Coca-Cola CEO, showed.

Case study: Economic rent at Coca-Cola

A 'brand' is a product name that people recognize quickly, which conveys its own marketing message to buyers regarding quality, reliability, value, enjoyment or delight. Brand names are assets, but generally are not listed on balance sheets—an example of a 'hidden benefit' discussed below.

The three most powerful, valuable brands in the world are Coke or Coca-Cola, Microsoft (Windows) and IBM. Each of these names is worth, in itself, billions of dollars. The products of each of these companies command higher prices simply because of their names. Coke's brand value was greatly strengthened by the late Roberto Goizueta, appointed CEO in 1981 (around the time GE CEO Jack Welch was first appointed). The story of how Goizueta built wealth for shareholders, using Economic Value Added as a key tool, is instructive.

Like Intel, Coca-Cola had an almost debt-free balance sheet. It paid for its capital investments out of its profits, which of course belong to the shareholders. On the profit-and-loss statement, only interest payments on bank loans or on bonds are listed, because these are sums for which cheques are written.

When he took charge Goizueta stressed the crucial importance of building wealth for shareholders. He explained that even if some divisions of Coke (a movie company, and a wine company, for instance) made an 8 per cent return on shareholders' capital, they were still destroying, rather than building, wealth. The reason: by his calculation, using the basic rate plus risk premium formula, Coke's opportunity cost of shareholders' equity capital was 16 per cent. That meant the following: Investments earning 8 per cent yearly doubled their value every 9 years. Investments earning 16 per cent doubled every four-and-a-quarter years. At 16 per cent return, shareholders could double their money *twice*, in an alternate use, in nine years. If Coke doubled it only *once* in that time period, Coke was destroying half the shareholders' potential wealth in less than a decade. This was unacceptable.

'We were liquidating our business,' Goizueta said, 'borrowing money at 16 per cent and investing it at eight. You can't do that forever.' Note a key lesson here: *If managers do not employ the opportunity-cost principle, and charge themselves for their own capital, at the appropriate rate, the profit-and-loss statement may give the illusion of profitability, while the bottom-bottom line notion of Economic Rent registers large losses.* There are few dangers greater than the illusion of perceived success and profit, which can mask an organization that is rapidly declining and destroying wealth.

Case study continued

Case study continued

Goizueta implemented a new policy. Every business unit or division had to attain the so-called 'hurdle rate' of 16 per cent. Those that did not were sold. 'When you start charging people for their capital, all sorts of things happen,' Goizueta said. 'All of a sudden inventories get under control [because inventories are a part of capital, and you must charge yourself for the capital sunk in them]. You don't have three months' concentrated sitting around for an emergency. Or you figure out that you can save a lot of money by replacing stainless-steel containers [an expensive capital charge] with cardboard and plastic.' Goizueta's policy was not to try to make capital budgeting decisions himself, using the opportunity-cost principle, but to structure the decisions of everyone in the Coke organization who used and spent company capital, to achieve the right result. Treat company capital as if it is scarce and expensive, was the message—because it is!

What was the result? To benchmark Goizueta's achievement, we need to define a supplementary tool, related to Economic Value Added.

Source: From S. Maital, *Executive Economics* (Free Press, 1994).

DEFINITION

Market Value Added (MVA): The market value of a company's shares—what investors would pocket if they sold all their securities—minus capital they invested, including equity and debt offerings, retained earnings and bank loans. If MVA is positive, management has made shareholders richer. If MVA is negative, it is destroying their wealth.

After 13 years as Coca-Cola CEO, by 1994 Goizueta had achieved a Market Value Added for Coke shareholders of $61 billion. This was about 10 per cent more than the wealth created by GE CEO Jack Welch, who used similar tools and approaches, in the same period—about $52 billion in MVA. At that time they led the corporate league in wealth-building. Coke then fell on hard times and lost its focus. By 1999, its premier place in wealth-building was grabbed by Bill Gates' Microsoft, followed by GE, Intel and Wal-Mart.[6]

For investors, Economic Value Added is a powerful tool. It tells them: put your money not into companies whose revenue grows quickly, but whose bottom-bottom line grows and you expect will grow further in future. Profitless growth (some of it duplicitous, based on revenues that were fictitious) was the basis of the dotcom bubble. Investors are now sadder and wiser. They now seek to invest in companies that will build real wealth, not imaginary future sales.

6.10 COLLECT THE RENT

Economic Value Added is the translation of a very old economic concept known as 'rent' into a management action idea. Rent, in everyday language, is what we pay for the right to live in a house we do not own, or to occupy office space we do not own. But *economic rent*, for some resource, is the difference between what the resource earns now, and what its opportunity cost (highest alternate income) is. Rent is excess, or above-the-norm, income. Basketball player Shaquille O'Neill earns many millions in rent, because the highest amount he could earn, say, playing baseball, is much smaller. Pop star Madonna earns rent as a singer, compared to what she commands as an author of children's books.

The task of managers is to generate substantial economic rent for shareholders' capital, above what that capital could earn elsewhere. This requires a benchmarking mindset for managers—constantly weighing best-practice industry profitability and measuring their organization's profitability against that. Investors, analysts, advisors and shareholders have this mindset, so managers must too.

Case study: GM–How hidden costs turn a cost reduction into a cost increase

General Motors weighed the following decision: Invest $1 million to develop a manual seat adjuster for a large vehicle, or install power seat adjusters as standard equipment (see Case study 6.1: Passenger power seat adjuster).

At first glance, the decision was a no-brainer. The power seat adjuster cost $80 more to make than the manual one, and was to be installed on 100,000 cars over a five-year period. It seemed like a case of investing $1 million in order to save $80 × 100,000 = $8 million—a very high eight-to-one rate of return. On closer inspection, GM engineer Robert Kruse found many hidden costs.

First, he considered the opportunity cost of shareholders' capital. Using 'hurdle rates' (risk-adjusted opportunity costs of capital) of between 14 and 18 per cent, he found that hidden capital costs would total between $1.9 million and $2.3 million over the five years. Second, there was the cost of the engineers' time spent on testing and evaluating the seat, amounting to another $5.3–$6.3 million (depending on whether the 14 or 18 per cent hurdle rate was used). This was an opportunity cost, as already-employed engineers would divert their time from other productive uses. Taking hidden costs into account made the decision to engineer a new manual seat adjuster rather doubtful.

6.11 OTHER HIDDEN COSTS

The cost of shareholders' capital is the largest, but not the only, hidden cost. There are many others.

Meetings

Consider a typical company meeting, with a dozen participants. According to expert Paul Strassman, a fairly brief hour- long meeting can cost $13,000, or $216 a minute: $6,000 in 'opportunity cost' time for the initiator or organizer; and $7,000 in opportunity cost for participants' time. Suppose a company has a profit margin of 8 per cent. It would need about $162,500 in sales revenue (resulting directly from the meeting) to justify the hidden cost. How many meetings can generate this much revenue? A good way to reduce hidden costs then, is simply to reduce the number of meetings, or charge the initiator with the explicit cost of the meeting as part of the expanded bottom-bottom line attributed to the project manager, by which he or she is measured. Or, at the least, make everyone aware of the high hidden opportunity costs of meeting time.

Shelf space

Have you wondered why it is so difficult to get retailers to agree to stock what seems to be a winning new product? Suppose Wal-Mart agrees to put your Purple-Green Lip Gloss product on its cosmetics shelf. Each yard of shelf space generates a known, and large, value in sales. Shelf space is a resource. Shelves that do not create sales cost revenues and profits. These are hidden costs—the lost opportunity of selling and making money. Sometimes retailers require suppliers of innovative new products, perhaps unfamiliar to buyers, to pay for shelf space.

Cognitive attention, or space in our brains

This is the hidden cost perhaps least considered. Modern times place enormous demands on our brains' capacity to process, store, sort and use information. Choosing a type of cereal in a supermarket alone can require looking at dozens of boxes, ingredients, and other types of information. With the proliferation of choice, brain capacity (or 'cognitive attention') has become a very scarce resource. Advertisers are well aware of this, as our brains are bombarded with selling messages on TV and radio, and in magazines and newspapers, and as a result develop the ability to block them out, with or without the remote.

A technology known as RFID, or radio frequency identification, which 'broadcasts' data on products, has a great future—put on cereal boxes, it can remind us as we walk by the supermarket shelf which cereal we bought last time. With cognitive capacity limited, simplicity becomes a great virtue. As a result, brand names grow in value, because they conserve enormous brain resources and serve as a kind of shorthand—the four letters S O N Y convey to us in a very economical manner what otherwise would take considerable processing capacity. (See Section 6.14, 'Hidden Benefits.')

Nirmalya Kumar[7] notes that, 'many corporations generate 80 per cent to 90 per cent of their profits from fewer than 20 per cent of the brands they sell'. He cites as an example Nestlé, which marketed more than 8,000 brands in 190 countries in 1996; the bulk of the company's profits came from only 200 brands, or 2.5 per cent of Nestlé's portfolio. Nestle has since embarked on a global programme to trim and optimize its brand names. The lesson here for companies is, he notes: 'Kill a brand, keep a customer.' The management side of this argument is powerful as well. For senior management, time and thought are scarce, and if spread too thin over too many issues, brands, products or divisions, they are wasted or used inefficiently. Conserve not only shareholders' equity and time but also your capacity for thinking—storing, processing and remembering information. Thinking, too, can be a scarce resource with a very high opportunity cost.

6.12 HIDDEN COSTS IN AMERICA: $1.3 TRILLION … OR CHINA'S GDP!

There are large hidden costs in every economy as well as in company financial statements and our family budgets. Among the largest is the hidden cost of higher education. A nation's investment in higher education does not reflect a very large hidden cost—the cost of the lost output, or income, that college students could generate if they were working rather than studying. Even for individuals, this hidden cost is generally larger than the measured explicit cost of college (tuition, books). This is not to say that higher education investment is not worthwhile—in fact, the return on such investment to society and to the individual is among the highest of all investments. It simply says that a large chunk of that investment is non-monetary and hidden from sight.

Other hidden costs, by one calculation, add up to an amount equal to nearly 13 per cent of America's GDP (gross domestic product, a measure of total national output or income), or the huge sum of $1,300 billion, roughly equal to China's GDP (Table 6.5).

Table 6.5
An estimate of hidden costs in the US economy

Item	*Hidden cost (reduction in annual gross domestic product) $ billion*
SPAM (junk email)	10
Trampolines (injuries)	1
Formosan termite	1
Animal-related traffic accidents	1
Poor English-speaking skills	1.2
Stress	300
Inactivity	8.9
Herniated disks (spinal problem)	16
Heightened security after 9/11	151
Other	810

Source: Jerry Useem, 'This Just In: Mystery Economics: The GDP and Stuff', *Fortune*, 27 October 2003.

Action learning
Your *Hidden Costs*

What do you spend—in cash, cheques and credit cards—in a week?

List some of the hidden costs you incur (in terms of time, or the opportunity cost of capital, such as the home and car you own).

Do *you*, too, have substantial hidden costs, like Intel and BP? How might measuring these hidden costs change some of your decisions or behaviour?

6.13 DEPRECIATION–ECONOMIC OR ACCOUNTING?

The cost of wear and tear of machinery, vehicles and buildings is another topic on which accountants and economists differ widely. Accounting depreciation is the cost of such wear and tear, approved and recognized as a business cost by accounting principles and thus deductible from income in calculating tax on corporate profits. It is not related to the true, or economic, cost defined as the reduction in value of assets owing to use and the passage of time (obsolescence). For companies with heavy investments in factories, depreciation is a very large cost, and strongly influences decision-making.

For example, Intel has some 24 semiconductor fabrication plants (known as 'fabs') worldwide. Such a plant today can cost as much as $6 billion.

So depreciation on this heavy capital investment is very large. When a fab is fully depreciated—that is, its full value has been deducted from earnings, as a business expense—its profitability suddenly rises. (True, taxable profits—and hence taxes—rise, but each depreciation dollar reduces gross profits by that dollar, while adding only about a third of a dollar to net profits.) Yet, this is solely because of the accounting conventions. As an asset, the fab is still valuable and productive, even though it no longer appears on the firm's balance sheet as an asset. Intel's ability to generate income and profits from 'depreciated' fabs—for instance, its Fab #8 in Jerusalem, fully depreciated long ago by reinventing the factory's purpose and use—is a source of considerable sums of profit. Fab #8, no longer able to produce microprocessors, now produces MEMS, or microelectronic mechanical devices, tiny devices that combine electronics and mechanical parts. Using assets that no longer have accounting value, but retain high economic value, can generate substantial profit for companies.

6.14 HIDDEN BENEFITS

Recall that our earlier definition of 'net income', in the profit-and-loss statement, included R&D spending as a cost. In accounting terms, spending on R&D is indeed a cost. But in economic terms, it is an asset, because through R&D organizations create winning new innovative products, and an asset is simply a resource that generates income or revenue. Why not, then, treat R&D as an investment, aggregate it, and then 'depreciate' or 'amortize' it (that is, reduce its value to reflect the fact that over time, R&D assets 'age' and hence are worth less than they were, say, a year ago) over a short horizon of, say, three years?

Accounting rules do not currently allow this. But when managers adopt the economic toolbox, and related hidden costs and hidden benefits approach, they value their R&D assets in their 'second set of books'. This approach is highly consistent with the management philosophy, prevalent in many organizations and embraced by top executives, that knowledge-based organizations' most valuable assets are their people: human capital or human resources. If so, why not then give these assets formal expression on an expanded company balance sheet? Accounting rules are slowly but surely developing a set of proposals that will recognize this principle, bringing accounting and economic definitions in line.

On the benefits or assets side of an organizations' balance sheet one of the largest items is brand value. The asset value of a brand is the aggregate present value of the profits that accrue directly from the brand itself. The aggregate value of the world's top 10 brand names is close to $400 billion (Table 6.6).

Table 6.6
Value of the top 10 global brands, 2005 ($ billion)

Coca-Cola	67.5
Microsoft	59.9
IBM	53.4
GE	47.0
Intel	35.6
Nokia	26.5
Disney	26.4
McDonald's	26.0
Toyota	24.8
Marlboro	21.2

Source: *Business Week*, bwnt.businessweek.com/brand/2005.

Action learning

Calculate Your *Organization's Brand Value*

1. Compute the percentage of your revenues credited to a brand.
2. Project five years of earnings and sales for the brand; take the annual average by dividing the total by five. Deduct operating costs, taxes and a charge for capital, to compute 'intangible' earnings. Choose a 'discount rate' that can be used to capitalize (i.e., turn an annual stream of earnings into a capital sum—a process known as 'net present value', discussed in Chapter 13). Apply this rate to the sum of annual earnings for the brand. (As a rule of thumb: for an opportunity cost of capital of R per cent, to capitalize an annual income stream, multiply by 100/R.)

6.15 RECONCILING GROWTH AND COST CUTTING

Managers and employees understand that you cannot grow a company solely by shrinking it (reducing its spending).[8]

According to Altman, Kaplan and Corbett, companies that lead in cost discipline *make clear the link between cost reduction and future growth*. They cite four key measures to clarify how cost reduction spurs growth.

Four steps to disciplined cost cutting–and growth

1. Tie cost discipline to growth strategy

A key way is to help people change the way they do their jobs. Consider this: 'A company that raises the efficiency of its employees from 65 per cent to 70 per cent gets a 5 per cent increase in productivity'—a huge gain, especially if that gain has not required any costly shareholder capital.

2. Empower the advocates

Since most managers are not wired for cost reduction, but rather focus on generating sales and growth, champions are needed who particularly relish cost reduction. Such champions make good use of benchmarking, data collection, and careful diagnostics.

Supermarkets are known to have razor-thin profit margins. Kroger, a major chain, introduced self-service checkout aisles in the mid-1990s. To its surprise, not only did costs fall, but customers came to Kroger's specifically for such aisles, their speed, privacy and convenience. Cost-cutting that slashes costs *and* boosts revenues is ideal. Kroger had champions who loved cost-reduction innovations in business processes.

3. Act quickly

Some cost-cutting requires up-front investment. Often, one-shot investments can yield continuing cost reduction like Kroger's self-service checkouts. United States businesses invested some $1,000 billion in Information Technology in the 1990s, without immediate pay-off and then saw enormous growth in productivity as the benefits of these systems finally kicked in and generated far lower costs.

4. There's always another dollar to be saved

'When everyone in the company thinks you've gone too far,' report the authors, 'there's usually one more layer of cost to take out—perhaps 'the most important lesson learned'. By making cost reduction a core-competency and discipline, strong competitive advantage is achieved. The case of Toyota Motor Corp., striving to become the world's largest car company, illustrates this.

Case study: Growth with cost-cutting at Toyota Motor Corp.

In 2003, Toyota Motor Corp. was the world's eighth largest corporation, with $153 billion in sales, just behind Ford, which was at #6 with $165 billion in sales. Toyota forecasts production of over 9 million

Case study continued

Case study continued

vehicles in 2006, compared with 6.83 million in 2003. Toyota's goal is a 15 per cent global market share, compared with 10 per cent today. Most of its profit comes from US sales, where it sells over 2 million vehicles. Toyota combines vigorous innovation—its Prius gas–electric hybrid is in such high demand that waiting lists are as long as seven months—with aggressive cost-cutting, which enables it to keep prices reasonable while improving quality and gadgetry. As of 2006, Toyota is poised to overtake GM as the world's largest automobile producer.

Source: Ginny Parker and Norihiko Shirouzu, 'Toyota Pushes Up Its Global Targets for Sales, Output', *Wall Street Journal*, 21 July 2004, p. A2.

6.16 GOOD TO GREAT: HOW MEASUREMENT CHANGES MANAGEMENT

In his book *Good to Great*, author Jim Collins describes 11 'great companies' that outperformed thousands of Fortune 500 firms. One of them is Fannie Mae, a company that buys mortgages, packages them, and then borrows money by selling bonds backed by the mortgages, while profiting from the interest difference between what it earns and what it pays. Fannie Mae began its life in deep trouble. Its management sought to maximize its profit per mortgage. This was disastrous. A change in management, and resulting change in measurement, led to a turnaround. The change was a slight one: from maximizing profit per mortgage to maximizing profit per unit of mortgage *risk*. That change led to efforts to manage risk better, a key variable that previously had been ignored (for example, by managing borrowing and lending over the interest-rate cycle, when rates rose and fell with Federal Reserve policy and business downturns).

The moral here is: Be careful what you measure, and how you measure it: *choose your measures to elicit the behaviour and results you seek*. Measuring accounting costs without considering hidden economic costs can lead to inferior results. In general, before you begin any project, large or small, decide in advance how you will know whether you succeeded; set the 'metric' or measurements that will tell you; and be sure those metrics are carefully aligned with the types of behaviour that will make the project successful.

Managers, according to management guru Peter Drucker, have only two functions: innovation and marketing. That is, developing new products and selling existing ones. Innovation can be very expensive, requiring commitment of large amounts of capital under conditions of great uncertainty. The same is true of marketing. As Jay C. Levinson notes in his book *Guerilla Marketing*, there is a measurement problem: judging marketing campaigns by CPM (cost per thousand viewers, or recipients) can be highly misleading, when the proper criterion should be cost *per potential buyer*—and one rarely knows how many viewers become potential buyers. Whether you are innovating or marketing, measurement is not an end in itself, it is a means to an end. Always be certain that your metrics help, rather than hinder, in attaining that end.

Action learning

Return on Equity

Return on Equity (RoE) is defined as: (Net income after tax / Shareholders' Equity) × 100

Examine the RoE values below and ask yourself which industries created wealth in 2005 and which industries destroyed it. What part of each RoE do you think is explained by higher risk? By the global recession or industry cycles? By 'structural' or long-term effects, such as excess production capacity? Do you foresee capital migrating from one industry to another based on these RoE values? The Table below lists RoE for the year 2005 for Fortune 500 companies according to industry. It is clear that RoE varies widely.

Industry	*Return on Equity (per cent)*
Pharmaceuticals	18
Beverages	18
Motor Vehicles	7
Airlines	0
Semiconductors	11
Median of all Fortune 500 companies	14.9

Source: *Fortune*, Fortune 500, 17 April 2006.

6.17 SUNK COSTS

Our last task in this chapter is to examine [2] in Table 6.1, where costs are *not* economic costs but *are* accounting costs. One instance of this is known as 'sunk costs'—sunk, meaning invested and unrecoverable.

Perhaps the single most difficult management decision is to close down a project. The more capital invested in a project in the past, the harder it is to end it. This is where managers truly earn their salaries. Often, there is a powerful—and fallacious—'sunk cost' argument used. It goes as follows: We have already invested $X billion; why not invest just $Y billion more, to complete the project? The fallacy lies in the utter irrelevance of the $X billion. It is 'sunk', spent. The sole thing that matters is the stream of revenue and costs, or net profit, extending only from the present into the future (see Visual Tool #2). Money spent and unrecoverable has a zero opportunity cost, and therefore is not an economic cost.

Economist Richard Thaler explains why sunk costs play such a key role in so many business decisions. Consider a person who buys a very costly non-transferable and non-refundable membership in an exclusive tennis club. Shortly after, she develops a painful tennis elbow, which makes playing tennis sheer agony. Will she continue to play? Logic dictates she write off the membership, it is 'sunk'. You cannot be happier by enduring more pain. But human nature being what it is, chances are she will play through the pain, even though playing tennis is far more pain than gain. To do so avoids the admission that the membership fee is a loss. But it *is* a loss—why not face it? Many managers, too, suffer from the tennis-elbow sunk cost syndrome. They avoid mentally writing off costly 'club memberships', even if they are worthless, and continue to invest larger and larger sums.

VISUAL TOOL #2 Piercing the veil of sunk costs

To make effective use of economic tools, managers need to know not only how to use them to make wise decisions, but also how to communicate those decisions and how they were reached, to others. That is why the most powerful decision tools are ones that lend themselves easily to vivid visual pictures.

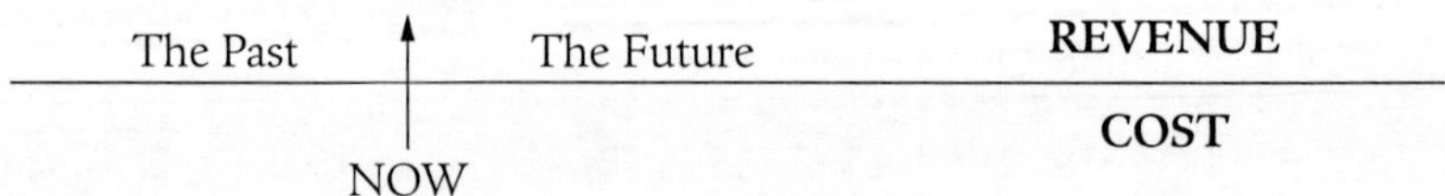

To avoid the sunk cost fallacy, use the above diagram. List revenues and costs *anticipated* for a project, extending only from the present moment to the future. Be sure to include hidden costs and hidden benefits. If the project is expected to yield a satisfactory economic value added, or rent, it should be continued. If under reasonable assumptions about the future, the project does not yield economic rent then it should be closed down and its assets sold. The fact that enormous sums have been invested in the project in the past should not be relevant. Those sums are indeed accounting costs; but because they have been spent already, they have no opportunity cost (they are 'water under the bridge', unrecoverable) and hence have zero economic cost. They should be ignored. To do so is of course exceptionally difficult; projects in which resources have been invested are also those in which time, energy, blood, sweat, emotion and self-respect are also invested.

Case study: Lockheed L-1011 TriStar

Between 1967 and 1971 Lockheed, under the direction of its chairman Roy Andersen, invested $1 billion in research, development, testing and evaluation of a new wide-body civilian aircraft to be known as the L-1011 TriStar. In 1971 Lockheed faced a hard decision: End the project and write off the $1 billion, or put the plane into production by building a costly new plant, in Palmdale, California. At the time Lockheed was undergoing a financial crisis, because of technology problems with a military plane, the C-5A, and appealed to the US Senate for a loan guarantee of $250 million. It was fairly clear at the time that stiff competition from McDonnell Douglas and Boeing would make it unlikely that the plane would become profitable. And indeed, in 1985, when the last TriStar was produced in Palmdale, calculations showed Lockheed lost money. But the sunk cost fallacy prevailed. US Treasury Secretary John Connolly and Anderson both argued that it would be an utter shame to 'waste' the $1 billion investment. The US Senate voted narrowly to approve the loan guarantee. Lockheed's losses in civilian aircraft nearly sank the company; it was rescued only when it changed course towards defence products in the period when President Reagan was sharply increasing US defense spending.

Source: Uwe Reinhardt, *The Journal of Finance*, 1973.

6.18 CONCLUSION

There is a familiar Quaker prayer that asks for three kinds of virtue: courage (to change what can be changed), serenity (to accept what cannot be changed), and wisdom (to know the difference). Managers too need three kinds of wisdom: the perceptiveness to charge themselves for hidden costs, including capital they and their shareholders own; the courage and honesty to ignore large sunk costs, and avoid investing further resources that delay the painful admission of loss; and the wisdom to know the difference between accounting costs and economic costs and to know when each is appropriate in their decision-making processes.

Readers are invited to view 'Pillars of Profit: Segment #2, Hidden Costs, Hidden Benefits' in the accompanying CD.

CASE STUDY 6.1

Passenger Power Seat Adjuster*

Case study discussion topics

1. How was the $1 million capital investment needed for the manual seat adjuster, originally treated?
2. What was the opportunity cost that Kruse estimated for the $1 million? What were the other hidden costs?
3. What was the major disadvantage, apart from cost, in equipping all cars with the power seat adjuster?
4. What is a 'hurdle rate', and how did Kruse make use of GM's hurdle rate?

When a new vehicle programme is being formulated, many factors are evaluated to determine if the proposed project will actually be executed. This case study focuses on three factors: piece cost, investment and return on investment (ROI) as compared with corporate hurdle rates for that segment of the market. The case highlights the analysis GM undertook to decide whether to engineer and tool a manual passenger seat adjuster for its vehicles, which were proposed for entry into the 'Large' market segment. Seat adjusters are of many types, but for the purpose of this case only a six-way power adjuster and a two-way manual adjuster have been considered.

Passenger power seat adjusters existed and found application in the 'Large Luxury' market segment. The segment specification for a 'Large' vehicle required a six-way power adjuster as standard equipment on the driver's seat. The passenger seat already had a two-way manual adjuster as standard equipment with a six-way power adjuster as an optional equipment. The projected market penetration was 80 per cent for this option and was provided as a standard equipment in the 'Large Luxury' segment. Cost pressure was greater in the 'Large' segment since it commands a lower price in the market than a 'Large Luxury' segment vehicle. GM's proposed entry into the 'Large' segment targeted to sell on an average 100,000 units over five years (20,000 per year) and the project

* This case study is a summary of the case authored by Robert Kruse, General Motors [GM].

Case study 6.1 continued

Case study 6.1 continued

was expected to continue for at least five years until another major programme was initiated in this segment. GM's proposed programme had a limited amount of total capital available.

Engineers at GM suggested the manufacture of a six-way passenger power seat adjuster as standard equipment for the new vehicles proposed for the 'Large' segment. They were of the view that this would save GM approximately $1,000,000 in capital as they felt that a manual seat adjuster would not need to be designed, tooled and tested by them, which would result in significant savings. The downside to this proposal was the added piece cost to a programme that had already exceeded its piece cost targets. The added cost was approximately $80 per unit, a manual adjuster costing approximately $40 per unit and a power adjuster around $120 per unit. GM's financial department considered this proposal and completed the analysis shown in Table 6.1.1.

Table 6.1.1
Analysis by the finance department

Annual volume	*Added unit cost*	*Annual cost of 20,000 units*	*Penalty over five years*	*5-year-programme life cost*
20,000	$80.00	$1,600,000	$8,000,000	$1,000,000

Accordingly, engineers were advised that saving $1,000,000 in capital was not worth the added costs over the life of the programme. Thus, it was thought that manual passenger seat adjusters should be made as standard equipment with an available option of a power passenger adjuster. In their enthusiasm to save capital, the engineering department at GM had failed to take into account the hidden cost of capital. Hidden capital cost is the appreciation that the capital might have earned if it were invested elsewhere and earned a rate of return. The cost of capital and the cost of engineering and testing a new manual seat adjuster were not considered in the analysis, and were thus considered to be 'free'. In reality, not only was there the cost of the engineering and testing, but also the lost opportunity cost by not investing those resources in other endeavours.

Analysis of cost of capital

GM had an expected ROI hurdle rate of 14–18 per cent for vehicles in the 'Large' market segment. Considering these rates to be the cost of capital employed, for a 14 per cent return, the five-year cost of $1,000,000 of capital would then become $1,925,415 (Table 6.1.2). In other words, when the cost of capital was considered to be 14 per cent the added unit cost for each power seat adjuster that replaced a manual adjuster would be

Case study 6.1 continued

Case study 6.1 continued

reduced by $9.25 or 12 per cent. For an 18 per cent rate the five-year cost of capital would grow to $2,287,778 (Table 6.1.2).

Table 6.1.2
Cost of capital at two different ROI hurdle rates

Volume	Added unit cost	Annual penalty cost	5-year-programme life cost	Cost of capital at 14 per cent	Cost of capital at 18 per cent
20,000	$80.00	$1,600,000	$8,000,000	$1,925,415	$2,287,778

For an 18 per cent cost of capital, the unit cost for each power seat adjuster that replaced a manual adjuster would be reduced by $12.88 or 16 per cent. When comparing the cost of tooling the manual seat adjuster plus the lost opportunity cost of $2,287,778 against the five-year incremental cost penalty of $8,000,000, creating a manual adjuster made more sense than to incur cost penalty to the base vehicle.

Hidden costs of engineering and testing the manual passenger seat adjuster

It would cost GM approximately $575,000 to engineer a manual seat adjuster (including $75,000 in prototype material) and additionally $1,200,000 in testing expenses. Considering the five-year cost of capital of $2,775,000, and 14 per cent rate of cost of capital, the total of capital costs, engineering costs and test expense would become $5,343,025 (Table 6.1.3). Considering a 14 per cent rate of cost of capital, the added unit cost for each power seat adjuster that replaced a manual adjuster would reduce by $25.68 or 32 per cent, taking into account only the lost opportunity cost of the capital, engineering costs and test expense. Considering an 18 per cent rate and five-year cost of capital of $2,775,000, the total of capital costs, engineering costs and test expenses would become $6,348,528 (Table 6.1.3). Considering cost of capital to be 18 per cent, the added unit cost for each power seat adjuster that replaced a manual adjuster would reduce by $35.74 or 45 per cent, taking into account only the lost-opportunity cost associated with capital, engineering costs and test expenses.

Table 6.1.3
Hidden costs of engineering and testing the manual passenger seat adjuster (in US$)

Capital cost	Engineering cost	Testing expense	5-year-programme price cost	Total cost at 14 per cent cost of	Total cost at 18 per cent cost of
$1,000,000	$575,00	$1,200,000	$8,000,000	$5,343,025	$6,348,528

Case study 6.1 continued

Case study 6.1 continued

The above highlights that it made financial sense for GM to engineer, test and tool a new manual seat adjuster. However, advantages of the above approach are substantially reduced when hidden costs of capital and engineering expenses are considered. GM could evaluate the added value that power passenger seats would provide to customers. This added value could be considered for a very nominal cost, i.e., costs could be reduced by as much as 45 per cent below the traditional costs of power passenger seats ($44.26 vs $80.00). From this perspective GM could conclude that power passenger seats should be made standard equipment, thereby reducing capital expenditures and providing customer value in relation to nominal incremental costs. Additionally, engineering resources would be conserved by not creating a manual passenger seat adjuster. This conclusion would then lead to another analysis before power passenger seats become standard equipment. GM's marketing department would need to evaluate the differential product pricing (utilizing another tool) between the 'Large' and 'Large Luxury' market segments, by specifically asking the question: 'Will making power passenger seats standard equipment in the "Large" market segment erode the ability to command higher prices in the "Large Luxury" segment?' If the answer to this question is 'No' or the net additional sales estimate offsets any loss in the 'Large Luxury' segment, then GM could conclude that power passenger seats should be made standard equipment in 'Large' segment vehicles. This discussion, however, has not been addressed in this case study. GM could also evaluate cost savings associated with standardization by considering reduced build variation in seat assembly (only one type of adjuster, not two). Obviously, there would be hidden costs here too.

Thus, consideration of 'Hidden Costs' is important in all business propositions. GM's case clearly highlights that not considering the cost of capital or engineering expense in the product cost analysis leads to poor decisions being made.

CASE STUDY 6.2

Comprehensive Trauma Consortium: Valuing Human Life

Road accidents in Bangalore city, like anywhere else in India, have become a common sight. To avoid being caught in subsequent police enquiries and legal hassles, many passers-by prefer to drive on. Due to

Case study 6.2 continued

Case study 6.2 continued

the gruesomeness of the situation, very few people extend a helping hand, and those who do are not familiar with handling trauma victims. Trauma is any kind of high impact energy that is applied to the body by any means leading to tissue destruction or damage in the body. Hence, often after the elapse of considerable time, an on-looker would bundle the patient in a passing three-wheeler (auto rickshaw) or van and deposit the victim in a hospital. Due to the poor handling in this process, often the patient's situation gets aggravated, causing irreparable damage. Often the victim's identity is not known as his valuables like wallet, etc., are stolen at the site of the accident. This results in the trauma victim being admitted to a hospital as a person whose identity is 'unknown.'

Careless driving is the prime cause of accidents

Roads buzzing with vehicles invariably driven carelessly are the prime cause of accidents. Vehicle populations that far outstrip the pace of infrastructural development, and bad road maintenance are additional factors contributing to accidents within city limits. The national highways are even more prone to accidents due to negligent driving, lack of roadway design features, and inadequacies in the application of traffic regulations and control. Every 12 minutes there is a death caused due to accidents on the Indian roads, and every 2 minutes there are accidents causing serious injuries. The total *reported* deaths on account of road accidents in the country are close to 80,000 a year, while people sustaining injuries caused due to accidents are 300,000. This number is fast exploding as vehicle population increases at a rapid rate. Bangalore alone witnesses 8,000–9,000 *reported* accidents every year. If unreported accidents are included, the annual death toll is over 20,000 in the Bangalore area alone. Around 15 per cent of the accidents result in deaths. The hidden costs to society from road accidents is surely staggering! Ironically, there exists no effective trauma care system in the country to rescue accident victims and provide them with necessary medical care. As for the emergency call numbers 102 and 103, it is a miracle if a caller happens to hear a voice at the other end of the 'public helpline', let alone receive timely help!

Realizing that the city, and at a broader level the entire country, needs an efficient trauma care infrastructure and system to be established on the lines of 911 in US or 999 in UK, Dr Venkataramana (Dr V), a neurosurgeon and Head, Department of Neurosurgery, Manipal Hospital, Bangalore embarked on an ambitious journey of implementing a 'pre-hospital care' or 'trauma care' system in the city in 1998. From available

Case study 6.2 continued

Case study 6.2 continued

statistics, Dr V analysed that 22 per cent of accident deaths in the country were on-the-spot deaths, 10 per cent deaths were during the transportation of the victim to the hospital, while an astonishing 68 per cent were delayed deaths occurring within three days after the victim was admitted to a hospital and provided treatment. This means that there is something wrong with the system, or with the treatment being provided or with the way trauma victims were being transported to the hospital. There were only a handful (5–6) hospitals treating trauma accident victims in the city in the early 1990s. Unlike on-the-spot deaths, delayed deaths had the possibility of being prevented, provided the victim was given immediate medical attention. The first hour after an injury, called the Golden Hour, is very critical. If provided with immediate and appropriate medical treatment within the Golden Hour, accident victims stand a greater chance of survival and the possibility of the victim succumbing to injuries is greatly reduced. Thus, safe transportation of the injured to the right hospital within the Golden Hour along with ensuring maintenance of ABC (airway, breathing and circulation of blood) has the potential to drastically reduce the percentage of delayed deaths.

To set up an efficient trauma care system in the city and provide on-site pre-hospital care to an accident victim, Dr V saw the need to have:

1. An exclusive, easily accessible and direct toll free number to which a person could call after witnessing an accident.
2. A control room to receive distress calls and respond suitably.
3. A fleet of medically well-equipped, dedicated ambulances.
4. A global communication network to facilitate on-site, pre-hospital care, which provides immediate care within the Golden Hour.
5. Collective participation of hospitals with an integrated approach to provide trauma care.

Having conceptualized the need for such a 'consortium' in 1998, Dr V was successful in establishing the Comprehensive Trauma Consortium (CTC) in March 2000, with a lot of hard work and perseverance. CTC was constituted as a non-profit voluntary organization.

Today, CTC has 25 hospitals accredited in the consortium, with a dedicated fleet comprising 32 ambulances (a number that is fast growing) providing emergency pre-hospital care to every nook and cranny of Bangalore. A distress call to the CTC-dedicated, toll-free number '1062' is received at CTC's control room, which operates round-the-clock. A wireless base station has been set up in the control room, while each of

Case study 6.2 continued

Case study 6.2 continued

the member hospitals of the consortium has been fitted with a wireless radio frequency device, thereby enabling an 'open loop' messaging system. Any distress call received at the control room gets simultaneously relayed through the entire network/consortium of hospitals, making it possible for each hospital to know the location of the accident, and the hospital to which the victim would be taken. Accordingly, that particular hospital gears up to provide trauma care to the victim.

To facilitate easy coordination, the entire city has been divided into seven zones, each of which has a representative main zonal hospital, area hospitals and first-aid centres. While main zonal hospitals attend to all injuries and mass casualties, area hospitals cater to minor injuries. The high-tech control room (which also has a digital map of the city) makes a broadcast over the wireless system, which is simultaneously received by all ambulances that are strategically positioned in different parts of the city through wireless handsets present in the vehicles. The driver in the ambulance closest to the accident location heads to the scene of the emergency and is given directions via the GPS unit fitted in the vehicle to enable the driver to take the shortest possible route to the nearest member hospital. The ambulances are fully equipped with sophisticated medical equipment like ventilators, automated external defibrillators, suction apparatus, spinal boards, first-aid medical kits, splints and other life-saving equipment. Also on-board the ambulance is a well-trained paramedic, who on reaching the location of emergency ensures there is no bleeding of any kind in the victim and that his blood circulation is normal. After making sure that the breathing channels are clear, the paramedic places the victim on the spinal board, without damaging the spine, the victim is then taken to the designated hospital and continues to receive medical treatment inside the ambulance, till it reaches the hospital.

Since its inception, CTC has carried out over 1,900 free rescues in Bangalore city, with only 13 of them resulting in death. CTC has also started a similar service on the national highways, by positioning its ambulances at various points on the main highways leading in to/out of Bangalore. So far, over 3,000 rescues have been undertaken on these highways. With the above services of CTC in place, the pre-hospital death rate has been reduced from 32 per cent before its inception to just 3 per cent in the city at present. Apart from providing succour to the families of the victims who survived the accidents due to CTC's prompt services, the latter have also prevented considerable social and economic loss to the country at large.

Case study 6.2 continued

Case study 6.2 continued

The challenges faced by CTC are largely related to its financial viability. The victims who are picked by CTC's ambulances are in no position to make any payments to CTC at the time of being taken to the hospitals. After being discharged from the hospitals, the victims are unable to pay CTC for service rendered, as they would have already paid heavily to the hospital for the treatment. The founders of CTC are still grappling with this issue.

There are *hidden benefits* that the society gets from CTC's life-saving services. Typically, the victims are the sole-earning members of their families. If they are not effectively transported from the accident site to the hospital, they may end up losing their lives or getting incapacitated for life. This would push a household of dependent family members with no viable source of income into living in penury. It is time the government realizes the hidden benefits of CTC's services and finds a way to compensate CTC. In fact, CTC has taken up a task which actually the government's responsibility. Is anyone in the government listening?

For another stakeholder concerned with the effective and timely treatment of trauma victims, there are huge *hidden costs* if CTC were to cease to exist. Why? In the absence of effective and timely pick-up of trauma victims, their situation would deteriorate rapidly, either resulting in their death or prolonged treatment in the hospital, if they manage to survive. In either case, the insurance companies that provide third party insurance to vehicle owners, have to make much larger payments to the victims in the absence of care provided by CTC. However, till date, CTC's efforts to convince insurance companies to pay for its services out of the third-party insurance cover of vehicle owners involved in the accident has fallen on deaf ears. In this case, the failure on the part of the insurance companies is due to myopia and short-sightedness. If they understood these hidden costs, they would promote more organizations such as CTC to continue to render the good service to the society as they have been doing, so that in the long run, their hidden costs are reduced.

Notes

1. The Thoreau quote is cited in Julia Cameron, *The Artist's Way* (New York: Tarcher, 1992).
2. The opening quotation is based on a line from an Oscar Wilde play, Lady Windermere's Fan, 'A cynic is someone who knows the price of everything and the value of nothing.' We have seen this epigram used to define economists. This is highly misleading—if economists do anything, it is to analyse and optimize cost and value in decision-making.

3. The early version of the first author's MIT students' survey was published in the article by Shlomo Maital, 'The problem approach to teaching elementary economics', *The American Economist*, Summer 1971.
4. Economic Value Added™ is a term that is a registered trademark, owned by the New York consulting firm Stern, Stewart, which pioneered in the management applications of this concept.
5. The bible of the Economic Value Added method is *The Quest for Value: A Guide for Senior Managers* by G. Bennett Stewart III (New York: HarperCollins, 1991).
6. Data on Market Value Added comes from 'The new champ of wealth creation', by Terence Pare, *Fortune*, 18 September 1995, and 'Americaís Wealth Creators', by Shawn Tully, 22 November 1999, sourced from www.fortune.com.

   The 'Meeting Meter' concept was invented by Paul Strassman, former VP Xerox and author of The Business Value of Computers.

   How to value so-called 'intangible' assets, such as R&D and human resources, is discussed in accounting professor Baruch Lev's book Intangibles (Washington DC: Brookings, 2001).
7. The 'Kill a Brand' article is adapted from Nirmalya Kumar, 'Kill a Brand, Keep a Customer', *Harvard Business Review*, December 2003; see in particular p. 2.
8. For the four steps for turning cost cutting into a core competency, see V. Altman, M. Kaplan, A. Corbett, 'Turn Cost cutting into a Core Competency', Harvard Business School Update, December 2002.

Chapter 7
Trade-offs: Optimizing and eliminating them

People face trade-offs .... Life is full of trade-offs.
—Gregory Mankiw, *Principles of Economics*[1]

There is no gain without pain.
—Presidential candidate Adlai Stevenson, and legendary American football coach Vince Lombardi

There is no pain without gain.
—Anonymous dentist

LEARNING OBJECTIVES After you read this chapter, you should understand:

- **How to define and measure trade-offs**
- **Why good managers optimize them, while great ones defy them**
- **What the difference is between efficiency and effectiveness**
- **How to create winning new products by using trade-off analysis to find new 'market space'**
- **Why great companies defy the trade-off between creativity and discipline**
- **How to make trade-off decisions in a team, using the even swap approach**
- **What the link is between globalization, global GDP growth, and trade-offs**
- **How to allocate tasks in a team using the comparative advantage principle**

TOOL

Managing trade-offs: Even swaps #3

7.1 INTRODUCTION

One of America's most distinguished economists, N. Gregory Mankiw, framed a set of 10 economic laws on which nearly all economists agree.

The first, and presumably most important, was: 'People face trade-offs'.

A trade-off is the balancing of two *opposing* qualities or benefits or goods, both of which are desirable. Managers face trade-off choices every day. Sometimes, they grapple with picking what they perceive is the lesser of two evils, or the best of two virtues—between cost-reducing layoffs and losing key personnel; time-to-market and product quality; cost and price, and product quality; short-term profit and long-term growth; product focus, and variety of offerings; and between discipline and creativity. Peters and Waterman, in their book *In Search of Excellence,* call trade-offs 'paradoxes' and cite managers' ability to deal with, and optimize them, as a vital element in managerial excellence.

The key point of this chapter is:

Good managers identify and optimize trade-off choices.

Tools for making optimal trade-off decisions, both individually and in teams, will be provided in this chapter. But truly great managers make trade-offs vanish. They want to have their cake and eat it too—and they find ways to defy Economic Law #1. They know that superior management and leadership can produce gain without pain. How this is done will also be discussed at length.

ECONOMIC LAW #1

Gregory Mankiw served as a presidential economic advisor. As an economist, he is undoubtedly ambidextrous—two-handed. Facing policy decisions, he must, on the one hand; surely ask

What are the benefits of this policy?

And, on the other,

What do we have *to give up* in order to implement it?

and frame his policy advice accordingly.

In general, trade-off choices are made by implementing the 'opportunity cost' concept explained in Chapter 6, by weighing pain and gain—what do I gain? What do I give up (pain)? And—is the gain more than the pain?

One can surmise that generations of leaders, executives, managers and ordinary people who rely on economists' advice sometimes yearn for less of Economic Law #1, balancing opportunity cost and value, and more 'one-handedness—Tell us the *one* answer. Do this. Period. Former French Prime Minister Pierre Mendes-France once said, '*gouverner, c'est choisir*' (to govern is to choose). But fortunately, economists do not govern, they generally advise. Defining, measuring and optimizing trade-off choices are economists' stock-in-trade.

There are times in the lives of managers when this skill is crucial. And there are times when a different skill is needed—defying trade-offs, in a way that makes them virtually disappear.

Action learning

Trade-offs in Life

Life is indeed full of trade-offs. Name the main tradeoff choices you face in your own life. For instance, time spent at work vs time spent at home with your family.

- Analyse how you make those choices. Do you make them, or are they made for you? Are you choosing well?
- Think about ways to eliminate the tradeoff and enjoy more of both of the two opposing benefits, or qualities.

We begin the chapter with some tools for optimizing trade-off choices, in the context of a recent difficult business decision—innovation in Intel's microprocessor.

Case study: Pentium M ('Centrino' ™)

Beginning with its first microprocessor, the 8086, Intel Corp. has pursued a single-minded strategy summarized in a single word: 'speed'! Each new microprocessor, from the 286, through the 486, and now the Pentium, has featured higher Megahertz (computing speed and power). Intel has harnessed the law named after one of its founders, Gordon Moore: The number of transistors packed onto a microprocessor doubles every 18 months. Intel's customers have been persuaded that more speed is essential. Each new generation of microprocessor has generated more heat and consumed more power, by packing incredibly large and growing numbers of transistors onto a small slice of polished silicon.

In 2003, with the announcement of the Pentium M mobile processor (branded as Centrino when combined with other devices), Intel shifted strategic gears. Perceiving the future in wireless computing, Intel sought to tailor its products to further that end, by reducing their microprocessors' size and power consumption, and then focusing on that 'mobility' feature.

Case study continued

Case study continued

'Notebooks never captured more than 10 per cent of the US market,' noted Stephen H. Wildstrom, in *Business Week*, because using one involved big tradeoffs, namely 'lower performance, shorter battery life or both'. Intel's Pentium M and Centrino sought to increase battery life to between five and eight hours, enabling all-day mobile computing. Some argue there was a tradeoff, against speed and performance. Intel claims there wasn't. Had Intel continued to focus on speed, they probably could have increased computing speed faster than was achieved with Centrino.

Intel's decision-makers were betting that the tradeoff decision they made in favour of longer battery life was one consumers would themselves choose. They made the decision as most trade-off choices are made—years before the product reached the market, without truly knowing for sure whether Intel customers really yearned for mobility, enough to make it a winner. In the end, it turned out they were right. Intel was aided by a very large marketing budget, to help persuade customers to 'Unwire your world'.

A major internal debate in Intel involved strategic focus—Intel built its brand, with the famous Intel Inside campaign, focusing on 'speed'. Would the new strategy blur the valuable brand by switching to a very different feature, mobility? Could the transition in consumer's minds from speed to mobility be made successfully? Long fierce debates were held on this, before the decision to proceed full-speed with Centrino was taken.

7.2 EFFICIENCY AND EFFECTIVENESS

How can engineer–managers know when to manage tradeoffs, and when to strive to ignore them? To answer this question, we begin with several definitions.

DEFINITIONS

- **Technical Efficiency: Producing the maximum possible amount of product, with given technology and resources (labour and capital). An organization is said to be 'technically efficient' if it is located on its 'efficiency frontier'—the curve that separates 'feasible' from 'non-feasible' outcomes. (This is also known as the production possibilities frontier.) Along this efficiency frontier, there are choices, all of which are termed 'technically efficient'. But only one of them is 'economically efficient'.**

Definitions continued

Definitions continued

- **X-efficiency: The late Professor Harvey Leibenstein termed X-efficiency the degree to which organizations were economically efficient. He called it that, because in his view most organizations are far from 100 per cent technical efficiency, but the reasons for the inefficiency were somewhat shrouded in mystery, hence 'X' for 'unknown'.**
- **Economic Efficiency: The choice pair, on the efficiency frontier, which is 'optimal'—usually, in the sense of maximizing profits. Economic efficiency for two products, say X (cars) and Y (minivans) is achieved, when the opportunity cost of a minivan (measured in terms of the reduction in the number of cars produced, to make one more minivan) is equal to the relative price, or value, of a minivan (minivan price, relative to the price of a car) (Figure 7.1). The condition for an optimal trade-off choice, attaining economic efficiency, is:**

  Opportunity cost = Relative value (or price)

For instance, an economically-efficient choice would be to make the number of cars and minivans, such that if the price of the minivan was twice that of a car, making another minivan meant giving up two cars.

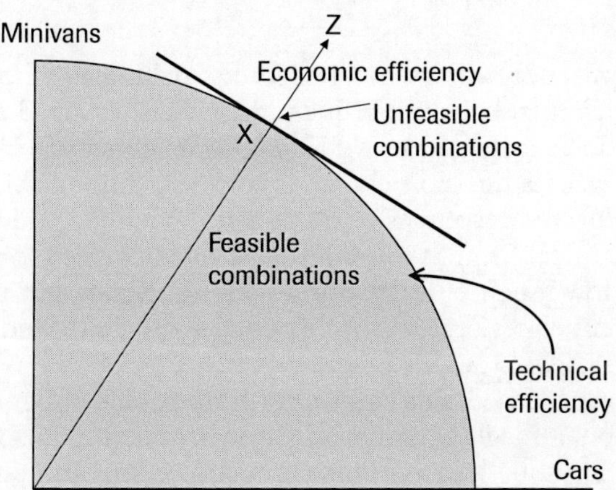

For a plant that makes minivans and cars, the shaded area shows the feasible combinations of the manufacture of both for a given technology and amount of resources (machines and workers). The border between the 'feasible' and 'infeasible' region is known as the technical efficiency frontier, or production possibilities curve. Only one point on this frontier is 'economically efficient', in the cost-benefit sense. At this point the opportunity cost of making one more minivan precisely equals the relative price, or value, of a minivan, compared with that of cars.

Figure 7.1
Trade-offs: Minivans vs cars

Definitions continued

Definitions continued

- **Effectiveness: The degree to which an organization's actual performance meets its projected goals or targets. The minivan/car factory, for instance, might aim for point Z in 2006, but might achieve only some point X. Its effectiveness, then, is OX, OZ, or about 90 per cent. Effectiveness is often related to the ability to *surmount* trade-offs and constraints, and push the production possibilities frontier outward. Some corporate leaders use the term 'stretch goals' to refer to setting high-performance standards.**

Case study: Trade-offs at Kodak

(The reader is invited to read a more elaborate version of this case at the end of the chapter.)

On 29 October 1993, George Fisher was appointed CEO and Chairman of the Board of Eastman Kodak. Prior to this he was CEO of Motorola, where he had anticipated the mobile phone boom and led Motorola to early market and technology leadership in this industry. Fisher, trained as a mathematician, faced pressing and complex trade-off problems at Kodak.

1. The organization was by most accounts technically inefficient, suffering from substantial X-inefficiency. Fisher acted at once to cut waste, reduce costs and move Kodak to its efficiency frontier.
2. He then faced a decision choice involving economic efficiency. Kodak allocated resources to its imaging business and to the pharmaceutical firm, Sterling Drug, it had acquired for some $5 billion. How much of its resources should Kodak put into pharmaceuticals? Zero, Fisher decided—and sold Sterling, greatly reducing Kodak's debt burden.
3. Finally, Fisher faced a difficult long-term trade-off between conventional imaging, based on silver halide film, and digital imaging. He sought to optimize this choice, investing in R&D in digital imaging while sustaining the highly competitive and profitable conventional film business. In this realm, Kodak struggled—and continues to struggle—because the competencies needed to succeed in electronics-based technology are utterly different from those possessed by a chemistry-based company. In 2003, Eastman Kodak had over $13 billion in sales, but attained razor-thin net income of $265 million, down 66 per cent from 2002 levels. In the ten-year-period 1993–2003, the average annual total return to investors (capital gains in share prices plus dividends) was a bleak minus 2.1 per cent.

Source: Information from Fortune 500 annual issue.

7.3 VALUE INNOVATION

One of the most powerful applications of trade-off analysis is known as 'Value Innovation',[2] and was developed by W. Chan Kim and Renee Mauborgne. The Centrino case described above is an example.

The basic idea of value innovation is simple. People never buy a product or a service. They buy a 'basket' or set of product features, or characteristics, each of which provides them with something they seek. A car for instance, comprises style, speed, convenience, ease of maintenance, fuel economy, comfort, and other features. There are trade-offs among features. For instance, power and price. You can buy a car with a very large V8 engine, but it will cost more than a V4 and burn more fuel.

One approach to innovation is to subtract, or diminish, some features, while augmenting others—seeking a 'market space' (i.e., a new set of features) that fulfils two conditions: it does not already exist, and it represents a new product people would happily buy if it were available. A common fallacy in product design lies in the constant effort to add or augment features. As a result software has become complex and cumbersome far beyond most users' basic needs.

Case study: Quicken (Intuit)

Quicken is cheque-writing software produced by Intuit. Its founder, from the outset, benchmarked its simplicity and ease of use, by defining the competition, *not* as other software, but as: the pencil. By making Quicken ultra-easy to use, Intuit found it used by millions of small businesses as their basic accounting software—a use they had not originally intended or expected.

Case study: Formule 1

The French budget hotel chain's co-Chairman, Paul Dubrule and Gerard Pelisson, challenged their managers to innovate. What would you do, they ask, if you could launch Accor from scratch? Their managers discovered that there was 'market space' for a low-cost hotel that offered nothing but a quiet, restful night's sleep. By moving along the 'hotel room feature' 'production possibilities curve', giving up things like room service, amenities and room size, they could provide a quiet room (by investing resources saved on amenities, in insulation) and a great

Case study continued

Case study continued

mattress. The innovation was based on the idea that those who chose to sleep in a one-star hotel basically wanted only to sleep there—so, the product he provided was 'a good night's sleep'. By subtracting product features people felt were inessential, and focusing resources to strengthen ones they thought were vital, he created a new market space—and a successful business (Figures 7.2 and 7.3). The key to this method lies in answering three questions:

1. What are the product's (or service's) essential features?
2. Which features now emphasized are perceived as inessential? Which features not emphasized are perceived as crucial?
3. What new product can be created by reframing the product, by finding a new place along the feature production possibilities curve?

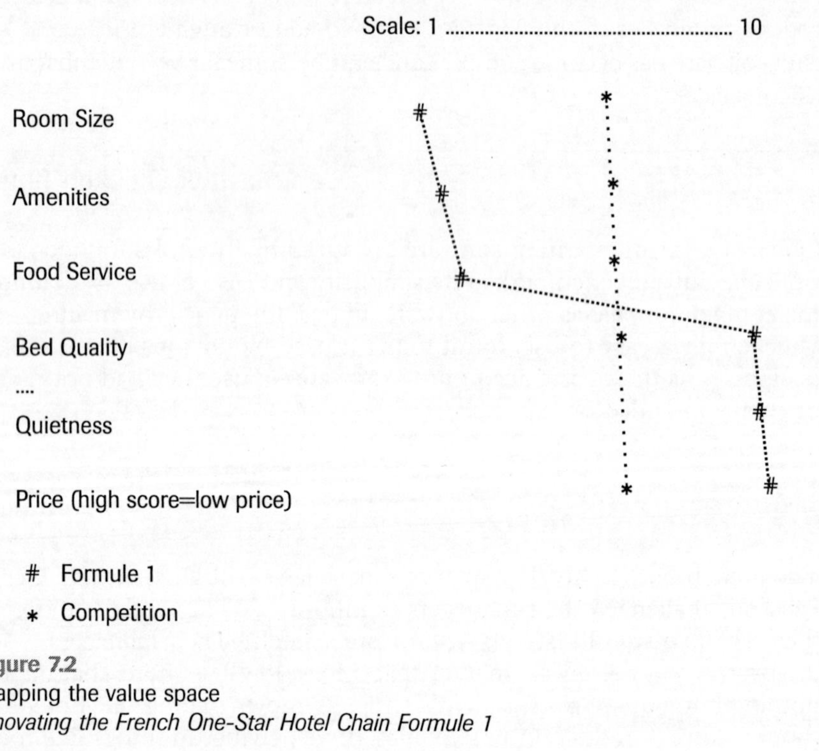

Figure 7.2
Mapping the value space
Innovating the French One-Star Hotel Chain Formule 1

Case study continued

Case study continued

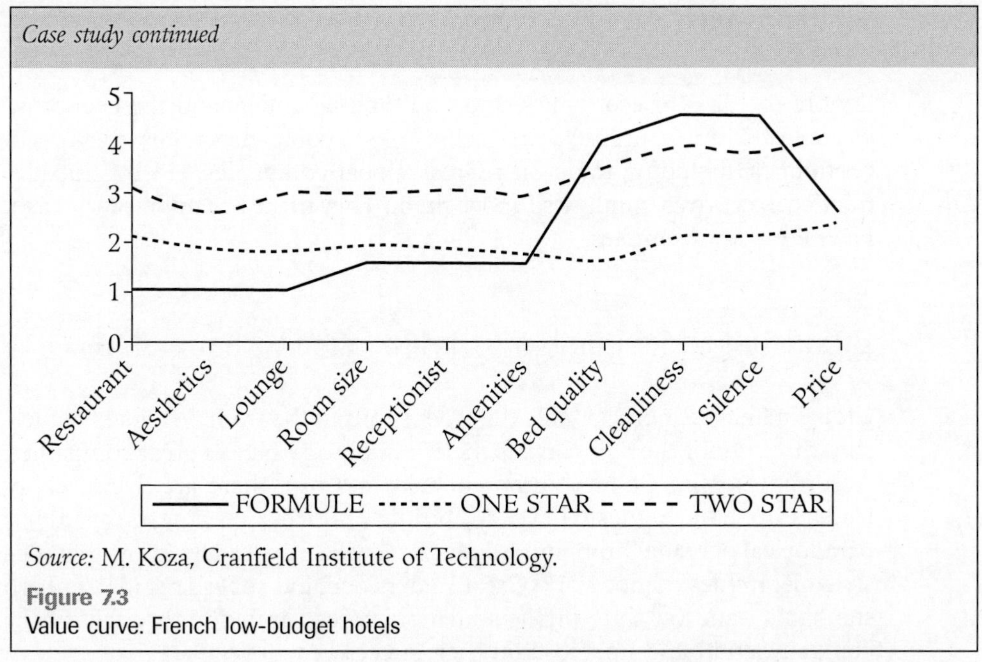

Source: M. Koza, Cranfield Institute of Technology.

Figure 7.3
Value curve: French low-budget hotels

TOOL #3 Mapping product space

1. List the key features of your organization's product, or a product or service of your choice. It is best to choose between 5 and 12 features—few products have more than a dozen or so crucial characteristics of importance to buyers.
2. Score each characteristic, on a scale of 1 to 10, or 1 to 5, where 5 is the best and 1, the worst. Do the same for competing products.
3. What does this 'product profile' reveal? Can you use it to discover open 'market space'—product profiles, such that, by trading off less important product features for improvements in more important ones, a winning new product can be created?

A French entrepreneur carefully surveyed the low-cost one-star hotel industry, and found market space—he found that an inexpensive hotel without frills (small rooms, no amenities or food service) but that offered a quiet restful night's sleep, would find a large market. He was right. The result: the successful Formule 1 chain.

7.4 DEFYING TRADE-OFFS

'Ignore the laws of economics, and you'll never understand the economy,' wrote Rob Norton, in *Fortune* magazine.[3] Good companies follow the laws of economics, including trade-offs. Great global companies, led by globally-minded executives, simply rise above them. They make key trade-offs vanish. Here are a few examples.

Broad-based leadership vs high-visibility leadership

Global managers need to 'rally the troops' out in the front, yet foster leadership throughout the company. Is there a trade-off? Not in great companies. According to Jim Collins, author of *Good to Great,* there are five levels of leadership. The highest, Level 5, 'builds enduring greatness through a paradoxical personal humility and personal will'. Top leaders know that old-style hierarchies do not work. Great leaders demand superb results, set high standards—and yet shun public adulation, spread ambition throughout the company, and build up and train their successors.

Great leaders never shun tough decisions, yet consult widely and build a powerful team of smart managers around them.

Short term profit vs long term growth

Good managers find the 'sweet spot' between investing in R&D, technology and product development, and quarterly profits. Great leaders want both. They spur workers and managers to find 'free lunches' that fatten the bottom line, while resisting stockholder pressure to cut R&D budgets, and while boldly venturing into new, growing markets.

Global companies tie cost discipline to a growth strategy. Toyota, for example, has aggressively slashed its costs to keep prices low. At the same time, Toyota pursues a long-term growth strategy, that may reach a 15 per cent world market share and overtake #1 automaker GM by 2006 (As of 2005, Toyota's global sales of $153 billion were just a few per cent below GM's). Toyota's President Fujio Cho is a trade-off-ignoring global leader. He has expanded his company aggressively worldwide.

'People are our #1 assets' vs 'whatever it takes'

When the techno-bubble burst in 2000/2001, many high-tech companies were forced to lay off key workers to survive. This was often done badly, in several waves rather than a single one. Workers who had invested 20-hour days for years felt their loyalty was betrayed.

Great leaders do not trade-off their focus on human resources against achieving corporate goals, but *link* the two closely. They attain their goals by fostering, developing and enhancing their people and by making sure their walk matches their talk.

Management experts Charles Hampden-Turner and Fons Trompenaars argue that 'wealth is created from conflicting values.' They focus on cultural values. Quoting Alfred North Whitehead, who said 'Everything was seen before by someone who did not discover it,' they observe that 'foreign cultures are ... *mirror images of one another's values, reversals of the order and sequence of looking and learning.*' For instance: Western culture tends to be individualistic; Eastern, communitarian or collective. The West is specific, the East is diffuse. The West is particular and analytic, the East is holistic, 'big-picture'. Such 'reversals' or trade-offs appear frightening to many global managers, born and raised in a specific culture but they need not be. Contrary to what Rudyard Kipling said, East and West *do* meet. Wealth is created when they do—when talented leaders build organizations that exchange the logical operation of 'either or', in cultural values, for 'both and'.[4]

Action learning

Managing Key Trade-offs in Your Organization

Here are three pair choices commonly regarded as opposing benefits or trade-offs. State how your organization scores for each trade-off (on a scale of 1 to 10), compared with industry best-practice; for each consider how you might act to score higher in both.

	Your Organization's Score	*Best Industry Score*
1. Short-Term, Long-Term:		
short-term profitability:	___	___
long-term growth	___	___
2. Leadership, Teamwork:		
High-profile visible leadership:	___	___
Senior Management teamwork	___	___
3. People, Goals:		
People-first policy:	___	___
Attain goals at all costs	___	___

Action learning

Perspiration: Meet Inspiration

Some organizations believe that there is a trade-off between two key organizational values: the culture of discipline (the ability of individuals to execute the work plans and ideas they are responsible for based on internalized values); and the culture of creativity (the ability of individuals to come up with useful viable new ideas that can generate profit opportunities for their organization) (Figure 7.4: From good to great—discipline and creativity).

1. Rate your organization's (company or business unit) culture of discipline on a scale of 1 to 10, where 10 is the industry best-practice: ___
2. Rate your organization's creativity, on a scale of 1 to 10, where 10 represents the industry's highest creativity: ___

Use these two numbers to locate your organization on the discipline/creativity trade-off curve.

— Where is your organization *now*, in the discipline/creativity space?

— Where do you want it to be, or where will it *have* to be, in three years?

— What change process and action plan must be initiated, to close the gap between where your company now is, and where you *want* it to be in three years?

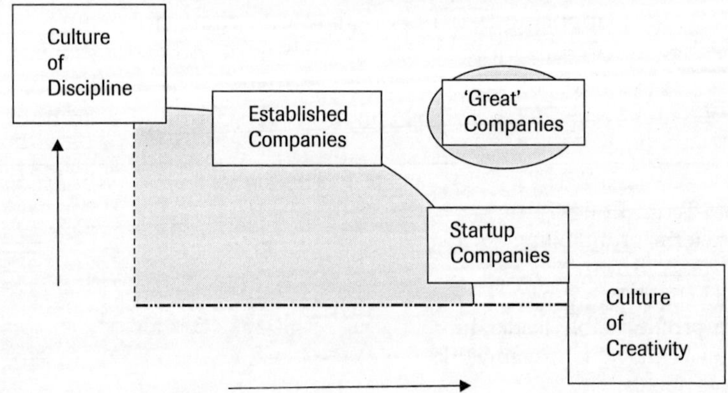

Figure 7.4
From good to great–discipline and creativity

In his book *Good to Great*, Jim Collins shows that the 11 'great' organizations he identified all excel in combining creativity ('the production of novel ideas that are useful and appropriate to the situation in any realm of human activity') with 'the culture of discipline' (an internal quality, such that individual members of the organization choose to meet rigorous operational challenges, deadlines, milestones, etc., in implementing creative ideas, not because of external controls or rewards but because they simply want to do so, because it is a core value that is a part of their personality and their thinking).

7.5 EVEN SWAPS

'I sold my dog—for $2 million,' said Tim.
'Mmm?' said his disbelieving father.
'Yeah. I got two $1 million cats for him.'

Market value is established by such swaps—though normally money, rather than dogs and cats, is involved. When value cannot be established in the marketplace, through free exchange and the forces of supply and demand, we can engage in 'what if' opportunity-cost simulations. This is the basis of the 'even swap' approach, developed by John S. Hammond, Ralph Keeney and Howard Raiffa. What is the most you would give up...? one should ask—and use this question to frame consensus trade-off decisions.[5]

The authors observe that most trade-off decisions—indeed, most crucial management decisions in general—are made collectively, rather than by a single individual. They stress the importance of organizing the two-handed decision process—weighing relative costs and values—in a manner that enables orderly, clear decision-making processes in a group context. (See Action Learning: The Wisdom of Teams). Most of us have been present at 'decisions by committee', in which heated arguments obscure the *reason* for the disagreement. The consequence, usually, is deadlock, wrong decisions, or a 'fog of battle' in which no-one really grasps why the committee cannot reach a decision. The 'even swaps' method separates clearly the discussion of relative value (the 'right hand' of the two-handed trade-off decision) from the relative cost (the 'left hand').

Action learning

The Wisdom of Teams

The British scientist Francis Galton proved the superiority of collective wisdom over a single brain with a simple experiment. He asked a group of farmers to guess the weight of an ox. None of the farmers individually came close. But the average guess for the group as a whole was 1,198 pounds. The true weight: 1,197 pounds.

Try this. Ask 10 people in your office to guess your weight. Take the average. See if the average is closer to any of the individual guesses.

Earlier, we noted how innovators at Intel created Centrino, a trade-off choice involving longer battery life in return for reduced speed or computing power. To understand the 'even swap' approach, here is an admittedly simplified example of how that decision might have been taken.[6]

Case study: Designing a new laptop

A product development team meets. It must choose between three different designs for a new laptop computer: #1, #2 and #3. The three key features are: speed, battery life and price.

Scores (on a scale of 1 through 10, as seen from the perspective of the consumer—a high score indicates low price):

Product features: Scores

Design	*A (speed)*	*B (battery life)*	*C (price)*
#1	8	6.5	3
#2	7	6	4
#3	4	4	5

The team must choose one of the three designs.

Step one

Eliminate the effectively-dominated design. A 'dominated' design is one that is inferior in all, or almost all, product features. On this basis, #3 can be eliminated. It is inferior in speed and battery life and superior only slightly in price. Unless price is valued above all else by customers, #3 is a non-starter.

Case study continued

Case study continued

Product features: Eliminate dominated alternatives

Design	*A (speed)*	*B (battery life)*	*C (price)*
#1	8	6.5	3
#2	7	6	4
~~#3~~	~~4~~	~~4~~	~~5~~

Step two

The first even swap. Ask the decision team: *In order for design #2 to achieve a score of '8' in speed, rather than '7', it is necessary to divert resources from 'battery life'. What is the maximum reduction in battery life (number of points) that you would 'swap', in return for a one point increase in 'speed', without lowering the perceived overall value of the design?*

A long, perhaps heated discussion results. At its conclusion, hopefully the team reaches a decision. Suppose it is: one point. We are willing to swap at most one extra 'speed' point for one less 'battery' point. The new modified points table is:

Product features: Swap for 1 speed point

Design	*A (speed)*	*B (battery life)*	*C (price)*
#1	8	6.5	3
#2	8	5	4
~~#3~~	~~4~~	~~4~~	~~5~~

Speed can now be eliminated, because designs #1 and #2 are even (hence the name, 'even swap') on this feature. The decision now boils down to two product features and two designs, #1 and #2:

Product features: Simplified trade-off

Design	*B (battery life)*	*C (price)*
#1	6.5	3
#2	~~5~~ 6.5	~~4~~ 3.5

Step three

Perform a second 'even swap'—Ask the decision team: *In order for design #2 to achieve a score of '6.5' in battery life, rather than '5', it is necessary to invest and hence raise the product price. What is the maximum increase in price (expressed as lower 'price' points) that you would 'swap', in return for a one point increase in 'battery life', without lowering the perceived overall value of the design?*

Case study continued

Case study continued

Again, after heated discussion, the answer emerges: a half-point, reducing C for #2 to 3.5.

The designs are now equal on 'B', but #2 wins on 'C'. Design #2 is chosen. It provides more value to the customer through its cheaper price.

Many readers will quickly see a much quicker, mathematical solution.

Step one

Find the relative importance, or 'weight', of each product feature, in the eyes of the consumers, on a scale of zero to one: say, a = 0.2, b = 0.2 c = 0.6, for features A, B and C, respectively.

Step two

Calculate the weighted score of each of the three designs:

$$a\,A + b\,B + c\,C$$

where
a, b, c are the weights,
and A, B and C
are the product feature scores

Design	*Weighted score*
#1	4.7
#2	5.0
#3	4.6

With the highest score, design #2 wins.

Why, then, go to all the trouble of the even swap process? There is a reason—the vast difference between the small and the capital letters. The small letters (preference weights) are *subjective*, representing consumer preferences. The capital letters (feature scores) are *objective*, representing technologically determined performance specifications. The key value of the even swaps approach is that it separates in the decision process, the conflict over 'subjective preferences' and 'objective performance'. It provides a soul-searching data-gathering process, in which consumer preferences and subjective trade-offs are determined, and separates this issue from the technological, or engineering feature trade-offs. In our experience, these two issues often mingle, blur and when they do, an effective trade-off decision is nearly impossible.

The even swap process can be adapted to build product platforms. When market segments differ in their subjective preferences, it may pay to develop a design for each set of preferences, provided the segment is sufficiently profitable. If only a single design is sought, decision-makers must be certain they are aiming for the right set of preferences.

Case study: Silver threads among the gold: The Honda Accord

The Honda Accord was once the best-selling automobile in the United States. Honda executives had the foresight to build manufacturing plants in Ohio, and were able to surmount car import quotas as well as the rise in the value of the yen relative to the dollar, which made Japanese-made Hondas costly for Americans. Over time, almost unnoticed to Honda executives, the average age of Honda buyers began to rise from mid-1930s to early 1940s. The Honda Accord's features, style, and design had aged. Meanwhile, the baby boom bulge of thirty-somethings created a rich, high-spending market, that Honda missed. The Accord gave up its #1 market position.

The Accord was quickly redesigned, with the target 'preference weights' now reflecting those of the younger market segment. While it did not regain #1 position, it did substantially rise in sales revenue and unit sales.

Case study: Is it worth the risk?

A team of engineers in a small Asian nation was assigned the task of evaluating two defence-related proposals presented in a bid or tender process. They summarized the projects in terms of two parameters: the expected 'returns' from the project, and the anticipated 'risk'. (In general, the trade-off between risk and return is the foundation of capital market analysis and successful investment; this will be discussed in Chapter 13.) They used an even-swap process to make their decision. One point in 'returns', they agreed, was equal in value to three points of risk.

	Alternatives	
Objectives	A	B
Returns	43.6	43.6
Risk	69 + (20.5 × 3) = 130.5	250

Case study continued

Case study continued

If the 'returns' for alternative A were increased by 20.5 points to 43.6, it would have risk equal to 69 (the original risk level) plus 3 times 20.5 = 130.5. After equalizing the returns of both A and B, a decision could then be made based only on the risk level of A and B. Since A has a lower risk than B, it is evidently the best trade-off choice among the two proposals.

Action learning

Can You Implement even Swaps?

The Table below shows scores for price, reliability and flexibility for four software packages as well as the preference weights for each attribute.

Construct an 'even swap' scenario, in which each of the four packages is eliminated, until a final clear winner emerges, *that is consistent with the preference weights given in the table.*

	Attribute		
Package	*Price*	*Reliability*	*Flexibility*
A	0	75	100
B	25	100	0
C	30	0	100
D	100	0	0
Preference weights:	*0.45*	*0.20*	*0.35*

7.6 COMPARATIVE ADVANTAGE

Earlier Gregory Mankiw's 10 Economic Laws were mentioned. Law #5 says 'trade can make everyone better off.' This principle, known as 'comparative advantage', dates back to Adam Smith's seminal book, *Wealth of Nations* (1776) and explains both a key fact about the global economy and a key issue in human resource management. Trade and specialization for countries and for teams are special cases of trade-off analysis.

Global trade

According to data from the World Trade Organization (WTO), in the period 1950–2002 world GDP grew by an average of 3.8 per cent annually. This is a remarkable figure—no other period in human history came close to achieving such a remarkable rate of growth. World GDP doubled three times in 50 years, from $5 trillion to today's value of $40 trillion. This is unprecedented in history.

The WTO data, shows the engine of growth was trade. The value of world exports grew by an annual average of 8 per cent for the same period—more than double the growth of GDP. The creation of a global economy, with more or less free trade, has been a tremendous boon to developing and developed nations alike.

Trade has made the world richer. Why?

In 1776, seeking to understand the burgeoning Industrial Revolution, Adam Smith described the parable of pin manufacture. By splitting the different operations required to make pins into 18 separate ones and assigning each task to a worker, great gains in efficiency were attained. By specializing, each worker became more proficient, and overall, the output of pins soared.

The principle underlying this efficiency gain was that of specialization according to comparative advantage—each worker did the task he or she did relatively best, even though there may be some workers who could do every task faster than others.

As trade-offs are always relative—what output is lost, when some worker polishes the pins rather than cuts them—*every worker always has* some *comparative advantage.* If a worker takes three times longer to polish pins than to cut them, compared to other workers, by definition that same worker takes one third the time to cut pins rather than polish them, compared to other workers.

This same principle applies to nations. Every nation in the world has a comparative advantage in producing and hence exporting some product or service. By organizing the world's economy along the lines of comparative advantage and export-import trade, rather than through autarchy ('every nation makes everything it needs by itself'), tremendous gains in efficiency and hence in wealth can be made.

Many rounds of trade negotiations have taken place under the old General Agreement on Tariffs and Trade (GATT) and its successor, the WTO; the latest being the Doha round of agricultural subsidy reductions and elimination of trade restrictions. These agreements have greatly reduced barriers to free trade. The result has been to make trade an engine of world growth.

The bitter protests against this process, known as 'globalization', stem from the fact that the losers are usually fairly small, cohesive and visible groups (those whose skills have been made obsolete by imports and global comparative advantage), while the winners (e.g., consumers who buy imported products at vastly lower prices than before) are diffuse and often are not fully aware of their gains under the free-trade system.

Managing people

Comparative advantage can be used in managing human resources as well as in organizing world trade. Much of today's work is done in teams. It is the nature of people that some are faster, better or smarter in every task than others. But because cost is measured in relative terms, every team member has a comparative advantage in some task, just as every country has a comparative advantage in some product or service. The task of a team leader is to discover each team member's comparative advantage and build the team work around it. When this is done, one can show that the team achieves 'technical efficiency' or full X-efficiency—that is, it performs on its production possibilities frontier, in the same way that the world achieves full efficiency when it organizes around the principles of comparative advantage, specialization and free trade.

Action learning

Running a Team

A team of three people has the task of assembling bookshelves. There are three separate tasks, each requiring one person: paint, sand and assemble. The three team members and the time they take for each task in hours, are as follows:

	Paint	*Sand*	*Assemble*
Bob	6	7	5
Pat	3	4	4
Mel	1	6	4

- Bob, clearly, has an absolute disadvantage in all three tasks. If Bob is drawing a salary, should he be assigned a task—or told to sit idle?
- Assign each of the three tasks to an individual, in order to minimize the total time required to assemble one bookshelf. What principle did you employ?

7.7 CONCLUSION

Managers always consider alternatives in their decision choices. They may do so intuitively, balancing costs and benefits (including the hidden costs and benefits described in Chapter 6). Or they may use analytical tools like those described in this chapter, quantifying opportunity costs and relative prices or values. They may accept existing constraints in their trade-off choices. Or they may defy them and boldly push their organization's capabilities outward, in every direction. Ideally they will be skilled at both.

According to a Hebrew saying, smart managers know how to escape from tight spots that wise managers avoid. One may adapt this to read: Smart managers optimize trade-offs that wise, bold ones defy.

In the next chapter, the topic is cost functions. We examine how a deep understanding of the various cost concepts—average, marginal, total, fixed, variable, and so on—can yield surprisingly powerful insights into the future course of a company and the industry in which it competes.

Readers are invited to view 'Pillars of Profit: Segment #3, Tradeoffs: Optimising and Eliminating them' in the accompanying CD.

CASE STUDY 7.1

Kodak's Trade-off Dilemma*

Case study discussion topics

1. Eastman Kodak had three reasons for acquiring Sterling Drug; and Sterling Drug had three reasons for wanting to be acquired by Kodak. What were these reasons for each company? How valid do you think each reason was?
2. Why do you think Eastman Kodak was surprised to learn that developing a successful drug and bringing it to market, after its potential was identified, could cost up to $500 million?
3. What were Kay Whitmore's three key trade-off decisions?
4. What was George Fisher's key trade-off decision? What were his reasons?
5. A new trade-off decision that Kodak is now struggling with is: conventional imaging versus digital imaging? Why is Kodak finding the transition to this new technology so difficult?

In 1988, Eastman Kodak Corp. (EKC) acquired Sterling Drug Inc. for $5.1 billion. Since the late 1970s, EKC had evinced interest in the biosciences and pharmaceutical markets with the formation of its Clinical Products unit. In 1984, EKC organized its Life Sciences Division in an

*This case study is a summary of the case authored by Lance Drummond.

Case study 7.1 continued

Case study 7.1 continued

attempt to expand its participation in the $110 billion worldwide pharmaceutical market. Prior to the acquisition of Sterling, most of its efforts had been focused on joint ventures and equity investments, but generally EKC was a minor player. By adding Sterling (which was enjoying one of its best years in recent history as can be seen from Table 7.1.1) to its portfolio, EKC became one of the top 20 drug companies in the world.

Table 7.1.1
Sterling Drug Inc. financial summary

	1986	*1985*	*1984*	*1983*	*1982*
Sales Growth (%)	13.5	1.6	–1.8	6.2	0.0
Income Growth (%)	11.8	8.5	6.8	3.1	0.0
Gross Margin (%) of Sales	66.1	65.1	64.1	62.7	60.9
SG&A (%) of Sales	46.0	45.6	44.7	44.2	41.7
R&D (%) of Sales	5.2	4.8	4.9	4.4	4.1
Income (%) of Sales	8.6	8.7	8.2	7.5	7.7

There were three primary reasons why EKC acquired Sterling:

1. The company was looking to reduce its dependence on the increasingly competitive traditional film business.
2. Pharmaceuticals appeared to be a natural extension of its chemical base, EKC having amassed a library of over 500,000 chemical compounds.
3. Sterling would provide an efficient delivery system for turning those compounds into profits.

Sterling's willingness to be acquired by EKC was driven primarily by:

1. EKC's strong cash flow from its traditional film business that could be used to fund more aggressive research.
2. The price EKC was willing to pay—$5.1 billion—met and exceeded Sterling's expected value.
3. EKC's apparent commitment to become a major player in the pharmaceutical business meant they were less likely to shed Sterling's assets and resources.

Almost immediately after acquiring Sterling, things started to come unglued. Competitive pressures within the film business intensified. This put significant pressure on price, drove gross margins down for

Case study 7.1 continued

Case study 7.1 continued

EKC followed by declining net income and cash flow (Table 7.1.2). The film market in developed countries became flat and in some countries started to decline. This was partially due to technology substitution (video cameras) and the start of a recession that affected disposable income used to purchase discretionary items such as film.

Sterling's R&D pipeline was marginal at best, due to its below-industry average investment in R&D (5 per cent of sales versus the industry average of 9–12 per cent). In addition, it was no longer intuitively obvious which of its 500,000 chemical compounds could be turned into the next blockbuster drug, without significant investment from EKC. Indeed, as the company later learned, it would cost $100 to $500 million and an average cycle time of 10 years to introduce a new drug. Finally, the overall decline of drug prices driven primarily by healthcare reform initiative reduced Sterling's profitability. As debt soared and cash flow plummeted, the then CEO Kay R. Whitmore, made a series of economic trade-off decisions. These trade-off choices will not be analysed as part of this case study, but it is important to note the key decisions taken:

1. Three restructurings were done, costing over $2 billion, reducing EKC's headcount by approximately 20,000 people since 1988, in order to improve productivity.
2. The chemical business, a $3.8 billion division, was spun off as Eastman Chemical Company (ECC), because EKC was unable to feed its appetite for cash to sustain growth. As a separate entity, ECC would have better access to capital markets and create more value for EKC shareowners.

These decisions however were not sufficient for EKC's board of directors. Whitmore was asked to step down from his position as Chairman and CEO in 1993 and was replaced by George M. C. Fisher

Table 7.1.2
Eastman Kodak–financial overview, selected years: 1975, 1980–84, 1990, 1995 and 2005 (US$)

	2005	*1995*	*1990*	*1984*	*1983*	*1982*	*1981*	*1980*	*1975*
Revenues	14.3 b.	16.8 b.	18.5 b.	10.2 b.	10.8 b.	10.3 b.	9.7 b.	8.0 b.	4.6 b.
Net Profit	–1,362 m.	557 m.	529 m.	565 m.	1,162m.	1,239m.	1,153m.	1,000 m.	630 m.
Market Value	8.5 b.	18.1 b.	12.9 b.	–	–	–	–	–	–
Fortune 500 Rank	155	143	18	30	26	28	29	30	32

Source: Fortune 500 (various years).
Note: m = million, b = billion.

Case study 7.1 continued

Case study 7.1 continued

whose first major decision in 1994 was to sell all of EKC's non-imaging businesses (approximately $3.7 billion in sales). George Fisher essentially made an economic trade-off decision when he decided to divest EKC's non-imaging businesses. He balanced gain and pain in a manner that would leave EKC in better health with the most gain for the least pain.

EKC's expected gains from the divestiture:

1. An improved balance sheet by significantly lowering debt—expected value from sale of non-imaging assets should exceed $5.2 billion.
2. Improved quality of future borrowings due to EKC's reduced leverage position.
3. Greater ability to exploit its imaging strengths by focusing all resources in that area.

The pains:

1. Loss of a profitable growth business that had recently started to contribute cash.
2. Disruption throughout the company caused by increased uncertainty affecting employees' livelihood.
3. Loss of access to a readily available talent pool.

Trade-off decisions have a time dimension. In 1988, EKC essentially made a decision to trade-off imaging for health, given the existing market conditions of both industries. In 1994, EKC made another announcement, which appeared to be the opposite of the trade-off choice made six years ago. Therefore, trade-offs tend to be made based on existing and forecast market conditions at specific points in time.

EKC's task of creating and managing trade-offs was related to the economic idea of efficiency. The company's inability to eliminate X-inefficiency and allocative inefficiency played a key role in Fisher's analysis leading up to his decision. Given the resources of EKC (over $20 billion in assets), could EKC have profited more by eliminating its X-inefficiency (failure to attain its efficiency frontier)? Indeed, had EKC been able to improve productivity, grow profitably, reduce debt and increase shareowner value, thereby achieving its full potential where the marginal opportunity cost equals the relative value line (Figure 7.1.1), the trade-off would most likely have been different. The company may have decided to keep its non-imaging businesses and perhaps acquire another

Case study 7.1 continued

Case study 7.1 continued

pharmaceutical company and shift the trade-off curve northeast (Figure 7.1.2). One can only speculate what could have happened had X-inefficiency been eliminated or at least significantly reduced.

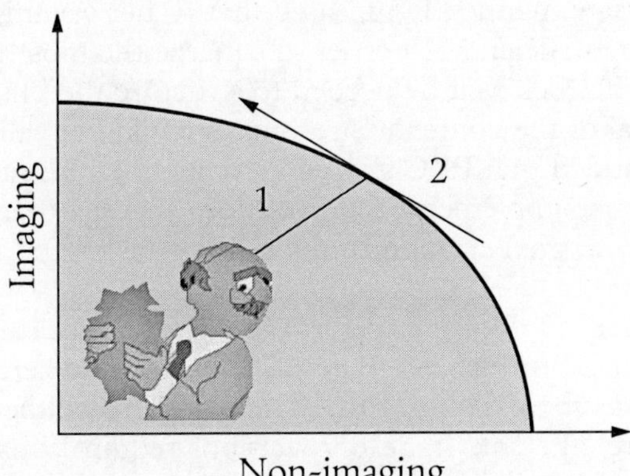

Kodak Strategy

Stage 1: Become efficient (cost reduction).
Stage 2: Refocus business on imaging: Sell Sterling Drug, non-imaging units.

Figure 7.1.1
Kodak trade-off decisions

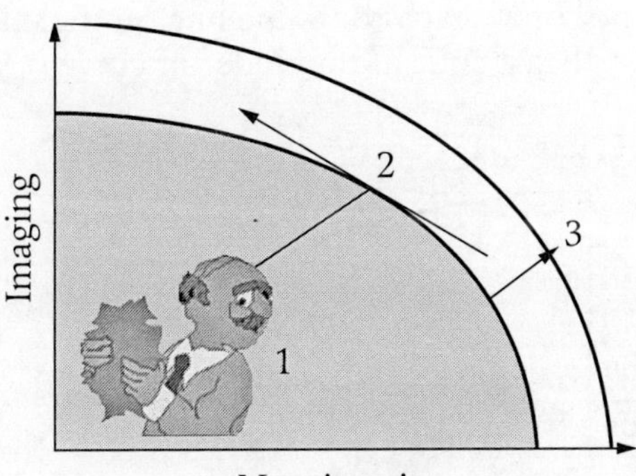

Kodak Strategy:

Stage 1: Become efficient (cost reduction).
Stage 2: Refocus business on imaging: Sell Sterling Drug, non-imaging units.
Stage 3: Growth—shift trade-off curve outward.

Figure 7.1.2
Trade-off curve shifts outward

Case study 7.1 continued

Case study 7.1 continued

EKC was unable to eliminate X-inefficiency, but the company faced an equally difficult task in reducing or eliminating allocative inefficiency (choice of the wrong strategic point on the frontier). In allocative inefficiency, resources—labour, capital, management time—are allocated in an inappropriate manner. It appeared that Fisher was highly concerned about allocative inefficiency. In order to squeeze the most that he could out of EKC, Fisher believed he needed to structure the business so that the full potential of the company's resources could be realized. He, therefore, concluded that EKC should commit its entire resource base to imaging and hence implemented a divestiture strategy that would provide each business with greater opportunity to grow faster and realize its potential.

Is Fisher's trade-off choice going to allow EKC to realize its potential? Only time will tell. But Fisher's trade-off choice would certainly have a long-term and lasting effect on EKC. The company will be smaller but most likely more efficient. Trade-off decisions require constant testing and reconsideration. Therefore, this issue will have to be revisited sometime in the near future. In fact, Fisher will immediately begin to face a new set of tradeoff choices between traditional film and digital imaging (Figure 7.1.3). Fisher clearly articulated his vision to all key stakeholders (customers, employees, shareowners, suppliers, etc.). His vision appeared to be a 'Back to the Future' strategy. However, EKC clearly has a comparative advantage in imaging. If EKC is able to reduce or eliminate its inefficiencies (X and allocative), it will not only reach the value line on the efficiency frontier, but will cause a northeast shift in the trade-off curve.

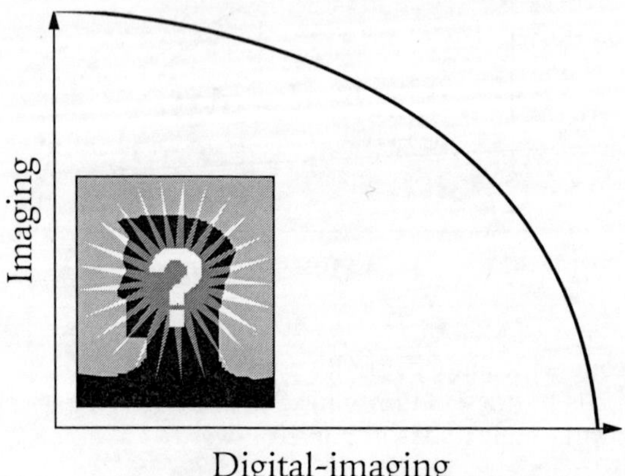

Figure 7.1.3
Choosing between conventional imaging (silver halide film) and digital imaging

CASE STUDY 7.2

Tata Consultancy Services—Trade-offs*

Roshan Kumar, the Relationship Manager at TCS, was assigned the task of taking charge of the Coopers & Brand (C&B) account, which was among the top 25 customers of TCS. Although, TCS and C&B had had a good working relationship over the past three years, given the competitive environment in which C&B operated, the C&B management had began to express concerns on two key issues which they felt TCS needed to address to sustain the relationship. Roshan was made responsible for setting things in order with regard to the C&B account.

TCS is one of the world's leading Information Technology (IT) consulting services, business process outsourcing and engineering services organization. With annual sales of $2.2 billion and net profits exceeding $500 million, the company employs over 50,000 people worldwide who work out of 32 countries. TCS services its clients through its network of delivery centres present in 10 different cities in India and other countries including USA, Canada, Brazil, Uruguay, UK, Hungary, China, Japan and Australia.

With annual sales exceeding $20 billion and operations in more than 50 countries, C&B is a leading global financial services firm with a commanding presence in several areas such as investment banking, institutional securities sales and trading, and investment and global asset management services. TCS has over the years grown to be the largest IT outsourcing vendor for C&B. TCS has two Offshore Delivery Centres (ODCs) in India—one at Pune and the other at Chennai. The two ODCs ensure that C&B is well served. TCS and C&B have a strong working relationship, with the former executing IT projects for multiple divisions of the latter. In short, TCS provides critical solutions and support to C&B's businesses worldwide.

In a meeting between Roshan and Bob Goldberg, the resident C&B manager in India, Bob had expressed two key concerns:

1. Need for increased support from TCS in handling the C&B account to meet increased service levels C&B customers expected from it.

*This case draws on the ideas presented in the case 'C&B Global Account Management' written in September 2005 by Susheel Vasudevan, Tata Consultancy Services. Names and other details have been disguised to protect confidentiality.

Case study 7.2 continued

Case study 7.2 continued

2. C&B expected TCS to do more to deliver value to the former through its various solutions, and was not very enthusiastic about paying more for these services, as it had offers from several other global IT service companies.

In addressing the first of C&B's concerns, Roshan faced the trade-off choice between cost and service quality. Roshan was keen to provide even better service quality and support to C&B and contemplated Bob's suggestion of providing a global 24 × 7 support for one of the settlement applications of C&B. As per the suggestion, instead of operating three shifts from a single India-based delivery centre (Chennai) for the new application as was being contemplated so far, it was better to have a two shift—two centre (2×2) strategy for this support. If TCS could, for example, have one delivery centre in Chennai and the other in North America, the two shifts to be operated in Chennai could support users of C&B in Tokyo, Hong Kong and London (morning) and similarly the two shifts in North America could support users in London (afternoon), New York and Tokyo (early morning). This way TCS would be able to provide C&B round-the-clock global support without having to run the third (night) shift in India. Setting up of such a dedicated centre in North America would require TCS to invest in additional (and costlier) manpower and infrastructure, thereby escalating costs.

Roshan faced a second trade-off choice between price and delivering value to C&B. With all the skills that TCS had in the company, there was no doubt that they could deliver extraordinary value to the customer. 'But at what price?', wondered Roshan. He and his group manager of 'Straight Through Processing' had come up with a few ideas for delivering new elements of value to C&B. One such proposal was to help improve the stability of the IT environment of C&B's 'Fixed Income Division' through process consulting. The Fixed Income Division did not even have data to verify and demonstrate their problem. As a first step, TCS decided that it could develop a set of business measures to determine the stability of the IT application and IT infrastructure of the Fixed Income Division, followed by an analysis of the data collected and finally take a decision on the various six sigma projects that need to be initiated within the division to improve the system performance. Roshan was confident that C&B would be willing to give TCS a chance to do this work and provide many other value-adding solutions to the company. Roshan was also aware of C&B's unwillingness to increase the price it paid to TCS for its services. The question before Roshan was how to do the trade-off between

Case study 7.2 continued

Case study 7.2 continued

providing superior value to the client and ensuring that TCS obtains a higher return for the higher value delivered.

After holding several meetings and discussions with the different TCS managers handling the C&B relationship and delivery managers in the Pune and Chennai ODCs, Roshan and the team were successful in *optimizing the trade-off choices*. As a result of this analysis and its subsequent implementation, the value of the work outsourced by C&B annually to TCS continued to grow.

Notes

1. N. Gregory Mankiw was the head of President George W. Bush's Council of Economic Advisors, on leave from Harvard University's Economics department. His textbook *Principles of Economics* His 10 laws are: 1. People face trade-offs. 2. The cost of something is what you give up to get it. 3. Rational people think at the margin. 4. People respond to incentives. 5. Trade can make everyone better off. 6. Markets are usually a good way to organize economic activity. 7. Governments can sometimes improve market outcomes. 8. A country's standard of living depends on its ability to produce goods and services. 9. Prices rise when the government prints too much money. 10. Society faces a short-term trade-off between inflation and unemployment (cited in Rob Norton, *Fortune*, 13 October 1997).
2. An account of Kim and Mauborgne's 'value innovation' is found in W. Chan Kim and Renee Mauborgne, 'Value Innovation: The Strategic Logic of High Growth', *Harvard Business Review*, 1997 (reprinted in 'top line growth' Best-of-1997 July 2004).
3. Rob Norton, article in *Fortune*, 13 October 1997.
4. The book by Hampden-Turner and Trompenaars is *Bulding Cross-Cultural Competence: How to Create Wealth from Conflicting Values* (Wiley: New York, 2000).
5. 'Even Swaps' is recounted in John s. Hammond, Ralph Keeney and Howard Raiffa, 'Even Swaps: A Rational Method for Making Trade-offs', *Harvard Business Review*, March–April 1998.
6. The even-swaps exercise (Intel's Speed vs. Battery life) is based on *Harvard Business Review* case study 9-396-307, 'Exercises on tradeoffs and conflicting objectives'.

Chapter 8
Cost functions: 'Survival of the fittest'

Each organic being is striving to increase in a geometrical ratio ... each at some period of its life, during some season of the year, during each generation or at intervals, has to struggle for life and to suffer great destruction .... The vigorous, the healthy, and the happy survive and multiply.

—Charles Darwin[1]

LEARNING OBJECTIVES After you read this chapter, you should understand:

- **How Darwin's 'survival of the fittest' and economics' 'theory of fierce competition' are related**
- **What average, marginal and total costs are**
- **What is the difference between fixed and variable costs**
- **Why firms in fiercely competitive markets practise marginal cost pricing**
- **When plants should be closed immediately tomorrow, operated for a year and then closed or operated forever**
- **How Wal-Mart's business model is built on three core types of cost reduction**
- **Why average cost curves tend to be U-shaped and why and how they must be 'flattened'**
- **How to use activity-based management to slash fixed costs**
- **Why innovation is crucial in a Darwinian competitive market**

TOOL #4 Cost functions

8.1 INTRODUCTION

Nothing in the world is more useful, it is said, than good theory and nothing, one might add, is less useful, or more destructive, than bad theory.

This chapter applies what we believe is good theory—the economic theory of highly competitive markets and the theory of cost functions—to building and running a business that achieves sustained profitability in the long run.

We will proceed from a set of rather uninteresting definitions of costs, to the economic version of Darwin's 'survival of the fittest'.

'Each slight variation, if useful, is preserved,' Darwin noted in 1859.

Only living things—plants and animals—able to change and adapt to their changing environment survive to reproduce themselves. Darwin was referring to variations in species. But products, too, compete. In the age of globalization and global competition, managers increasingly face a fierce process of Darwinian 'natural selection', in which only products that are supremely suited to their customers' needs and wants endure and prevail. In fact, as we will see later, Darwin himself got the idea for his path-breaking theory from an economist.

In business, the impartial cruelty of natural selection is only partly softened by the fact that only products and companies die, rather than people. People, in fact, do lose their jobs in this process, though it can be claimed there are more winners than losers in the long run. Herbert Spencer, to whom Darwin attributes the phrase 'survival of the fittest', applied it literally to human society. 'We have unmistakable proof', he wrote approvingly, 'that throughout all past time, there has been ceaseless devouring of the weak by the strong.' Earlier, he had written, 'the poverty of the incapable ... and the starvation of the idle ... are the decrees of a large, farseeing benevolence.'[2] While few would embrace Spencer's extreme vision of capitalism, it is hard to deny the fruits of global competition, even while noting the suffering of those unable or unwilling to pluck them.

Good theory?

How does one know whether theory is good or bad? The test commonly used in science is that of prediction. Build a set of definitions, frame a hypothesis based on them, then make a prediction that derives from the hypothesis—what should we find, if the hypothesis is true? Next, gather data. If the data is not consistent with what we expect to find, then we reject the original hypothesis and start from scratch. This approach, known as the scientific method, has great power as a system for learning about the world (see Chapter 11).

But in management education, a different criterion for good theory applies. One of Harvard Business School's early Professors Arthur Stone Dewing, once said, '[Management education] asks not how a person may be trained to know ... but how a person can be trained to *act*.' That is why we prefer the social psychologist Kurt Lewin's test for good-or-bad theory: A theory is good if you produce the desired result when you use, or act upon, it. *Creating,* Lewin said, *not predicting, is the true test of validity.*[3]

The reader will test the bread-and-butter notion of economics—the theory of competitive markets—according to the insights it provides for working managers struggling to compete successfully against their counterparts.

8.2 CONNECTIONS: FROM MALTHUS TO GLOBALIZATION

Author James Burke once wrote a celebrated column called *Connections* in 'Scientific American', in which he showed links among seemingly-unrelated discoveries and inventions across continents and centuries.[4] A kind of *Connection* exists between economics and Darwin. How are the 18th century economist J. M. Malthus, Charles Darwin's *Origin of Species* and the fall of the Berlin Wall on 9 November 1989, marking the rise of the global economy, connected?

In his celebrated *Essay*, written in 1798, Malthus expressed the pessimistic view that mankind could never sustain a standard of living above subsistence. His reasoning: If there is an economic surplus (income per head above that needed to sustain life), it will lead to a higher birth rate, lower death rate and hence to population growth. But, Malthus showed, because of agricultural 'diminishing returns' the incremental, or 'marginal', food output from an extra pair of hands working on an acre of land tends to decline, the more 'hands' there are. Overpopulation, then, creates rising competitive pressure to obtain food resources, creating many disaster scenarios, including wars and famines and plagues, in what he called 'the perpetual struggle for room and food' (reminiscent of Darwin's 'struggle for existence'). Population then declines to the level sustainable with available resources. This dismal view of human progress led to economics being labelled 'the dismal science'.

In the middle of the 19th century, scientist Charles Darwin travelled the world on *The Beagle.* He saw many different species and wondered how they originated. In his book *Origin of Species* Darwin explained that all living things compete for scarce resources, just as Malthus had said about humans. Species best able to change and best adapted to their surroundings survive to reproduce.

> Mutations occur. Most are not successful. But once in a while, a mutation will give a living creature an advantage, making it better able to compete than others. This helps it reach reproduction and create more of itself.

Darwin himself attributed the idea behind his theory, known as 'natural selection', or 'survival of the fittest' (a phrase he himself did not invent) to Malthus.

On 9 November 1989, the Berlin Wall fell. This was a signal that the entire world was embracing the economic notion of 'survival of the fittest' (free and open competition in free markets) as its organizing principle. A link, or connection, was thus established, between Malthus, Darwin and the Fall of the Wall. The world now organizes not only its economy, but also its society, around the notion of competition.

Allow entrepreneurs and managers to create innovations—economics' version of 'mutations', or new ideas for products and services—and let competition in the marketplace choose among them. The 'fittest' ideas win, when people 'vote' for them by buying them with their money. Profit, then, becomes the signal that a product mutation (like the Formule 1 hotel chain) is successful and suited to its environment. Note the resemblance between the economic democracy of Darwinian competition and the political democracy of one-person-one-vote.

A deep understanding of this important economic theory is vital for all engineer–managers, because during their lifetime they will doubtless experience this model first-hand. Understanding how it works and how to use its key metrics may be crucial for the business to survive, along with the jobs of those employed in it.

Case study: Wal-Mart

A breakthrough innovation can quickly convert a competitive market into one dominated by one or two large players. Wal-Mart, the world's largest company (as measured by sales revenue) is an example. Once, Americans bought much of their goods and services at small retail establishments (locally owned drugstores, grocery stories, or convenience stores) and at chains of discount department stores. Then, Sam Walton, in Bentonville, Arkansas (to this day, Wal-Mart's global headquarters) invented a new business model based on one simple principle: 'delivering low prices by concentrating on lowering operating costs', using information technology and cost-reduction through size and scale, in huge 100,000 square feet stores sited outside population centres. Today, Wal-Mart generates one out of every 10 dollars in US retail sales in its 3,000 US stores; 30 per cent of the US population shops at Wal-Mart. Wal-Mart now sells 25 per cent of all toys and 20 per cent of clothing in the US and is rapidly expanding into groceries. The Wal-Mart 'mutation' has made other business models into obsolete dinosaurs. Many retail chains and single stores have closed down as a result.

Their owners have lost while consumers have gained, by gaining a wide variety of choice at lower prices.

8.3 COST FUNCTIONS

The key metrics in fiercely competitive markets are those related to cost and cost functions. So, as usual, we begin with some definitions: three ways to measure costs (total, average, marginal) and two different types of costs.

DEFINITIONS

Three Ways to Measure Costs

- **Total Costs: The total amount of money spent on producing a good or service.**
- **Average Costs: Total Costs divided by the number of units of the good produced.**
- **Marginal Costs: The increment, or addition, to Total Costs, caused by making one more unit of the good. The term 'marginal' derives from the phrase 'at the margin', meaning, at the last unit; marginal here means not 'unimportant', as in common language, but 'at the edge', as in the margins or shoulders of the highway. Indeed, the 'marginal' or last unit is often the most important, because it shows the current trend of costs.**

DEFINITIONS

Two Types of Costs

- **Variable Costs: Costs that originate as a direct result of production, and change when the amount of production changes (e.g., raw materials, and labour costs for assembly workers).**
- **Fixed Costs: Costs that do not change when production changes, but remain constant (e.g., building rent, managerial personnel).**

One last definition is needed, that of 'cost functions'.

- **Cost Function: A function in mathematics is a kind of 'map', mapping the link between one variable and another. Cost functions 'map' from the amount an organisation produces in units (cars, phone calls, dollars of sales) to the cost of making and selling the product.**

8.4 THE CASE OF THE DATA THAT DID NOT BARK

It is ironic that the most intriguing, and dramatic, of economic theories, that of competitive markets, is often taught or explained in a very humdrum fashion, that loses its flavour and excitement. To remedy this, let us join the famed detective Sherlock Holmes and his assistant Dr Watson in solving The Case Of The Data That Did Not Bark.

Like all living things, Holmes has had to adapt to changing times or disappear. So seeking competitive advantage in the overcrowded private investigator business, he added business consulting to his sleuthing skills. In his most famous recent case, the two were combined in classic fashion.

Someone was murdering the boulangerie (bakery) owners, one after another, in the picturesque French village of St Paul de Vence, a lovely beautifully-preserved town perched on a mountain, just northeast of Nice. The Chamber of Commerce called in Holmes. Maigrit was considered, but Holmes' understanding of management tools tipped the scales.

The data

'This is absolutely all the data I could glean,' said Dr Watson, Holmes' faithful assistant. 'I have reason to believe that the six total cost numbers [Table 8.1] reflect the cost situation of each of the bakeries in the town. *But frankly Holmes,'* said Watson, *'the data do not bark.* They are too sparse. We can, I'm afraid, learn nothing from them.'

Table 8.1
Holmes' basic data
Cost data for typical bakery in St Paul de Vence

Loaves per day (cartons)	*Total cost (old French francs,'000)*
0	10
1	15
2	19
3	24
4	30
5	40

Action learning

Be Your own Holmes

For your own organization (it need not be a for-profit organization—it could be a school, or a club) collect data on costs, for several data points (levels of service or output), as in Table 8.1. As Holmes pursues the murderer in The Case Of The Data That Did Not Bark, pursue his reasoning for your own organization—though, hopefully, without the need to find the perpetrator of a crime.

Holmes looked at the numbers carefully. He scratched a few calculations on the back of his National Insurance envelope (his pension was getting increasingly smaller, he thought), sucked on his unlit pipe, and then announced: Quite to the contrary, my dear Dr Watson. The data bark rather loudly. I have already solved this case using the basic principles of economic competition. Inform the French. And Watson: the barking dog metaphor is rather old tired, I fear. Everyone uses it. Please retire it.

Rebuked, Watson looked stunned. He sat down and listened to Holmes' logic unfold before him. When Holmes was finished, it all seemed crystal clear to the faithful Watson. He was happy that the six cost figures he felt were so inadequate had in fact told the entire story to the economics-savvy Holmes.

Spreading the overhead

Fixed costs are rather high, mused Holmes. *They are the costs you incur even if you do not bake a single loaf of bread,* Pay rent and so on. So total fixed costs are 10. We can fill in this column (Table 8.2) as well as the total variable costs which are by definition the difference between total costs and total fixed costs. So from only six cost figures, we have now deduced a total of 18 figures. Elementary.

Table 8.2
Holmes' deduction of full total cost data

Loaves per day (Cartons)	*Total cost (TC)*	*Total fixed cost (TFC)*	*Total variable cost (TVC)*
		(old French francs, '000)	
0	10	10	0
1	15	10	5
2	19	10	9
3	24	10	14
4	30	10	20
5	40	10	30

Now, said Holmes, we must look carefully at unit costs (or average costs), found by dividing total costs by the number of cartons, to get per-carton cost (Table 8.3). This is most interesting. Note, he said, the phenomenon of 'spreading the overhead'. By spreading the fixed costs of 10 over larger numbers of output, average fixed costs (AFC) decline (Figure 8.1). Many businesses (for instance, pharmaceuticals, which spend heavily on R&D, a component of fixed costs) have high 'overhead'. For their products to be profitable, they have to sell high volumes of them, to 'spread the overhead' across large numbers of output.

Table 8.3
Holmes' deduction of total, average and marginal costs

Loaves (Cartons)	*Total cost (TC)*	*Total fixed cost (TFC)*	*Total variable cost (TVC)*	*Av. fixed cost (AFC)*	*Av. variable cost (AVC)*	*Av. total cost (ATC)*	*Marginal cost (MC)*
	(old French francs,'000)						
0	10	10	0	–			
1	15	10	5	10	5	15	5
2	19	10	9	5	4.5	9.5	4
3	24	10	14	3.3	4.6	8	5
4	30	10	20	2.5	5	7.5	6
5	40	10	30	2	6	8	10

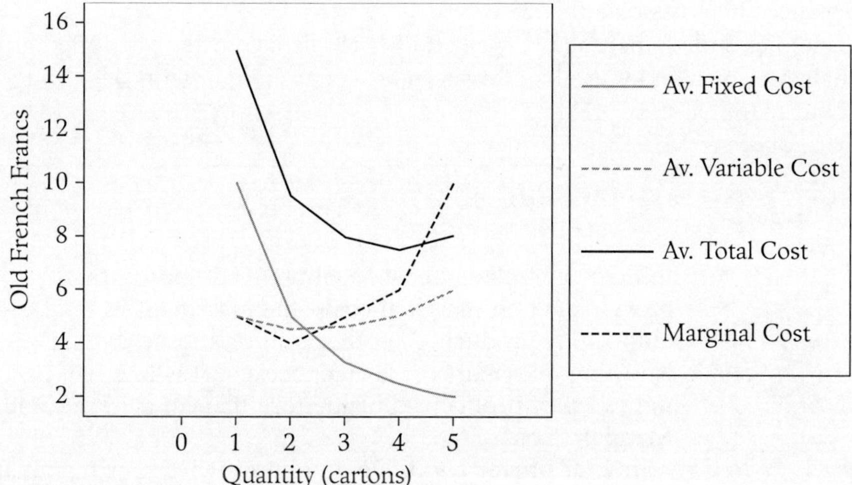

Figure 8.1
Holmes' cost functions (for typical St Paul de Vence Boulangerie)

Marginal costs hold the key

I presume these bakeries are efficiently run, said Holmes, otherwise they would have gone bankrupt or sold out. I therefore know how many cartons of bread per day each is making.

How can you possibly know that? asked Watson. None of the boulangeries would reveal this.

Elementary, said Holmes. The price of a carton of baguettes is 6,000 old French francs. True, said Watson. And that price is set by competitive market forces, beyond the control of any individual boulangerie, Holmes continued. Agreed, said Watson.

So, continued Holmes, a bakery will make and sell an additional carton, only if its price exceeds *the cost of making that particular carton.* Which is the 'marginal cost', said Watson—the incremental cost of that additional carton, measured as the difference in the total cost of, say, 3 cartons and 4. If you get 6,000 francs for it, and it costs you 7—it does not pay to make it. If you get 6 and it costs you 5, you make a profit of 1.

In economics, this is known as marginal-cost pricing. It is a powerful management principle. Produce up to the point where the price of your product equals your marginal cost. Any less, and you can increase total profit. Any more, and your total profit declines.

Therefore, said Holmes, pacing restlessly, and referring to Table 8.3 and Figure 8.1, each boulangerie will produce 4 cartons per day. The price and marginal cost of the fourth carton are both 6.

Brilliant, Watson said, but how does knowledge of what each boulangerie produces help us solve this case?

Holmes smiled inscrutably, walked over to his favourite overstuffed arm chair, sat down and was silent for several suspenseful moments. He thought about marginal-cost pricing.

Action learning

Find Your Marginal Cost

In many companies, cost accountants do not normally provide data on marginal cost—the increment to total cost induced by producing another unit or another batch. Knowing marginal cost is vital, because it is one half of the two part profit-maximizing formula: equate Price and Marginal Cost.

In your organization: Do you know what your marginal costs are? If not, can you calculate it, using average-cost data normally generated by the cost accountants? Is your MC rising or declining, as more units are produced?

Another famous corollary of economic theory is that investment in added production capacity is worthwhile, even BEFORE the plant reaches its minimum-average cost optimum. Such investment, however, depends crucially on demand being sufficient to absorb the output produced by such extra capacity.

Regarding overcapacity problems: How has your firm managed the dilemma, between: (*a*) the high rate of return on investment in added capacity in good times, when you can sell more and are able to expand production, and (*b*) the negative return on such investment when the economy contracts and demand declines? (See Case Study 8.1 for a real-world example.)

Case study: Airlines and phone companies

Modern air travel owes much to entrepreneur Juan Trippe, founder of Pan American Air Lines. Trippe sought to make air travel affordable for all and global in nature. He invented tourist class and slashed New York to London fares. He was tossed out of the International Air Transport Association cartel but ultimately all airlines fell in line. But Trippe was still inventing Darwinian 'mutations'. He understood that creating a mass market for air travel meant cutting prices, and that, in turn, meant slashing costs. He worked with Boeing to build an aircraft (the 747 Jumbo) that would cut seat-mile costs by 30 per cent from their current level of 6 cents.

Airline deregulation meant that anyone could rent a few planes and launch an airline. This led to fierce competition. Some airlines began practising marginal-cost pricing. They first sold 'expensive' seats (to business travellers), then sold remaining seats at ever lower prices, right down to the point where the ticket brought only the marginal cost (the incremental cost of flying that passenger). Soon other airlines sprang up that knew how to slash costs—Ryan Air, Easy Jet, and so on. The Darwinian model of 'survival of the fittest' kicked in, as terrorism and high jet fuel prices cut demand for travel; old-line airlines unable to cut costs, burdened with expensive labour contracts and redundant labour went into bankruptcy.

The first of these was Pan Am. Its founder Juan Trippe did not keep pace with changing market conditions; Pan Am expired in 1991.

Telecommunication companies face a different problem. They are an infrastructure industry—once phone lines are in place, it costs very little to supply an additional phone conversation, whose marginal cost is near zero. In fact, it costs more for companies to bill for that call than it does for them to supply it. But putting those lines in place is expensive. Sprint, for instance, spent over $1 billion in laying fiber-optic cable in the US. Marginal cost pricing suggests pricing at zero. That, of course, brings zero revenue. So telecommunication companies are searching for innovative pricing models based on 'subscriptions'—flat fees that give subscribers almost unlimited call, voice and data services during a month. Another feature of infrastructure industries, where fixed costs

Case study continued

Case study continued

dominate variable ones, is that of innovation. Once the infrastructure is in place, providing higher volumes of services costs very little extra. So high profit accrues to companies able to innovate, and invent new types of services that generate revenue from the in-place infrastructure. SMS (short message service up to 160 characters) is an example. Invented a decade ago, today 360 billion text messages are sent annually from cell phones—a billion a day, or one for every six people on earth.[5] Because the marginal cost of providing an SMS is near-zero, so is the price—yet billions of SMS messages generate substantial revenue in aggregate.

Source: Richard Branson, *Time Magazine*, Special Issue, 'Builders and Titans', 7 December 1998, p. 135. (Richard Branson is the founder of Virgin Airlines.)

Case study: Northwest Airlines

One of America's oldest (and fourth largest) airlines, Northwest faces bankruptcy. Its $227 million operating profit in 2nd Quarter 2004 was due mainly to asset sales and a government handout of $209 million. In 2002 Northwest lost $798 million. To survive, it has to buy new planes (Airbus A330) that burn 30 per cent less fuel than existing aging DC-10s—but that takes money, which it does not have. Northwest wants to slash $950 million, or 24 per cent, from the pay of unionized employees. But low-cost airlines with which it competes are non-union. Northwest may do what other airlines have tried—enter bankruptcy under Chapter 11 and use the threat of that, or bankruptcy itself, to batter workers into accepting lower wages. Changing market conditions for air travel occurred years ago. Many of the old-line airlines have been very slow to react to them.

Note: Data on Northwest Airlines is from 'Northwest: No Profit Predictions', *Business Week*, 12 August 2003.

Do-or-die

Holmes at times was insufferable, purposely prolonging the suspense or those for whom he was solving a crime. But now, he tired of the game and quickly laid out his reasoning to the patient Dr Watson.

It is a case of do-or-die, Holmes said. The boulangeries in St Paul de Vence are each making 6 (old French francs ['000] per carton) × 4 cartons = 24 old French francs ('000) daily in revenue. In this, they are making an operating profit of 24 – 20 = 4 because their revenues exceed their total variable cost of 20.

Excellent, exclaimed Watson, who himself dreamed of owning a little bakery.

No, awful, said Holmes. You see, they have fixed costs of 10. And in the end, they do not make sufficient profit to pay for them. And remember, Watson, those fixed costs include the opportunity cost of the invested capital—the money each owner sank into ovens, kitchens, and other equipment. So each boulangerie is not achieving its 'hurdle rate' (see Chapter 6). The net income is a miserable loss of 6: operating profit of 4 minus the fixed costs of 10.

Well, blustered Watson, why then do the bakers bother getting up so early in the morning (they all rise at 3:30 A.M. so that the peaceful citizens of St Paul de Vence can have their fresh-baked baguettes at 6 A.M.)? Why not stay in bed?

Because, explained Holmes patiently, they have to pay their fixed costs of 10 in any event, whether they rise and shine (and bake) or loll in bed. So the bitter choice is between working hard and losing only 6 each day or not working and losing 10.

What will happen? asked Watson.

According to the economic theory of competitive markets, said Holmes, which closely resembles Darwin's theory, there are insufficient resources to 'feed' all the bakeries, or in other words, there are too many bakeries. Some will go bankrupt and disappear. This will reduce the supply of bread and lead to a rise in its price. Ultimately, in the long run, the price will rise so that bakeries can just cover their average total costs, including the opportunity cost of capital.

What if *too many* bakeries disappear? asked Watson.

In that case, Watson, explained Holmes, there will be excess profits. The price of bread will (temporarily) exceed the average total cost. The capital invested by the bakery owners will begin bringing an economic rent, or Economic Value Added. And we know what *that* means.

Yes, said Watson. New bakeries will be set up, attracted by the lure of profit. Supply of bread will rise. That will drive down the price and eventually eliminate the economic rent. In precisely the manner that population grows when there is a surplus of food, whether of humans, rabbits or kangaroos.

Of course, said Holmes. That brings us to the resolution of the murder case. It is 'do-or-die'. Do, meaning existing bakery owners must reduce their costs, become more efficient and eliminate their short term losses of 6. Die, meaning one of those bakery shop owners is either unable or unwilling to do this, and is trying to help his own survival by violently eliminating some of the competition, 'die'.

But who? said Watson. Who?

I suspect the boulangerie on Rue de la Place, said Holmes. I bought a loaf there yesterday. It contained margarine rather than butter, and tasted as if it were made of frozen dough. Anyone who would do that, would not hesitate to commit murder in order to survive. Case closed.

Action Learning

Closely Watched Costs

The first author has this personal experience to narrate:

> I use two post office branches. One has three workers, who are pleasant but rather slow, and the lines are often long. Another, with equal volume of traffic, has a single worker, who is remarkably fast and efficient. Lines are long but move very quickly. She is a superb multi-tasker, sending faxes, giving out forms, selling stamps and weighing packages in a blur of motion. I often wonder what her incentive is, since postal workers earn pretty much the same. I also wonder whether the head of the Post Office is aware of her efficiency; if he was, he would bring other branches to visit her, and observe and try to transmit her best practices to other branches.

Practise close observation when you visit your bank, post office, dry cleaner and other organizations that provide you with services. Notice differences in service, efficiency and cost. Think about what *you* would do if you ran these organizations. Think about how important it is for senior managers to 'manage by walking around', visiting their installations and observing them. For instance, Northwest Airlines President Douglas Steenland, struggling to turn around his company, flies on Northwest planes once to four times a week, and also flies on competitors' planes to benchmark them and 'to get a view of how they're approaching things'.

8.5 THE ECONOMICS OF COMPETITIVE MARKETS

With more and more markets becoming global in nature, and fiercely competitive, the economic theory of how such markets work is a powerful tool for managers. In the short run, when many businesses produce essentially identical products, profits are maximized (or, losses are minimized—mathematically, these two concepts are identical) by choosing to produce that amount of output that makes the marginal, or incremental, cost equal to price. Even if there are losses, it pays to produce *something* (rather than shut down), because the operating profit (difference between price and average variable cost times the number of units sold) can offset fixed costs. But in the long run—a period of time long enough to sell fixed assets, like buildings and machinery, and extract the invested capital—price must cover so-called 'fully allocated costs', or average total cost including the opportunity cost of capital. Otherwise, the owners of the capital will liquidate and shift their investment elsewhere.

The power of mapping costs, or cost functions, lies in their ability to help managers dissect the likely future developments in competitive industries. Airlines' enormous operating losses suggest that some airlines will go bankrupt and disappear, while those who survive will be ones able to reduce costs and operate in the black.

This theory applies to individual businesses or factories. Many products and services face a natural process known as commoditization. In this process, innovative products and services capture large profits when they first reach the market and achieve high success and popularity. Eventually imitators emerge. The product becomes standardized, as consumers 'vote' with their dollars or euros or rupees and indicate precisely which product specifications they prefer. Prices then begin to fall as more entrants produce the standard product and the competitive game shifts from innovation to cost reduction and manufacturing efficiency. Plants that once were profitable suddenly find their existence endangered as they no longer cover their full average total costs. Managers and workers alike then struggle with the question: Should we operate this plant tomorrow? Next year? Or should we send the workers letters of dismissal.

Case study: Air Liquide

This French company was a market leader in supplying industrial gases. But by the early 1990s gas had become a commodity. Only price differentiated Air Liquide from its competitors. Prices fell and so did Air Liquide's operating income. It responded by doubling R&D spending to innovate. But there were few successes. Air Liquide then reinvented itself. From being solely a supplier of gas, it became a provider of

Case study continued

Case study continued

chemical and gas management systems, by building a new system for manufacturing gas on its customers' sites! Since service profit margins are high, and with nearly a third of its revenue coming from such services, Air Liquide is again profitable. It fought commoditization by escaping that zone and selling a differentiated service.

Source: 'Don't laugh at gilded butterflies', *The Economist* (Website), 22 April 2004.

Action learning

Operate the Plant? Close it?

You are the CEO of XYZ Co. which has a small plant that makes computer monitors. The F.O.B. (free on board) price of each monitor is $45. The plant's land and buildings are worth $9 million at market value. A global recession and excess capacity cause the F.O.B. price to fall to $32.

Output ('000 units per year)	*TVC*	*TFC**	*TC*
40,000	900	500	
50,000	1,100	500	
60,000	1,350	500	
70,000	1,645	500	
80,000	1,976	500	
90,000	2,430	500	
100,000	2,950	500	

AVC AFC ATC MC $'000 per unit.

Note: TVC—Total variable cost; TFC—Total fixed cost; TC—Total cost (TVC+TFC); AVC—Average variable cost; AFC—Average fixed cost; AC—Average total cost (AVC+AFC); MC—Marginal cost.
*Depreciation only; does not include opportunity cost of capital.

Questions:

1. Calculate TC, AVC, AFC, ATC, and MC for each output level. (Hint: Where should the opportunity cost of shareholders' capital find expression?)
2. For the short run (a period of time too short for the land and equipment to be sold): Should the plant

remain in operation? If so, how many units should be produced? Why?

3. For the long run (a period of time long enough for the land and equipment to be sold): Should the plant remain in operation? Why/why not? What steps might you take to make this plant viable in the long run and save the jobs of its workers?

8.6 THERE ARE NO FIXED COSTS

Slashing fixed costs is often crucial. Companies quickly become overburdened with unnecessary layers of management. Once mid-level management had the key function of processing and analysing information. Today, information technology produces computer screens that CEOs can call up in one key stroke, making an entire level of managers utterly redundant. Reducing fixed costs can greatly lower the level of output and sales needed by an organization to cover its costs and break even. In the early 1990s IBM found its 'sales, general and administrative' expenses were over 25 per cent of its sales while competitors had that ratio down to 15 per cent. This hurt IBM's ability to compete. A major effort got IBM's fixed-cost ratio down to that of its competitors.

How can fixed costs best be reduced?

One approach, invented by Harvard Business School Professor Robert Kaplan, is known as Activity Based Management (ABM).[6] In this approach, the fundamental principal is: There *are* no fixed costs; all costs are variable. By this, Kaplan means that under his system, every dollar of cost has some manager who is responsible for it and therefore has a strong incentive to reduce or eliminate it. ABM asks that everyone in the organization analyse precisely what they do and how and in particular measure their consumption of such fixed cost services as corporate services, marketing, purchasing and so on, and allocate that 'consumption' to specific product lines. This is often frustrating and time-consuming, but the very process of analysing such activities generates, in our experience, enormously valuable data.

Often, conventional cost-accounting systems allocate fixed costs to products based on arbitrary unrealistic assumptions. Once generated, this cost data is treated as real and accurate by the organization, creating a distorted picture of profitability. The result: Products that managers *know for certain* are highly profitable appear on the books as losers, simply because they have been allocated an unjust share of the fixed costs. ABM insists that fixed costs be allocated based on true consumption, not based on rule-of-thumb assumptions.

Once true and accurate bottom-line figures exist for each product line, based on accurate allocation of fixed costs, far better strategies can be developed to strengthen winning profitable products and to eliminate needless fixed costs. Enormous 'pools' of fixed costs, for whom no one except perhaps the CEO is directly responsible, are hard to reduce. But the moment individual managers find those fixed costs in their own profit-and-loss statements, by which their performance and bonuses are measured, suddenly creative ways are found to cut or eliminate such fixed costs without impairing the organization's product or performance.

Case study: NEC, Nagano

Yuko Watanabe was Professor Maital's Management of Technology student at M.I.T. A soft-spoken engineer for the consumer electronics firm NEC, she told him and the class how she had saved the jobs of workers at a large factory in the Japanese city of Nagano, famous for recently hosting the Winter Olympics. (See Case Study 8.1 for a more detailed discussion.)

Yuko made effective use of the cost function tool. She was sent to Nagano because the NEC's plant there had high costs. It was a case of either reducing those costs substantially or closing the plant. The first thing Yuko did was to go to work herself on the assembly line—rather unusual for a senior manager. Yuko knew that in many cases, both the nature of the problem and its solution are clearly known to line workers but somehow do not get transmitted to senior managers closeted in their comfortable offices on the fortieth floor of glass towers. Yuko discovered that NEC Nagano's cost curves were U-shaped (like the French boulangeries), and as a result were highly inflexible. Unless the NEC Nagano plant produced the equivalent of precisely 'four cartons' (the output level that minimized the average total cost of bread), costs would be very high. If it made less than the optimal amount high overhead would raise costs. If it produced more than the optimal amount, there would be rising variable costs (overtime, etc.). The problem, she saw, lay in the very long inflexible production line, over 100 metres in length. Increasingly, in competitive global markets for consumer electronics products, demand is highly variable. Sometimes, it shrank. Other times, it boomed, when consumers had to have a new attractive product. Nagano's long Ford-like assembly line could not adjust either to shrinking demand or growing demand without seeing costs explode.

Case study continued

Case study continued

Yuko redesigned production. Instead of one long production line, she created several smaller lines. When demand shrank, only two or three of the lines were operated. The redundant workers, who had retrained, did other tasks—some of them were even able to do functions such as marketing. The remaining lines were simply shut down. When demand boomed, all the small lines were operated, and all the workers focused on production and assembly tasks. The result was to flatten the average cost curve and eliminate its 'belly'. By taking a small flexible production line, with a flat cost curve, and then replicating it several times, the aggregate cost curve too was relatively flat. The result was to save the jobs of Nagano workers, and create a model for flexible manufacturing that NEC replicated in some of its other plants.

Yuko may simply have gained some time for Nagano. Fujio Mitarai, head of the Japanese giant Canon, told *The Economist* he had a 'cut off' rule—anything for which labour costs comprise more than 5 per cent of total production costs should be done in China or some other low-wage country rather than Japan.[7]

8.7 COMPETITION AND EVOLUTIONARY NICHES

Fierce global competition has been disastrous for some companies, and has proved an enormous boon for others. An example is electronics manufacturing services companies (EMS), firms that do contract manufacturing for other global companies. One way to cut costs, electronics companies have found, is to close their own plants and contract out (outsource) manufacturing to firms whose sole expertise is lean efficient production. This saves capital and focuses management attention on the key processes of marketing and R&D. This has created a kind of Darwinian niche, or market space, for EMS firms. This relatively new type of company sprang up because there was a need for it created by global competition.

The leading EMS firm is Singapore's Flextronics International, which sells $13 billion worth of products yearly, producing Nortel routers, Ericsson cell phones and Microsoft Xbox game consoles, among others. Flextronics takes orders from companies such as Hewlett-Packard or Xerox and ships their products directly to their customers.[8]

Case study: Wal-Mart revisited

Wal-Mart's competitive model is based fundamentally on tugging downward both its fixed and variable costs. According to a leading consultant the three key sources of Wal-Mart's cost advantages are: low corporate overheads (fixed costs); efficient supply-chain management (variable costs) and, above all, low labour costs (variable costs). Wal-Mart calls its employees 'associates'. A new hire, despite the high-level name, might earn as little as $8 an hour, 20–30 per cent less than workers in unionized retailers. Wal-Mart employs some 1.4 million workers. With its low wages, staff turnover is high; once 60 per cent (6 of every 10 workers) quit each year, that ratio has fallen to 40 per cent lately; nonetheless, 600,000 new workers have to be hired every year to replace those who leave. Cost reduction alone is not sufficient; Wal-Mart's core model calls for passing on cost savings to customers, in the form of lower prices, and making money on increased sales volume, rather than pocket cost reduction savings through higher bottom line profits. Some of Wal-Mart's competitors have fallen, but others have thrived in the increased competition—Costco, for instance, and Target. All offer low prices, like Wal-Mart, with 'something else on top', such as convenience or luxury goods.

Source: 'How big can it grow?' www.Economist.com, accessed on 15 April 2004.

Case study: Innovation is (again) the answer

One of the world's leading experts on business strategy, Gary Hamel, notes why in a Darwinian competitive business environment, innovation is so crucial. 'Many companies are reaching the point where it will be impossible to raise prices, grow the top line, or even significantly reduce costs without innovation,' Hamel notes. 'The challenge is ... to reinvent the core of your company, ... where any company that's not constantly renewing itself is simply becoming irrelevant.' He cites many examples. Starbucks got its customers to pay for their coffee weeks in advance using debit cards. Nobody had thought of doing that. At W. L. Gore (maker of Gore-Tex fabric) employees take up to 20 per cent of their time working on experiments and new ideas. Much innovation occurs 'from the customer backwards'—innovating on both the demand and

Case study continued

Case study continued

cost sides. Hamel cites W. E. Deming, pioneer of quality management, who insisted every employee should be an empowered quality-control officer 'able to shut down a million-dollar line'. Individual employees should similarly be empowered to come up with creative ideas. Toyota has done this and is now the world's #2 car-maker, heading for #1.

Note: Gary Hamel's insights on innovation are from 'Innovation Special: Dos and Don'ts', by David Kirpatrick, www.fortune.com.

8.8 CONCLUSION

Companies, like Darwin's 'organic beings', are struggling to increase in geometric ratio (i.e., grow their top and bottom lines, sales and net income) in competition with other organic beings for resources (market share or sales). As in Darwin, the vigorous, the healthy and the happy survive and multiply. When Wal-Mart's CEO Lee Scott was asked whether his firm was trying to take over the world (vastly understated, in view of an Internet photo purporting to come from Mars Exploration Rover, showing a Wal-Mart on Mars), his answer was, 'I don't think so, all we want to do is grow.' The less vigorous, healthy or happy disappear.

More and more organizations will find themselves locked in fierce competitive combat as more countries join the global economy. Banks, telecommunications, retailing, coffee shops all have global giants that replicate in many countries. The result of this competition is to create many winners—lower prices, better service, wider variety of products—and some losers—those who worked in now-bankrupt businesses. The process itself creates huge protests, because the benefits are somewhat amorphous without a cohesive clear constituency, while the costs are visible, highly publicized and somewhat narrowly concentrated.

For good or for ill, Darwin's 'survival of the fittest' in the realm of business competition is probably here to stay. Managers who understand it well enough to turn it to their organization's advantage will survive, endure and prevail. One of the key tools they can enlist is that of cost functions—mapping costs, then acting to reduce them. By visually presenting an organization's cost curves, relative to those of competitors, it is possible to enlist organization-wide support for cost reduction. Survival is a remarkably powerful goal for focusing minds and generating cohesive cost-reducing team-work.

Cost per unit of output is simply the inverse of productivity—output per unit of resources (labour or capital). So cost reduction and productivity growth are two sides of the same coin. In the next chapter, we introduce a relatively new way of looking at productivity measurement, known as free lunch productivity, and examine how managers can use it effectively to make their organizations profitable and efficient.

Readers are invited to view 'Pillars of Profit: Segment #4, Cost Functions—NEC Nagano' in the accompanying CD.

CASE STUDY 8.1

The Innovation Programme at Nippon Electric Company (NEC), Nagano*

Case study discussion topics

1. Why was NEC considering closing its Nagano plant?
2. What are the main elements of the 'lean production system'?
3. What are the advantages of 'small flexible (production) lines' over larger lines?
4. By how much did NEC Nagano reduce its costs?
5. What did NEC (Nagano)'s new cost curve look like, compared with the old one? What explains the change?

NEC's plant at Nagano produced PCs, word processors, printers, scanners, monitors and TVs. NEC's total sales growth had been decreasing since 1989, and in 1993, NEC faced the crisis that its sales were going down by more than 20 per cent because of the economic recession in Japan and the price wars in the Japanese PC market. NEC Nagano had to reduce costs for its survival. Further, there was also an increasing urgency to innovate in the production process to achieve productivity improvement.

*This case study is a summary of the case authored by Yuko Watanabe.

Case study 8.1 continued

Case study 8.1 continued

An analysis performed by NEC Nagano on the structure of costs of each product revealed that more than 85 per cent of the costs were 'Direct Material' costs. This meant it would be difficult to reduce costs only by improving productivity. Generally speaking, mass production is a good method to reduce direct material cost but as the demand was decreasing in Japan, Nagano had to consider other methods of reducing costs.

Inventory statistics at Nagano revealed that in the 3rd and 4th quarter of 1992, the inventory (147 million ¥) was about 13 per cent of the sales (1,163 million ¥). The finished goods inventory was written in the balance sheet as an asset, but it had the possibility of becoming dead stock because of the short life of the products. These goods also needed more storage space. Therefore, it was decided to reduce the finished goods inventory as much as possible. On analysing the reason for the big size of the finished goods inventory, it was found that the sales divisions were ordering more products than needed to avoid the risk of shortage. Second, in order to increase productivity, the Nagano plant was manufacturing goods in large lots.

Techniques such as 'kanban', 'reducing waste' and 'visible Management' were implemented to reduce finished goods inventory. But the most effective of them all was the 'small flexible lines' approach. To ensure the co-existence of small lot production while retaining productivity, large inflexible conveyer assembly lines were done away with and many small flexible lines made of aluminium pipes and junctions were rebuilt in their place. The previous line was 36 metres in length, occupied a floor area of 192 square metres and employed 14 labourers, whereas the new small flexible lines were 20 metres in length, occupied 70 square metres floor area and employed 10 labourers. This change resulted in 122 square metres empty floor area and reduced 4 direct production workers while retaining the same productivity. One small line had the capability of manufacturing half the quantity that a large line could. This meant goods could be manufactured in small lots. The advantages of this new line were:

1. Small space

By replacing large lines with smaller ones, a 2,000 square metres empty floor area was created in 1993.

2. Small lot production

Decreasing the capacity of production per line made the production lots smaller.

Case study 8.1 continued

Case study 8.1 continued

3. Reduced initial cost

The cost of a new line was only 400,000 ¥ while the cost of the old one was 30,000,000 ¥.

4. Simplified production planning

Small lot production by using small lines made the production planning easy. The production planners calculated only how many lines they needed in order to manufacture the day's order. They did not have to make complex calculations for the planning. If the order of product A was reduced abruptly, planners would plan to have some lines continue to manufacture product A and other lines would be made to manufacture other products or stop manufacturing altogether. They did not have to worry about large idle fixed costs when they stopped manufacturing because of the low initial cost of the new small flexible lines.

5. Retain learning effect

Small lot production yielded the same learning effect as in the case of mass production because the line could continuously manufacture one kind of product in a whole day.

6. Continuous improvement

The flexibility of the new line was a big advantage and contributed towards continuous improvement. When there was a need to change the line to improve its productivity, workers could easily change it themselves.

Since the simplification of the production management made much of the indirect labour unnecessary, the structure of Nagano was reorganized to reduce overhead cost. The production management division was eliminated, with this function being transferred to the manufacturing division. The division's employees were transferred to the manufacturing division and the newly-formed sales division at NEC Nagano. This change yielded a lot of manpower in the manufacturing division, reducing the direct labour cost relating to the sub-contract. Using promotional videos on the 'small flexible lines' programme and talking about the success of this programme to all of the managers at NEC gradually changed the mindset of managers of the sales divisions at

Case study 8.1 continued

Case study 8.1 continued

NEC. NEC managers decided to cooperate in reducing the finished goods inventory. They set the maximum quantity of the stock for each product and promised to order in small lots when the stock was short.

Reduced costs analysis

Assuming that in 1992 Nagano retained the same amount of inventory and 10 per cent of this became dead-stock, the hidden cost would have been 9,700 million × 0.1 = 970 million ¥. However, Nagano successfully reduced the inventory and also the percentage of dead-stock. After the reduction in inventory if it was to be assumed that 1 per cent of the finished goods inventory became dead-stock, the hidden cost would be reduced to 3,000 million × 0.01 = 30 million ¥ (3,000 million Yen: estimated finished goods inventory in 1994).

NEC Nagano started a new business, CD-ROM assembling and also planned other new businesses, by using the manpower and space that was freed up by the process described above. The estimated cost of the new business in 1994 was 1 billion ¥. Initial cost of assembly lines for the new business was 1 million ¥. Assuming the rate of direct materials to total cost to be about the same as other products (85 per cent), the profit of the new business was estimated at 1 billion × 0.15 – 1 million = 149 million ¥ for the first year. Moreover, the CD-ROM assembling business had the possibility of growing into a big business in the future.

Cost savings for the first year due to small flexible lines have been summarized in Table 8.1.1. It includes initial cost, as effective costs become higher after the 2nd year. As changing lines reduced 2,000 square metres of the floor space, NEC Nagano broke the contract with a warehouse that cost 48 million ¥ per year (monthly: 2,000 ¥ per square metres).

Table 8.1.1
Cost reductions achieved (¥)

Reduced cost of warehouse	48,000,000
Cost for new small flexible lines (16 lines including installation cost)	–3,200,000
Cost for old inflexible conveyer lines (abandonment)	–30,000,000
Reduced dead stock (hidden profit)	940,000,000
New business (hidden profit)	149,000,000
Reduced labour cost (subcontracts)	2,000,000,000
Continuous improvement	161,000,000
Total effective cost reduction	3,264,800,000

Case study 8.1 continued

Case study 8.1 continued

Reduction in dead stock and labour costs, as well as profits from the new business were the hidden benefits for the small flexible lines. Labour costs of sub-contracts reduced by 2 billion ¥ (500 men). The accelerated productivity improvement was 2 per cent. The direct labour cost was about 7 per cent of the total goods cost (115 billion ¥). The impact on profit due to continuous improvement was 115 billion × 0.07 × 0.02 = 161 million ¥.

Cost functions

Replacing large inflexible conveyer lines with small flexible lines resulted in significant benefits to NEC Nagano. NEC Nagano's net income exceeded the budget (by more than 600 million ¥). Figure 8.1.1 below shows average cost curves for one of the types of Word Processors manufactured at NEC Nagano using the previous manufacturing method, compared to the subsequent change to the Lean Production System. It confirms that small flexible lines were better than the large lines.

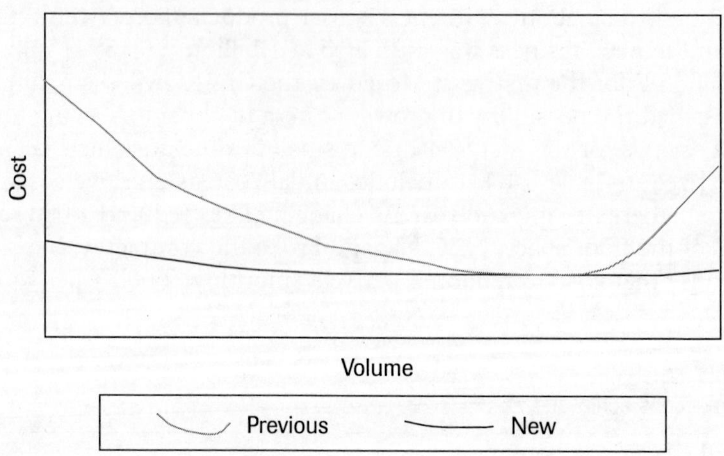

Figure 8.1.1
Cost curve

CASE STUDY 8.2

Moser Baer–Survival of the Fittest*

Recognized as a world-class high-technology developer and manufacturer of removable data storage media, Moser Baer India Ltd. (MBI) is one of India's top optical disc (recordable CD, DVD, etc.) manufacturing companies with an annual turnover of Rs 17.25 billion ($400 million), commanding a 16 per cent share of the global recordable optical media market. Established in 1983 in New Delhi, the company today employs close to 7,000 people, has five highly sophisticated manufacturing units in India and its products are available to customers in over 82 countries through its well-developed domestic and international marketing network. The company's comprehensive product portfolio includes floppy disks, compact discs (CDs) and digital versatile discs (DVDs), with over 2 billion CDs and DVDs being supplied annually to global markets and to well-known OEM brands. MBI has subsidiaries in India, Europe, the US and Japan.

MBI stands out as a stellar example of the very few high-tech manufacturing companies in India that has survived and succeeded in the global arena in an industry where few in India have stepped in. The strong belief of the management that an Indian company can take on the world's best and prove victorious has placed MBI as the world's third-largest manufacturer of optical storage media. In order to survive and emerge as the fittest in an industry characterized by rapid growth and short market and product cycles, MBI initiated and ensured the following:

1. It emphasized a strong focus in improving systems and processes in all the production units. These manufacturing plants today hold certifications for quality management and have a host of tools and techniques (Six Sigma Methodology, Statistical Tests, Taguchi methods, Failure Mode and Effect Analysis, etc.) to continuously improve quality and process capability. These initiatives have helped MBI to successfully face global competition in product quality and price, seemingly making it the only manufacturer that supplies to all the top 12 leading OEMs scattered around the globe.

*Sources of material from various Websites.

Case study 8.2 continued

Case study 8.2 continued

2. The company made efforts towards accomplishing exceptional and world-class manufacturing status, including excellence in manufacturing line and post-manufacturing practices in order to achieve global competitiveness and high levels of customer satisfaction.
3. It consistently kept itself abreast of technological changes in the optical media industry that from time-to-time threaten to change the shape and format of what the company was manufacturing.
4. MBI was always one step ahead in identifying and developing the world's future formats of media storage. A strong focus on R&D coupled with a capable R&D facility enabled MBI to not only continuously evolve its products but to be the first to introduce new products in the market. Along with building a rich pool of in-house research talent, MBI collaborated with well-known international companies to jointly develop innovative products and processes. This resulted in MBI manufacturing almost all its products in-house using proprietary manufacturing processes, leading to significant cost savings. Leveraging upon its R&D capabilities and core skills in material science, thin film coating, etc., MBI pioneered a series of new products and formats into the market, and effected further improvements in speed and capacity of its products and enhanced the reliability of its products.
5. Being part of an industry where technological changes are fast and continuous, MBI's deep understanding of markets, accurate predictions of technological changes and timely investments in additional capacities facilitated the company to be on the forefront to develop and launch new niche products very early in the market.

Thus, MBI gained a leadership position and has successfully put India on the global map for optical discs manufacture through excellence in world-class manufacturing. It did this through process efficiencies and significant investments in R&D programmes. Since the tectonic shifts in technologies are never-ending, the company, looking into the medium-term future, sees that the optical disc market will soon stabilize and perhaps stagnate, as other methods of storing and moving data, such as Internet and Pen drives become increasingly more common. The company is hoping to leverage its strengths in a sunrise industry, the solar energy industry, by manufacturing solar panels, solar photovoltaic cells and solar modules, which promises huge opportunities for the

Case study 8.2 continued

'early birds.' The MBI case study is an apt illustration of *Survival of the Fittest*, clearly demonstrating how the company continues to flourish in intensely competitive markets.

Notes

1. Darwin's 'natural selection' quote is from *On the Origin of Species*, 1859, chapter 3.
2. Herbert Spencer's quote is from his *First Principles* (1861).
3. The quote by Kurt Lewin, is 'If social scientists truly wish to understand certain phenomena, they should try to change them. Creating, not predicting, is the most robust test of validity-actionability.' He is cited in Robert Kaplan, 1999. 'Innovation action research: Creating new management theory and practice,' *Journal of Management Accounting*.
4. James Burke, 'Connections', *Scientific American*, various issue.
5. Data on SMS are from Nicola Clark, 'Wireless: text messages come by the billions now,' *International Herald Tribune*, 30 August 2004 (Website version).
6. R. Kaplan, 'Introduction to Activity-based Costing', Harvard Business School, Case 9-197-076, rev. 5 July 2001.
7. See 'Weathering the Tech Storm,' *Business Week*, 5 May 2003, for the article on EMS manufacturers and Flextronics.
8. The quote from the head of Canon is from Economist.com, 'How are Japan's manufacturers faring against low-cost competition from China?,' www.economist.com.

Chapter 9

People, knowledge and machines: In search of a free lunch

There is no free lunch.
—Milton Friedman[1]

LEARNING OBJECTIVES After you read this chapter, you should understand:

- **Why people are the key element in any business design**
- **What the difference is between an adaptive challenge and a technical problem**
- **How to measure FLP—free lunch productivity**
- **Why it is better to beg forgiveness than to ask permission**

TOOL #5 Free lunch productivity™

9.1 INTRODUCTION

> People are our most valuable asset. We are a people company. Here, in this company, people come first.

In our years of consulting and teaching, we never met a CEO who did not subscribe to the 'people first' value, nor a single successful organization that did not believe that its human capital was a key success factor. Yet some of those same people-first CEOs have been known, in the same breath they praise their human resources, to announce massive lay-offs.

As with the Ten Commandments, there is often a gap between practice and theory, in managing, developing, enhancing and celebrating human capital. This chapter provides some tools for closing this gap. The central tool is an approach for measuring what we call Free Lunch Productivity (FLP), a way of measuring how smart people generate productivity gains that are costless and hence fly right to the organization's bottom line and enhance it.[2]

9.2 THE FIVE KEY ELEMENTS OF A BUSINESS

Professor Jay Galbraith is a pioneer of organizational design, a discipline that shows how best to structure an organization to achieve its goals and to 'fit' its culture and industry. He developed what he calls the 'star' model, showing the six key elements of any business: strategy (the plan that when implemented will achieve the organization's goals), structure (the chain of command in the organization and how its parts are linked), people (the human assets or human capital), process (the various systems and procedures the business uses to market, produce, distribute and ship its products) and reward (how the organization compensates its managers and workers) (Figure 9.1).[3] Normally, he presents these five elements in the shape of a star, with each point connected to the four other 'points', showing how each is closely related to the other. We prefer, however, to present this model as a 'sun and planets', with people at the center of the 'solar system' and the other four elements revolving around them.

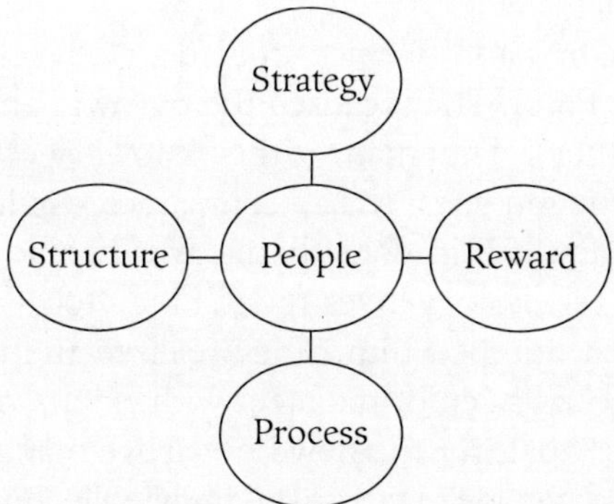

Figure 9.1
The five key elements of an organization's business: people, reward, process, strategy, structure. People are central.

For most organizations, this is an accurate portrayal. People *are* their core asset and embody their core competencies. There are four reasons.

First, for many organizations, it is knowledge that conveys competitive advantage; the people possessing that knowledge thus become the key.

Second, innovation is becoming increasingly important in attaining and maintaining competitive advantage, and innovation is embodied in creative, empowered people. Third, following the theory presented in Jim Collins' book *Good to Great*,[4] great organizations are those in which the 'right' people are assembled, 'put on the bus', and then the strategy, structure, reward and process are shaped around them. Far too many organizations are like Cinderella's sisters who tried to shape the slipper (people) to their feet (strategy and structure) rather than vice versa. Fourth, leadership—people (not necessarily CEOs or even senior management) with leadership skills and potential can drive an organization forward, when the lack of such leadership can lead to stagnation and failure. We now turn to leadership and examine the key elements of what makes a successful business leader and what differentiates true leaders from managers.

9.3 ADAPTIVE LEADERSHIP

Harvard Kennedy School of Government Professor Ronald A. Heifetz has argued, in two powerful books, that 'the single most common source of leadership failure we've been able to identify—in politics, community life, business or the non-profit sector, is that people ... treat adaptive challenges like technical problems.'[5]

For example: The first author once studied a global engineering and construction company, Fluor. They realized their growth and profits were being hampered because they did not manage their knowledge well across countries, regions and construction sites. Many companies would diagnose this as a technical problem and call in consultants, who would then recommend a costly Information Technology investment. Fluor, too, called in an expensive consultant and then dumped him. They realized the problem was one of leadership. They picked a senior manager with extensive line experience; he established business goals for the new knowledge management system, and then built it, 'selling' the idea by painstakingly collecting and disseminating success stories about how sharing knowledge made the company and its workers better off. He showed leadership by realizing that company attitudes had to change and then took the right steps to create that change in the minds of its managers and workers. He understood this was not a technical problem at all.

Case studies: Fannie Mae, Walgreen, General Motors and New York Archdiocese

These four great organizations were all headed by great leaders, who achieved success in a highly personal, individual and unique manner. Much can be learned from each. Each led processes of adaptive change.

Alfred P. Sloan led General Motors to defeat Ford, in the late 1920s, by innovating—producing cars with closed bodies, choice of colours, powerful engines, etc., when Ford dominated with the all-black Model T.

Francis Cardinal Spellman took a bankrupt archdiocese and built it into America's most powerful and prosperous Catholic diocese through his quiet personal leadership. Management guru Peter Drucker called this perhaps the most impressive management achievement of this century.[6]

Charles Walgreen III abandoned tradition and took Walgreen's drugstores completely out of food-service operations (even though Walgreen's had invented the malted milkshake), to focus on what it did best—convenient drugstores.

Finally, David Maxwell took over Fannie Mae (Federal National Mortgate Corp.) in the early 1980s. Designed to buy packages of mortgages from banks, and 'securitize' them by issuing bonds, Fannie Mae was burdened with high-interest debt. Maxwell and his team rebuilt Fannie Mae into a leading Wall Street player, with expertise in measuring and managing mortgage-based risk and generated stock returns eight times higher than the stock market average in the coming 15 years. He did this by inventing new financial measures; redefining Fannie Mae's business as 'risk management' rather than mortgage packaging, hiring the right people, and by never losing sight of the goal—to make Fannie Mae the #1 company for packaging and managing mortgage-backed securities. Maxwell was assisted in inducing change, because everyone at Fannie Mae knew the alternative was bankruptcy.

Often however, adaptive change must be implemented by leaders precisely when the organization perceives itself as hugely successful, a result of the rapid pace of change in global markets. This is the ultimate in leadership challenges: getting everyone in the organization to change what is perceived as a winning formula.

Action learning

Suppose You are John Akers

In 1990, the Chairman of the Board of IBM, John Akers,[7] announced that his company had achieved record profits of $5 billion. No other company in history had ever made so much money in a single year. Just two years later, the same John Akers announced that IBM had broken another record—this one, a more dubious one—piling up *losses* of $6 billion in a year, also an all-time record.

Suppose you are John Akers. In 1990, just after you announce the record profit, suppose an angel whispers in your ear that in just two years your company will lose $6 billion unless something drastic happens. Your company, IBM, has half a million talented managers, workers and engineers, who are basking in the warm sunshine of success. What can you say or do, that will induce IBM to engage in the radical change process necessary to prevent the near-disastrous loss two years down the road?

In the hyperdynamic pace of change in the global economy, managers often need to lead painful radical processes of change, precisely when the company perceives itself to be highly successful. Implementing change in an atmosphere of crisis, loss and failure is much easier than implementing it when everyone believes they are successful; this is a major test of leadership.

9.4 FORGIVENESS? OR PERMISSION?

True leadership sometimes involves exceeding one's authority. Case Study 9.1, on the Patriot anti-missile missile, is an example. The Air Force colonel who initiated changes in the missile's software code that transformed it from an ground-to-air anti-aircraft missile (its original purpose) to an anti-missile missile did so without formal permission from his superiors. He knew that getting such permission would take so long, that the project would never be completed in time for action in the Gulf War. He had a saying on his wall: It is easier to ask forgiveness than to get permission—a highly unusual saying for a senior officer in a military organization where chain-of-command and discipline are paramount, one that typifies adaptive leadership. Case Study 9.1 tells his story, through the eyes of a former student of the first author, who worked on the Patriot Missile project.

Action learning

Key Decision Nodes in Your Career

Examine your own career. Think about the key 'nodes' or decision points. Looking backward in hindsight: when might you have acted, against 'orders' or authority, without permission, if you had a chance to relive this decision? When have you shown adaptive leadership? When *might* you have shown such leadership but perhaps missed the opportunity?

9.5 FINDING FREE LUNCHES: FINDING NEW WAYS TO MEASURE AND MANAGE PRODUCTIVITY

There are no free lunches, Nobel Laureate Milton Friedman once said. He meant that every time we consume real resources, there is an economic cost; *someone* always provides and pays for the food. But growing numbers of companies are using an economic concept known as FLP, or free lunch productivity—also known, boringly, as multi-factor productivity—to identify and capture enormous free lunches. They do this by squeezing more production and sales out of existing resources. The beauty is, when they succeed the results go directly to the bottom line. In times of global deflation, when falling prices put severe pressure on profits and profit margins, FLP free-lunch gains are positively life-saving.

9.6 THE ORIGINS OF FLP

MIT Professor Robert Solow won the Nobel Prize in economics in 1987 for 'contributions to the theory of economic growth'. Solow asked: Why are some countries wealthier than others? He noted two answers: (*i*) the Marxian answer: 'Wealthy countries saved more and accumulated mountains of physical capital' (e.g., Singapore), and (*ii*) the Solow answer, 'Wealthy countries found smarter ways to use their resources and make them more productive' (e.g., Hong Kong). He invented the equation that partitioned per cent change in output per worker into two components, (a) and (b), and found (b) was far larger (see the FLP calculator below).

FLP: Crunching the Numbers

1. Start with the conventional measure of labour productivity growth:

   year-to-year per cent change in value added per employee
   (*if you are using annual-report data: replace value added with sales revenue.*)

2. Subtract from this the part of productivity growth caused by higher capital investment:

   Subtract:
   0.4 times year-to-year per cent change in capital assets per employee
   Equals:

3. The result is: year-to-year per cent change in FLP (Free Lunch Productivity)

   Example:
   GE increased its sales revenues by 16 per cent in 2000 with essentially the same number of employees and with an increase of only 8 per cent in its capital assets per employee (see the table FLP change at GE: 2000). The result: A very large increase in 'free lunch' productivity (FLP).

	FLP Change at GE: 2000		
	2000	*1999*	*% Change*
GE Basic Data			
Sales	$129 billion	$111.6 billion	+16.3
Employees	341,000	340,000	
Assets	$437 billion	$402 billion	
Change in Sales per employee:	+16%		
Change in Assets per employee:	+7.5%		
FLP change = 16% − 0.4 × 7.5% = 16% − 3.0% = 13%			

Per cent change in Output per Hour of Work =

(a) Gain due to Workers having more capital, equipment, tools, computers +
(b) Gain due to Workers 'working smarter' (better methods, motivation, management, etc.)

Component (a) is 'Marxian', attributable to physical capital; and component (b) focuses on human capital—better skills, motivation, management, etc. For the United States, (b) has been found to be twice as important as (a), for 1948–2001 (Figure 9.2).

Solow agrees that the same tool can be applied to discovering why some companies are wealthier than others. When this is done, the same answer (not surprisingly) is discovered: Growing profitable companies have higher rates of FLP growth.

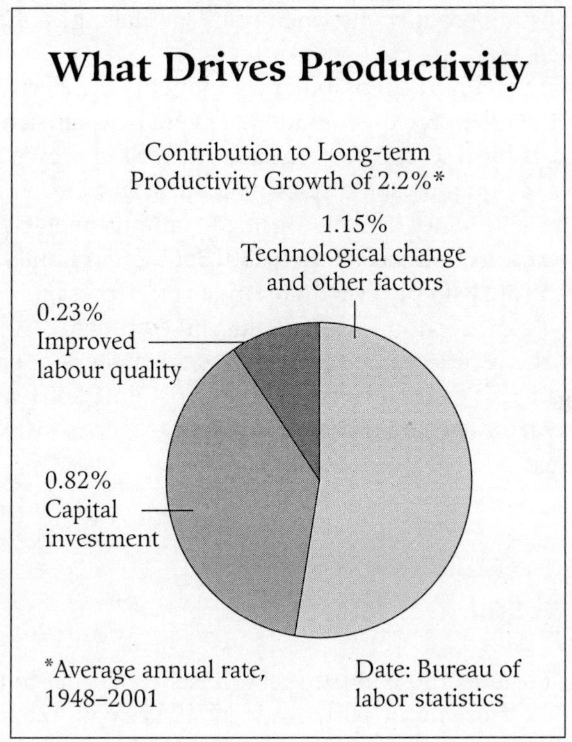

Figure 9.2
Free lunch productivity and expensive lunch productivity: What drives productivity?

According to the Bureau of Labor Statistics, America has enjoyed long-term growth of labour productivity (output or value added per hour of labour) of 2.2 per cent annually during 1948–2001. A little more than one-third of that was attributed to capital investment (0.82 per cent). Slightly less than two-thirds was attributed to 'free lunch productivity' (improved labour quality and technological change). This means that FLP is twice as important as ELP (expensive lunch productivity). FLP is somewhat of a hyperbole—technological change may be initially costly, but ultimately it does yield a bumper crop of productivity gains without further investments.

Why productivity is crucial in the age of deflation

Managing and measuring productivity are important for all companies at all times. But in times of global deflation, shrinking demand and falling prices squeeze profit margins. *Only if costs fall faster than prices can profit margins grow.* This is achieved by getting more output out of fewer resources. So for many companies boosting productivity when prices are falling is often a matter of life and death.

Consider manufacturers of computer components and electronic assembly. In this sector, the price erosion is about 6 per cent per year, hence companies have to cut costs by at least 6 per cent per year or see profits decline.

For example, a liquid crystal display panel firm in Singapore told us that the price of the 'screen' for a game console (a famous one) fell by more than half, in three years, from US$ 2.80 to $1.30. For this firm unless productivity grows rapidly, profits simply evaporate under price pressure.

Conference Board economist Ken Goldstein comments: 'A profit squeeze helped set off the recession. So business has taken steps ... productivity (in America) began rising significantly in the 3rd Q. of 2001 and continued through the year ... as a consequence, profits recovered $100 billion of the $200 billion lost prior to the recession.'

FLP among Fortune 100 companies: Key ways to find free lunches[8]

In examining Fortune 100 companies, we discovered that in the recent US recession, unlike those in the past, productivity has continued to rise. Companies no longer stockpile labour and ride out the recession. They act at once to slash redundant labour and squeeze out unnecessary costs. Here are some examples:

Use technology

Health care wholesalers McKesson, that distributes drugs to drugstores and hospitals, slashed its distribution centres from 50 to 30, while boosting revenue from each by five times. A small example of an almost-free lunch, according to CEO John Hammergren: warehouse workers wear laser scanners on their wrists that tell them where every item is in the warehouse; no time is wasted on prolonged searches, as in the past. The scanners were not free but paid for themselves within weeks. McKesson's productivity-boosting activities were so impressive, Wal-Mart, itself an obsessive productivity booster, named McKesson a supplier of the year and turned its pharmaceutical bulk packaging over to a McKesson facility in Tennessee.

Save time

At General Motors, when assembly lines broke down, technicians once looked up the problem from a library of manuals. Now, touch screens right at the assembly line produce immediate diagnoses, shortening line shutdowns.

Stopped lines cost $5,000 a minute, so those saved minutes add up to big savings.

Dump unproductive businesses

PepsiCo spun off ailing low-productivity units Taco Bell, Pizza Hut and KFC restaurants, focusing on high-profit beverages and snack foods. For 1996–2000 FLP gains averaged 33 per cent yearly.

Refocus on high-productivity businesses

AutoNation concluded that capital and labour tied up in used-car superstores was a dead asset. By closing them and reinvesting the capital on new-car sales, it achieved FLP gains averaging 75 per cent yearly in 1996–2000, as its shareholders' capital and workers focused on more productive businesses.

Innovate, innovate

The single biggest source of free lunches for companies is hot new innovative products that boost sales without added resources or inputs. Global 500 firm Nokia increased its sales in 1996 by 20 per cent with stylish new cell phones cleverly marketed; but the number of Nokia employees fell slightly and invested capital rose only by about 1 per cent. The result: growing profitability and profit margins. GE did the same in the year 2000 (see 'Crunching the Numbers' on page 281).

How Does FLP differ from existing metrics?

Many companies use a variety of individual metrics to measure the productivity of capital and labour.

- EVA (economic value added): Measures the productivity only of capital; not suitable for companies whose human assets are more important than capital assets
- RoI (return on investment): Focuses only on capital
- Value added per worker: Doesn't tell whether the gain in labour productivity came from higher capital assets or from the free-lunch variety, and *why* it happened

Many companies focus single-mindedly on capital productivity, using rate-of-return measures such as RoI, RoA or EVA. This is particularly true of European firms. Such measures are highly misleading, because they often ignore key dimensions of productivity gains, accruing from more productive *labour* and finding free lunches (FLP).

FLP is a metric that distils data into a single measure that shows bottom-line profitability gains and reflects how productive *both* capital and labour are.

Why FLP is no panacea

It is very important for managers to realize that their quest begins with the FLP metric, rather than ends with it. Large FLP gains raise the question: Where precisely did they come from? New products? More motivated workers? Spinning off unproductive SBUs? And how can the FLP momentum be preserved? Poor FLP growth, of course, raises the question, why? Why are resources not more productive? Does the problem lie with wasted labour? or wasted capital? How can this waste be eliminated? Only when those questions get systematic answers will the FLP metric lead to structured changes that perpetuate those gains.

Singapore and Hong Kong: Lessons for managers

Singapore and Hong Kong are each city states, limited in their land areas and similar to successful businesses; each has achieved rapid growth and high per capita GDP of around $25,000. But a study by economist Alwyn Young,[9] using the FLP concept, reveals a surprising difference: If Singapore had 'shareholders', they would be exceedingly unhappy, while Hong Kong's 'shareholders' would be in seventh heaven. The reason: Singapore's growth was achieved the expensive, hard way, with enormous capital investments and with no FLP growth, hence very low capital profitability, while Hong Kong's growth was mainly of the free-lunch variety. According to Young's study, 'fully 56 per cent of the increase in output per worker in Hong Kong between 1971 and 1990 is attributable to FLP growth' [i.e., the 'free lunch']; 'in the case of Singapore FLP growth contributed minus 8 per cent' [i.e., there was absolutely no free lunch].

FLP among high-tech firms: Take the long view

A study of FLP growth among high-tech firms in Singapore, by Nicholas Baratte (JP Morgan) reveals that firms can be classified into three groups:

- The consistently bad—low or negative FLP over a number of years

- The inconsistent—huge variations in profits, margins ... making the FLP growth quite difficult to interpret
- The consistently good-firms with positive FLP

In research done on performance and FLP growth of companies by the first author, most of the firms studied had one or two bad years over the period of 6 years ... (for Intel, this occurred when implementing a new technology, such as a 300 millimetre Silicon wafer). Conclusion: it is dangerous to look at a single-year of FLP growth and draw conclusions. But over longer periods of time (say, five years) FLP growth shows very good correlation with other indicators of good management (such as high margins, low working capital, high ROE and ROIC). So FLP is probably a component of competitive advantage of a firm and is also a positive barrier to entry. Its advantage over other conventional metrics is that tends to lead them in time—higher FLP growth is generally followed by higher profitability in later years.

The European angle

With Europe's economy growing slower than elsewhere, some observers have claimed that European companies are less innovative and less productive than those in Asia and America. A FLP study by Forrester Technology[10] reveals that FLP growth among leading European companies matches that in the United States. The conclusion: Rigidities in European goods, capital and labour markets, regulation, bureaucracy and bloated public sectors and government-owned firms are a major cause of European stagnation, and not private-sector firms.

Case study: Free lunch productivity: Smucker's Peanut Butter and Jam

Name the only company that simultaneously made it to three prestigious lists: Fortune 1000 (the one thousand largest American companies); Best Companies to Work For (it is #1—the first manufacturing company to achieve this distinction); and 100 Fastest Growing Companies (#92).

Clue: It is not a software or high-tech firm. Another clue: Chances are your children love this company. A final clue: The company is older than your grandfather.

This is a great free-lunch company that literally makes large free lunches from peanut butter and jam—Ohio-based J.M. Smucker. This

Case study continued

Case study continued

venerable 107-year-old company has been family-run for four generations. It has come alive in the past four years, acquiring the JIF peanut butter brand from Procter & Gamble (along with Crisco shortening) and doubling its revenues in three years to $1.3 billion.

In 2003 it achieved FLP growth of 1.1 per cent. While this sounds very modest, recall that it did this while achieving rapid growth (often harmful to productivity) and making several major acquisitions, in an industry (food) known for slow growth. In 2003, Smucker's earnings per share grew 30 per cent, its revenue rose by 35 per cent, and total return to investors (dividends and capital gains) averaged a high 20 per cent in the past three years. As a result, Smucker shares rose from just over $30 in early 2003 to today's level of $45. All this, in a company that sells high-carbohydrate high-sugar jam, when Americans are obsessed with Atkins Diet and low-carb foods.

How does Smucker create FLP gains? Says Richard Smucker: Give 'love and attention' to brands. Their brand-building grew Smucker's food-spread market share by an average of 1 per cent a year—a major achievement in the hidebound jam industry. Another secret: 'guerilla marketing'. Smucker's sponsors a small daily department on the NBC Today Show in which weatherman Willard Scott congratulates people celebrating their 100th birthday. The checkered Smucker brand thus links itself to longevity, good health and respect for old age, at a very low cost.

Action learning

Calculate Smucker's FLP Growth

Use the data below and the FLP calculator to compute J.M. Smucker's FLP growth for 2003.

	2004	*2003*
Sales	$1.417 billion	$1.312 billion
Employees	2,950	2,775
Capital	$1.211 billion	$1.124 billion

9.7 CONCLUSION

We began this chapter by noting the five key elements of all businesses: strategy, structure, reward, process and people. One version arranges these five elements in the shape of a star, with each point linked to each other point. We chose to place 'people' at the very centre. In the end, as nearly all the case studies in this and other chapters show, great organizations invariably have great people at their core—highly motivated, energetic, creative and caring workers and managers, from the most junior to the most senior. Strong managers and leaders choose good people, inspire them, then empower them and let them perform. The resulting 'free lunches', in the end, drive sterling top line growth and bottom line excellence. Of all the formulas for managerial excellence, this one is perhaps the easiest to state, and the hardest to implement.

Readers are invited to view 'Pillars of Profit: Segment #5, People, Knowledge, Machines' in the accompanying CD.

CASE STUDY 9.1

The Patriot Missile Story*

Case study discussion topics

1. How did the Patriot missile—the PAC-2 version—acquire the capability to operate against other missiles, beyond just aircrafts?
2. Who made the decision to put the PAC-2 into production, when and why?
3. How many PAC-2 missiles were available for the armed forces, when the Gulf War broke out on 17 January 1991? What were the factors that made it possible to field those numbers?
4. What problems were encountered in employing the PAC-2 missiles to intercept and destroy incoming Scud missiles?
5. Did the 'value' created by the missile justify its $600,000 average cost?

Without a doubt, the Patriot anti-aircraft and anti-missile missile system was the most spectacular and well-known US Army missile used during the Gulf War of 1991. After the first combat firing in January 1991, the system became known worldwide as the 'Scudbuster' because of the Patriots firing at Iraqi Scud surface-to-surface missiles, which were capable of carrying chemical warheads.

The US Army Patriot Missile System, originally designed as an anti-aircraft system, provides high and medium-altitude defence against aircrafts and some tactical ballistic missiles, for the army theatre and corps

*This case study is a summary of the case authored by Steven Messervy.

Case study 9.1 continued

Case study 9.1 continued

levels. Patriot's fast reaction capability, high firepower, and the ability to operate in a severe electronic counter-measure environment are features that were not previously available in the systems that Patriot replaced. The Patriot design eases the field logistics burden since its overall performance is achieved with fewer resources and repair parts than previous systems.

The Patriot battery (i.e., the basic firing unit) consists of phased array radar, an engagement control station, computers, power-generating equipment and upto eight remotely located launchers, each of which holds four ready-to-fire missiles. The single phased array radar provides all tactical functions of airspace surveillance, target detection, and track and missile guidance. The Raytheon Company's Missile Systems Division is the prime contractor for the Patriot system. Martin Marietta Corporation is the principal sub-contractor and assembles the missile in Orlando, Florida. Each missile costs about $600,000 and each fire unit is priced at about $82 million. The system is in its 13th year of production and is fielded with the US Army in the United States, Europe, Southwest Asia, and most recently, in South Korea. Production of the US fire units is complete. US missile production deliveries include the Patriot Anti-tactical Missile (ATM) Capability Level-2 (PAC-2).

In the mid-1980s, it was recognized by the Warsaw Pact nations that tactical ballistic missiles were proliferating throughout Europe. The US started a programme to improve the Patriot system to give it capability against these missiles. Up until then, Patriot was considered an air defence (aircraft) weapon only. A software called Patriot Advanced Capability 1 (PAC-1) was developed and put into production. The PAC-1 improvement allowed the radar to orient into a high altitude search mode for surveillance track and launch the missile against incoming tactical ballistic missiles. PAC-1 was designed to give Patriot batteries a self-defence capability in Europe. This gave the original Patriot missile the ability to intercept a missile and knock it off-course. To destroy a tactical ballistic missile warhead, a more powerful warhead was needed.
As the threats increased and time marched along, a capability to destroy the incoming missiles and defend high-value assets became necessary. The PAC-2 missile was developed with an improved fuse and warhead. Software changes were made both to the missile and the radar, which would allow the missile to intercept other missiles. The new PAC-2 was built and put into production in 1989. The missile had a production lead time of over 24 months, with the missiles for testing at White Sands Missile Range, New Mexico, to be delivered in early 1991.

When the 11th Air Defense Artillery Brigade at Fort Bliss, Texas received an alert order on 6 August 1990, only three pre-production

Case study 9.1 continued

Case study 9.1 continued

missiles were ready, and they were on the White Sands Missile Range for testing. The production of some of the parts had not even begun in the US. The commander of the brigade called up Col. Garnett, the Patriot project manager, on 7 August 1990 and told him he needed PAC-2 missiles to counter the Scud threat in Saudi Arabia. The project manager had already given the contractors verbal orders to begin 'surge' production and accelerate their delivery of the missiles. He would get them to the tactical units as soon as he could. Col. Garnett did not even have authority to accelerate production and obligate the government to finance the production. However, Col. Garnett knew the gravity of the situation, knew that timing was critical, especially with the 15 January deadline that had been set for Iraq's withdrawal from Kuwait. When interviewed later and asked how he took such a decision without proper authorization, Col. Garnett pointed to a board in his office, which read, '*It is easier to beg forgiveness, than ask permission.*' Two days later, the commander of the brigade shipped out the three pre-production missiles (that had been trucked non-stop to Texas as per Col. Garnett's orders) and loaded them into C-5A transport planes. Subsequent authority was given to accelerate production, resulting in an adequate number of missiles arriving on time. Consequently all of the Patriot missiles that were fired for the defence of Israel and Saudi Arabia were PAC-2 missiles. By the time the air campaign commenced on the 17 January 1991, 460 PAC-2 missiles were in the hands of troops in Southwest Asia. The acceleration task involved the coordinated efforts of US government agencies as well as contractors in several states and Germany. By the end of August, missiles were rolling off the production line, with the lead time condensed from six months to two weeks. Raytheon took significant business risk and shipped the missiles. Missiles that came out of the factory were directly loaded onto trucks that stood at the Martin Marietta dock. These trucks immediately proceeded to Patrick Air Force Base (next to Cape Kennedy), where the missiles were loaded onto aircrafts that carried them to Saudi Arabia. The overall *production was accelerated not once but five times* before the war in the Gulf was over. Raytheon was working 8-3-7 (three 8 hour shifts, 7 days per week).

Another major consideration during the Gulf War was the declaration by Iraq that they would wage war on Israel. The Scud threat was apparent to Israel, since it was within striking distance of the ballistic missiles. The threat of chemical warheads hitting the population of Israel was very real. On 18 January 1991, Haifa was hit with seven Scuds and a day after, Tel Aviv was hit with three missiles. The next day, US announced that it was sending Patriot batteries to Israel to protect populated areas as well as

Case study 9.1 continued

Case study 9.1 continued

military targets. During the six-week Gulf War campaign, 158 Patriot missiles were launched to intercept Iraqi Scud missiles. Additional software changes to the Patriot system were made during the Gulf campaign. Based on initial intercepts of Scud missiles, data was fed back to the US and analysed. Software was modified at least six more times during the hostilities. The improvements were possible because the missile and radar were very 'software intensive' pieces of hardware. The missile alone had over 1 million lines of code built into various components. Upgrades to the software (many times done with limited data and over the weekend) allowed the Patriot system to predict Scud trajectories more accurately and to have more precision in its own trajectory. The minimum engagement altitude was raised to avoid Patriot having to engage warheads too close to the ground, to reduce radar clutter and also to account for false targets being generated by radar energy reflected off buildings.

Initially, Army sources claimed an interception success rate of 95 per cent for both Saudi Arabia and Israel, which was subsequently revised downward to a 70 per cent success rate for Saudi Arabia and a 40 per cent rate for Israel. A special report released by the Centre for International and Security Policy Studies not long after the cessation of hostilities stated that although the Patriot '... demonstrated for the first time in combat, that it is possible to hit a bullet with a bullet, the interceptions also demonstrated the limits of the Patriot, even against primitive ballistic missiles such as the Scud. Patriot missiles hit the Iraqi missiles at too low an altitude and with insufficient power.' Almost a year after Operation Desert Storm, an article in the *Boston Globe said*, '... there is mounting evidence that the missile, the supposed high-tech hero of the war, failed repeatedly and may not have succeeded even once—and that the Army and Raytheon have been trying to discount that evidence.'[11]

Regardless of the technical performance of the missile system, the deployment of the Patriot system in Saudi Arabia and Israel added tremendous value to the citizens of the US, Saudi Arabia and Israel. Some sources credit the deployment of Patriot for use with the Israeli Defence Force as a factor in the Israeli decision not to enter into hostilities. Several sources also talk of the reassurance that the Patriot system gave to the population as a whole during the campaign of terror started by Iraq. Undoubtedly, the value added by each missile was more than its average unit cost of $600,000.

CASE STUDY 9.2

Tata Steel's Merchant Mill Gets a Second Life

Tata Steel's Merchant Mill (MM) was installed in 1960. It produces 16 mm to 40 mm bars, which are used in construction projects such as high-rise buildings, bridges and highways. Although at the time of its commissioning, MM was the most modern plant in the company, it is now one of Tata Steel's oldest plants. For most of the 1980s and 1990s, the performance of MM had been dismal for a variety of reasons, such as shortage of electric power to feed the mill, other priority products for the marketing division of the company, etc. The annual production during that period varied from 90,000 tons to 150,000 tons. By December 1997, when Nandji Pandey took over as Chief of Merchant Mill, the plant looked like an ideal entity for closure.

The 1990s was also the time when the company embarked on major modernization. All unviable plants, which were mostly the older plants, would have to be closed. The Rolling Mills (RM1 and RM2) that supplied 75 mm × 75 mm billets (long bars that had a square cross-section) were old and in a rundown condition. The company had by now implemented continuous casting (CC) from the LD furnaces, to cast billets (100 mm square as well as 127 mm square) and slabs through the more modern CC method. The MM design would not allow use of such large-sized billets to be used as feedstock in place of the 75 mm square billets for which it was designed. The management of the company was unwilling to make any further capital investments into the MM, which by all accounts, was essentially a dying plant. RM1 was closed in 1998, being old and unviable operationally. By 1999, it was clear that there was no other option but to close down RM2 as well, for similar reasons. Accordingly MM was expected to close by 2000–2001. There were about 400 employees, including 12 officers at the MM. Most of the employees were in the workmen category and their careers were at stake.

Soon after taking over as its chief, Mr Pandey was obsessed with trying to find a way to prevent the certainty of closure. He addressed his workers in the local colloquial Hindi dialect:

> Every once in a while in the life of man, one gets an opportunity to do extraordinary things. I realize our situation in the MM plant is very bad. The plant is very run-down. Production has been very low and the

Case study 9.2 continued

Case study 9.2 continued

> plant has been losing a lot of money for our company. Our management has been patient for the last several years. Given the age of the plant, which is already about 40 years old, they are in no mood to sink more money into it. However I believe in the capabilities of each of you. You are the people who know most about the process. I believe that as a team we can achieve miracles. All the work that has to be done in this plant has to be done by you and you know best what needs to be done. So far, in the 30 years of my career in Tata Steel, I have not accepted defeat. In fact, I have not accepted defeat in my life. People who know me in this company tell me that whatever I get into my head, I will go all out to achieve it. I have had considerable success in facing many challenges in the company in my previous assignments. I have never done these relatively difficult things in anticipation of any reward or promotion. I believe together we can demonstrate spectacular results in the MM plant. This will need sustained teamwork over the next many months. I am willing to give my best. Will you work with me on this exciting opportunity?

There was a thunderous round of applause from the group of workers. Unanimously all of them affirmed their faith in Mr Pandey and told him that they would follow where he led them.

Mr Pandey realized that the only way to prevent closure of the plant was to bring the plant back to financial health quickly, without seeking incremental investment and to do this, the only way was to rapidly ramp up the production levels in the plant. Mr Pandey motivated his team of officers and workers to bring their best ideas so that they could continue to operate the plant using the 100/127 mm square billets, which were supplied by the continuous caster, in place of the earlier 75 mm square billets from RM2. The team came up with several ideas and implemented them systematically. None of these required any significant incremental investment. Whatever little money was needed to implement the ideas generated by the MM team was spent from the revenue budget of the mill. The steps taken included: frequent and thorough maintenance, changing the design of the hydraulic pushers to take care of the large sized billets, changing entry and exit guides to the furnace, improving mixing of fuel gas and air in the burners to create a better swirling effect and improving the material handling and logistics in the plant. Most important, however, was the change in mindset of the workforce and inculcating a 'can do' attitude among the workforce, which Mr Pandey systematically embarked upon. The team also rationalized the product mix and eliminated products that did not have adequate margins.

The average production of the MM plant had been in the range of 300–500 tons per day for the last several years, before Mr Pandey took over as

Case study 9.2 continued

Case study 9.2 continued

the Chief of the Plant. Based on the steps he took to motivate his team, the production on 20 December 1997 was a record of 1,298.1 ton. This was a major turning point for MM. It showed people that with focus, determination and teamwork, it was possible to make the mill economically vibrant again. In his usual characteristic style, Mr Pandey addressed a meeting on the shop floor to celebrate this achievement on the following day,

> You have seen what is possible to achieve in a short span of just three weeks. Together we can move mountains. Whether the mill will close or not from now on depends on each of you. Will you join me to work together to make our mill a healthy milk-giving cow which gives milk to the rest of the company?

His manner of speaking, sincerity, language, choice of analogies were down-to-earth and appealing to the largely semi-educated workforce. He led the battle from the front. He met every one of the 400 people in the MM plant during the first few days of his taking over as Chief, MM.

Whenever there was any achievement, however, modest, by anyone in the plant, Mr Pandey made it a point to acknowledge the contribution of those people who made it possible. He did this by calling for an impromptu meeting on the shop floor. Genuinely celebrating little achievements became a hallmark of his style. For any record that was broken and bettered, such as breaking a previous production record for a working shift, or a breaking a previous day production record, he ensured that sweets were distributed to the entire workforce of the MM plant.

Apart from direct face-to-face communication on every possible occasion, he sent written messages in his earthy style in Hindi, to every one of the 400 members of the team. When the top managers of the company sent messages to him, congratulating him for the progress being made at the plant, he ensured that individual copies of these messages were given to all the 400 team members. He conducted unscheduled meetings daily on the shop floor, with small groups of employees, nudging them to achieve even greater heights. He could be seen in his elements at any time of the day or night, through the week in the shop floor of the plant.

The sea-change in the mindset of the MM team can be seen from the fact that although there was no significant capital expenditure on the mill from December 1997, the production was on a steep climb. During April 2003 to March 2004, production reached an all-time record high of 300,000 tons, which was considerably higher than the rated capacity of the plant, and significantly higher than the production of about 150,000 tons in the year before he took over as Chief of the mill. This made the Managing Director of the company, B. Muthuraman, comment that 'The

Case study 9.2 continued

Case study 9.2 continued

capacity of a plant is not on the name plate of the equipment but in the minds of the people running it!'

When asked to comment on the secret of his success, Mr Pandey with characteristic modesty replies:

> Basically, I am a maintenance person who has moved into operations. A maintenance person is trained to be analytical. Hence grasping technical issues is not a problem for me. I spend a lot of time on the shop floor with my boys. There is a total change in their mindset. These changes are irreversible. They will achieve extraordinary things even if I move from this position to another assignment in the company. The mill is now stabilized and my team does everything.

Mr Pandey gives a lot of emphasis on training his team. He gives tremendous importance to the people at the lower level. He talks to them in their language. He never loses his temper at people working at the grass-roots level. Some of the 12 officer-cadre team members in the mill may be occasionally treated in a harsh manner by him, but never any of the workers. Perhaps, this is attributable to his humble background in a rustic village. His style is natural. It can not be taught. The workers in the mill work in conditions of intense heat. They appreciate him as someone who comes down to their level and speaks their language. Often he invites groups of his team members and their families to his home or to small get-togethers at other locations. Without any hesitation he often indulges in sharing tea and snacks on the shop floor with his workmen. These are small things. Most managers feel that these gestures go unnoticed and hence maintain distance from their workers. In reality all this has a lot of impact.

People see the genuineness of his approach, his sense of ownership of the mill and understand that he practises what he preaches. They are willing to give their all and emulate his example without any thought of reward or promotion. It is visible from the spectacular results in the MM plant.

To sum up, Mr Pandey did manage to extract a *'Free Lunch'* out of the Merchant Mill. This was possible through many small innovations that came from each of the 400 employees of the Merchant Mill. What Mr Pandey succeeded in doing was to motivate his entire team of *People* to innovate, leveraging their *Knowledge* of the *Machines* in the Merchant Mill to produce spectacular results.

Notes

1. www. quotationspage.com
2. FLP™ is a registered trademark of TIM,Tel Aviv, Israel.
3. Jay Galbraith's star model is found in a number of his writings; see *Designing Complex Organizations* (1973), *Organization Design* (1977), both published by Addison Wesley, Reading, MA, and *Designing the Global Corporation* (San Francisco, CA: Jossey-Bass, 2002).
4. Jim Collins' book is *Good to Great* (New York: HarperCollins, 2001).
5. Heifetz's books are: Ronald A. Heifetz and Marty Linsky, *Leadership on the Line: Staying alive through the dangers of leading* (Boston, MA: Harvard Business School Press, 2002) (the quote is on page 14) and Ronald A. Heifetz, *Leadership Without Easy Answers* (Boston, MA: Harvard Business School Press). See also John P. Kotter and Dan S. Cohen, *The Heart of Change* (Boston, MA: Harvard Business School Press, 2002).
6. Peter Drucker, *Lessons in Leadership* (San Francisco, CA: Jossey-Bass, 1998).
7. The action-learning exercise for IBM Chair John Akers was invented by MIT Professor Lester Thurow.
8. FLP calculations have been done for Fortune 100 companies each year, since 2000, in *USAToday*; see 'Productivity Grows in Spite of Recession', *USAToday*, Monday, 29 July 2002, Money Section, pp. B1–2, and *USAToday*, Money section, pp. B1–2, 13 August 2003.
9. Alwyn Young, 'A Tale of Two Cities: Factor Accumulation and Technical Change in Hong Kong and Singapore', in Olivier J. Blanchard and Stanley Fisher (eds), *NBER Macroeconomics Annual* (Cambridge, MA: MIT Press, 1992).
10. Charles Homs report is 'Understanding IT's Impact on Productivity', Forrester Associates: TechnStrategy™ Report, November 2002.
11. Ross Kerber, 'MIT Professor Faults Operation of Patriot Missile', *Boston Globe*, 30 April 2004.

Chapter 10
Scale and scope: Scaling markets of one

Scale and scope: friends, foes, allies, enemies .... Great managers persuade them to lie down together.
—Anon

The lion and the lamb shall lie down together .... But the lamb will not get much sleep.
—Woody Allen[1]

It was the development of new technologies and the opening of new markets, which resulted in economies of scale and of scope ... that made the large multiunit industrial enterprise come when it did, where it did, and in the way it did.
—Alfred D. Chandler[2]

LEARNING OBJECTIVES After you read this chapter, you should understand:

- **How to define and measure economies of scale and economies of scope**
- **Why both scale and scope economies have driven key global industries like oil refining and chemicals for over a century**
- **Why scale and scope are close allies and sometimes fierce enemies**
- **How, why and when 'mass customization' replaces 'mass production' as the driving business model of capitalism**
- **How to overcome an incumbent market leader's advantage in 'scale' by innovating and creating 'markets of one' (mass customization)**
- **What 'platform leadership' is and how to implement it**

TOOL #6 Creating and measuring economies of scale and economies of scope

10.1 INTRODUCTION

In their book *How the West Grew Rich*, Nathan Rosenberg and L.E. Birdzell summarize hundreds of years of history and answer the key title question in a short passage. Their 'bottom line' conclusion:

> The West has grown rich, by comparison to other economies, by allowing its economic sector the autonomy to experiment in the development of

new and diverse products, methods of manufacture, modes of enterprise organization, market relations, methods of transportation and communication, and relations between capital and labor. The market institutions that developed within this context made it possible to capture high rewards for successful innovation and threatened those who failed to innovate with decline and demise.[3]

Under capitalism, entrepreneurs and CEOs have become modern versions of Vasco da Gama, Magellan or Captain Cook—exploring technology and global markets. They find ways to *scale* their products and services, to compete in global markets, and to expand the *scope* of their product offerings. As they do so, they face major obstacles, among them, the lion-and-lamb dilemma: How to make the lamb of creativity, innovation and scope lie down with the lion of scale, and sleep well, when both are absolutely vital for global success.

The topic of this chapter is 'scale' and 'scope', or, volume and variety. We will argue that the link between the two is exceptionally complex, ranging from hostility to strong complementarity. This creates *complexity* with which engineers and managers must struggle, in order to create a simple, powerful, memorable product offering for customers—one that comprises an experience customers will seek to buy again and again. This chapter will provide tools that help achieve this. We begin by defining 'scale' and 'scope'. We then explain why scale and scope are simultaneously enemies and friends and why understanding the processes that drive them is so crucial.

DEFINITIONS

- **Scale: Economies of scale [are] those that result when the increased size of a single operating unit producing or distributing a single product reduces the unit cost of production or distribution.**
- **Scope: Economies of [scope] are those resulting from the use of processes within a single operating unit to produce or distribute more than one product, and reduce input costs.**

These definitions focus on cost savings resulting from scale and scope. A broader interpretation would relate to 'value creation' as well as to 'unit cost reduction'—that is, innovation and value creation that stem from either size and scale, or from broadening product lines using existing technology and processes. Economies of scale as the fundamental driving force underlying capitalism date back to Adam Smith's *Wealth of Nations* (1776). His famous 'pin factory' example shows how, when 18 separate pin-making operations are each given to a single person, specialization and efficiency slash costs, compared to a situation in which a single pin-maker tries to do all the 18 tasks himself.

Action learning

Scale and Scope within Your Family

Nobel Prize Laureate for Economics Gary Becker, Professor of Economics & Sociology at University of Chicago, has developed what is known as Household Economics—application of economic theory to understanding relationships and behaviour within families.[4]

Consider your own family. (*i*) Examine economies of scale—what savings do you experience, because you purchase for a family rather than separate individuals? (*ii*) Examine economies of scope: what is made possible by operating as a household, in terms of the range of products, services and experiences you create, purchase and enjoy, that would not be possible if the household operated as separate individuals?

Are there diseconomies of scale and scope for your household?

Take into account not only *cost savings* but also value creation. What can families do, in scale and scope, that collections of individuals may not?

Case studies: Economies of scale and scope

Scale: Standard Oil Trust

In 1882, John D. Rockefeller's Standard Oil Company created the Standard Oil Trust. (Trust comes from the word 'trustee', not from 'faith' or 'belief'; a board of *trustees* was formed.) Its goal was not to create a monopoly. Standard Oil was one already, controlling 90 per cent of America's kerosene, the product used to light lamps that was then the main use of petroleum. *The goal was to reorganize and streamline kerosene production, to make the monopoly virtually unassailable and nearly global.*

The Trust built three huge refineries, each with capacity of 6,500 barrels per day (huge in those days, not today!), triple the size of existing refineries. As a result, average cost per gallon of kerosene fell from 2.5 cents to 1.5 cents. Profit margins doubled, from half a cent per gallon of crude in 1884 to a full cent in 1885. Rockefeller was able to refine kerosene in New Jersey, ship to Europe and under-price Russian-made kerosene produced almost on the spot. It is important to understand: the economies of scale in kerosene production were not automatic! They arose from managerial and organizational skill, in running huge facilities, coordinating shipping, production, marketing and distribution

Case study continued

Case study continued

seamlessly. More than once, huge scale economies are ruined because managers simply cannot handle the complexity of efficiently running a huge facility.

The scale economies created by the Standard Oil Trust over 120 years ago endure, creating one of today's largest companies, Exxon-Mobil, even though anti-trust legislation broke up Standard Oil into several pieces, as it did to AT&T many years later. Standard Oil's business model, built on managerial skill in managing large-scale production to capture cost reductions, was so powerful that its impact has endured for much longer than a century.

Scale: Container ships

Some economies of scale are so simple, they can be understood using grade-school physics, and then employed to predict the future direction of a huge industry (shipping) for the next 40 years. In the 1970s, container technology was introduced. The idea was simple: Ship things in standard-size boxes rather than as bulk cargo. This enabled automated handling of the containers, lowering costs and improving speed of loading and unloading. The standard container was 20 feet long; a double container was 40 feet. Initial investments in ships and equipment were heavy but they quickly paid for themselves.

Consider container ships. The value of a ship (its revenues) depends on how many containers it can carry. Suppose, for simplicity, the container hold is a cube, of dimensions $a \times a \times a = a^3$. The value of the ship, then, varies with its cargo hold volume, or a^3.

The capital cost of building the ship depends on the quantity of steel. The total area of the cargo hold is the surface of the cube with dimensions a on each side, or six squares each with surface area a^2, or $6a^2$. Hence, the ratio of 'value' to 'cost' is $a/6$, which means that the bigger the ship, the more money it makes relative to the cost of building it (Figure 10.1).

Using these two simple formulae, then, for volume and surface area, we could easily predict the 40-year history of the container ship industry, and shipping in general—'the race for size'. The bigger the ship, the cheaper and more competitive it is. This indeed has been the case. From ships carrying a few hundred containers, the industry has evolved to the use of massive container ships carrying 7,000 containers or more, that can dock in only a few huge ports such as Hong Kong or Singapore. *Only shippers able to build and operate such ships can compete.* We could have foreseen this right from the outset

Case study continued

Case study continued

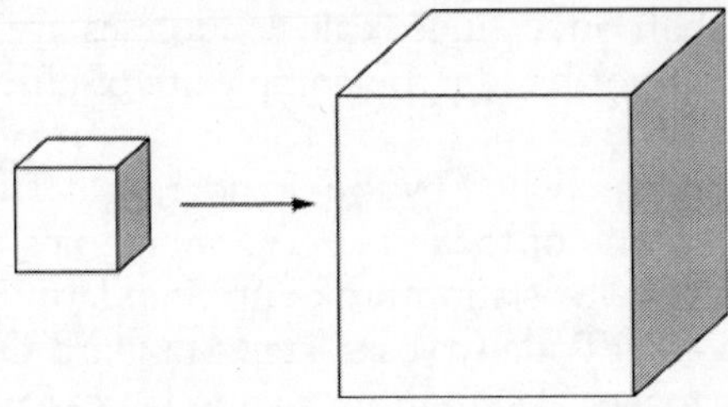

The volume of a cube with side 'a' is a^3, while its surface area is $6a^2$. The ratio of volume to surface area is $a^3/6a^2$, or a/6. This means that the ratio of 'value' to 'area' varies directly with 'a'. If the cost of the cube varies with its surface area (i.e., the cost of the steel, or cardboard, or plastic), while its value varies with its volume, then the bigger the cube, the bigger the value/cost ratio. This is the physical foundation of many economies of scale related to capacity—for shipping, oil tanks, and pipelines, for instance. The same principle applies to pipelines. The volume of a cylinder varies with the square of the diameter, i.e., it is proportional to πd^2, while the surface area varies with the circumference, i.e., it is proportional to πd. Doubling the pipeline diameter creates huge savings in the ratio of value (volume) to cost (surface area of steel).

Figure 10.1
Scale economies through volume/value

Economy of Scale—Example

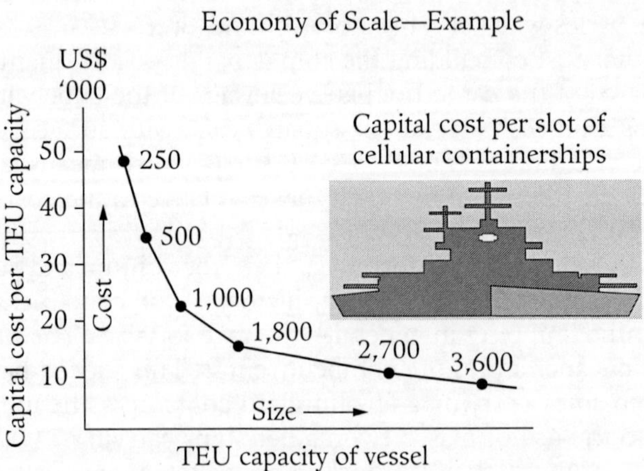

Figure 10.2
Capital cost per twenty-equivalent-unit (TEU) capacity for container ships

Case study continued

Case study continued

(see Figure 10.2). Managers and entrepreneurs who understood this would gear their company from the outset for rapid growth and large-scale financing. Note, at the same time, that scale economies created niche opportunities. Some shipping lines ply between small and large ports, 'feeding' the large ports where gigantic container ships dock. This 'niche', too, could have been predicted long ago. Wise managers could have built their strategies based either on global competition or niche competition.

The capital cost per container slot for container ships is less than one-fifth for huge ships (5,000 containers or more), than it is for small ships (250 containers) because of massive economies of scale. The underlying dynamics of many industries that have scale economies thus becomes a race for size and scale.

Source: Alfred Chandler, *Scale and Scope: The Dynamics of Industrial Capitalism* (Cambridge, MA: Belknap Press, 1990).

While oil pipelines are very different from cargo ships, they are driven by very similar economies of scale. The volume of oil a pipeline carries depends on its volume (the square of its diameter), while the surface area of the pipeline (and hence the cost of the steel) varies with its diameter, similar to the volume/area physics of the cube. So the bigger the pipeline, the cheaper it is to build per barrel of crude oil or million cubic metres of natural gas. We would thus expect huge pipelines to be built even if their capacity is little-used initially and this is in fact the case. This is examined in greater detail later in the chapter.

The fibre-optic 'pipelines' (fibre optic networks built to carry voice, data and video) are closely similar to oil pipelines. It is said that some 99 per cent of the world's fibre-optic lines are 'dark' (have not carried even one light beam even once). Is this a sign of wasteful overspending? Perhaps but perhaps not. If you are digging fibre-optic ditches, why not put in huge capacity from the outset, reap economies of scale and avoid costly digging again when you run out of network capacity? Most infrastructure investments are characterized by scale economies provided that the management skill exists to operate huge facilities efficiently. This is not always the case. General Motors' Lordstown automobile assembly plant was huge and had state-of-the-art technology but was hard to manage and even harder to work in (pin-factory tasks were minute, boring, repetitive and ultimately unsustainable). The factory reaped no economies of scale at all.

Case study: Bayer-Hoechst-BASF: Economies of scope

At the time Standard Oil Trust was being formed, German dye makers were making huge investments to exploit economies of scope. The huge plants could make hundreds of different dyes and pharmaceuticals based on the same raw materials and feedstock. The companies that joined in this effort—Bayer, Hoechst, BASF—slashed the cost of one product, red alizarin dye, to 1/30 its previous level.

As Chandler notes: 'The first company to build a plant of minimum efficient scale (and scope) and recruit the essential management team remained the leader in its industry for decades.' Bayer, Hoechst, BASF remain dominant global chemical and pharmaceutical companies to this day.

Source: Alfred Chandler, *Scale and Scope: The Dynamics of Industrial Capitalism* (Cambridge, MA: Belknap Press, 1990).

10.2 NETWORK ECONOMIES

A modern version of scale and scope economies is known as 'network economies'.[5] Services and products based on groups of users—e.g., Internet service providers, portals, even cellphone users—get better and cheaper as more people join, because the number of people in the network who can be accessed is a vital 'quality' parameter. This too is based on high school math. A network with 'n' members has (n)(n–1) / 2 possible connections between two people. If six people network, there are (6 × 5) / 2 = 15 possible links. If 12 people network: there are (12 × 11) / 2 = 66 links. Doubling the number of people in the network raised the number of links by more than four times! *In general, the number of links rises approximately with the square of the number of network members.* Yet the *cost* of adding one more member is negligible (the fibre-optic cable and computer servers are already there). This has led to a phenomenon known as 'winner take all'—the biggest network swallows, ultimately, all the users and customers, because it is the most valuable. Many of today's leading-edge businesses (cellphones, Internet, eBay) are indeed based on network economies. While modern analysis has regarded 'winner take all' as a relatively new idea, Chandler in fact shows that it is at least a century old, dating back to Standard Oil, Bayer and BASF.

10.3 MEASURING ECONOMIES OF SCALE AND SCOPE

In order to measure economies of scale and scope, and fully understand the intricate lion–lamb relationship between them, engineers and managers will need one of two tools: A matrix table showing Total Cost of producing two or more products, depending on the total amounts of each product produced, distributed, sold and maintained; or, an algebraic cost function TC(X,Y), showing the total cost of making X units of product x and Y units of product y.

Using Cost Matrices: When a matrix cost table is used, scale and scope is measured as follows:

Economies of Scale: $TC(2X,2Y) < 2TC(X,Y)$
Economies of Scope: $TC(X,Y) < TC(X,0) + TC(0,Y)$

These ideas are explained in detail in the following.

DEFINITION

Economies of scale exist when doubling the scale of operations (i.e., doubling both X and Y) leads to an increase in Total Cost less than double:

Total Cost for 2X units of x, and 2Y units of y is less than two times Total Cost (for X units of x, Y units of y)

For instance (see Table 10.1): Two thousand units of X and two thousand units of Y cost \$27 million. Four thousands units of X and four thousand units of Y cost \$34 million. While output has risen by 100 per cent, total cost has risen by only about 26 per cent. This is a substantial saving. The cost matrix in Table 10.1 reveals considerable economies of scale. Big companies will have a major cost advantage over small ones. (Small companies, facing this, will need to be innovative in order to compete.)

Table 10.1
Calculating scale and scope economies

		Total cost of selling X and Y (\$ million)				
		Amounts of X ('000 units per day)				
		0	1	2	3	4
Amounts of	0	10	15	20	25	30
Y	1	15	19	23	27	31
('000 units	2	20	23	27	29	32
per day)	3	25	27	29	31	33
	4	30	31	32	33	34

DEFINITION

Economies of scope exist when producing X and Y together costs less than producing them separately, in separate facilities or businesses:
Total Cost for X units of x and Y units of y, produced together is less than the Total Cost for X units of x and zero units of y, plus the Total Cost for Y units of y and zero units of x.

In Table 10.1, making four thousand units of x and four thousand units of y *together* costs \$34 million. Making, marketing, selling and distributing the same output separately would cost \$30 million plus \$30 million. (Cost of [zero X, 4,000 Y], plus cost of [zero Y, 4,000 X] or \$60 million.) So there are major economies of scope in the cost structure shown in Table 10.1.

Note that scale and scope here are allies or complements. Scale may make economies of scope possible, for instance, to use the same sales force that sells X to sell Y as well. This is related to 'platform leadership' (building a 'platform' from which many new products can be spun off). The reader might ask: Are not scale and scope economies always present? The answer is, no. Companies, for instance, that dilute their brand definition by trying to sell products outside their traditional lines will encounter broad *diseconomies* of scope. Companies whose management cannot handle scale will find that unit costs rise rather than fall, as the company scales upward. Ultimately, scale and scope result not from technology but from good management.

10.4 USING COST FUNCTIONS

When an algebraic cost function is available, scale and scope are measured as follows:

DEFINITION

Economies of scale are present when: $TC(2X, 2Y) < 2TC(X, Y)$

Economies of scope are present when: $TC(X, 0) + TC(0, Y) < TC(X, Y)$

TC = Total Cost

Case study: Scale in oil pipelines

Leslie Kookenboo has found that the formula for the amount of daily oil throughput through a pipeline is given by:

$$\text{Throughput} = CH^{0.37}\ D^{1.73}$$

where c = constant, H = horsepower of the pumping motors, D = diameter of the pipe.

Note that the volume of a cylinder is given by the length of the cylinder multiplied by the area of its cross-section. The latter, a circle, is given by: $\pi(D/2)^2$.

This means that when the scale of the pipeline doubles (i.e., diameter is doubled), the volume of oil it carries rises by four times. (The coefficient in Kookenboo's equation is 1.73, not quite 2, because of complex viscosity factors and friction.)

Case study: Scope in food and clothes

As Wal-Mart grew to dominate large-store retailing, it could have been predicted that it would expand to include groceries as well, in the same stores, because of economies of scope. Suppose X is clothes, Y is food, and the Wal-Mart cost function is:

$$TC(X,Y) = 5X + 6Y - 0.1XY$$

Selling 10 units of X and Y separately would cost $5 \times 10 + 6 \times 10 = 110$. Selling them together, under the same roof, purchasing unit, etc., would cost $5 \times 10 + 6 \times 10 - 0.1 \times 10 \times 10 = 110 - 10 = 100$. Economies of scope bring 10 per cent cost savings. In groceries, this is substantial. Grocery supermarket chains like Krogers should have been fastening their seat belts many years ago, preparing for Wal-Mart's entry into food retailing.

Case study: Music and the music business

Economists William Baumol and William Bowen explain, in their book *The Economics of the Performing Arts*, that art, music, theatre and ballet for

Case study continued

Case study continued

years faced an inherent disadvantage: lack of scalability. You need four musicians and 25 minutes to play a Haydn string quartet. That is a given. As overall wages rise, you need to pay the musicians more. Yet their output remains the same. So their 'product' becomes more and more expensive. Productivity gains cannot reduce unit costs. Suddenly, recording technology (magnetic tape) emerges, and makes it possible to record and sell that Haydn quartet to the whole world. A huge new industry is born, based on scale and scope (you can record and supply *all* Haydn's quartets, as well as Bach's, Beethoven's, etc.). Then that industry falls asleep and is nearly wiped out by a predictable emerging technology: person-to-person Internet music downloads, that takes scale and scope of music to a new level, by digitizing it and providing it as bits and bytes.

It is vital for managers to understand that contrary to common opinion, technology revolutions do not occur overnight. They are largely predictable. The music industry was complacent at a time when it should have sounded alarm bells long ago.[6]

Action learning

Products and Industries with Dis-economies of Scale and Scope

The relationship between scale and scope is like that between parents with teenagers—highly complex and hard to manage. Consider steel. In its Great Leap Forward, the People's Republic of China encouraged backyard steel mills. In an industry with huge economies of scale the result was predictably disastrous. Two decades later, along comes the innovative American steel company Nucor, with its 'mini-mills'. These smaller flexible steel mills gained cost and quality advantages over their competitors, exploiting *dis*economies of scale by becoming smaller. As Jim Collins notes in his book Good to Great, '... During 1973–88 Nucor shares outperformed the general rise in the stock market by 5.16 times!'.[7]

Think of two or three products and industries where there are major diseconomies of scale and diseconomies of scope—where small is beautiful.

Think about technologies that could disrupt this situation and reverse it, creating cost savings and value creation with size.

10.5 WHY SCALE AND SCOPE ARE ENEMIES–AND FAST FRIENDS

On 9 November 1989, Jorma Olylla, a mid-level manager from a Finnish firm called Nokia, was vacationing with his family in Southern France. At the time Nokia was a highly diversified unfocused company that at various stages in its 150 year history had made paper, rubber boots, electronics and other products. Olylla watched the fall of the Berlin Wall on television. Unlike others, he had a vision, based on a kind of feedback loop that he built in his mind. (a) The Fall of the Wall, he reasoned, will bring German unification; (b) That will bring European unification. (c) That will create a huge European single market. (d) That will create the need for communication Europe-wide. (e) That, in turn, will create demand for mobile phones and related services. (For some reason, feedback loops of this sort work best when there are five steps ... fewer is oversimplifying, more than five seems to lead to wrong forecasts.) Olylla returned to Finland, persuaded Nokia to focus its resources on the fledgling mobile phone industry and became its CEO and Chair. Nokia is today a global company.[8]

Nokia uses its scale—selling up to a third of the 400 million mobile handsets sold worldwide each year—to cut costs and fund R&D. It uses scope to offer customers a wide variety of cellphones, covering every possible need and taste. In this sense, scale and scope are close friends. Scale enables companies to become global—in fact, in many industries, such as financial services, scale is vital for survival. Scale enables scope, it permits integrated financial services organizations, like Citicorp, to provide a complete array of financial services—commercial and investment banking, trading, brokerage, underwriting, even insurance that large organizations seek today. You need scale to enable scope and you need scope to make scale truly pay.

But there is a sense in which scale and scope are enemies. Scale and size are enemies of innovation. And scope is driven by innovation. For instance, when Sprint spent $1 billion on a US-wide fibre-optic network, its managers and engineers had to dream up new services—economies of scope—that customers would want, in order to make the investment profitable. Many organizations that begin as startups (such as Intel, or Apple) grow rapidly, and as they do so, their very size dampens the chaotic creative spirit that drove them to initial success; more and more creative individuals find the bureaucratic atmosphere of the big company stifling for their ideas. So scale becomes a double enemy. It stifles creativity precisely when it is most needed. And it destroys profitability, by turning products into standard commodities, one like another, like peas in a pod.

The latter process is known as 'commoditization'. It occurs in nearly every industry where innovative products spring up, compete, and ultimately become standardized.

10.6 MEET THE ENEMY: 'COMMODITIZATION'

Some readers will recall the early days of PCs, featuring names like Apple, Commodore, Atari, Osborne and others. Each PC looked very different from all other models, and all were incompatible with each other. Within a short period of time, an 'election' was held. Consumers voted for different PC versions with their dollars by buying them. In August 1981 the IBM PC was produced. It became the gold standard of PCs. Soon 'clones' appeared, looking and operating exactly like the IBM version. It became hard to compete by innovating new PC features—so producers competed by becoming efficient and reducing costs. The PC was on the way to becoming a commodity. The race then becomes one of cost reduction and scale.

This process is known as commoditization, whereby an industry with vastly different versions of the same product undergoes standardization, a standard common set of product features emerges that are necessary to remain in the market and are demanded by consumers; then product prices fall as economies of scale production kick in and the product becomes much like flour or sugar—each unit looks, tastes and performs very much like every other unit. This process is shown in Figure 10.3.

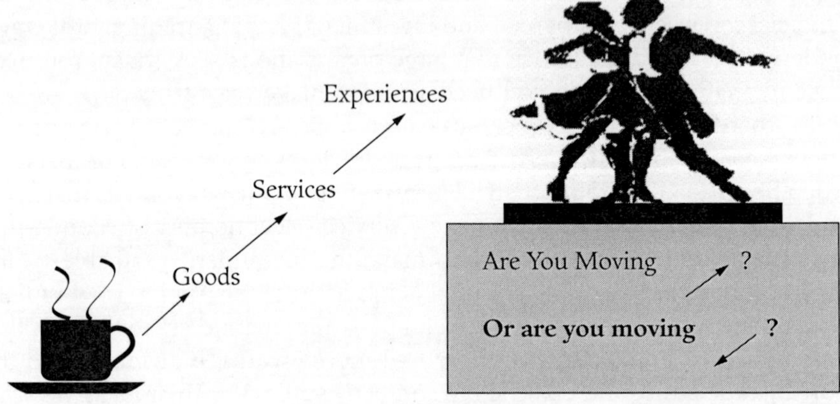

Figure 10.3
From commoditization to experiences

Source: Gilmour and Pine, *The Experience Economy* (2000).

Companies face continual downward pressure on their products and services, as commoditization pushes them downward on the 'experience to commodity' ladder. The lower you are on the ladder, the greater the price sensitivity, the fiercer the downward pressure on prices and the smaller the profit margins. Resisting commoditization is essential. It is done by creating unique product offerings that incorporate 'branding' (persuading customers to pay more for a product simply because it has a few letters on it, say, S-O-N-Y or I-B-M); superb customer service; or even, a remarkably memorable customer experience different from all others. The case of Jordan's Furniture is an example.

Goods can be placed on a scale starting from 'commodities'. Commodities are undifferentiated products, e.g., salt or flour, bought largely on the basis of price, where competition largely focuses on lowering production costs. Goods are differentiated (e.g., Morton's Salt, which contains iodine) and branded. Services are processes that satisfy wants, resolve problems or needs and are person-specific. Finally experiences are services that are memorable. The higher the product is on this scale, the less price sensitive it is and the higher the profit margins.

Case study: Jordan's Furniture

Furniture stores are similar and in general sell commodity-like items. The Teitelman Brothers took their father's Boston furniture store, risked a major investment and created a unique experience. They built a small version of New Orleans' Bourbon Street at the entrance to their store and invited people to come see it. Furniture showrooms are placed to the right and left of the Bourbon Street attraction. People come to see 'Bourbon Street', enjoy the experience—and often remain to buy a sofa they had not really intended to purchase. Of course, furniture quality, service, delivery, etc., are vital. But the key issue of how to get people into your store first (you cannot sell furniture unless people come in to the store) was resolved in a highly creative way by Jordan, who thus also defeated commoditization.

According to B. Joseph Pine (2000), a new business model is now conquering capitalism: mass customization. Whereas Henry Ford pioneered mass production, today Michael Dell has pioneered mass customization: 'markets of one', the tailoring of product offerings to each individual customer's wants and needs. It is a proven successful way to battle the inroads of commoditization on profit margins and market share.

10.7 FROM MASS PRODUCTION TO MASS CUSTOMIZATION

Henry Ford is said to have got the idea from a Chicago meatpacking plant, where carcasses of cows and pigs were strung up and moved along an overhead pulley line and workers processed the carcass at two dozen points or more along the line. He built a similar 'assembly line' for Model T cars. Once cars were assembled individually from a pile of parts on the floor. Ford pulled the chassis along a line with workers putting on individual parts (engine, lights, steering wheel) at each point on the line. It was his version of Adam Smith's pin factory. The result: enormous cost savings, reduction in prices and essentially, a way of inventing capitalism (see Figure 10.4). Russia's Joseph Stalin, who succeeded Lenin, copied Ford's mass production River Rouge factory near Detroit, building a much larger version of it near Moscow in the 1930s. Communism hated capitalism but tried its best to adopt its mass production scale economies.

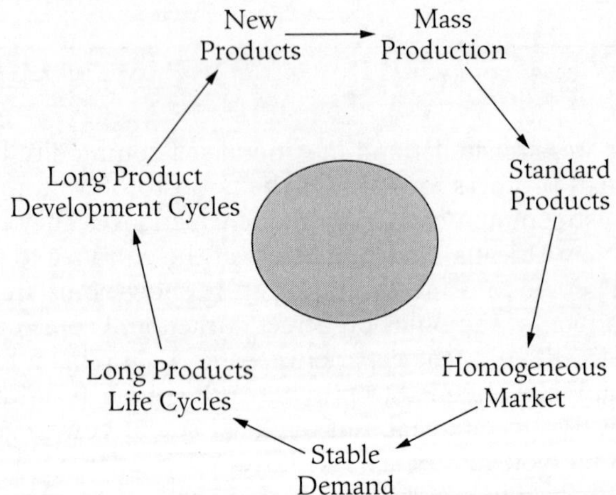

Figure 10.4
The old system (Mass production)

Ford had built a business model based on a virtuous cycle: mass produce standard products, slash costs, slash prices, make new products affordable and create new markets as a result and continue this process by leveraging profits and reinvestment. Ford's Model T dominated the market in 1925. But the mass production system was vulnerable to innovation. It is ironic that just when Joseph Stalin was embracing the model for Russia, it was being made obsolete by one of history's greatest managers, Alfred P. Sloan.

Sloan founded General Motors by pulling together several small car producers (Chevrolet, Buick, Cadillac, Pontiac) under one roof. He fought Henry Ford's standard black Model T with closed body cars, a variety of engines and different colours, in other words, partial customization. In 1927–28, facing slumping sales, Henry Ford closed the River Rouge plant for over a year to retool and customize his cars. Ford lost market share to General Motors, skated to the edge of bankruptcy and it took decades for the company to recover. Only the success of its Taurus model in Europe generated profits to keep the company alive in the 1950s.

Today a new business model is coming to dominate capitalism, made possible by global markets and technology: Mass Customization. In this model, innovative products emerge rapidly and frequently and are tailored to the unique wants of individual market segments and customers. Demand is fragmented, rather than mass and management complexity is enormous (see Figure 10.5). The virtuous cycle of mass production changes both in nature and direction. This powerful trend pervades industries as different as hamburgers and personal computers.

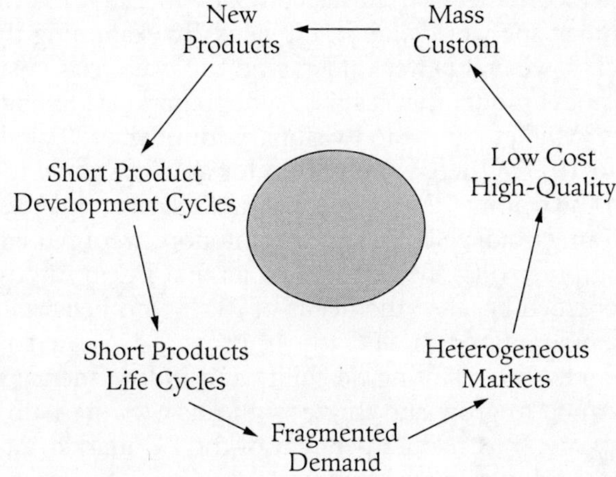

Figure 10.5
The new system (Mass customization)

10.8 FROM COMMODITIZATION TO EXPERIENCES: TWO CASE STUDIES

In the global bridge game of competitive strategy, customization often trumps mass production. Here are two examples.

Case study: 'Have it your way'

How do you compete with hamburger chain McDonald's and its large-scale system with thousands of franchises? The same way Sloan fought Henry Ford: customization trumps mass production. Competitor Burger King ran a campaign called 'Have It Your Way'. Customers can *choose* how they want their hamburger (rare, medium, well done) grilled. 'Have It Your Way' is a mass customization answer to mass production. The ability to 'design' your own hamburger creates a personal experience and gives customers a sense of control over what they purchase.

Case study: Michael Dell and the PC industry[9]

If Thomas Edison symbolises the explosive growth of the 19th century, Michael Dell, founder of Dell Computers, is the symbol of free markets in the 20th century, perhaps more than even Bill Gates, the most often-cited capitalist icon. Dell started his company in 1984. In only 17 years, it become number one worldwide in PC sales. By examining this especially interesting case, we will better understand the way mass customization can be a business model that leads to global market domination.

Ken Olsen, MIT graduate and visionary founder of Digital Equipment Corp., said in 1977: 'There is no reason for any individual to have a computer in their home.' As he was saying this, start ups such as Apple Computer, Tandy/Radio Shack and Commodore were pioneering the Personal Computer (PC). IBM launched its first PC in August 1981. The IBM PC succeeded because the heads of IBM, who believed only in mainframes, quarantined the 'PC toy' in its own division, far from the IBM mainframe. The resulting flexibility and independence enabled IBM's PC branch to grow and thrive within its own start-up culture. Within two years, IBM had 42 per cent of the PC market. At this juncture, IBM did two crucial things.

- IBM commissioned a tiny start up called Microsoft to write the operating system, known as DOS (Disk Operating System) for its PC.
- IBM published the specifications for its PC system, thus enabling software developers to write programmes for the PC, encouraging other companies (like Compaq) to 'clone' the PC by making PC-compatible machines and fostering compatible peripherals like printers.

Case study continued

Case study continued

This open system created a new industry that grew explosively. Ultimately, though Apple had better technology and a better product, the PC standard conquered the world, simply because by 'closing' their architecture and refusing to reveal it, Apple erased the enormous passion and enterprise that software and hardware entrepreneurs could have generated. For Apple founders Steve Jobs and Steve Wosniak, this was a $559 billion (660 billion Euro) mistake. At its peak, Microsoft's market capitalization was equal to that sum. Apple's market capitalization went to near-zero before Jobs returned to rescue it.

In 2001, Dell Computer Co., founded in 1984, became No. 1 worldwide in PC market share. Dell has no unique technology. It holds no crucial patents. It makes PCs that are like PCs made by other companies. Yet its growth has been astonishing. Dell Computer Co. is today 36th in the US Fortune 500 list of companies, with total sales of $35.4 billion ($41.8 billion Euro) worldwide, and net income of $2.122 billion (2.50 billion Euro) (for 2002). Because it minimizes its fixed assets, Dell earned a staggering 44 per cent Return on Shareholders Equity, even though 2002 was a global recession year. During the 10-year period 1992–2002, Dell's earnings per share rose at a compounded annual rate of 35 per cent; total return to investors for the same period was 43 per cent annually. Dell employs 39,100 people worldwide. Its global headquarters are in Round Rock, Texas, just outside Austin. Here is the story, as told by founder Michael Dell in a speech at MIT in 1998.

Dell is growing at an incredible rate: There are only 82 companies that have had revenue growth for the last three years (1995–98) of at least 10 per cent per year. There are only 11 companies that have had revenue growth for the last three years of 30 per cent per year. There is only one company (DELL) that has had revenue growth for the last three years of greater than 50 per cent per year (Dell actually had 55 per cent growth). Dell has no distribution channel conflicts because we have no distribution channels! Dell designs, manufactures and distributes its own computers and has created tremendous value for the customer and his company. Though Dell didn't get into the consumer market until several years ago, Dell's consumer business is operating in 35 countries via direct distribution without problems. Dell built 2 million PCs in the last quarter alone (3Q 1998) and only maintains seven days of inventory stock. The fact that we only have seven days of inventory on hand provides a direct financial payback because PC supplies typically depreciate at a rate of 1 per cent per week. Unlike other PC manufacturers and distributors who are forced to 'guess' what customer demand will be and 'guess' what

Case study continued

Case study continued

the right product mix is to send to their distributors, Dell is intimately involved with its customers and knows exactly what their customers want. The guessing is removed, we build exactly what the customers are ordering/buying and this is a competitive advantage. The Dell theme is 'lower overall cost for sales and support'. We first started out in direct personal selling, then added phone and now internet sales. We are now booking over 10 million dollars a day in internet sales (20 per cent of our sales are currently online) and we are looking for that to grow to at least 50 per cent online in the near future. Two million visitors go to our Websites each week. We introduced the concept of Premier pages where they dedicate a specific set of Web pages to a particular company that has pre-selected configurations, prices, etc., which a company can direct their employees to choose their work PC from these pages. We have over 8,500 of these Premier Web pages. Eighty per cent of our on-line business is to large business and institutional customers. Eighty per cent of Dell's components are purchased from only 20 suppliers, so we have a very tight link with our suppliers. We are convinced you can replace physical assets in the distribution channel with Information Assets and this strategy has worked all over the world. We started with desktops, then added laptops, now servers and we will continue to add more offerings as it makes sense. Dell is now growing at a rate of five times the growth of the industry. Business in Europe this year is $5 billion, growing at a rate of 68 per cent last quarter, some quarters have seen 80 per cent growth. Dell went from 2 per cent to 20 per cent US market share in 2.5 years surpassing HP and IBM, without any specialized service and support infrastructure of our own. Open PC standards have really allowed the Dell model to work and as standards settled in, cost became a greater factor and we have capitalized on this. The next phase of expanding our business will depend on improving the quality of the total product including service and support—the total customer experience.

Action learning

Create a 'Market of One' for a Mass-produced Standard Product

- Choose a standard, mass produced product. *Construct a business model that will create value, and manage cost, by creating a 'market of one'—customizing the product for each user.* For instance: 'mass customize' jeans; prescription eyeglasses or bicycles. See the end of the chapter for how innovators customized these products.

- Many automobile makers are considering applying Michael Dell's direct-sale model to their business, to 'build to order' (BTO). BMW already does so. You can order your tailor-made BMW, get a production date, and just days before it you can still alter your order (for instance, the color you choose). The cost of switching from build to sell, to build to order, is very high, but so are the advantages. Imagine you are running General Motors. *What are the management implications of shifting to BTO? Would you implement it fully, or partially, or not at all?*

10.9 PLATFORM LEADERSHIP

In her book *Platform Leadership*, Professor Annabelle Gawer (together with co-author MIT professor Michael Cusumano) shows how leading global companies build and innovate not individual products, but product platforms—'engines' that generate broad and deep product lines that come to dominate their industry and continue to spin off new and successful product generations.[10] To do this, such companies (as Intel and Microsoft) invest to spur innovation in complementary areas that strengthen their product platforms—Intel, in wireless technology that makes their Centrino chip more useful; Microsoft, in software that builds on their Windows operating system. Platform strategies are a sophisticated special case of economies of scope. They arise when innovative managers and engineers give careful thought to the architecture of the product and seek to attract a wide population of developers, innovators, buyers, peripheral suppliers and adherents.

Case study: MAC vs PC

IBM employed platform leadership when it used open architecture for building PCs, enabling other companies to copy ('clone') it and creating a huge new industry. Apple failed to do it. Its Macintosh operating system was simple and by far the best available (copied, Apple alleged in a losing court case, by Bill Gates' Windows). But it was closed: Apple sought to capture the value and profit inherent in software, a reasonable strategy, and thus did not permit independent software developers to obtain its MAC operating software code. This turned out to be fatal.

Case study continued

Case study continued

Ultimately software was developed for PCs and Windows. Microsoft at one point was the company whose shares had the world's largest market value. And Apple nearly became extinct rescued only by the return of original founder Steve Jobs.

10.10 TWO MORE ECONOMIES: SPEED, SPAN

According to Ross Mayfield, there are two additional key 'economies':

1. *Economies of speed* are achieved by using an asset to produce outputs at a higher rate of throughput. Through a decrease in the time required to produce an output, per-unit costs decline. Digital signal processors and parallel computing are examples of technology assets that realize economies of speed. In an age when 'time to market' is crucial, methods, ideas and technologies that can get products to market faster confer enormous advantage. Chandler has said that in a sense, economies of scale are ultimately economies of speed.
2. *Economies of span* are achieved by efficient coordination, or sequenced use, of assets. Through the decreased transaction costs between stages of production, per-unit costs decline. Control and logistics systems are examples of technology assets that realize economies of span. IBM saved $3 billion in 'economies of span' by streamlining the way it runs its purchasing and supply-chain mechanism. Nestle achieves economies of span by running its global operations seamlessly, leveraging physical assets and brand assets in every part of the world. American businesses have achieved economies of span by turning to PBAs (Pharmaceutical Benefit Associations) to purchase pharmaceuticals for their health care plans in bulk quantity, thus lowering their costs.

Case study: Cogentrix

Many business opportunities arise when the 'rules of the game' change, often through legislation and regulatory policy shifts. Wise entrepreneurs track changes in government policy and legislative acts carefully and act even before they take effect. An American entrepreneur named George Lewis anticipated the 1978 PURPA (Public Utilities Regulatory Policy Act), that required power companies to buy co-generated power from

Case study continued

Case study continued

private suppliers (e.g., industrial plants that generated steam and used some of it to make electricity). Lewis, experienced in building large-scale power plants, realized this would create demand for small power-generating units that could make both steam and electricity. He founded Cogentrix and got a year's jump on the competition. He harnessed both scale and scope. Scale: by making his units modular and standardized he could mass-produce them and then assemble individual plants from those units. This cut costs by 30 per cent. Scope: because he could tailor each cogeneration unit to the needs of the specific customer—markets of one. For a time, Cogentrix was one of America's fastest-growing small businesses. (See Case Study 10.1: Cogentrix: Development decision for a start-up company.)

10.11 CONCLUSION

In his widely-read book *Innovation: The Attacker's Advantage*, longtime McKinsey consultant Richard Foster notes how innovation is a vital strategy weapon against marketplace incumbents who have leveraged scale economies, size and learning with experience.[11] The next chapter focuses on learning: Learning curves as a management tool and how to build a learning organization. Learning curves are quite different from, though related to, scale economies; they are the foundation stone of many huge profitable global companies, such as Intel. We now look at another facet of the scale and/or scope, or 'volume and/or variety' issue, that relates to the basic behavioural question: how do organizations learn and how can the core competency of learning confer a vital strategic advantage?

Readers are invited to view 'Pillars of Profit: Segment #6, Scale and Scope: Scaling Markets of One' in the accompanying CD.

POSTSCRIPT

Mass customizing jeans, eyeglasses, bicycles:

- Levis tried stores where customers rather than pick off-the-shelf jeans, were measured and chose a style of jeans. Measurements were sent to a factory, which produced tailor-made jeans. The finished jeans were then shipped to the customer. While the idea was appealing, this experiment did not succeed.
- A computer programme captures a customer's face, then electronically fits various types of eyeglass frames to that face, so the customer can

actually see how the frame will look on his or her face. Any myopic reader who has had to choose eyeglass frames while squinting near-sightedly into a mirror will appreciate this innovation. It has been very successful.

- Bicycles: Japan's National Industrial Bicycle Co. (a branch of Panasonic) measures the body dimensions of a buyer, then builds the bicycle to those dimensions. Buyers get the bicycle two weeks later. Note a cultural difference here. Japanese buyers love the waiting period, because during it they anticipate and imagine receiving the wonderful new product. American consumers are impatient, and tend to want immediate gratification—a two-week waiting period for a product, or even the three-day wait for the Levis jeans, are often a kiss of death for customized products.

All these customized products confer the advantages of differentiation, 'memorable customer experience', higher profit margins and lower price sensitivity on their innovators.

CASE STUDY 10.1

Cogentrix: Development decisions for a start-up company*

Case study discussion topics

1. What is electricity cogeneration?
2. How did a decision of the Supreme Court (USA) create the industry of building cogeneration facilities? How did the founder of Cogentrix, George T. Lewis, Jr., anticipate this decision?
3. Why did 'economies of scale' go the 'wrong way' for Cogentrix?
4. How did Cogentrix manage to enjoy both 'small plants' and 'volume discounts', i.e., both scale and scope?
5. How is Cogentrix using 'economies of scope' to extend its current core operations?

A new market for private power generation was opened up by the US Congress through the passage of the Public Utility Regulatory Policy Act

*This case study is a summary of the case authored by William C. Campbell, III.

Case study 10.1 continued

Case study 10.1 continued

(PURPA) of 1978. The US Supreme Court issued its ruling in May 1983, upholding the legality of the Act. In anticipation of the Supreme Court ruling, Cogentrix of North Carolina was incorporated in April 1983 with the sole intention of building small cogeneration (providing two forms of energy from a single process) facilities that could provide inexpensive electricity to the local utility and inexpensive steam to a nearby industrial host. The company founder George T. Lewis, Jr., hoped to design and build compact, well-engineered, economical, yet small power plants in order to generate economies of scale.

Paucity of funds forced Cogentrix to secure third-party financing to set up its first plant. This made it important for Cogentrix to minimize the capital cost of the facility if it was to attract investors and deliver a high rate of return on the capital. There were complications in contracting with the public utility to sell the electricity from the plant. According to PURPA regulations, the utilities did not have to pay more than their 'avoided cost rate' (the cost to the utility to provide additional generating capacity to their system) for electricity from a cogenerator.
A utility could choose how it would fill its future power needs, thus setting the 'avoided cost rate'. Cogentrix discovered that the avoided cost was extremely low if the utility did not want to do business and lower than its actual cost from its large-scale power plants, if the utility was in desperate need of additional power. Obviously, the utilities did not want to pay more than what was absolutely required for new generation. The economy-of-scale was going the wrong way for Cogentrix.

Cogentrix wanted to utilize coal as the fuel for its plant since PURPA regulations encouraged the same, coal being the most abundant natural resource in the US. The initial infrastructural cost to utilize coal is far more expensive than for oil or natural gas, since the life cycle of the equipment can be twice as long. However, as cost of fuel was a vital parameter to the project's viability, stable prices of coal made this option more attractive. The volume of coal needed, however, was not sufficient to utilize unit trains and achieve economies-of-scale that competitive utilities were enjoying.

To fully utilize tax benefits provided in PURPA regulations, Cogentrix's facility had to provide a minimum of 5 per cent of its net thermal output to be used for something other than producing electricity. Thus, the plant needed to be a cogeneration facility. In order to persuade industry to give up the security of its own steam-generating equipment, the price of the steam had to be below the host's cost. The Cogentrix plant had to also ensure uninterrupted supply of steam to the industrial host.

Case study 10.1 continued

Case study 10.1 continued

A series of interdependent decisions had to be made on the kind of plant to be built and its size. Multiple economic tools were used to facilitate this decision but the concept of scale was by far the most important tool used. Cogentrix wanted to build small plants with multiple boilers to service industrial hosts. But the company also wanted to take advantage of the cost reductions that came with scale, in order to compete with larger utilities. There were limits on what Cogentrix could charge for its products (electricity and steam). The cost of fuel was not competitive in small quantities. Thus, the answer lay in scale. Cogentrix could have both small plants and volume discounts only if it could build multiple plants of the same kind.

Standardization became the watchword for Cogentrix. Engineering design was initiated on a two-boiler, 35 megawatt (MW) coal-fired unit, in a compact arrangement to minimize space and cost without sacrificing quality. Envelopes were included in the design for all major equipment to allow products of multiple manufacturers to fit in without re-designing. This saved on design time and facilitated competitive bidding. The design drawings were standardized wherever possible. The overall engineering cost was reduced to less than 2 per cent of the total cost of the plant, as against the industry average of 8 per cent.

To achieve economies-of-scale on the coal supply, Cogentrix built multiple plants simultaneously. With standardized drawings and multiple-unit equipment order, the task was very manageable and actually reduced the administrative overhead. Three plants were built to achieve scale-factor discounts throughout the project. All three sites were located in Eastern North Carolina within close proximity for centralized coal delivery. To take advantage of scale economy in construction, one general contractor was awarded all three jobs.

The projects benefited from increased efficiency in specialized crew utilization. The boiler erection was staged to allow crews to move from one plant to another in a modified assembly-line fashion, virtually eliminating congestion on the site and increasing crew efficiency with the setting up of each successive boiler. This style of construction was complemented by an economy-of-scale with Cogentrix's equipment manufacturers. The price of the boilers was reduced by 30 per cent, as the boiler shop was able to streamline the production of the components in an assembly line at their end. When the boilers were put up for sale, pricing was requested for orders of 2, 6, 12 and 22 boilers, although only six boilers were needed for the project at hand. The economy-of-scale was working so well that an order for all 22 boilers was placed resulting in

Case study 10.1 continued

Case study 10.1 continued

significant savings for Cogentrix and a fair profit for Foster Wheeler (the company that was involved in the Cogentrix projects as a reputed global engineering and construction contractor, and power equipment supplier), at a time when the boiler market was flat. All equipment purchased by Cogentrix, from boilers to steam turbines were in bulk, resulting in significant savings.

The result of scaling through standardization on these three plants alone resulted in 30 per cent reduction in cost while also procuring high quality, branded equipment for the facilities. The time to build them was reduced dramatically. The financing from General Electric Credit Corporation for $93.5 million was finalized in October 1984, and electricity was flowing from the first plant within 14 months. This had the added benefit of reducing the cost of interest during construction. Thus, all of these measures resulted in a total cost of less than $1,000 per kilowatt of installed electrical generating capacity, versus the industry average of $1,500 per kilowatt. In addition, Cogentrix was the very first independent cogeneration facility to be put on line under the PURPA regulations. The company was the first to market electricity under these new regulations.

Standardization continued to benefit Cogentrix through an economy of scale in operating the plants. Employee training was streamlined and staffing was reduced to levels needed for operations only. Major-maintenance outages were handled by collecting experienced crew from other identical facilities to come and help out. In turn, when better operating procedures were discovered at one facility, it was shared with the other two. Spare-parts inventory was also centralized to eliminate large numbers of expensive spare parts.

Cogentrix has gone forward with the economy-of-scale concept to achieving cost advantage through standardization and is currently operating 27 facilities. These comprise over 1,000 MW and more than a billion dollars in investment. The second generation plants are composed of 55 MW modules that can be linked together to form a plant of any size, needed by either the utility or the industrial host. The 55 MW module is itself an adaptation of the original plant with one additional boiler added. Costs of these facilities have remained low due to economies-of-scale. The plants have been tailored to the needs of individual buyers, creating economies-of-scope. The market responded positively and Cogentrix experienced explosive growth. Cogentrix was the fastest growing private company in America in 1989, and again in 1990.

Case study 10.1 continued

Case study 10.1 continued

Over the last several years, Cogentrix has been working on using its manpower resources and applying its expertise to businesses similar to its core business. The company has explored the resource recovery business, the contract operations business, the consulting engineering business and the environmental consulting business. The optimal situation has yet to present itself to complement its core operations and thus, achieve a true economy of scope.

CASE STUDY 10.2

Reliance Industries–Economies of scale*

Reliance Industries Ltd. (RIL) is one of India's leading private sector enterprises with a turnover of over $20 billion. With businesses in exploration and production of oil and gas, petroleum refining and marketing, petrochemicals and textiles, the group has its 'footprint' in more than 100 countries.

Having started in fabrics and yarn trade in the early 1960s, RIL's founder Dhirubhai Ambani ventured into manufacturing nylon fabrics (manufacturing unit at Naroda, Ahmedabad) for exports in 1966. He started importing polyester in 1971. With phenomenal export turnovers and profits and to meet the increasing demand for polyester fabrics in India, RIL expanded its manufacturing facilities and imported state-of-the-art technology and machinery. During the late 1970s, RIL focused intensely on the domestic market and rolled out high quality fabrics under the Vimal brand, which included sarees, dress materials and suitings. By the early 1980s, RIL had become the largest producer of fabrics in India.

Between the years 1980 and 1994, RIL was involved in the backward integration of its operations. Today it manufactures hundreds of products: textiles, Polyester Filament Yarn (PFY), Polyester Staple Fibre (PSF), Linear Alkyl Benzene (LAB), Fibre intermediates, high-density Polyethylene (PE) and Polyvinyl Chloride (PVC), a large variety of petroleum products at its world-class petroleum refinery and has a significant presence in oil and gas exploration. All its plants are world-class in terms of size.

*This case study is based significantly on the writings of Sumantra Ghoshal, Gita Piramal, Sudeep Budhiraja and more particularly draws on the ideas published in their book *World Class in India—A Case Book of Companies in Transformation* (2002).

Case study 10.2 continued

Case study 10.2 continued

In the implementation of all the above projects, RIL adopted several strategies, which served to be drivers for the company's phenomenal growth over the years.

Continuous investment in additional capacity

RIL ensured that the size of its facilities, be it Patalganga or Hazira, is huge and almost 15–20 times larger than what the markets may have demanded at that time. Instead of building capacities in line with the projected demand, RIL opted to create world-scale capacities in order to compete on cost and quality norms on a global basis. Driven by the ambition of achieving great things by doing the extraordinary, Dhirubhai Ambani always spoke of world-class status for RIL by building international capabilities. Most companies use traditional economic calculations to forecast future demand. Generally, these companies conduct a market survey to arrive at the current usage and this usage is projected into the future to forecast demand. Based on the company's anticipation of its market share, it sets up a facility with appropriate capacity. In contrast, RIL's approach was to create capacity much ahead of existent demand. It sought to dominate the markets that it chose to operate in, through sheer volumes that would immediately render uncompetitive any smaller players in the market. Simultaneously, RIL meticulously eliminated the hurdles that constrained the demand.

For every business that RIL sought to enter, it installed massive, world-scale plants of capacities far greater than what domestic competitors at the time possessed. RIL continuously modernized and augmented the capacity of its plants to garner all incremental market growth, in an effort to make the company the absolute leader in the respective industry that it operated in. Thus, the company came to occupy a position among the top 10 producers of major petrochemical products in the world. It also became the world's largest producer of polyester yarn and fibre. The continuing capacity augmentation in its textiles and petrochemical plants enabled RIL to emerge as the lowest-cost producer in the country and in the world for some of its products like polyester. It also sought to straddle the entire value chain through aggressive backward and forward integration giving it tight control on the entire chain.

Besides the cost advantage that RIL enjoyed from investing in huge capacities, these large capacities also enabled the company to enhance customer service. For instance, in its textile business, its large capacity facilitated diversification of the range of yarns that it produced for the local market resulting in the introduction of new yarns. RIL's customers (companies in the textile and garment industries) gained from these new

Case study 10.2 continued

Case study 10.2 continued

product introductions because it helped them further expand their own product portfolio. Further, RIL's large capacities facilitated meeting huge orders of big customers, which most of its competitors were unable to satisfy on account of their smaller capacities. Creating world-class capacities was closely tied in with operational excellence once the plants were operational and this resulted in very tight control of manufacturing costs on an on-going basis. The company had innovated greatly both in project implementation and in operational excellence as the following instances demonstrate.

Executing projects with speed

While making huge investments in installing capacity, RIL always tried to keep the 'cost of time' parameter as low as possible in implementation and execution of its massive projects. RIL did everything required to set up its projects speedily. Often, its manufacturing plants were up and running in record time. For instance, its PFY (polyester filament yarn) plant project was completed in an amazing 14 months after the licence was granted, a world record.

Financing of projects

Whether it was finance required for its foray into new manufacturing plants or finance needed for modernization of its facilities, RIL always sought to mobilize funds by directly approaching the investing public. This was in contrast to the practice followed by the majority of Indian businesses, which approached public financial institutions to finance their projects through debt funds. Consequently, RIL did not have to pay interest on the funds it mobilized from the public during the gestation time of the projects.

From oil exploration to textiles, RIL does it all, on a scale that is second to none in the world, truly delivering to it, *Economies of Scale*. The company appears to be never satisfied with its already vast scale of operations. For instance, its petroleum refinery at Jamnagar in Gujarat, complete with port facilities, has been designed to be versatile in terms of the type of crude oil it can handle. After implementing India's largest refinery with a capacity of 30 million tons per annum, it is now set to double the capacity, making it the largest single site petroleum refinery in the world. And as usual, the project will be completed in world-record time.

CASE STUDY 10.3

The Himalaya Drug Company—Economies of scope

Driven by a vision to bring Ayurveda (the 5,000-year-old traditional Indian system of medicine) to society in a contemporary form, Mohammad Manal founded the Himalaya Drug Company (HDC) in 1930. In 1934, Himalaya became the pioneer of the world's first anti-hypertensive drug Serpina, that could reduce blood pressure. The company has since converted Ayurveda's herbal tradition into a complete range of proprietary herbal formulations backed by a strong scientific research team, sophisticated manufacturing facility (in Dehra Dun and Bangalore, India) and state-of-the-art herbal medicine R&D centre (in Bangalore, India), with the founder's son, Meraj Manal aggressively driving the company's growth. With an annual turnover in excess of Rs 3,500 million (about $80 million) in 2004, Himalaya today enjoys a commanding presence in the domestic and international contemporary herbal healthcare products market. It operates in over 74 countries, reaching consumers through a network of exclusive and multi-brand retail outlets.

The company's basic product line is pharmaceuticals or drugs, and until the early 1990s it was a pharmaceutical company manufacturing a range of therapeutic products marketed mainly through the doctor-prescription route. In 1999, HDC made a strategic decision to expand to the OTC (over-the-counter) segment in addition to selling drugs through the doctor-prescription route.

Towards the end of the 1990s, new trends emerged in the domestic and global pharmaceutical industry. While the allopathic market (both domestic and global) was growing in single digits, the herbal market was growing at a rapid rate of 25 per cent annually, triggered by a paradigm shift in the perception of health amongst consumers. Globally, consumers were moving away from the management of sickness (curative) to the maintenance of well-being (preventive). Herbal supplements were gaining popularity as preventive supplements. Thus, the concept of preventive care coupled with the rising use of herbals as preventive supplements was a major reason for the relatively rapid growth of herbal medicines over allopathic drugs.

Another major segment where herbal products outperformed allopathic drugs was in the segment of 'lifestyle disorders'. The increase in lifestyle disorders like diabetes, joint pains, stress, increased levels of cholesterol, etc.,

Case study 10.3 continued

Case study 10.3 continued

caused individuals to consider herbal remedies, as these diseases were lifetime problems and using herbals in conjunction with allopathic products would reduce the allopathic dosage and thereby reduce the incidence of side effects. Many others used herbal products to delay the onset of diseases associated with lifestyle disorders.

A shift from prescribed medication to self-medication was yet another significant shift. As prescription products proved to be very expensive, consumers in the US bought only OTC products. Many herbal products started appearing in OTC form, hence these products benefited.

The changing trends in the pharmaceutical industry encouraged Himalaya to expand its scope within the herbal healthcare space, both at home and overseas. The strategic progression involved extending its competencies to the entire spectrum of herbal healthcare such as personal care, well-being and even animal health. By positioning itself as a 'head-to-heel' herbal healthcare brand, with a vision to provide 'wellness in every home through herbal healthcare', Himalaya was able to exploit the existing scope within the business. As compared to other manufacturers of herbal medicine in India, Himalaya had several strategic assets that it could leverage in its quest to expand scope.

Research and development

The core strength of Himalaya is its strong research base. The strong focus on science distinguishes it from other players in the market. Its research activities include exhaustive surveys of ancient classical medicinal texts and scientific literature by a team of herbalists; studies in pharmacognosy (the science dealing with the sources, physical characteristics, uses and doses of drugs) to establish the authenticity of the plant material, finally making polyherbal formulations of herbs to provide a broader scope of pharmacological and cosmetic activity. The Research and Development (R&D) department of the company focused on product development, quality control and standardization. It deployed the best people and adopted best practices and technology in developing new products. Each of the company's offerings resulted from years of primary research and most of the products took several years to launch as they had to undergo several tests before being introduced into the market. Himalaya's R&D facility is one of the best available for herbal medicine anywhere in the world.

Quality assurance and quality control

Himalaya is one of the very few Indian herbal drug manufacturers that complied with Good Manufacturing Practices (GMP), Good Laboratory

Case study 10.3 continued

Case study 10.3 continued

Practices (GLP), Good Clinical Practices (GCP), Good Agricultural Practices (GAP) and Good Harvesting Practices (GHP) in developing and manufacturing all its products from pharmaceuticals to personal care.

Manufacturing facility

Himalaya's manufacturing plant is efficient, state-of-the-art, scale-intensive and built to serve its rapidly expanding domestic and international herbal market. The standardization of herbal medicines is a relatively tough process compared to allopathic medicine. Formulating tablets of herbal medicine is arduous involving multiple granulating, processing and coating variables. The manufacturing plant at Himalaya uses automatic, high-speed tablet punching, coating and filling machines. It has the largest tablet coating facility in Asia. The plant produces nearly 5 billion tablets and 60 million bottles of liquids annually. Principles of GMP are rigorously followed in the plant, which enables Himalaya to maintain batch-to-batch consistency, ensuring that customers get the same high-quality product regardless of where it was purchased. The general-purpose nature of its manufacturing machines allows for rapid changeover of products, commensurate with the need to cater to its large portfolio of products.

Himalaya's decision to expand its scope across the herbal wellness spectrum also stems from an understanding of the current and future trends within this space. As people become more conscious of the importance of well-being, the differentiation between personal care and healthcare will gradually cease to exist. 'Looking good' will become a part of the more encompassing concept of 'Living Well'. Accordingly, Himalaya has taken the approach of establishing its personal care products as a clear extension of the wellness spectrum. The personal care range is backed by clinical tests with crisp claims on what the product can deliver to the user.

The economies of scope have resulted in significant cost savings to the company. It has also successfully created a new 'integrated' brand identity for Himalaya, one that carries with it the promise of good health and well-being. Its robust product suite today includes:

- Pharmaceutical (health maintenance, eye, cardiac, skin care, and cough control)
- Personal Care (general health care, oral care, hair care, skin care and baby care)
- Well-being (consists of Pure Herbs—a range of individual herbal extracts in ready-to-use capsule form)

Case study 10.3 continued

Case study 10.3 continued

In short, from its modest beginnings several decades ago, Himalaya today covers the entire gamut of herbal products. Its vision of becoming a herbal healthcare products company that provides remedies and care from 'head to heel' has become a reality. It is not uncommon that a middle-class family in India uses eight to ten Himalaya products. It has thus truly leveraged the power of *Economies of Scope*.

CASE STUDY 10.4

Ruf & Tuf Jeans–'Scaling markets of one'*

Established in 1931, the $500 million Arvind Mills Ltd. is a dominant player in the Indian textile industry. It set up its Denim Division in 1987 and the company today has emerged as one of India's top three producers of denim in the world. Besides supplying to the Indian market, the company exports denim to over 70 countries around the world.

Arvind Mills found the Indian domestic denim sales to be limited. Branded jeans such as Levi's, Pepe, etc., manufactured in India by MNCs sold at $40–$60 (Rs 1,800–2,700) a pair, which was unaffordable for a majority of Indians. Unable to predict the return on investment, many of the Indian players and MNCs in the textile industry hesitated to build the required linkages in order to cater to the Tier-4 market (bottom-end) segment. Their distribution systems were designed to service Tier-1 (top-end) markets, leaving out the small rural towns and villages where poor rural customers existed who were keen to buy denims, but could not afford to buy them. Arvind Mill's innovative strategy to notch a sizeable share of this market for jeans was a departure from the prevailing practice.

Recognizing the revenue potential at the 'bottom of the pyramid', Arvind Mills embarked on an ambitious project that eventually catapulted it to the status of the largest seller of jeans in India. It developed and introduced a new brand—Ruf & Tuf jeans, which was a ready-to-make kit of jeans components (denim cloth, zipper, rivets and a patch). Ruf & Tuf carried a very affordable price tag of $6 (Rs 270). Distribution of the jeans kits was done through a strong network of 4,000 street-tailors, many of who were stationed in small rural towns and villages. It was pure self-interest on part of the tailors that encouraged them to market the kits in a big way.

* Material from Websites in the public domain.

Case study 10.4 continued

Case study 10.4 continued

Ruf & Tuf was an innovative product developed to cater to the wants of the Tier-4 (bottom-end) communities. As the tailor stitched the jeans to measurement, an individual got jeans of perfect fit and did not have to go through the tiresome process of alterations, usually necessary on standard sizes of branded jeans. Second, the vast number of people who were often physically and economically cut off from buying 'ready to wear' jeans, now had easy access (through their local tailor) to a pair of branded jeans that was reasonably priced, and to top it, would fit each of them perfectly.

Further, Arvind Mills created an entire ecosystem at the bottom of the pyramid making it difficult for other players in the industry to replicate the Ruf & Tuf success story. Levi's had rolled out their concept of custom-made jeans in India, wherein a customer walking in to any of the Levi's retail stores could provide his/her measurements and a list of his/her preferences according to which the jeans would be stitched. But this concept posed hardly any challenge to Arvind Mills' customized low-cost jeans in India. Although Ruf & Tuf was priced almost 80 per cent below that of Levi's, the strategy still engaged legions of local tailors who single-handedly served as stockers, marketing agents, distributors and service providers. This saved the company the need for employing a large number of people directly on its payroll to perform these functions. The mode of production and distribution in the case of Ruf & Tuf provided jobs for many tailors, increased their incomes, and developed them as the company's 'new customers'. The Arvind Mills strategy was a winner, as the company's financial results over the years have demonstrated. This is a perfect example of innovating by *Scaling Markets of One.*

CASE STUDY 10.5

Adarsh Builders—Mass customization in the housing industry*

With a sales turnover of over Rs 1,500 million ($35 million), Adarsh Builders is a leading construction company in Bangalore, India. The company has brought to life the concept of 'great living experiences' through the creation of its spectacular residential properties, for instance

* Material from Websites in the public domain.

Case study 10.5 continued

Case study 10.5 continued

the Adarsh Court, Adarsh Hill, Adarsh Nivas and Palm Meadows. The company has also constructed landmark commercial properties such as Adarsh Regent and Adarsh Opus, which are hi-tech complexes in Bangalore that house many blue-chip technology companies. Every venture of Adarsh Builders stands testimony to the company's commitment to deliver properties of international quality with maximum facilities in an eco-friendly environment.

Recognizing the high revenue potential for international quality real estate in Bangalore, arising out of the growing number of consumers with large spending power coupled with the consumer's desire to live in dwellings of international quality and standards, Adarsh Builders embarked on an ambitious gated community residential project called 'Palm Meadows' in 1997–98. In an effort to establish mass-customization, the builders presented Palm Meadows as a combination of mass-produced housing with significant customer influence. The project attempted to build villas according to the desires of the individual consumer for a premium.

Spread over 55 acres, Palm Meadows housed close to 260 elegant villas designed on the finest international concepts and standards. The buyer could choose between 10 different modules. These 10 modules were further customized. To begin with, Palm Meadows constructed a model villa for two of its modules to demonstrate to a buyer the quality of construction common to villas in all its modules. These two units were open for inspection as model units by buyers. Brochures of villas of the remaining eight modules were printed to give buyers an idea of how these villas would look on completion. On selection of a particular type of module, the buyer was given as much latitude as possible to further design the villa to his/her tastes. The project provided an architect, with the help of whom the buyer could custom design the villa. Construction materials that conformed to the quality standards of the Palm Meadows project were also put on display for buyers to choose from.

The buyer was given freedom to choose between multiple possibilities, varying from a floor plan to colours for the interiors of the villa. However, villas of each of the modules had a broad set of specific standard features that the buyer had to retain and could not change. In other words, the biggest influence the buyer had was on the size of the villa, wherein he/she could opt for more segments or blocks according to the given design but the villa would be based on a particular pre-determined structure. Further, the buyer was given very limited options in the choice relating to the façade of the villa, so that there was significant standardization

Case study 10.5 continued

Case study 10.5 continued

relating to the external looks of the villas. However, as far as the interior of the villa was concerned the buyer enjoyed maximum leeway. Therefore, there were certain standard features built into each of the modules, with Adarsh Builders having a broad control over styles and designs and reasonable customization was made to suit the buyer's specific needs.

Although some of the buyers chose not to tamper with the original module designs, majority of the buyers (over 90 per cent) opted for customized houses without having to compromise on quality or project completion times. The incremental costs for such customization were reasonable, compared to the alternative of the buyer having to build such a villa on his/her own. Exquisitely landscaped gardens overlooked each of the villas. Palm Meadows complex offered luxurious privileges in its club house spread over 5 acres and had badminton courts, a squash court, a fully-equipped health club, a swimming pool, two tennis courts, billiards, a restaurant, and a departmental store. Palm Meadows stands as a benchmark for the gated community residential complex in the city of Bangalore.

Adarsh Builders offered its customers adequate flexibility by allowing them (within reasonable limits) to design their own homes, rather than giving them mass-produced houses, thus allowing for *Mass customization*.

CASE STUDY 10.6

Vishalla Restaurant—Creating an experience*

Located in scenic splendour, is Ahmedabad's popular get away restaurant, Vishalla. The sprawling premises of the bistro overlooks a wide expanse of greenery. The recreated village-like ambience at the restaurant brings to life the charming splendour of rustic Gujarat. Amidst the wonderful atmosphere of peace and calm, one cannot but unwind. One can spend the entire day at this 'timeless zone' experiencing a variety of entertainment besides great food that the restaurant offers.

Vishalla welcomes each guest with a spray of fragrant *gulabjal* (rosewater) and a rose bud, rejuvenating the true spirit of hospitality which is uncommon in most restaurants. This is done by a host dressed in ethnic attire, who welcomes the customer. Invariably, the dining room of

* Material from Websites in the public domain.

Case study 10.6 continued

Case study 10.6 continued

Vishalla has a full house, and while one awaits his turn, a quick bite at the adjoining stalls 'Tazagi' and 'Barfila' leaves a lingering taste in the mouth. The two counters together offer a mélange of authentic homemade Gujarati snacks, fresh-fruit juices and delectable ice creams. The elaborate Gujarati meal in the dining room, both in variety and quantity, leaves the diner completely surprised and gratified. It has everything from salads, to rice, to sweets. An 'army' of traditionally dressed hosts (waiters) ensure service is prompt and homely. While the dining rooms are covered with traditional village-type roofing made of leaves and grass to protect against the rain, the restaurant is open-air (with provision for a makeshift covered roofing in the monsoons).

Everything is authentic and homely about Vishalla. One sits cross-legged on a mat laid out on the floor and is served food on a leaf plate placed on a slightly elevated wooden platform that serves as a table. Water and buttermilk are served in earthenware pots. A craftsman with the potter's wheel produces these pots within the premises. Unlike most restaurants that run on electricity, Vishalla uses solar generators. Lanterns of adequate intensity help customers find their way around, while at the same time representing a rural ambience. Deep freezers are a common sight in the kitchens of most restaurants, but the kitchens at Vishalla have done away with deep freezers, ensuring that the guests get to eat healthy, farm-fresh food being cooked from fresh vegetables and groceries (the restaurant serves only vegetarian fare). The food is prepared by ladies who have to this day retained their 'rustic touch' and spirit of traditional Indian hospitality. This explains the 'home made' taste that the cuisine at Vishalla carries. The simple leaf plates and wooden spoons used as crockery and cutlery are disposable, thus ensuring high levels of hygiene.

While most restaurants are focused on satisfying the customer's appetite for food and cuisines, Vishalla has adopted a holistic-entertainment approach. As enthusiastic as Vishalla is about serving delicious Gujarati food (which is very local to that part of the country) to customers, it has also focused on offering its customers unique experiences. Vishalla's 'Manoranjan programme' stages live folk music and dance performances within the restaurant. The puppet show 'Jadoo ka Khel' is an unusual programme that keeps children and elders amused. Handicrafts directly sourced from local artisans can be bought from the small outlet 'Vibhusa' in the restaurant premises. The Vishalla complex houses a unique 'Utensils Museum', which has a mind boggling collection of over 3,500 antique utensils from different parts of India, dating back to several thousands of years, making it a star attraction for customers.

Case study 10.6 continued

Case study 10.6 continued

Vishalla like most other restaurants offers attractively-priced (though not cheap) wholesome meals and efficient services. However, customers come there not only for the food alone, but for the total experience. Before and after the meal, customers can lounge on a village-type *charpoy* (village cot), use the *jhoolas* (swings tied to trees), or sit in a tree house in the company of their friends and family. Customers typically spend 3–4 hours at Vishalla. At the end of a hearty meal, when one has eaten to his/her fill, the customer can partake of a traditional *paan* (made with betel leaf and a mixture of condiments) from a large variety of *paans*; or loll around on the *charpoy* smoking *hookah* (hubble-bubble), enjoying its soothing, gurgling sounds; or simply relax in utter contentment. A gong, periodically sounded by a turbaned 'villager' announces the time. When it is time to go (and one reluctantly makes his way home late into the night) a 'turbaned' host offers a mouth freshener and bids you adieu with a sonorous *Aavjo, Ram Ram* (meaning 'Bye, God Bless!', in the local Gujarati language), that lingers in your ears for many days thereafter.

What makes Vishalla stand apart is the unique experience that it creates for its guests. Each and every facility that Vishalla offers in this 'restaurant complex' (the museum, handicrafts outlet, the puppet show, etc.) is geared to make one's visit as pleasant and memorable as possible. Many other restaurant entrepreneurs have tried to emulate Vishalla, but even today, after over 30 years since its inception, no one has been able to replicate its success as Vishalla continues to innovate and create new experiences for the customer. The whole *Experience* lingers on in the mind of the customer over a lifetime, and leaves one with an unmistakable feeling: the desire to come again!

Notes

1. The Woody Allen quote was taken off the Web, from a site that features selected funny lines by him.
2. The Alfred Chandler quote is from his book *Scale and Scope: The Dynamics of Industrial Capitalism* (Harvard University, Cambridge, MA: Belknap Press, 1990), p. 18, as are the definitions of 'scale' and 'scope' (Harvard University, Cambridge, MA: Belknap Press, 1990), p. 16.
3. Nathan Rosenberg and L.E. Birdzell, Jr., *How the West Grew Rich* (New York: Basic Books, 1986).
4. Becker's 'household economies' is summarized in Gary Becker, *A Treatise on the Family* (Boston, MA: Harvard University Press, 1981).
5. For a fine discussion of network economies, see Carl Shapiro and Hal Varian, *Information Rules: A Strategic Guide to the Network Economy* (Boston MA: Harvard Business School, 2000).

6. For a study of mismanagement of scale and scope in the music business, see the Public Television Frontline video *The Day the Music Died* (PBS, 2003).
7. Jim Collins' quote about Nucor is on p. 7 of his *Good to Great* book.
   For an ode to the beauties of small, see E.F. Schumacher's book, *Small Is Beautiful: Economies As If People Mattered* (London: Blond & Briggs, 1973).
8. For more about Nokia, see Dan Steinbock, *The Nokia Revolution: The Story of an Extraordinary Company That Transformed an Industry* (New York City: AMACOM, 2001).
   The source of the 'commodities to experiences' diagram is James Gilmour and B. Joseph Pine, *The Experience Economy* (Boston, MA: Harvard Business School Press, 2000).
   Economies of 'speed' and 'span' are defined by consultant Ross Mayfield, in his Website.
9. The Michael Dell case study is based in part on: 'Matching Dell', HBS case study 9-799-158, June 1999; Joan Magretta, 'The power of virtual integration: An interview with Michael Dell', *Harvard Business Review*, March–April 1998; and the first author's own transcript of Michael Dell's address at Wong Auditorium, MIT, 19 November 1998.
10. A. Gawer and M. Cusumano, *Platform Leadership* (Boston, MA: Harvard Business School Press, 2002).;
11. R. Foster, *Innovation: The Attacker's Advantage* (New York: Summit Books, 1986).

Chapter 11
Learning curves are made, not born

The only sustainable competitive advantage is the ability of an organization to learn faster than its competitors.

—Peter Drucker[1]

LEARNING OBJECTIVES After you read this chapter, you should understand:

- **How powerful learning curves at the heart of 'magic circle' business models can help you dominate your competition or enable them to dominate you**
- **How to calculate the slope of your organization's learning curves**
- **How to make 'telling the truth' an integral part of organizational learning**
- **How to attack a competitor's superior learning curve through innovation**
- **When to 'switch horses'—leap from a mature product (and learning curve) to a new one**
- **How to employ learning curves to carry out 'break even analysis' for a project or product**
- **How leading organizations learn, and leverage knowledge globally**

TOOL #7 Building and measuring learning curves

11.1 INTRODUCTION

This chapter is about learning, learning organizations and learning curves as powerful tools for achieving market competitiveness.

If an engineer or manager asked us, 'I have time to read only one chapter of your book, which shall I read?' we would choose this one, Chapter 11, in a close race with Chapter 5. There are several reasons.

One reason is the wise observation by Peter Drucker that opens this chapter. Ultimately, management is about attaining and sustaining competitive advantage. In this, learning curves are essential. A second is the neglect of learning curves in conventional microeconomics texts. The best-selling text gives learning curves a bare five pages out of a total of 700 pages, or less than 1 per cent. A third is the cautionary tale told throughout this chapter, showing how quickly a business can go from dominant to bankrupt, in a large profitable market, when it faces competitors' superior learning curves. The tale is about the British motorcycle industry and how it fell victim to a learning curve.

Case study: Norton, Villiers, Triumph ('Not Very Triumphant')

In early 1975, Eric Varley, British Minister of Trade, urgently summoned America's leading business consultant, Bruce Henderson, a partner in Boston Consulting Group, to the United Kingdom. On the face of it, Henderson's mission was to report to Varley and to Parliament on why Britain's motorcycle industry, led by once-dominant brand names like BSA, Norton, Villiers and Triumph, was collapsing and to suggest what might be done about it.

In fact, Henderson came to Britain to perform an autopsy. In just three months he submitted his report, titled *Strategic Alternatives for the British Motorcycle Industry,* on 30 July 1975.[2] We believe it was one of the finest, and for some, saddest, consulting reports in history. It showed how Honda, Yamaha and Kawasaki—Japanese motorcycle companies—took away Britain's lucrative American market for heavy bikes in just four short years and bankrupted Britain's firms (Figure 11.1).

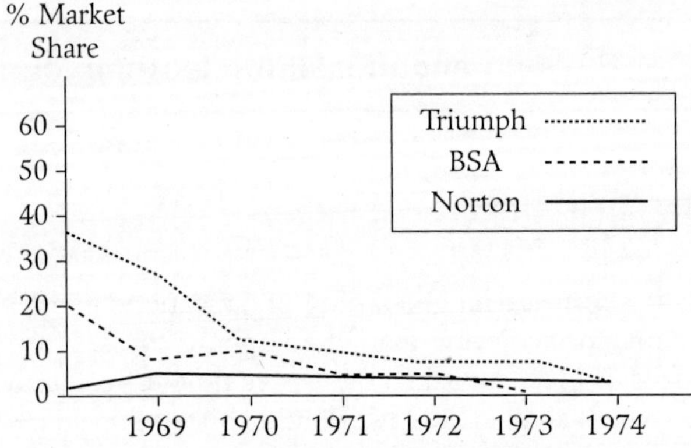

Figure 11.1
Collapse of British motorcycle firms' US market share, 1969–73

Henderson revealed the core of Japan's competitive strategy, based on powerful, steep *learning curves*. Despite the word 'alternatives' in its title, his report showed clearly there *were* no alternatives for the British motorcycle industry. Of course, as a wise consultant, Henderson *did* give three alternatives—one with 'extremely low pre-tax returns on assets', one with 'modest pre-tax returns', and the last, with pre-tax returns between the first two. However, said Henderson, 'it is most unlikely that private capital to fund the necessary investment would be forthcoming'. It wasn't. All that remained was for Henderson, Varley and the British Parliament to recite a hushed eulogy for the once world-leading brand names: BSA, Norton, Villiers, Triumph, NVT—it now stood for 'Not Very Triumphant'.

11.2 NVT–R.I.P. REST IN PEACE. BUT WHY? AND HOW?

The Japanese firms had created a powerful feedback loop known as 'the magic circle'—higher sales brought lower production costs, which permitted lower prices, which increased sales, which further lowered costs and prices... (Figure 11.2). Once that loop kicks in, competitors drop like flies.

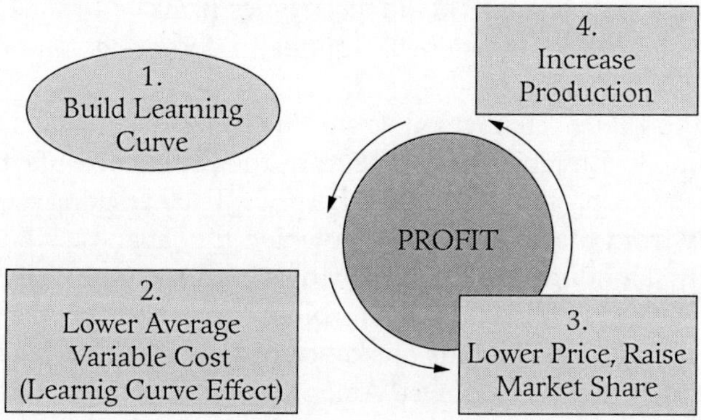

Figure 11.2
The magic circle

Bruce Henderson described precisely how the Japanese firms accomplished this.

> The profit pressure experienced by British manufacturers results '... from a cost position which is fundamentally *uncompetitive* with that of the Japanese.' This, in turn, stems from the fact that 'the competitor with the highest annual model volumes can benefit from methods which embody

up-to-date technology and which rely on scale effects for their cost superiority.'

When a learning curve exists, higher production volume leads to lower average costs, which in turn permits lower prices *without impairing profit margins, vital for generating funds for continued investment*. In turn this price decline boosts demand and sales and increases market share, leading to higher production, even lower costs, lower prices ... and so on.

But wait! It was the *British* who were once the high-volume producers. So, what went wrong? Henderson continues: 'Honda ensures the secrecy of their developments by maintaining a 1,400-man subsidiary which manufactures machine tools for Honda [only].' The British motorcycle makers, noted Henderson, 'use low productivity general purpose equipment' obtained as cast-off machine tools made for car producers. Honda too could buy them—but why would they?

'The disastrous commercial performance of the British manufacturers in this decade [i.e., the 1970s] is the final result of their failure to respond effectively to the strategic implications of the economic relationship between volume and costs in the motorcycle business.' Translation: They slept through the class on learning curves. Nor were they alone. American car companies did the same a decade later. So did electronics firms.

The signal for NVT's disaster was sounded a decade ago. But British managers turned a blind eye.

'During the 1960s,' Henderson wrote, 'in any model in which the industry was confronted with Japanese competitors, the British manufacturers found it difficult to make profits at a competitive price. Their response was essentially to withdraw from the smaller bikes in which the Japanese were competing so effectively.' Honda, in particular, began its market conquest by dominating the US market for small 100 c.c. motorbikes. 'You meet the nicest people on a Honda', was Honda's famous market campaign, invented by an American MBA student who won a contest. American and British motorcycle manufacturers willingly gave up this low-end of the market because profit margins were low.

'The success of Honda, Suzuki and Yamaha in the States has been jolly good or us,' said Eric Turner, board chairman of BSA Ltd., the leading British firm. 'People here start out by buying one of the low-priced Japanese jobs. They get to enjoy the fun and exhilaration of the open road and frequently end up buying one of our more powerful and expensive machines.'[3]

'Basically, we do not believe in the lightweight market,' said William H. Davidson, then president, and son of a founder, of Harley-Davidson, a leading American firm. Both were smart, experienced managers. What they failed to understand was people who buy and love cheap small Honda motorbikes, when they are poor and young will buy expensive big Hondas when they are older and rich. And with each passing year, they get older and richer. If you cede the low end of the market, ultimately you will give up the high end as well and much faster than you believed possible. Like Attila the Hun rolling back and conquering complacent European countries one by one, year by year a new-age cohort arrives that is already locked in by your competitors. Year by year, you lose your market. Precisely the same business model later worked to perfection for Japanese automobile firms. American automobile executives did not benchmark the disaster of the motorbike firms.

Market share and RoI

The magic circle business strategy is based on an empirical finding that there is a direct relationship between market share and pre-tax Return on Investment (RoI) (Figure 11.3).

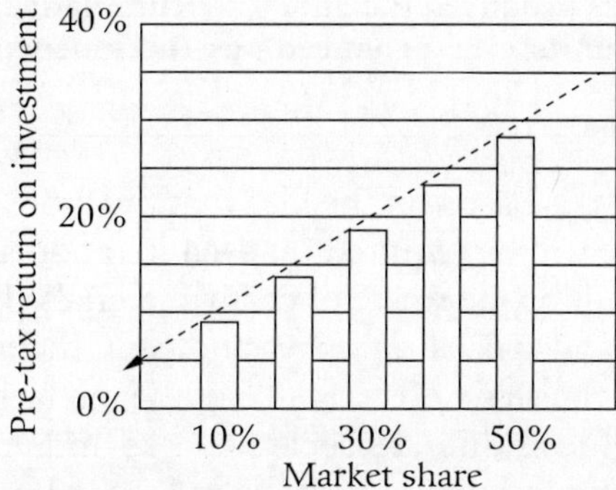

Figure 11.3
Relationship between market share and pre-tax return on investment (RoI)

Market shares above 40 per cent move products into 'Economic Value Added' territory, where large rents and significant wealth are created for shareholders. This is the major reason that legendary General Electric CEO Jack Welch insisted GE be either number one or number two in markets where GE competed.

Henderson's report should have helped alert managers in Britain and America benchmark and draw conclusions for other industries. But they were asleep at the helm. Precisely the same strategy that led Japan to dominate motorcycles was soon applied to give Japan domination in motor cars and to some extent, consumer electronics. Conquer the low end, move up to the high end. Toyota took this to an extreme. Ultimately, they moved upscale to challenge Mercedes with their Lexus and succeeded against all odds. Had the heads of General Motors, Chrysler, Ford and other companies read Henderson's report and realized its implications for their businesses, they might have sounded alarm bells and revamped their strategies. However they did not, until a dacade later when it was almost too late. To paraphrase Santayana: *Those managers who forget the past—who do not carefully benchmark best practices, in particular, and who ignore the history of Magic Circle learning curves—are doomed to repeat it, and their workers and shareholders will endure great pain as a result.* At the heart of the Magic Circle lies the learning curve. We now examine this powerful concept in depth.

DEFINITION

- **Learning curve: (a) the relation between the average variable cost (or average production cost) of a product (defined in Chapter 8), measured over the entire production history of the product, from the very first unit to last, as the dependent variable 'y', and (b) the number of units of the product ever produced (i.e., the total cumulative or lifetime output or number of units ever produced), as the independent variable, 'x', where y depends on x.**

The learning curve is based on the idea that the more often a task is done, the less labour time will be required on each iteration as skill and expertise grow and smaller will be the waste of costly materials. The link between repetition, efficiency and specialization was noted in the previous chapter and goes back to Adam Smith's 1776 example of the pin factory, where breaking pin-manufacturing down into 18 separate tasks and letting a single expert specialize in each, led to huge reductions in labour hours per million pins.

History

The concept of the learning curve was first introduced by an American aeronautical engineer, Thomas P. Wright, in an academic journal article in 1936. *He observed that the cost of producing airplanes follows a regular mathematical curve, with average variable cost declining by about 15–20 per cent each time aircraft production doubles.* He also observed that this relationship was stable across different types of aircraft, a fact that remains true to this day. Were he alive today, Wright might be surprised to learn that his 'law' applied equally well to Henry Ford's Model T, to the Lockheed 1011 Tristar wide-body passenger aircraft, to F-15s and F-16s, to the space shuttle, shipbuilding, machine tools, VCRs, welding and plastic even though the production technologies used in making these products are very different. (Figure 11.4 shows the learning

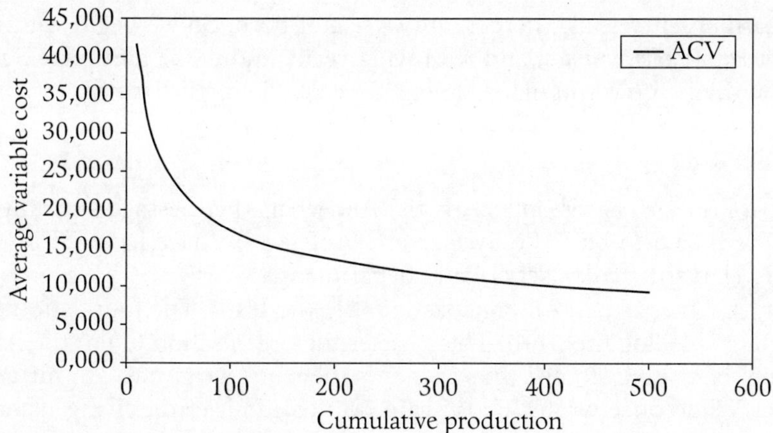

Figure 11.4
Learning curve for the Lockheed 1011 TriStar

curve for the Lockheed Tristar wide body aircraft.) Bruce Henderson was the first to apply this concept as a strategic management tool, rather than as an engineering concept, in the 1960s.

Arithmetic example

Lockheed 1011 Tristar[4]: One of the first widebody civilian jet aircrafts. The first production model rolled off the assembly line in Palmdale California in 1973; then-Governor Ronald Reagan cut the ribbon. The production cost for that first plane was a stiff $100 million; but a steep 77 per cent learning curve was created, meaning that Average Variable Costs (AVC) fell 23 per cent each time production doubled, i.e.,

$$AVC(Q = 2) = 0.77 \times AVC(Q=1).$$

By the time the 500th plane was produced, workers were so adept at the work that the average production cost (averaged over all the 500 planes produced) was only about $10 million. Slashing production costs by a full order of magnitude is not unusual for products driven by learning-curve effects! This is computed as follows: for a 77 per cent learning curve,

> average variable costs for two planes are 0.77 times $100 million or $77 million.

After production doubles,

> nine times (512 planes = 2^9) average variable cost declines to 0.77^9 times $100 million = 0.095 × $100 million or only about $9.5 million, 10 per cent of its initial level.

Learning curves, like heroes, are *made,* not born. So we begin with their *behavioural underpinnings*, and with what seems more like a Sunday School lesson than a powerful management concept, 'telling the truth'.

Tell the truth

Who is Professor Christopher Argyris? And what is his message—so universal that he is said to be the only Harvard Professor to have lectured in every single Harvard faculty, school and department?

Argyris' message is: All organizations seek to learn. The foundation of all learning is telling the truth. The smarter the organization, often the harder telling the truth becomes. 'Experience is the name we give to our mistakes', Oscar Wilde once wrote. Those who do not admit error, giving names to their mistakes, do not learn. And, notes Argyris, it is precisely those who are very smart and very successful who have the hardest time to learn, because they find it hard to admit error.[5]

American schoolchildren learn the apocryphal tale of George Washington, who, when confronted as a child, confessed to chopping down a cherry tree, saying: 'I cannot tell a lie. I did it with my own little axe.' According to Argyris, telling the truth is not only a moral principle and the Ninth Commandment—it is the First Commandment for organizations that seek to learn and the foundation for building valuable knowledge assets. For over 40 years, in books, articles and workshops Argyris taught managers how to foster truth-telling and showed why this is exceptionally difficult.

Argyris studied 6,000 managers and administrators around the world. He discovered a fundamental paradox: *The smarter and better-trained people are, the tougher it is for them to learn*. The reason: Smart, successful people are more reluctant to admit errors and mistakes. They are experts at defence behaviour—at shifting or evading blame. Conclusion: Teaching organizations to tell the truth and make truth-telling part of the corporate DNA culture is the first step toward creating a learning organization.

Case study: Einstein: 'I was wrong'

Argyris observes that smart people often have a hard time admitting error. But truly clever people overcome this. Perhaps the smartest person of our age was Albert Einstein. Here is an account, by Simon Singh, of how he admitted error—and ultimately profited tremendously:

Case study continued

Case study continued

When Einstein invented his general theory of relativity (his theory of gravity), he encountered a tough problem. If gravity is an attractive force—attracting comets to the sun, and coins to the ground—why then hadn't gravity caused matter in the universe to collapse inward on itself? Einstein posited an 'antigravity' force, that would maintain the overall stability of the universe. The universe, in this view, was eternal—always was, always will be.

In the 1920s, a band of renegade cosmologists suggested that the universe was not eternal but had been created at a finite moment in the past. They posited that the universe was once a primeval 'superatom' that ruptured and exploded and became the current universe. This became known as the Big Bang theory. In 1929, an astronomer named Edwin Hubble—who came from one of America's poorest regions, the Ozark Mountains—used the Mount Wilson Observatory telescope to show that all the distant galaxies in the universe were racing away from one another, as if from a huge explosion. Einstein quickly grasped the implications. 'This [the Big Bang theory] is the most beautiful and satisfactory explanation of creation which I have ever listened,' he said, calling his antigravity repulsive force 'the biggest blunder of my career'.

There is a twist to this tale. According to then contemporary theory, the Big Bang should be slowing, because the force of gravity attracts the receding galaxies to one another. But in 1998, astronomers found that the universe is actually accelerating, expanding outward *at an increasing rate!* The only way to explain this is Einstein's antigravity—so, notes Simon Singh, 'even when Einstein thought he was wrong, he turned out to be right.'

'[Einstein], the world's smartest person, was prepared to admit he was wrong.'

'Perhaps humility, more than anything, is the mark of true genius,' concludes Singh.

Source: Simon Singh, 'Even Einstein had his off Days', *New York Times*, 1 January 2005.

Action learning

Seven Things You *Can Do to Foster Truth-Telling*

1. Truth starts at the top. If mid-level managers tell the truth but their CEO does not deception soon makes a comeback. Instiling the truth-telling value starts with top management.
2. Encourage people to confront their own ideas and re-examine basic assumptions. Help them 'create a window' into their own minds and experience.
3. Challenge your own positions, principles and values and examine them constantly.
4. Be aware of how and when you, as an individual, react defensively to criticism and take steps to avoid this response.
5. Encourage others (and yourself) to say what they know, even when they are fearful of doing so. Foster the notion that questioning others' reasoning is not a sign of mistrust or an indication of disloyalty but a valuable opportunity for learning.
6. Ensure that the penalty for error and mistakes is not so severe, that managers and employees avoid revealing or admitting them at all costs. There is an optimum here—sanctions for error should not be so tiny that it results in carelessness, nor so huge that they are desperately concealed.
7. Debrief after every event, project or major process; examine what went wrong and what went right without mercy.

11.3 SINGLE-LOOP AND DOUBLE-LOOP THINKING

Argyris invented the notion of 'double-loop' and 'single-loop' thinking.[6] Most learning and thinking is 'single-loop', he claims, while one should aspire to the 'double loop' variety. Argyris' metaphor is that of a thermostat. A sensor measures room temperature and activates heating or cooling, which in turn changes the temperature. This is one single closed loop. Double-loop learning soars above the single loop, asking, for instance: do we *need* a thermostat at all? Perhaps opening a window would suffice. Such thinking adds a second loop that questions the need for the first, or inner, one. Double loop thinking is loosely referred to as 'out of the box thinking', though this is inaccurate; all businesses operate within 'boxes' or constraints, the question is, which are truly binding and which can be ignored?

All businesses need to be good at single-loop learning. But many are trapped by it, and never advance to a higher level. Quality control is an example. Once companies checked for defects at the end of the production line, and discarded them—a single-loop system. Total Quality Management gurus like Deming and Juran then noted how costly this was and urged double-loop thinking: Find the *source* of the defects, and eliminate it; aim for zero defects.

Why accept the existence of *any* defects? It is 'double loop' thinking, because you add a loop that asks: do we need the inner, single loop at all? Or is there a better way?

Double-loop thinking often requires admission of failure or error, Argyris explained. For example: A high rate of defects requires a very smart and experienced production manager or VP (Production) to accept responsibility for flaws in the assembly line and commit to eliminating them. Often, this does not happen. Smart people are unaccustomed to failure. Recognizing, admitting and accepting responsibility for failure in front of fellow workers is one of the hardest things in the world for accomplished people, such as R&D experts, to do. When others suggest their performance may have been below-par, they react with feelings of guilt and anger and become resistant to change. This behaviour is widespread, endemic and hard to uproot.

No manager or CEO would knowingly chop down their companies' invaluable tree of knowledge. Yet they do it all the time when they and their employees fail to tell the truth. If experience is indeed what we call our mistakes, then hiding those mistakes erases the potential benefit of our experience. In this we pay twice—once for the mistake, a second time for discarding the lessons it could teach.

Case study: Model T learning curve

Henry Ford, pioneer of modern mass production, revolutionized industrial production forever by creating a powerful learning curve and associated Magic Circle. He had the brilliant idea (said to have come from visiting a Chicago meat packing plant, where carcasses were hung from a pulley and moved along a production line), of pulling the Model T car chassis along an assembly line and giving each production worker only one task (e.g., install the bumper or the steering wheel). Previously, cars were assembled one by one, by dumping a heap of parts onto the

Case study continued

Case study continued

floor and having workers assemble them into a car. By making tasks repetitious, workers gained speed and proficiency. The result: Model T average cumulative variable costs fell by 15 per cent each time production doubled. Ultimately, over 16 million Model Ts were produced—24 doublings, since 2^{24} is about 16 million units. Average production costs fell by 15 per cent, 24 times, once for each doubling. The rapid reduction in cost, and hence in price, transformed cars from a luxury item to an item of mass consumption affordable by the middle classes (Table 11.1). It also made a huge fortune in profit for Ford and his Ford Motor Company.

Table 11.1
Price of Model T cars (adjusted for inflation)*

1909: $4,000	1911: $2,500	1912: $2,000	
1918: $1,500	1921: $1,000	1923: $900	1928: $500

Source: Abernathy and Wayne, 1974.
Note: *Measured in constant 1958 dollars.

Henry Ford encountered two major obstacles in implementing his earning curve strategy. The first, he surmounted easily. The second proved fatal.

The first hurdle, encountered at the outset, was the sheer dulling boredom of performing a single assembly-line task dozens of times a day, for 10–12 hours, day after day, month after month. Workers quit in droves. [Readers may recall Charlie Chaplin's brilliant parody of mass production, *Modern Times*, in which Chaplin, an assembly line worker, tightens a bolt thousands of times a day, working faster and faster as the line speeds up and then goes home with his arm locked in a repeated bolt-tightening motion that he cannot stop.] As a result, new workers had to be retrained. The learning curve disappears when worker turnover is high.

Ford's answer to the problem: double wages, to $5 an hour and buy loyalty. It worked. Money trumped tedium. Ford was a despotic stingy capitalist but self-interest and the profit motive made his wage policy seem benevolent.

The second hurdle almost led to Ford Motor Co.'s bankruptcy. It was what Abernathy and Wayne call the 'Limits of the Learning Curve'.[7] There is one major way to attack a competitor who has raced ahead of

Case study continued

Case study continued

you down the learning curve—continual innovation! Former McKinsey principal Richard Foster calls this 'The Attacker's Advantage'.[8] If you cannot catch a competitor far ahead of you on the learning-curve ski slope move to another mountain and make him or her chase you! The founder of General Motors, Alfred P. Sloan, used this approach with consummate brilliance.

11.4 ATTACKING LEARNING CURVES

In his book *Innovation: The Attacker's Advantage*, former McKinsey principal Richard Foster uses the notion of the 'S-curve' (Figure 11.5). The S-curve shows the cumulative sales (number of units ever sold) of a product, from start to finish. The typical pattern for a product is this: Initially cumulative sales grow slowly, then grow more and more rapidly as the product catches on, then the rate of growth of sales slows, because almost every household has at least one unit, and finally becomes zero as the market reaches saturation. This occurred with the Model T.

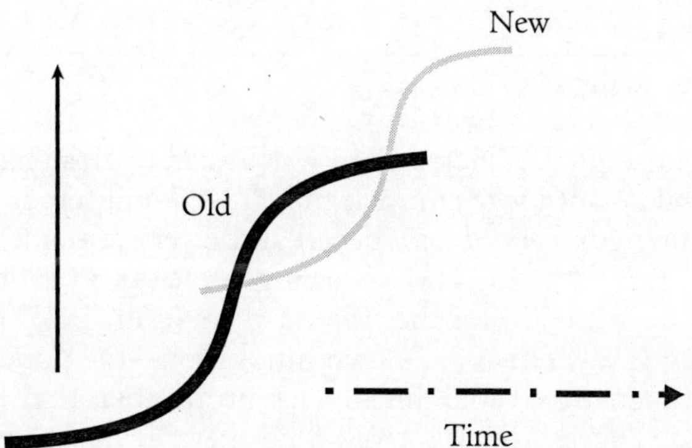

Figure 11.5
The 'S-curve': How to time transition from old products and services to new ones

There is a major management dilemma embodied in the S-curve. Often profits accrue not in the early stages of the curve (when costs are still high) but in later stages, when costs are low owing to moving down the learning curve, brand names are well known and market positions are secure. Abandong this 'cash cow' seems like folly. Yet precisely at this stage of the mature S-curve, it is vulnerable to attack by an innovator. Great managers know that if they do not destroy their mature product, a competitor will. This is what happened to Ford.

Case study: GM vs Ford

Faced with Ford's venerable Model T learning curve in the 1920s, Alfred P. Sloan, CEO and Chairman of General Motors, knew he could not catch Ford on the existing learning curve.[9] His only hope was to make Ford shift to a new one, *and pursue GM*, rather than have GM pursue Ford. So he created slick new models, with a variety of colours, closed bodies and engines and gave consumers a choice. Under Sloan's guidance, GM's companies—Pontiac, Chevrolet, Cadillac, Oldsmobile—competed fiercely with Ford, and even with one another, pushing innovative designs. The new GM models were a big hit. Ford's market share peaked at 62 per cent(!) in 1924, and in just three years dropped to only 13 per cent, reminiscent of NVT R.I.P. (Table 11.2).

Table 11.2
Ford market share for automobiles: US, 1909–27

1909: 11%	1912: 27%	1913: 49%
1929: 55%	1924: 62%	1925: 53%
1926: 44%	1927: 13%	

Source: Abernathy and Wayne, 1974.

As a consequence, Henry Ford was forced to close his River Rouge automobile plant for over a year in 1928–29 and retool. This destroyed his learning curve. Ford now began at the very top of a new and costly learning curve, chasing GM's learning curve. As a result Ford struggled to catch up with GM for the next 35 years (until 1965) and almost went bankrupt. It was only Ford's own innovation—the popular Taurus Ford model designed and sold initially in Europe, then translated to worldwide success—that revived the venerable company.

There are two mistakes associated with S-curves, and each can be life-threatening. One is prematurely dumping an old, familiar S-curve to leap to a new one, before the market and the technology have matured. Like cross country skiers breaking trail for those who follow, often being second or third in such markets is optimal. A second, more common mistake is the opposite: Clinging to an old S-curve for far too long, when you should have leaped onto an innovative new one. Wise managers know when to dump an

S-curve by innovating and moving onto a new one, and when to continue to ride an old, profitable 'cash cow' S-curve—or, at times, how to maintain both old and new in the same product portfolio. Great companies, like Proctor & Gamble, know how to avoid both errors, by maintaining product portfolios that include venerable old hags (Ivory Soap, a 120-year-old brand) and snazzy new chicks (Oral B toothbrushes).

It is ironic that precisely at the time when the mass production system of capitalism invented by Henry Ford was being assaulted by Alfred P. Sloan's General Motors and his innovative skills, a Georgia-born Russian dictator and Socialist named Joseph Djugashvili (Stalin) was instructing his subordinates to find the most efficient factory in the world and benchmark against it. Of course, they found and copied Ford's River Rouge plant. A similar but much larger plant was built near Moscow to produce cars and trucks and it was referred to as River Rouge (Red). (Stalin liked the colour Red.) Russian industrial progress and socialist planning never did move beyond the stage of mass producing huge standard quantities of goods, while capitalism progressed from mass production to mass customization (see Chapter 10); ultimately socialism was defeated. Henry Ford, who for a time sympathized with Fascism, would have gained great satisfaction knowing that the Communists failed by blindly copying him. By embracing the capital-intensive mass production model at the precise moment in time that it became obsolete, communism gave capitalism a decisive edge.

11.5 LEARNING CURVES IN BREAK-EVEN ANALYSIS

Learning curves enable us to predict the life history of production costs with considerable accuracy, even before a single unit has rolled off the assembly line. This feature leads to one of the most useful ways to use learning curves: Break-even analysis, the analysis of the time it takes to recover a capital investment.

DEFINITION—BREAK-EVEN ANALYSIS

- ***Calculation of the number of units of a good or service we have to sell and the time it takes to make them, in order to balance costs and revenues.*** **Very often, investors, CFOs or CEOs, have to consider whether or not to sink money into a new idea or venture. They want to know how long it will take for the investment to pay for itself. Break-even analysis based on learning curves provides some answers. There are actually three break-even points, one for each concept of 'cost' (marginal, average variable and average total).**

- **The learning curve is the relationship between average variable cost AVC(Q) and cumulative number of units of a good or service ever produced, Q. From the learning curve, one can also derive the marginal cost curve MC(Q), which shows the cost of the last, or Qth, unit produced. By adding the fixed costs (such as Research and Development) to production costs, one can compute the average total cost curve ATC(Q),**

  ATC(Q) = AVC(Q) + (TFC / Q) (TFC is Total Fixed Costs)

- **The three cost curves generate three break-even points. They are, in order of their occurrence:**
  - **'cash flow break-even', the value of quantity Q where price intersects marginal costs; the notion here is that if the price covers the cost of making the last product, then for that product cash flow is zero and about to turn positive, because marginal cost is falling. At this point, a toast of Coke is in order, though overall the project is far from being profitable.**
  - **'short run break-even', the value of quantity Q where price intersects (i.e., equals) average variable costs; at that value of Q, and at that point in time, operating costs are covered by revenue, so the project is about to reach an operating profit but still has not recovered its fixed costs. A toast of white wine is called for as workers and managers celebrate this milestone. And your banker begins to sleep better at night.**
  - **'long run break-even', the value of quantity Q where price intersects average total costs. Now, revenues indeed cover all costs. Champagne is called for, because further sales begin to generate significant rents (economic value added) and create shareholder wealth.**
- **Break-even points are defined in terms of units of production and sales Q. But if the *rate* of production per month is known, say 'q', then the time it takes to reach each break-even point can also be calculated simply as Q / q months.**

Here is an example of break-even analysis, used by Professor Uwe Reinhardt to predict that Lockheed's new widebody aircraft, the L-1011 TriStar, would ultimately lose money. For a fuller mathematical exploration of this case, see Appendix to this chapter.

Case study: Lockheed 1011 TriStar

The L-1011 TriStar was one of the first wide-body civilian airliners. Design work began in 1968 and the first production model rolled off the

Case study continued

Case study continued

assembly line in 1973 in Palmdale, CA. The aircraft was technologically advanced and successful; but almost drove its producer, Lockheed, into bankruptcy. In 1972, Lockheed's CEO Roy Anderson asked the US Congress for a loan guarantee of $250 million to enable Lockheed to build a plant and put the plane into production. The request was hotly debated; it was approved in the US Senate by one vote. When the last plane was produced in 1985, it emerged that Lockheed had lost billions of dollars. Uwe Reinhardt, a young professor of finance at Princeton University in 1972, analysed the business prospects of the TriStar when the US Senate debated providing a loan guarantee to Lockheed. He used the learning curve, and with no inside information from Lockheed, accurately predicted that the plane would lose money. Here is a simplified version of his analysis.

Assumptions

There is a 77 per cent learning curve (similar to that of other aircraft). The first production model will cost $100 million ($AVC_1$ = $100 million). The average price per aircraft is about $14.5 million (Fierce competition among the DC-10 of McDonnell Douglas, the Boeing 747 and the TriStar brought prices down). Table 11.3 is generated by using

Table 11.3

Learning curve for the L-1011 TriStar

($ million)

Q	*AVC*	*ATC*	*MC*
1	100	1,100	100
2	77	577	49
4	59	309	38
8	46	171	29
16	35	98	23
32	27	58	18
64	21	37	14
128	16	24	11
256	12	16	8
512	10	12	6
1,024	7	8	5

Note: Q = number of planes of that model ever produced; AVC = average variable cost (averaged over the cumulative number of planes Q); ATC = average total cost (including fixed costs for R&D, etc.); MC = marginal cost, i.e., cost of producing the last, or Qth, plane.

Case study continued

Case study continued

the learning curve expression (see Appendix to this chapter). Using it, first find the cash-flow break-even point by running your finger down the MC (Marginal Cost) column, until MC is about equal to price, or \$14.5 million; this occurs at around Q = 64. Next, find the short-run break-even point, by running your finger down the AVC (Average Variable Cost) column, until AVC = P = \$14.5; interpolating, this occurs at around Q = 185. Finally, the long-run break even point, found by equating ATC and Q, is at around Q = 325.

Lockheed did create a strong steep learning curve for the TriStar, with a 77 per cent coefficient. But it did not succeed in racing down the learning curve, and capturing its profits speedily. Learning curves are about the economics of speed. Lockheed's rate of production at Palmdale of two planes per month was only half of what was needed for profitability. In the 1980s, when managers sought to speed up production, they hired new workers. But the new workers had to be trained and the result was to push Lockheed back up the learning curve rather than race down it. Only a strategic decision in the 1980s to shift Lockheed heavily into defence and aerospace-related products, at a time when Ronald Reagan (the ex-ribbon-cutting governor, who became President) was boosting military spending, saved Lockheed from bankruptcy.

Lockheed did pay back the \$250 million loan guarantee from profits made in defence-related businesses. The TriStar was its last civilian airliner. The TriStar was a safe, comfortable aircraft—a technological success, but a business failure.

Technology leader vs market leader

One of the main lessons of the TriStar case is an exceptionally important one: *Technological innovation and engineering superiority do not necessarily lead to market success and profitability.* The L-1011 was a fine, comfortable and popular plane, with a fine safety record. But competitive forces and market shifts (for instance, the 1973 and 1979 oil shocks and consequent rise in jet fuel prices) doomed it. The lesson: Never let technology alone drive your business model. Avoid the fatal 'Field of Dreams' syndrome. *Field of Dreams* was a 1989 movie, starring Kevin Kostner, about an American farmer who hears voices telling him to build a baseball diamond (baseball playing field) in his corn field. He is ridiculed. But the voices tell him: 'if you build it, they will come'—'they', meaning the ghosts of all-time great baseball players. He builds the diamond. And 'they' come, indeed, including legendary players of the Chicago Black Sox. Field of Dreams has become a 'mantra' for the 'if you build it, they will come' approach—if you create a technologically-superb product, buyers will beat a path to your door. Better to begin with the market and market needs, not with the technology. Harness technology to meet needs rather than exhibit engineering virtuosity. Understanding market demand is the topic of our next chapter.

11.6 MANAGEMENT BEGINS WITH MEASUREMENT

'Never begin a project', advises MIT Professor Lester Thurow, 'unless you have a system in place to tell you whether you succeeded or failed, when the project ends. Otherwise, you will not learn.'[10] A learning curve measurement system is often vital for project learning. Here is an Action Learning project to measure and improve your organization's learning curves.

Action learning

Learning Curve Arithmetic—The Calculator: How Steep is Your *Learning Curve?*

- Choose a repetitive task done in your organization.
- Measure the labour time it takes you to do it each time and, from the first time note the number of times you have done the task.
- Graph the learning curve as shown in Figure 11.6; estimate the learning curve coefficient 'b' as the slope of the line joining the data points. Use the Appendix to convert 'b' to β, the standard Beta learning curve coefficient.
- How might you improve this learning curve? How do you think it compares with similar curves of your competitors? How do you know?

11.7 PRICES VS COSTS: AND THE WINNER IS ...

Typically, in industries driven by learning curves, the race is not only to get production costs below those of competitors but also and perhaps even more important, one between costs and market price. In the real world, learning curves compete in a race between the ability to ramp up production and lower production costs, and the tendency of prices to fall as innovative products become commoditized and as new entrants come in to the market. Creating a steep learning curve is crucial to profitability, in order to keep

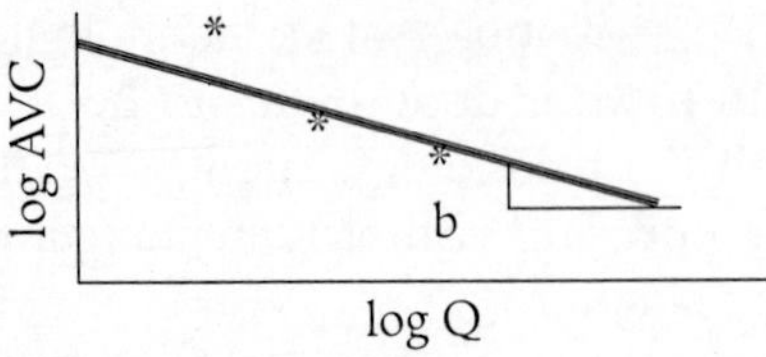

Figure 11.6
Estimate learning curve slope coefficients

Note: AVC = average variable cost; Q = cumulative number of units ever produced; log = logarithm. The learning curve slope coefficient 'b' is the slope of the line joining the data points, or 'log AVC divided by log Q'. The base number of the logarithm is of no consequence as the slope will be the same, provided the same base is used for both numerator and denominator. See Appendix (page 361) for how to convert the 'b' coefficient to the standard Beta learning curve coefficient.

costs falling faster than prices and maintain profitability. Competitive strategy calls for cost leaders to slash their prices below their competitors' costs and thus drive them out of business, while still maintaining profitability. 'In the [motorcycle] size classes where they competed,' noted Bruce Henderson, 'the Japanese ... essentially dictated price levels over the past 15 years' because they had superior learning curves and rapidly falling costs.

In our TriStar break-even analysis, we assumed a constant market price of P = $14.5 million. In practice, of course, market price (especially in consumer electronics) falls rapidly. The price of the TriStar fell even before the first plane was produced owing to fierce market competition. The curve showing the relationship between cumulative production or sales for the company's product and market price is known as the Price Experience Curve. Table 11.1 shows how the price of the Model T fell sharply over time, as falling costs driven by the learning curve drove prices down. Typically, innovative products reach the marketplace in a plethora of shapes, sizes, colours and styles. Soon, consumers 'vote' their preferences and such products become standardized. They then become commoditized, in that one version looks like another and market competition focuses not on innovation or value creation but on cost reduction. The battle then becomes a race down the learning curve, to see who can cut costs faster than price fall.

Case study: Intel

While some observers believe Intel's competitive advantage lies in its creativity and innovative ability, others believe strongly that in fact Intel's competitiveness lies in its manufacturing skill—the ability to create steep

Case study continued

Case study continued

learning curves and race down them rapidly before falling prices erase profitability. Companies like Intel live or die on their ability to create a new microchip, for example, debug it, ramp up production and capture profits while prices remain high, before competitors reach the market with similar products and 'commoditize' them. While Intel rightly prides itself on continual creativity and innovation—for instance, the recent introduction of the Centrino (Pentium 5) chipset—some observers think Intel's true core competency lies in debugging new chips, then ramping up production, creating a steep learning curve, producing millions in a short time and capturing profits, and then making its own product obsolete by introducing a new one and repeating the process. Intel regularly leaps from an old S-curve (e.g., Pentium 3) to a new one (Pentium 4) even while profits from the old one are still strong. It does this as a core competitive strategy, because it keeps competitors off balance. No sooner have they reached the market with a competing version of the Pentium 3, than Intel dumps it and introduces Pentium 4, making competitors' investment in time, and R&D capital, a sunk cost. Intel's manufacturing skill is superior to that of many of its competitors; their products, in their design, are clever and competitive, but fall short as their manufacturing process is slow and clumsy.

An obvious but crucial point about learning must be made. Learning is necessary but far from sufficient. You have to implement what you learn. Jeffrey Pfeiffer and Robert Sutton argue convincingly in their book *The Knowing-Doing Gap*[11] that the key management problem is *not* managing knowledge, but rather using it. Most companies learn, from themselves and from others, and know what they should do. But somehow, they fail to do it. There is a huge gap between knowing what to do and actually doing it.

11.8 KNOWING AND DOING

The numbers are striking. In the US, note Pfeiffer and Sutton, $60 billion a year is spent on management training, yet much of it is ineffective and has to be repeated often. Some 80,000 MBAs graduate yearly, however translation of management research and education into practice is slow and unreliable. Organizations spend $43 billion yearly on management consultants but that advice is seldom implemented.

Why? The authors suggest that up to 70 per cent of workplace learning is 'informal'—transferred by stories, gossip and watching others. Yet many knowledge management systems are tailored for *codified* written information only. There is a trend to create specialized functions for knowledge management; yet, the authors argue, knowledge management works best when those who generate the knowledge are also those who store, process and transmit it to others. The amount of 'tacit knowledge'—learning that has not been formally written down, processed and organized—far surpasses overt knowledge in most organizations, yet few have systems in place to analyse and exploit it. 'Do you know what you know?' is a powerful question every organization must ask itself. All too often, the answer is, well, we don't really know.

People learn best, argue Pfeiffer and Sutton, by doing. This recalls the Chinese saying: I hear, I take note; I see, I pay attention; I do, I understand. Or, as medical residents learning a new procedure are taught: hear one, see one, do one. The answer to the knowing-doing gap is deceptively simple, they argue—embed more of the process of learning *in the actual doing of the task*, and less in formal training programmes that are often ineffective. Learning by doing is almost always superior to learning by listening. It is a lesson we are striving to implement in this book, in the action-learning exercises.

The first author encountered a powerful example of learning by doing. On a visit to the US Navy aircraft carrier *Theodore Roosevelt*, he was told that one-third of the ship's crew of 5,000 sailors changes completely every year. Onboard, sailors work eight-hour shifts, train for eight hours daily, and eat, sleep and rest for eight hours. Veterans teach rookies. The vessel is able to launch and land jet aircraft at the same time, even at night, in pitch darkness, and in bad weather. The combination of learning and doing creates high performance, in high-pressure situations where an error will almost certainly cost lives.

Case studies in effective organizational learning

1. The little teddy bear

Good managers create successful products; great ones produce whole new industries. Procter & Gamble (P&G) created a new industry, fabric softeners—liquids or special small sheets you put into washing machines and dryers to make the clothes and towels soft, static-free and fragrant—and persuaded people it was a 'must' purchase. Its brand, Downy, dominated the market. Unilever tried everything to snatch market share from Downy and failed. Taking on a P&G brand is like climbing Everest; recall that P&G pioneered in organizational structure built around

Case study continued

Case study continued

brands, rather than around businesses, products or divisions. Then, in Germany in 1970, Unilever introduced fabric softener with a teddy bear on the package, and called it *kuschelweich* (German for teddy bear). Now, everyone has had a teddy bear as a child, and so everyone instantly associates that symbol with softness and gentleness—precisely what fabric softener tries to convey. *Kuschelweich* was an instant success. Unilever reacted by doing what *New York Times* columnist Thomas Friedman calls 'glocalization' (taking a global idea and adapting it, all over the world, to local conditions). For English speakers, they called the product Snuggle. The teddy bear image was identical to *kuschelweich*. There were Spanish and French equivalents. Unilever quickly leveraged its Snuggle brand to a strong #2 position, challenging Downy. The lesson here is clear. Managers should ask themselves: Can I quickly identify a 'local' success, and organize to transmit it rapidly throughout the organization, while changing and adapting it where necessary to regional differences in culture, tastes and markets? In the end, this is what effective learning is about. It is about bottom-line ability to spread successful ideas anywhere, everywhere. It is this ability that distinguishes between a multinational organization, operating in many parts of the world, and a truly global 'transnational' organization, able to leverage successful ideas anywhere in the world and transmit them to all parts of the organization seamlessly. Unilever knew what it knew—it knew how to 'brand' fabric softener in a way that touched a universal human heartstring. The fact it discovered this heartstring in Germany was of no consequence. Unilever eventually sold its teddy bear brand to P&G for a tidy profit.

2. PAM: From Holland to Calgary, Houston and New Delhi

'PAM', in this context, is not a girl's name. It stands for Project Activity Model. It is a learning-and-knowledge-management story that has immediate bottom-line consequences at Fluor, a $10 billion global engineering and construction company. In 1999, senior Fluor manager John McQuary told the first author[12] that Fluor had embarked on building a new knowledge-management system. There was a practical reason. Large numbers of their baby-boomer engineers would retire in 5–10 years. 'We had to create a culture that would attract and retain younger engineers,' he explained, while capturing the knowledge of retiring ones. 'Knowledge management is not technology driven but technology enabled—it is about connecting people,' he stressed. One of Fluor's key lessons: Always harness knowledge management to clear business principles and strategy.

Case study continued

Case study continued

Fluor's knowledge management goal was to transform itself into the premier engineering and construction knowledge-based company. Fluor's office in Haarlem, Holland had developed a project-planning tool called PAM (project activity model). This tool specified all the activities necessary for each engineering discipline, across all phases of a project, including project initiation, scope and definition, preliminary engineering, detailed design, construction, etc. Each component contains a 'Knowledge Pack' with documents needed for anyone involved with a new project. *It was quickly recognized that PAM, developed in the Haarlem office, was widely useful for the whole Fluor global organization.* PAM was placed on-line, and was soon finding wide use across the whole organization. Like *kuschelweich*, PAM was a bottom-line idea that proved itself in one place and quickly was transmitted, by the knowledge management system, to all places. Learning was rapid, global and efficient.

A powerful part of Fluor's knowledge management is the concept of 'communities of practice'. These Web-based systems are each built around functions, such as structural engineering, electrical engineering, materials management, project management, etc. Each function has a 'leader'—someone responsible for content. There are some 37 of them and they include more than 13,000 members in over 90 locations. They permit any Fluor employee, for instance, to ask a question ('How close can a concrete barrier be placed to a flare?'). This question got a first response in 30 minutes and three more responses within a day. The system requires everyone not only to use knowledge, but also to share and contribute it—uploading knowledge other Fluor employees will find useful. Fluor tracks the system, known as Knowledge OnLine™, with extensive statistics (42,200 home page reads per month, 3,500 daily searches).

[Chris Argyris relates that he once took part in an award ceremony in which a line worker got a prize for an idea that sharply reduced costs. When he asked the worker how long he had known about this cost-cutting idea, the worker said ten years. Why didn't you come forward sooner? Argyris asked. No one ever asked me, said the worker. Learning is often present among the foot soldiers but it struggles to get to the staff officers, especially those who never visit the front lines but huddle in their cozy carpeted 40th floor corner offices.]

An American TV advertisement for college funding says: 'A mind is a terrible thing to waste.' So is a great idea. Fluor is a best-practice benchmark for ways to prevent this in large global organizations.

11.9 BUILDING A LEARNING ORGANIZATION

We begin and end with the same key issue: Building an organization that can learn fast and well. In the Case Study later, 'Racing Down the Learning Curve', Motorola's Kevin Christenson struggles with an organizational learning problem many managers will find familiar. Two subgroups exist. One deals with a new, upcoming technology, not yet profitable. The other deals with an old, fading technology that is still highly profitable. There is some antagonism between the two. Those working on the new technology need the wisdom of those who know the old one but why would these people share it? They, after all, are in a company backwater. There is little incentive for knowledge to travel between the two groups, hence learning is slow and painful, hurting Motorola's competitiveness. Christenson found a good solution, one that created a powerful learning curve where none existed previously. Readers are invited to come up with their own solution (see Case Study 11.1).

11.10 CONCLUSION

The chapter title deserves repeating. Learning curves, like heroes, are made not born. Do not be deceived by the similarity of learning curves across such diverse industries as plastics, cars, aircraft and electronics. They do not just happen. All of them were built by great managers, who built learning organizations, by telling the truth, and by instilling constant learning and sharing of knowledge as a core company value. Few strategies succeed without such learning. The cautionary tale of NVT that accompanied us in this chapter should be remembered. Those who fail to build steep learning curves and then fail to race down them rarely survive to tell the tale.

Readers are invited to view 'Pillars of Profit: Segment #7, Learning Curves are made, not born', in the accompanying CD.

APPENDIX: LEARNING CURVE ARITHMETIC

The words 'average variable cost decline by 15 per cent with each doubling of production' describe a simple mathematical function, known as a negative exponential curve. The mathematical formula for a learning curve—relationship between average variable cost and cumulative production measured over the entire life of the product, from first to last unit produced can be expressed in two different ways:

$$[1]\ AVC(Q) = AVC_1\ \beta^n$$
$$[2]\ AVC(Q) = AVC_1\ Q^{-b}$$

where: Q—cumulative (lifetime) production; AVC_1—average variable cost of the first production model; AVC(Q)—average variable cost after Q units are produced (averaged over the entire production history of the product, from the first to the Qth unit); n—number of times output has doubled, i.e., $Q = 2^n$, β—learning curve coefficient: interpreted as, after doubling production, from Q to 2Q, the new value of AVC for 2Q units is β per cent that of the previous value of AVC for Q units or, AVC declines by (1 – β) per cent each time cumulative production Q doubles; b—exponent of the negative-exponent version of the learning curve; related to β by the formula $\beta = 2^{-b}$.

When [2] is expressed in logarithmic form, we get:

$$[2']\ \log AVC(Q) = \log AVC_1 - b\log Q$$

Once you know the learning curve, you can also compute two additional curves: Total Variable Cost (TVC) and Marginal Cost (MC) curves:

$$[3]\ TVC(Q) = Q^*\ AVC(Q) = AVC_1Q^{1-b}$$
$$[4]\ MC(Q) = d[TVC(Q)] / dQ = (1 - b)\ AVC_1Q^{-b} = (1 - b)AVC(Q)$$

And, once you know Total Variable Cost (TVC), you can compute the Total Cost (variable and fixed) Curve TC by adding Total Fixed Cost (TFC) to TVC:

$$[5]\ TC(Q) = TFC + TVC(Q) = TFC + AVC_1Q^{1-b}$$

Translating from β to 'b'

Learning curves are often described using the β coefficient, e.g., 90 per cent learning curve, or 85 per cent learning curve. (The learning curve coefficient for the Model T automobile, produced from around 1909 through 1928 turned out to be 85 per cent.) But the negative-exponent form of the learning curve is more convenient to use in calculations. It is easy to shift from one formulation to the other using the following equations and conversion table (Table 11.4).

$$[3]\ \beta^n = Q^{-b} = 2^{-bn}$$
$$[4]\ \therefore\ \beta = 2^{-b} \text{ or}$$
$$[5]\ b = -\log \beta / \log 2$$

Table 11.4
Translating b to β

β	90%	85%	80%	77%	75%	70%
b	0.15	0.23	0.32	0.377	0.42	0.51

Action learning

The Two Per Cent Solution

Very small changes in the learning curve coefficient are sufficient to generate very large increases in lifetime profits accruing from a product. To see this, try the following exercise:

1. Assume a product price P of \$14.5 million (the market price of Lockheed's TriStar aircraft in 1973); and assume that lifetime production and sale of planes Q amounted to 600. Assume a 77 per cent learning curve. That means that if β is 77 per cent,

   then $b = -\log \beta / \log 2 = 0.377$ (Table 11.4).
2. Calculate the total amount of operating profit earned over the lifetime of the TriStar [(P times Q) – (Q times AVC(Q)].
3. Now: Assume a 75 per cent learning curve (b = 0.42). Calculate operating total profit again. What increment to total profit accrues to an improvement in the learning curve coefficient of just 2 per cent?

Case study: Break-even analysis: Lockheed 1011 TriStar

Cash-flow break-even point

('Incremental cash flow' break-even)—this is the point, where the marginal cost of the TriStar equals its price; after this value of Q, each additional plane produced and sold brings in more revenue than it costs to produce, and ongoing incremental cash flow becomes positive. To find this point, solve for Q:

$$MC(Q) = P = \$14.5 \text{ million}$$

$$MC(Q) = dTVC / dQ = d[QAVC(Q)] / dQ$$
$$= d[AVC_1 Q^{1-b}] / dQ$$
$$= (1 - b)\, AVC_1 Q^{-b}$$

$$\text{or } MC(Q) = (1 - b)AVC(Q)$$

Case study continued

Case study continued

Note that for the learning curve, marginal cost is always a fixed proportion of average variable cost, with the proportion equal to (1 – b).

For a 77 per cent learning curve, b is 0.377 and MC is 62 per cent of AVC. Since for the TriStar, AVC_1 was \$100 million:

$$MC(Q) = 0.62(100)Q^{-0.377}$$

solve for Q* to find the cash-flow break-even point:

Q* = about 50 planes

[see Figure 11.7: intersection of P=14.5 with MC(Q)].

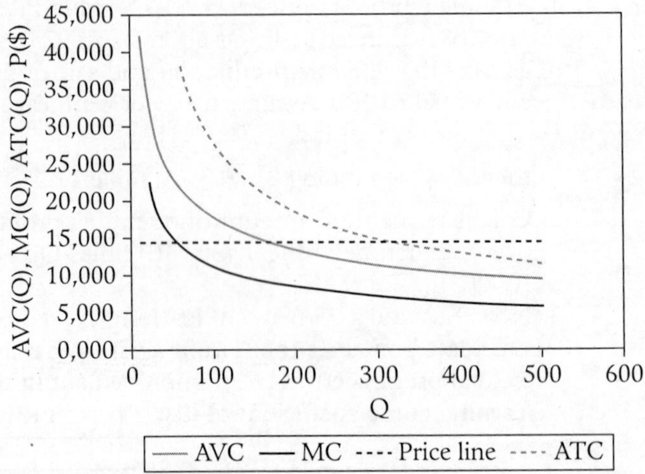

Figure 11.7
Break-even analysis using learning curves

Lockheed was producing about two planes a month at its Palmdale plant; so cash-flow break-even would occur after about 2 years, or 50/2, i.e., 25 months.

Short-run break-even point

A zero operating profit is attained, when Average variable cost equals Price. Beyond this point, operating profit becomes positive. To find this point solve for Q:

$$AVC(Q) = P = \$14.5 \text{ million}$$
$$AVC(Q) = AVC_1\, Q^{-b} = \$100\, Q^{-0.377} = 14.5 \text{ million}$$
Q** = about 175 planes

[see Figure 11.7: intersection of P = 14.5 with AVC(Q)].

Case study continued

Case study continued

After some 175 planes are produced, the aircraft begins making an operating profit—production costs fall below the price and total revenue from sale of planes is greater than the total costs of making them.

However, this is still not an overall profit, because the development costs (Research, Development, Testing, Evaluation or RDT&E) have to be covered. They amounted to some $1,000 million.

Long-run break-even point

In 1968, when the decision was being made to invest in designing a new wide-body plane, long-run break-even analysis was the tool to be used: how many planes and how long will it take in order for the project to make an overall profit?

The long-run break-even point occurs when:

$$ATC(Q) = P = \$14.5 \text{ million}$$

where ATC is the average total cost per plane, including the production costs (AVC) and the fixed costs (AFC), where ATC = AVC + AFC, and AFC is equal to TFC / Q .

The fixed Research, Development, Testing and Evaluation costs for the TriStar were reported by Aviation Week to be about $1,000 million ($1 billion).

Therefore:

$$ATC(Q) = \$1{,}000 / Q + AVC^1Q^{-b} = \$1{,}000 / Q + \$100Q^{-0.377} = 14.5$$
$$Q^{***} = 325 \text{ planes}$$

It would take the sale of 325 planes to reach overall break-even. [Figure 11.7: intersection of P=14.5 with ATC(Q)].

Note that this analysis is only approximate; it is true only if all 325 planes are produced and sold instantly. If production and sales revenue take place over time, it is necessary to take into account the opportunity cost of money; that is, profit on a plane sold in 1985, say, $2 million, is worth less than $0.4 million in 1968, when its present value in 1968 (or, 17 years earlier) is computed, using:

$$\text{present value of \$2 million in 1968} = (\$2 \text{ million}) / (1 + R)^{17}$$

where R is the weighted average cost of capital for the firm, and R is about 10 per cent for Lockheed. The concept of present value will be

Case study continued

Case study continued

explained more carefully in Chapter 13. This is also referred to as 'time value of money'.

Taking into account this 'present value', Uwe Reinhardt computed Lockheed's breakeven point at well over 585 planes. Lockheed actually did manage to make about this number of planes. But it took them far too long; they never did succeed in getting the rate of production up from two to four planes a month at their Palmdale plant. Efforts to accelerate production ruined the learning curve—new 'hires' lacked the skill and knowledge of veterans, shifting the system back up the learning curve rather than continue to race down it. Learning curves not only have to be steep—organizations have to race down them headlong, as fast as they can, like champion downhill skiers. Lockheed did not succeed in this. (Prices too fall over time, often rapidly, and further force companies to contain their costs even more tightly.)

CASE STUDY 11.1

Resource Allocation between Two Technologies*

Case study discussion topics

1. How was Motorola's Application Specific Integrated Circuit (ASIC) division originally organized? What were the advantages and disadvantages of this organization?
2. Why did knowledge not migrate easily from technology A group to technology B group, and vice versa? What were the consequences of this?
3. How did the management team change the 'methods of running and organizing the ASIC business'? Specifically, what organizational changes did they make, to create a 'learning organization'?
4. How did this change affect the ASIC division's tradeoff curves?

Motorola's Application Specific Integrated Circuit (ASIC) division was confronted with the problem of allocating and fixing resources between

*This case study is a summary of the case authored by Kevin G. Christiensen.

Case study 11.1 continued

Case study 11.1 continued

two technology platforms. ASIC supplied semi-custom chips utilizing two different technology platforms (referred to as technology A and technology B for the purpose of this case). The semi-custom nature of the business made short life cycles a norm. A very high level of engineering resources had to be maintained to develop each technology, service the designs and to assure quick prototype and product deliveries. Motorola now faced the dilemma of balancing resources between maintaining its existing high-margin technology in declining markets, but where it was the dominant player—versus penetrating a much larger and growing competitive low-margin market with a technology where strong competitors already existed. This apart, new product families were being released on both technologies. Table 11.1.1 highlights the market situation surrounding the two products. In the short run, the ASIC division had to maintain technology A to remain profitable and continue to finance the expansion into technology B. In the long run, it would be required to channelize resources towards technology B, as it would become dominant. At the time of developing the case the ASIC division split its resources almost equally between the two technologies; adding more resources to either technology was not feasible.

Table 11.1.1
Market and technology comparisons of technology A and technology B

Market issues	*Technology A*	*Technology B*	*Relationship*
Market size (MS)	Small	Large	MS_a=(1/10) of MS_b
Future market	Shrinking	Growing	
Market position	1	4	
No. of competitors (NC)	Few	Many	NC_a=(1/12) of NC_b
Strategic customer Base (SCB)*	Small	Large	SCB_a=(1/5) of SCB_b
Financial status	Solid but deteriorating	Break even	
Product profit margins	High	Low	
Developmental cost (DC)	High-doubles with each new product family	High-doubles with each new product family	$DC_a = DC_b$
Product/Package variations	Low	High	

* Strategic customers that are, or, that could be significant contributors in A or B or in both A and B.

The ASIC division was horizontally organized along functional lines under the general manager, who had under him the departments of

Case study 11.1 continued

Case study 11.1 continued

manufacturing, test, quality assurance, production planning/product support, marketing, new product development, finance and administration; and two separate operations—one each to service technology A and B. Product operations organizations were responsible for the profit and loss of products stemming from their respective technologies. Each of the product operations had dedicated resources to address issues confronting their technology. These dedicated resources created economies-of-scale to meet demands of competitive markets. The arrangement was duplicated for both operations and many of the resources in the operations duplicated functions being performed by other departments within the division. This allowed the division to meet the market demand of each technology and assured quick design and prototype turnaround.

Each product operation was broken down vertically into four main areas of functional responsibility: sustaining products, pre-production products, future products and programme management. Each product area had a product manager who had a dedicated group of product test, option development and design engineers, and manufacturing specialists reporting to him. The existing organization structure made the transfer of resources from one group to another within an operation very slow. An impenetrable wall existed between the two groups, impeding resource movement from one operation to another. It created a dead-end career path for the personnel working on technology A, and a non-productive situation for personnel working on technology B who did not benefit from the expertise developed in producing technology A. The ASIC division had to find a way to service both technologies, respond to new market opportunities, while remaining profitable and providing a career path for all employees. Given that this was an organization designed for economies-of-scale, the management team faced the challenge of pushing out the trade-off curve of the two technologies, while holding the number of resources constant by improving the creation and transfer of knowledge between the two technology groups.

The tools of trade-off curves, scale versus scope and learning curves were used to describe the problem of resource allocation between the two technologies at the ASIC division.

Trade-off curves

A trade-off or production-possibilities frontier curve is a tool to describe the dilemma of trade-off between choosing to produce or utilize more of one product or resource against another. It defines the maximum

Case study 11.1 continued

Case study 11.1 continued

amount of goods or services that can be produced with a given set of resources (machines, manpower, technology and methods). In the case of the AISC division, it is an application of resources to service technology A versus turning them onto technology B, in which the X-axis relates to Technology B and the Y-axis relates to technology A. The first curve in Figure 11.1.1 shows the representative trade-off curve for technology A and B. To expand production as shown by the second curve in Figure 11.1.1 requires the expansion of machines, manpower, technology or methods.

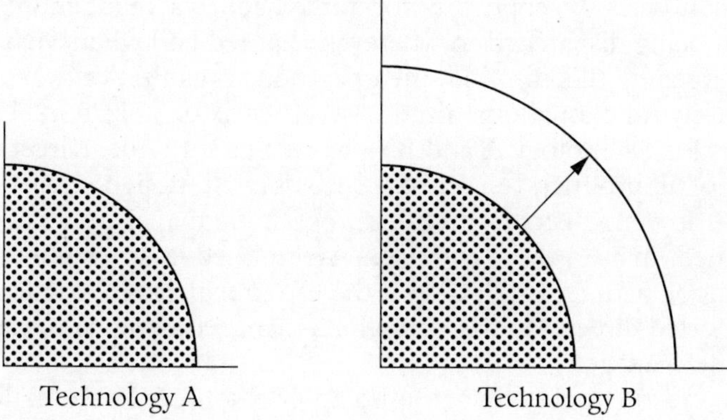

Figure 11.1.1
Trade-off curves for technologies A and B

Scale vs scope

The tool of scale versus scope is a productivity measure. It describes how resources can be mobilized to produce a wider variety of goods and services to meet the demands of the market. The challenge of scale versus scope is to try to maximize high-volume production (scale), while at the same time provide a product suited to the specific requirements of the customer (scope). The use of this tool allows a manager to determine if a particular scenario is achieving economies of scale, scope, or multi-product economies of scale. If economies of scale exist, it means a manager is getting more output at lower cost per unit or at lower marginal costs with higher-output volumes. If economies of scope exist, it means a manager is getting more output at lower cost per unit or at lower marginal costs from two or more products being produced or processed by sharing resources than he/she would get if they were produced separately. If multi-product economies-of-scale exist, it means

Case study 11.1 continued

Case study 11.1 continued

total costs will be less than double when production of both products is doubled. This is a result of combination of single-product economies of scale and economies of scope.

Application of the tools

Pushing out the trade-off curve and broadening the scope of the business required additional machines, manpower and improved technology, which was not possible given the financial constraints of the ASIC division. Therefore, the only way to achieve this was to change the division's ways of running business and its organization structure. To achieve economies of scope, the workforce had to be made more mobile, capable of being dispatched to wherever required and whenever required. Keeping this in mind, the operations organization was changed from a purely functional organization to a matrix organization. The two operations for technology A and B were merged into one. Direct reporting of all product, test, option development, design and manufacturing engineers to product/programme managers was discontinued. Instead these engineers were placed in an engineering resource pool, with a team leader at the top to manage it. The team leader reported directly to the operations manager along with the programme managers.

The engineering pool was set up to apply resources horizontally across the functional areas, which allowed resources to be applied on a need basis in real time. Under the new structure, each key customer and programme had a programme manager servicing it. The team leader controlled the assignment of resource to the various projects, decided where best to apply the resources and had the last say. Each engineer worked on cross-functional projects and was typically assigned to one or two key projects and some minor tasks. Engineers were allowed to work on projects they were excited about and on more than one technology or functional area. Senior engineers were given opportunities to be project leaders on significant projects. The new organization structure provided new opportunities for engineers, provided them a career path and created plenty of room for them to develop their desired skills. Through the new changes made, the trade-off curve for technology A and B were pushed out considerably. Figure 11.1.2 compares the trade-off curves for technology B before and after the organizational change.

Case study 11.1 continued

Case study 11.1 continued

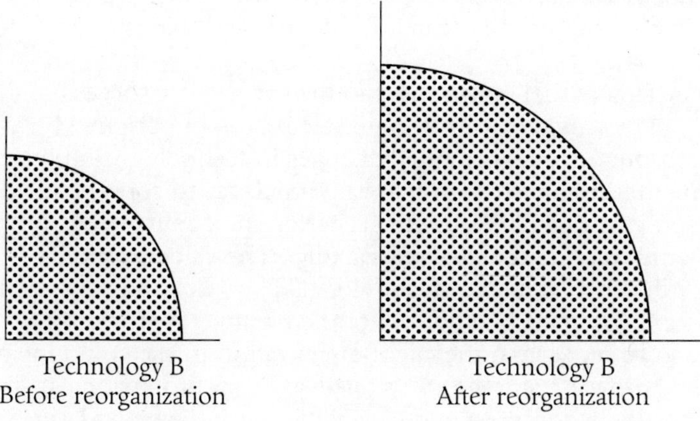

Figure 11.1.2
Trade-off curves for technology B before and after the organizational change

Results from the change
Duplication of activities between technologies were eliminated. Completion cycle-times on key projects was reduced by approximately 30 per cent. There was approximately a 20 per cent increase in the total number of projects started and completed and a 5–10 per cent rise in the average satisfaction level in customers as revealed by customer satisfaction surveys. In the past, the pre-production of new product families for both technologies A and B were understaffed and releases to production schedules were way behind schedule. Since the organization change, both schedules were brought back on track without lowering the service level on other projects. Two new efforts to develop previously untapped markets were started.

CASE STUDY 11.2

Infosys Technologies: Migrating up the Value Chain

Infosys Technologies Limited (Infosys), founded in 1983 and headquartered in Bangalore, is one of India's top IT service providers, providing software services to many leading global corporations. Recently, the company crossed an annual sales turnover of $2 billion.

Case study 11.2 continued

Case study 11.2 continued

The company constantly seeks to come up with strategies that will enable it to get out of the commoditization spiral that is a reality for any business today.

The key factors that contributed to the spectacular success of the company are its ability to attract and retain best and brightest employees, quickly adapt to rapid changes in technology and business paradigms, and establish high maturity processes to consistently deliver quality software in a high-growth scenario. The company has over 50,000 employees (and increasing rapidly). The value pyramid for a company in the information technology (IT) services business consists of at least three layers. At the bottom of the pyramid is providing infrastructure services to the client organization (these could include providing hardware, storage and skilled software professionals). Today, Infosys has limited interest and capabilities here. The next layer of the pyramid consists of offering application design, integration and maintenance services, which has been the traditional strength area of Infosys for the last several years. However, the competition for these types of services is intense as more companies in various countries, other than India (such as China, the Philippines, Russia, Ireland, etc.) are also vying for a share of this market. The top layer of the notional 'value pyramid' is to provide business applications and business consulting in the client's industry/domain. This requires the service provider such as Infosys to have considerable 'domain' and 'business' expertise. Infosys seeks to increase its presence here.

As may be anticipated, competition for these top-end services (which are more difficult to render, since they call for high-end expertise) is less and consequently profit margins are higher. The other significant reality of Infosys' business is that the knowledge in all the domains where it operates is changing at a rapid rate, making it essential for Infosys to track, capture and deploy this knowledge on an on-going basis. In order to provide these high-end services, Infosys created a business consulting group manned by several hundred professionals with strong consultancy background in industry verticals such as insurance, banking and manufacturing. Apart from its current strengths, Infosys seeks to continuously add new services, to 'stay ahead of competition'. In order to be able to offer high-end solutions, Infosys initiated several steps. These include: on-site investment in people, end-to-end solutions and offering full-line of solutions, brand building, education and training, on-site hiring and creating an organizational mindset for the consultancy business.

Case study 11.2 continued

Case study 11.2 continued

For offering these high-end services to its clients, Infosys has to reckon with competitors both from India (such as WIPRO and Tata Consulting Services) and the US (such as IBM Global, Accenture and EDS). The India-based IT service providers like Infosys have certain intrinsic strengths—strong talent management, high quality execution, perfected global delivery model, strong customer relationships, ethical and value-based approach to business and a lean organization. The global majors have readymade solution sets, deep high-level relationships with clients, the right mindset and a track record of offering end-to-end services for their clients. In order to be more cost-competitive, global majors have embarked on several measures such as investment in offshore facilities including in India, reducing layers of fat thereby shifting the centre of gravity lower down the organization, relocation of resources, investment in processes, addressing organizational issues and billing rate reduction.

Given that the company had traditionally been offering various IT services, particularly in the relatively lower end of application software development and maintenance, moving up the value chain raises many challenges. Infosys has to contend with a long history both within and outside the company, in terms of competencies of its employees and perceptions of its client base. Concerted and deliberate action on various fronts, both within the organization and with clients, needs to be taken to relocate the company higher up along the value-chain.

Finally, from a marketing perspective, Infosys has to redefine its value proposition. The company seems to want to move away from its current reputation as an 'offshore IT outsourcing firm' and towards one that is geared to improving and helping its customer firm to be successful in its line of business.

Will Infosys choose to span the entire spectrum of IT-services offering, right from low-end to high-end? It is clear that customers are increasingly looking at end-to-end solutions. Is it possible for Infosys to be equally good in providing all types of services (low-end to high-end) with equal finesse? Well, Infosys has succeeded in making this transition up the value chain, while being capable of providing its clients with 'end-to-end' solutions. It has done this through the creation of a very strong organization that values learning. It has, perhaps the largest training facilities for any corporation anywhere in the world at Mysore, about 130 km south of Bangalore.

Given the nature of its business, which changes rapidly, the management recognizes that creating an organization which is willing to learn is at the core of its business. In this sense, the ability of its

Case study 11.2 continued

Case study 11.2 continued

employees to learn both on the job and through formal learning programmes is central to its success. The software industry is characterized by a lot of 'churn' of its employees and creating, capturing and deploying knowledge is a vital skill Infosys has mastered. It has done this through elaborate and structured processes. Rapidly moving down learning curves and quickly changing 'horses' from existing learning curves to new learning curves that relate to technologies and services in the distant horizon, is a skill that is vital for the company's continued growth. The Infosys case study illustrates that indeed, *Learning Curves are Made, Not Born.*

Notes

1. Peter Drucker, cited on www.ngrain.com/solutions/articles
2. Bruce Henderson's report, *Strategy Alternatives for the British Motorcycle Industry*, was published by Boston Consulting Group: Boston in 1975. It is one of the first intensive uses of learning curves in analysing competitive strategy. The quoted passages are from the prolog to the report, p. xi.

   The text mentioned on conventional microeconomics is Robert S. Pindyck and Daniel L. Rubinfeld, *Microeconomics* (Fifth Edition) (Upper Saddle River, New Jersey: Prentice-Hall, 2001).
3. The quotes by Eric Turner and William Davidson are from Harvard Business School Case Study 9-384-049, 'Honda (A)', p. 3.
4. For the analysis of the Lockheed 1011 TriStar, see: Uwe Reinhardt, 'Breakeven analysis for Lockheed's TriStar: An application of financial theory', *Journal of Finance*, 1973.
5. A seminal article by Chris Argyris on truth-telling and learning is: 'Teaching Smart People How to Learn', *Harvard Business Review*, May–June 1991.
6. For double-loop learning, see Chris Argyris, 'Double loop learning in organizations', *Harvard Business Review*, September–October 1977.
7. See William Abernathy and Kenneth Wayne, 'Limits of the Learning Curve', *Harvard Business Review*, September–October 1974.
8. Richard Foster, *Innovation—The Attacker's Advantage* (New York: Summit Books, 1986).
9. See Alfred P. Sloan's brilliant biography, one of the best management books ever written, *My Years with General Motors*, for an account of his Ford-killing strategy.
10. Personal conversation with Professor Shlomo Maital.
11. Jeffrey Pfeiffer and Robert Sutton, *The Knowing Doing Gap: How Smart Companies Turn Knowledge into Action* (Boston, MA: Harvard Business School Press, 2000).
12. The Fluor case is based on a personal site visit by the first author.

Chapter 12

Where is the money? Markets, demand and customer intimacy

Good managers create winning products; Great managers create whole new industries.
—S. Maital, 1994[1]

The best way to predict the future is to create it.
—Peter Drucker[2]

LEARNING OBJECTIVES After you read this chapter, you should understand:

- **What price-sensitivity of demand and income-sensitivity of demand are**
- **What determines them, how they are measured and why they must constantly be tracked**
- **Why people are all the same at times and very different at others**
- **What 'bandwagon' and 'snob' effects are and how they are created by talented managers**
- **How to build product platforms, rather than individual products**
- **How to link value, demand, and profit, by using the 'profit pool' tool**
- **How to attribute industry profits to each part of the industry value chain and examine where those profits will migrate in 3–5 years**
- **What the logical connection is among markets, demand, value, profit and wealth creation**

TOOL #8

Price and income sensitivity: Profit pools

12.1 INTRODUCTION

Markets are driven by two forces: supply and demand. Market price is determined by demand and supply and the 'rules of the game' that underlie them. Managers must understand global markets in general, not only those in which they specifically operate and so must have a masterful grasp of the underlying drivers of both demand and supply.

The truth must be told: Economists do not understand well the underlying forces that drive customer demand. (The first author is an economist and we say this in sadness.) The reason is largely because at the individual and market level, demand is a highly psychological phenomenon, based on perception and social interactions. Understanding these key elements—how consumers perceive products and how they influence one another—requires behavioural tools of psychology, sociology and anthropology, tools economics does not in general employ though there are notable exceptions.

We evaded this awful truth for seven full chapters in Part-II of the book, which focused largely on costs and the supply side of markets. But the demand side can no longer be shoved aside. Thus, since this is a book about *economic* tools for innovation and growth, the authors find themselves in hot water. And not for the first time. When the first author wrote *Executive Economics* (1994), Chapter 7 was a list of 'ABC's of market demand': aptness, bubbles, bandwagons, cost or price, demographics, elasticity, fads, greed, habit, income, jazz, knowledge, loyalty, minds and money. It was the weakest chapter of all and a source of much embarrassment to him over the years. He vowed this would not occur again.

In the past decade, he has learned that there *are* those who understand consumers and demand. They are the scholars and practitioners of the business discipline known as marketing and the psychologists who support them. Their articles and books contain valuable tools for managers. Their work is in general studiously ignored by economics textbooks and economics scholars. The leading microeconomics textbook has in its index a third of a page of entries on markets and related topics but not a single entry titled 'marketing'.

We believe marketing is an 'enemy' that must be joined, not fought. Much of what follows in this chapter was gleaned from what we have learned over the years from marketing practitioners and educators. Their focus in understanding markets and demand is always on *people*—their desires, tastes, whims, habits, and values, how they choose products as individuals and in groups. Their goal is *customer intimacy*—knowing your customer perhaps better than the customers know themselves. 'Customer intimacy' tools are the focus of this chapter, and are a necessary condition for successful innovation.

The first chapter of Part-II of this book (Chapter 5) was about the Price-Cost-Value framework. In that trio, value is by far the most important. Ultimately demand is about creating value. And value, in turn, is highly psychological, subjective and often mysterious. Managers who are successful at innovation invariably create high differential value generating high and enduring profit margins. This chapter discusses how to do this.

12.2 PRICE–COST–VALUE REVISITED

To set the stage for our discussion of demand, let us pay a return visit to price-cost-value, and view it from a slightly different perspective than that of Chapter 5.

There are two polar-opposite ways to build a successful, profitable business. One is to be a cost leader. Producing a relatively low-value product, at low price and low cost, yields small profit margins but can generate large total profits if sales volume is large. (This is product 'a' in Figure 12.1.)

The second is to be a value leader. Producing a high-value product, sold at relatively high price and at higher cost than the cost leader (this is product 'b') can generate large, enduring profit margins if and only if the relative value of 'b', compared to 'a', is proportionately higher than the unit cost of 'b' compared to 'a'.

We recommend 'b'. Innovating is more fun than cost-cutting. And in the end, we believe more enduring. Cost cutting is often based on methods and technology that sooner or later find their way into the hands of your competitors.

Implementing 'b' requires a deep, abiding understanding of customers—what marketing experts call customer intimacy. It requires creation of a powerful *unique value proposition*.

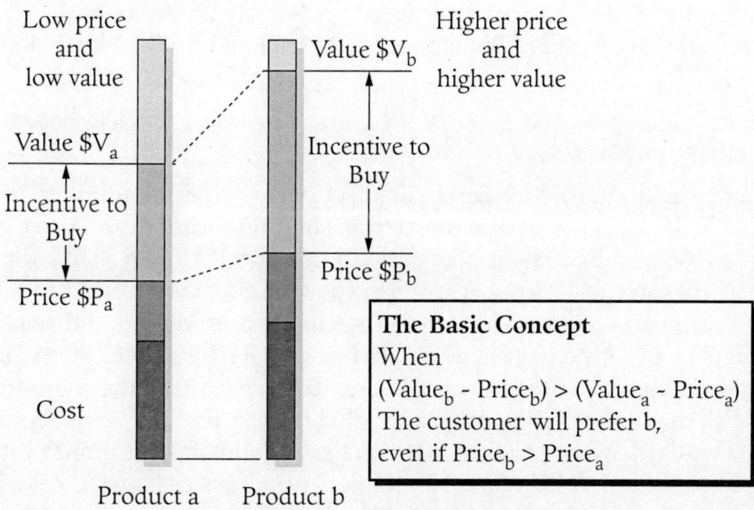

Figure 12.1
Price, value, cost, profit

The dark bar indicates *unit cost*. The medium bar is the *profit margin*, the difference between *unit price* and *unit cost*. The lightly shaded bar is

figure 12.1 continued

figure 12.1 continued

relative value: the difference between the maximum sum the customer *would* pay for the product and the actual price. This 'relative value' concept is highly subjective, differs from customer to customer and is not easy to measure.

Product 'a' has low price, low cost and relatively low value, compared to Product 'b'. Product 'b' is more expensive but because it creates relatively higher value, creates a higher incentive to buy and generates a larger profit margin.

DEFINITION

- **Unique value proposition (UVP): A short terse sentence stating how your product or service creates value for customers in ways that competitors do not.**

Powerful innovative UVPs can create entire new industries. Two examples are Walkman and iPod.

Case study: Sony Walkman

Like many great products, the Sony Walkman was born by accident. Sony's tape recorder division was pressed to 'market something soon' or face 'consolidation' (polite word for elimination). They took a monaural portable cassette recorder called a Pressman, slimmed it down by removing the recording apparatus, added a pair of earphones and—presto, stereo Walkman. The first Walkman was completed on 24 March 1979.

Its UVP?

We let you listen to your favourite stereo music anywhere, anytime without disturbing anyone else.

There was no market research. Said Akio Morita, Sony founder, to *Playboy* in 1982: 'The market research is all in my head! You see, we *create* markets!' Morita had taken his family to live in the United States for several years in the 1950s, because he knew that he would need to achieve *customer intimacy* with Americans, in order to design and sell Sony products to the American market. He knew Americans loved music and would love a product that let them listen to it without bothering others. The Walkman would probably have failed market research tests, because people would have rejected the strangeness of sticking earphones into their ears. In its first 20 years, 186 million Walkman units were sold. The only product to rival its global conquest was iPod.

Source: www.pocketcalculatorshow.com/walkman/history.html. Sales data are from www.tuaw.com (the unofficial Apple Weblog). See also 'The meaning of iPod', *The Economist*, 10 June 2004 (www.economist.com).

Case study: Apple iPod

In November 2001, Apple released a digital music player weighing just 6.5 ounces, containing 1,000 songs. It was not the first MP3 player. But it was smaller and held more songs. Its price was $400, prompting one sceptic to say, iPod stands for 'idiots price our devices'. He was wrong. It was a smash hit. In late 2004 it was selling 4 million units every quarter and after three years on the market was 1 million units ahead of Walkman at a similar stage. Its UVP?

> *Cool-looking device, ultra-simple—spin one wheel to scroll your songs, select the one you want, use the wheel to set volume—and presto.*

After being booted out of Apple, the company he founded, Steve Jobs returned to rescue it, pioneering iPod. He says: 'People think it's this veneer—designers are told, "make it look good". That is not what we think design is. *Design is how it works.*' And iPod works by creating value, in turn created through Jobs' deep customer intimacy. Jobs knew what people wanted when he led the design of the Macintosh. And he did it again, with iPod.

Source: Rob Walker, 'The guts of a new machine', *New York Times*, 30 November 2003 (www.nyt.com) and 'The meaning of iPod', *The Economist*, 10 June 2004 (www.economist.com).

Action learning

UVP: Unique Value Proposition

What is the UVP for your company or organization? Does everyone, including the receptionist and cleaning staff, know that UVP? When asked for the UVP, does everyone come up with the same answer? Do your customers all know your UVP? How can it be strengthened? How should it be changed, to meet imitators and challengers?

Creating differential value is the objective of innovation.

What tools exist in the economic armoury that can help managers attain customer intimacy and build winning UVPs to create new industries like Walkman and iPod?

What follows is an attempt to describe several such tools and show how they can best be used to attain enduring competitive advantage and sustained profitability.

12.3 PRICE SENSITIVITY: PEOPLE ARE ALIKE

In some ways, in analysing demand people are much alike. In other ways, people are exceedingly different. Here are two brief cases to illustrate.

Case study: People are the same

Famous Players is a Canadian movie chain, wholly owned by Viacom, with 84 locations and 794 screens across Canada. It is 85 years old. Like movie houses everywhere, *Famous Players* struggles to compete with TV and DVD rentals.

In early 2005, an experiment was attempted at movie houses in Winnipeg and Edmonton. Previously, the price of a movie ticket was C$ 13.99. The price was slashed to C$9.99 (C$8.50 for students and senior citizens). This is a steep 28.6 per cent price cut. The hypothesis underlying the experiment was this: The price cut will increase the sales of movie tickets by 30 per cent or more. Otherwise, sales revenue (price times quantity) will decline. In these two cities, revenue increased significantly. The hypothesis was confirmed. As a result the experiment was replicated in other cities, including the main market, Toronto. The results were similar. Sales revenue rose.

Source: *The Toronto Star*, 25–26 January 2005.

What *Famous Players* managers learned was that all over Canada, there is a significant market segment of movie-going people, who are the same—they are price-sensitive to movie tickets. Demand for movie-going rises more than the decline in price.

DEFINITION

- **Price sensitivity of demand, or as economists misleadingly call it, price-*elasticity* of demand, (though it has nothing whatsoever to do with the physical notion of *elasticity*) is the ratio of: (*i*) the percentage change in the quantity demanded of a product or service, and (*ii*) the percentage change in the price of that product or service, other things held constant (such as the quality of the product, etc.).**

A ratio exceeding one (ignoring the sign, always negative, since demand and price move in opposite directions) indicates price sensitivity; a ratio less than one indicates lack of price sensitivity. Revenue is demand (quantity) times price. If demand rises by more than price falls, revenue grows. If demand rises by less than price falls, revenue falls.

Example

Suppose demand for movie tickets rises by 50 per cent in the wake of a 28.6 per cent price cut. Then the price-sensitivity of demand for *Famous Players* movie tickets is:

50% / 28.6% = 1.75

Sales revenue will rise as a result of the price cut by some 7 per cent:

$(1 + 0.50) \times (1 - 0.286) = (1.5) \times (0.714) = 1.074.$

Generally, price sensitivity is *greatest* when there are substitutes. And there are many good substitutes for movie-going. Price-sensitivity is *lowest* when there are few or no substitutes. That is why innovative managers strive to develop new product offerings that are so different and superior to existing offerings, that people feel *they must have them.* This perception of value permits high prices and high profit margins.

It is absolutely vital that managers and entrepreneurs know and constantly track the price sensitivity of demand for each and every product they make and sell. Price sensitivity is subject to rapid change like the weather. Products that are price-insensitive suddenly become price-sensitive when recession, for instance, makes people more price- and value-conscious in the face of falling disposable income, or when new products appear that are potential substitutes. Note that if demand for your product is price-insensitive, you can raise prices and by doing so increase sales revenue. This does not mean that in all cases it is desirable to do so.

Action learning

Estimate Your Product's Price Sensitivity

If you work for an organization that sells a product or service, ask yourself: What is the price-sensitivity of this product? High or low or medium? Write down the answer.

Then ask: what would happen to the number of units sold if I lowered the price by 10 per cent. Try this question on a few customers. Calculate the price-sensitivity coefficient. Did your initial hypothesis check out? Are the answers

similar? Or do you have highly price-sensitive market segments and price-insensitive segments?
Ask: how can I make my product less price-sensitive? Nearly always, the answer is: finding ways to create value for my customers that competitors or substitutes cannot match.

Case study: Rate reduction? Or investing in a future network? The issue facing Japan's NTT (Nippon Telegraph and Telephone)

Like many countries, Japan deregulated its long-distance call industry. The dominant company Nippon Telegraph and Telephone (NTT) faced new entrants. To cope with the fierce 'rate reduction war' that developed between NTT and the New Common Carriers, NTT had to aggressively slash its long-distance call rates, reducing its revenues by over $10 billion. Initially, the price sensitivity of demand was greater than unity. Hence NTT could cut rates and see its revenues rise. But later, with more entrants, NTT had had to continue to cut rates, with a big loss in net income. Long-distance rates have dropped dramatically, from 720 ¥ for a three-minute call to only 180 ¥! Demand became price-insensitive.

How should NTT respond?

(See Case Study 12.1, at the end of this chapter.)

DEFINITION

- **Income sensitivity of demand or income-*elasticity* of demand, is the ratio of: (*i*) the percentage change in the quantity demanded of a product or service, and (*ii*) the percentage change in the per capita income of buyers, those in the product's market segment. It is also the ratio of (*i*) the fraction of each *additional income dollar* spent on the product, and (*ii*) the part of *total income dollars* spent on the product, i.e., the ratio of marginal to average spending on the product.**

It is as vital to know income sensitivity of demand for your product, as it is to know price sensitivity. If your market segment is growing wealthier, and your product is income sensitive—for example, health club membership, which is regarded as a luxury good, one we spend on proportionately more as income rises then your sales will rise. If your product is income-sensitive and there is an economic downturn, so that people's per capita incomes stagnate or fall your product will do poorly.

12.4 MARKET SEGMENTATION: PEOPLE ARE SIMILAR

DEFINITION

- **A market segment is a group of customers who are similar in important ways, e.g., sex, age, income, tastes.**

Each market segment may require a different product offering. Be sure you know clearly the key parameters that define your market segment and how your product creates appropriate benefits for that segment. This is an essential condition for maintaining customer intimacy. Be aware continually of how your market segment is changing. Honda once sold more Accord vehicles than any other car in America. It woke up one day and found it had lost its #1 position, because the age of Accord buyers had risen sharply and Honda had lost the lucrative youth market. It had failed to 'youthen' its designs to appeal to a key market segment. It took a major effort at redesign and remarketing to repair the damage.

12.5 ... BUT ... PEOPLE ARE *DIFFERENT*: CREATE 'PLATFORMS'

Suppose your goal is to capture several market segments that *differ* from each another. After all, people are different. How does one achieve the goal of reaching customers with very different tastes and needs?

Case study: People are very different

In the 1970s, a food engineer named Howard Moskowitz was given an assignment by his employer, Pepsi-Cola[3]. Find the right degree of sweetness, one that optimally hits the target for our customers—doubtless influenced by the Three Bears and their hot, cold and medium porridge.

Howard rounded up some Pepsi-drinkers and ran experiments, trying different versions of Pepsi with varying sweetness on them. What he found was quite obvious. Some people liked very sweet Pepsi. Some liked it medium-sweet. Some liked it barely sweet at all. There were very large differences, distributed around a normal curve with fairly wide dispersion. Howard's proposal—that Pepsi offer a variety of degrees of

Case study continued

Case study continued

sweetness—was rejected. But later, he applied his 'people are different' principle for Prego spaghetti sauce. He proposed four different types, including mushroom, meatless, chunky, etc. Prego became a dominant spaghetti-sauce brand. Howard's mass-customized four varieties gave Prego more supermarket shelf space, met customers' varying needs and became a model for other products. *Segment your market, differentiate and tailor your offering and capture a wider variety of customers.* This is sometimes known as a platform strategy. Prego became a platform for a variety of spaghetti-sauce products rather than a single product.

DEFINITION

- **'A high-tech "platform" [is an] evolving system made of interdependent pieces that can each be innovated upon.' Some companies *own* the whole platform. Other companies supply parts of it.**

Example

The PC consists of a microprocessor, operating system, application software and hardware (keyboard, monitor, motherboard). If Microsoft and software companies failed to supply ever-more powerful, value-creating software, Intel's increasingly more powerful and expensive microprocessors would not find a market. The model of tacit cooperation between Microsoft (Windows) and Intel is sometimes known as Wintel. The PC is a platform, whose interdependent pieces are closely linked. Intel's Architecture Lab strives to encourage innovations that build and support demand for its Pentium microprocessors.[4]

Action learning

Platform Your Product

What changes could you make in your product or service to make it into a *platform* and thus reach a wider market. Can this be done in a cost-effective manner? What market research information would you need?

12.6 BANDWAGONS AND SNOBS

Case study: People buy what they see others buy–or see that others *don't* buy

More than 50 years ago, the late Harvard University economist Harvey Leibenstein (a maverick, and a powerful, almost unique exception to our claim that economists do not understand consumers or demand) wrote a classic article, with two powerful insights: the *bandwagon effect* and the *snob effect*.[5]

DEFINITIONS

- **Bandwagon effect: People buy what is widely being bought.**
- **Snob effect: People buy what is not being widely bought; it becomes more desirable because fewer people can afford it or can find one.**

The term 'bandwagon' comes from a circus wagon with a band on it; when it arrived in town, all the townspeople turned out and followed the bandwagon in droves.

Managers can build powerful businesses on the foundations of either of these social psychological traits. Here is how the bandwagon effect makes the owner of a meat dumpling food stall in Shanghai's marketplace wealthy.

Case study: Shanghai meat dumplings

The following is a narration by the first author to illustrate the bandwagon effect.

On a trip to Shanghai in November 2004, I visited the Shanghai marketplace where food stalls offered visitors various kinds of food. One group of stalls sold meat dumplings, a favourite food in Shanghai, prepared in advance and then cooked when ordered. One stall had a very long queue. Other stalls sold what looked like identical dumplings, and identical prices but had almost no customers.

My host, a local, explained that it was known that this particular stall made the very best dumplings and that people were willing to wait for them. But, I wondered, what about out-of-town strangers like me? Why don't they go to one of the other stalls? Would I?

Case study continued

Case study continued

No, I thought. I would not, for the same reason that I gravitate to restaurants with long queues outside. A queue indicates there is excess demand. That is important information. It shows new buyers that other people who have presumably consumed it in the past want the product enough to wait for it and to invest substantial opportunity cost in lost time.

New dumpling customers join the long queue, or bandwagon, for that reason. They are not familiar with the dumplings made by each stall. Nor, perhaps, do they have the time, leisure and money to try each. They need reliable information. What information is more reliable than a long queue? The length of the queue sends a message, saying: *We are busy and impatient and hungry nonetheless, we are willing to wait for this stall's dumplings.* So they must be really good, worth the wait. Why not join us?

If you can *create* a bandwagon effect, you have a powerful marketing tool. The queue, or its equivalent, is a powerful advertisement that costs nothing. That may be why some businesses *like* to have excess demand for their product, and choose not to follow conventional economic wisdom by raising prices to reduce that excess demand. Excess demand creates *more* demand. Some brilliant marketers actively try to engineer a scarcity effect. Some restaurants *like* to have long lines outside their doors, though they could eliminate them by raising prices or adding tables.

What puzzled me about the dumplings was why the owners of the noncompetitive stalls did not benchmark their product and figure out what was their dominant competitors' special appeal?

The answer was clear. The people working for them in their stalls did not seem to care. Fewer customers simply meant less work for them. And the *owners* of the idle stalls were nowhere to be seen. Had they been there, they would surely have been troubled and humiliated by the human histogram for their competitor's product. This is a classic example of the importance of managing by 'being there'.

Harry Potter books, marketed skillfully, are an exceptionally strong example of the bandwagon effect.

Case study: Harry Potter

Few examples of customer intimacy are more powerful than the Harry Potter books written by author Joanne K. Rowling. The first book,

Case study continued

Case study continued

Harry Potter and the Sorcerer's Stone, was published in Britain in June 1997 as a juvenile-fiction title. It quickly hit the top of Britain's adult best-seller list—and did the same in the US. There were ultimately to be seven such books. Rowling, now one of England's wealthiest individuals, says she was writing an adult novel during a 1990 train ride when 'Harry Potter strolled into my head fully formed'. Working on Harry Potter taught her how easily she could tap into her childhood memories. I really can think myself back to 11 years old (Harry's age when the series opens). You're very powerful and kids have this whole underworld that to adults is always going to be impenetrable.' Empathy can be one of the most powerful tools for innovation and customer intimacy. For we ourselves are customers, and understand ourselves, hence we can understand our customers through our own selves.

Source: 'Wild About Harry', *Time* magazine, 20 September 1999.

Once in a rare while, an especially brilliant manager and innovator uses both snob and bandwagon effects. Here is an example.

Swiss watches

Some products are profitable because they are exclusive. Snob appeal is created. Watch brands (year of birth in brackets) such as Longines (1832), Omega (1848), Piaget (1874), Movado (1881) and Rolex (1908) have snob appeal, built by history, craft and legend and very high prices.

Talented managers can find ways to make opposites, like lions and lambs, lie down together such as Nicholas Hayek, pioneer of the Swatch, whose product innovation almost achieved the impossible, generating both bandwagon and snob effects at one and the same time.

Case study: Swatch: Bandwagon + Snob = Profit

'Swiss' and 'watch' were once synonymous. In 1946 Swiss watchmakers had 80 per cent of the world market. But with the advent of electronic quartz technology that enabled cheap accurate timepieces, companies like Timex (US), Seiko and Citizen (both Japan) used it to grab half of Switzerland's watch market share. Swiss companies, who ironically had pioneered quartz technology, rejected it as a 'passing fad'—not the first time that the inventor of a winning technology failed to understand its business implications.

Case study continued

Case study continued

In 1983, Swiss banks forced a merger of two nearly-insolvent watch companies, SSIH and ASUAG and put the banks' watch-industry consultant Nicholas Hayek in charge as CEO. Hayek's initiative was Swatch ('Swiss' and 'watch'). It was quartz, made in highly-automated Swiss factories (because Swiss labour was very costly) and encased in plastic. It had only half the parts of normal watches and could be made at a staggeringly low cost of under 10 Swiss francs per unit, hence could be sold at a price low enough to attract buyers yet high enough to leave substantial profit margins.[6]

'You can build mass market products ... only if you embrace the fantasy and imagination of your youth,' Hayek said, a very un-Swiss opinion. Swatch watches featured outlandish designs with brash, intense colours. There were dozens of models to choose from; each 'collection' featured 70 Swatch designs, and each design was produced in limited numbers (note: snob effect). Even smash hit designs were not produced beyond the initial production run. Swatch Collectors' Clubs sprang up. New models hit the market often; consumers sometimes bought dozens of different Swatch watches. The market exploded; everyone had to have one (bandwagon effect). Hayek reinforced the bandwagon by spending 30 per cent of the retail price of Swatch on advertising—double the industry standard. The $40 price tag was low enough to encourage impulse buying, yet high enough to be profitable and Hayek kept that price constant for an entire decade. Swatch buyers were intensely loyal, perhaps because there was no real substitute, the acid test of innovation.

'Everything you do, and the way you do it, sends a message', said Hayek. His message to Swatch shareholders: Swatch sold 26 million watches in 1992!

Note how Hayek orchestrated a perfect combination of cost, price and value, found a unique new market space and created a new industry.[7]

12.7 WHERE IS THE MONEY? WHERE WILL IT BE IN 3–5 YEARS?

The goal of a business is to make a profit for its shareholders. Customer intimacy and value creation stemming from it are a means to that end. But creating unique value for customers is not synonymous with making a profit. Often, profit is captured by those who play a seemingly minor role in the value-creation process.

For example, in 2003 General Motors had sales of nearly $200 billion, placing it 3rd among American companies. Its after-tax profits totalled $3.8 billion. Hundreds of thousands of GM workers produced millions of cars and sold them all over the world. But it is estimated that two-thirds of GM's profits came from GMAC, General Motors Acceptance Corp., the GM company that lends people money to buy GM cars. General Motors, it turns out, is really a bank. Its profit margins come from lending money, not from making cars. In fact, GM's car-making troubles are hurting GMAC's credit rating and thus impairing its ability to borrow and lend.

DEFINITIONS

- **Value Chain: The series of actions, processes and steps required to bring the finished product to the ultimate consumer; for instance, for the PC industry: components, microprocessors, assembly, shipping, software and operating systems, maintenance.**
- **Gross profit margin: Gross profit (sales revenue minus cost of goods sold) as a per cent of sales revenue.**
- **Operating profit margin: Operating profit (sales revenue minus cost of goods sold; sales, general and administrative costs but not including finance charges) as a per cent of sales revenue.**
- **Net margin: Net profit after tax as a per cent of sales revenue.**

Leading Bain & Co. consultant Orit Gadiesh, along with James L. Gilbert,[8] have developed a tool to help managers analyse precisely where profit margins are highest to enable them to better strategize their products and migrate their companies' resources, products and competencies toward those high margins. Revenues are not synonymous with profit, the authors note. Mapping profit margins for each link in the value chain is a valuable exercise. The result is a powerful visual presentation, often surprising, showing where the money is and who is making it. Here is how to do it:

1. Define the value chain for your industry (of which your company is a part): list the value chain components and all the activities necessary to bring the end product to the customer.
2. Estimate revenues and profits for each link
3. Calculate profit margins (y-axis) and revenue share (x-axis) (per cent of total industry revenue) (use whichever of the three profit-margin concepts you think is most appropriate).
4. Graph the profit pool diagram, plotting 'profit margin' (y-axis) against 'revenue share' (x-axis).
5. Do this profit pool diagram, at least roughly, as you think it will be 3 to 5 years from now. What strategic conclusions can be drawn from it?

Case study: Profits in air conditioning

Revenue and profit in the part of the air-conditioning industry that uses 'absorption chiller-heater' technology arises from three sectors: Parts, Manufacturing, Maintenance.

The profit pool diagram showing profit margins charted against total revenues as they exist at present is shown in Figure 12.2.

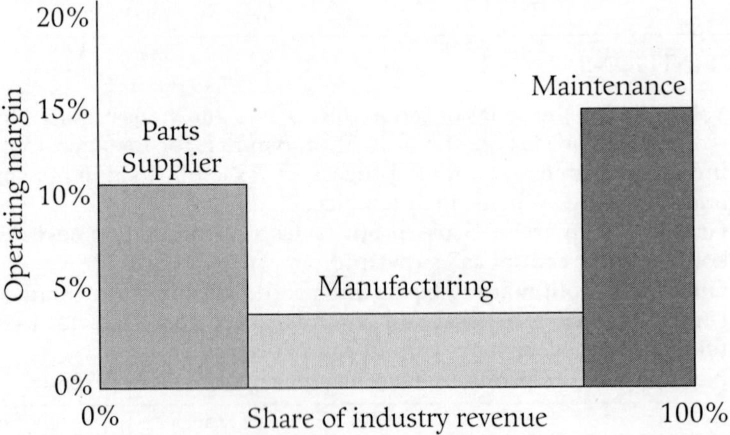

Figure 12.2
Profit pool: Air-conditioning (absorption chiller-heater) industry

It is clear that higher profit margins accrue to parts and maintenance than to manufacturing. Parts suppliers, for instance, make equal total profits on less than half the revenue than manufacturers. This is often the case, when certain parts become 'choke points', in the sense that manufacturers absolutely need them—especially parts that embody proprietary technology. This suggests that manufacturers should include both ends of the 'value chain', parts and maintenance, in their business design or forego significant profits and be doomed to continuing low profit margins. Software companies often find, to their surprise, that their customer-service centre—initially treated as a costly albatross around their neck—becomes a major profit centre, when warranties expire and customers begin to buy service contracts. They may make more profit from such services than from the actual software sale itself. *Knowing this is vital to constructing a winning, profitable business strategy.*

Action learning

Build Your Industry's Profit Pool

1. Choose one of *your* organization's most profitable products or services, or, choose a product you like to buy.
2. List the series of value chain steps, beginning with raw materials, that get the finished product into the hands of the customer. (Use the template shown below.)
3. Build the profit-pool diagram, by using the template given below: (a) how is the total revenue generated by this product divided among each value-chain step? (b) what is the profit margin for each value-chain step, and where is the money? (i.e., who is making the money?).
4. How do you think this profit pool will change in the near future, say, 3 to 5 years hence? What must your organization do to capture profit as value and profit migrate owing to market changes and technological advances?

Profit pool exercise

Product or Service:
Value Chain Components:

	Sales	% of Total Industry Sales	Profit Margin
1.__________			
2.__________			
3.__________			
4.__________			
5.__________			
6.__________			
7.__________			
Total: ________			

Graph:

profit margin

% of industry sales

12.8 THE UPSIDE-DOWN PROFIT POOL: FROM FROWN TO SMILE

Many companies have noticed a major long-term shift in 'where the money is' in their industry. High profit margins once accrued to manufacturers—those who actually made and assembled products. The profit-pool diagram was shaped like a frown—those in the centre (manufacturers and assemblers) had high profit margins, while those who supplied components and peripheral products, at the beginning and end of the value chain, had low profit margins.

Then came Asia. The newly-industrialized Asian nations invested enormously in manufacturing plants for TVs, cars, PCs and consumer electronic products. Excess capacity emerged, profit margins fell. Today, in most industries, the profit-pool curve has become inverted, with the frown shifting to a smile. High profit margins now accrue, in PCs, to companies that make microprocessors (Intel), at the start of the value chain and to companies that make software operating systems and applications (Microsoft), at the end of the value chain. In the middle, profit margins are razor thin. This is characteristic of many industries. It is one reason why companies like Nike, for instance, build business strategies that focus resources heavily on design and R&D, at the start of the chain, and on marketing, at the end—and outsource manufacturing, in the middle.

Case study: Microsoft, IBM

In 1980, IBM commissioned Microsoft to make DOS (disk operating system, software that ran the PC). On 12 August 1981, IBM introduced its Personal Computer which used Microsoft's 16-bit operating system, MS-DOS 1.0, plus Microsoft BASIC, COBOL, PASCAL, and other products made by Microsoft. IBM perceived that its value creation for customers was in the computer hardware. They willingly gave up the part of the value chain that was 'peripheral', the software and operating system. Result: Microsoft's market value (of its shares held by the public) as of 17 March 2005 was $267 billion on revenues of $36.8 billion, while IBM's market value was just over half that of Microsoft, at $147 billion, on revenues almost three times those of Microsoft, $96 billion.

Some experts prefer the term 'value network' to value chain, because a value chain has links that are joined linearly, while a value network is

Case study continued

Case study continued

often highly non-linear and involves complex systemic collaboration and cooperation among many different companies. For instance, Dell Computer Co. is the world's #1 PC producer, selling directly to customers and achieving operational excellence by building a smooth, highly integrated value network that includes its just-in-time suppliers.

Part of Dell's value chain is DHL, UPS and FedEx, overnight parcel shippers, who see to it that Dell's customers get their computers very soon after they are ordered. A significant part of the industry's profits accrues to those shippers. Federal Express sales revenue, for example, in 2004 was $24.7 billion, with profits of $838 million.

12.9 CONCLUSION

There is a simple, straightforward logical link between markets, demand, value, profit and wealth creation.

Products and services are bought and sold in markets. In free, open and competitive markets, customers signal their demand by 'voting' with their dollars, pesos, euros, rupees or other currency. Those dollars generate sales revenue, which is based on the differential value created by the products consumers buy, *as perceived by those customers.* It is very important to understand that value is *always* perceived value, as seen by the customer or buyer. If it is not perceived, it does not exist. Profits result from unique value propositions embodied in products whose value and price exceed by a wide margin the overall cost of producing them. High profit margins, in turn, build wealth for shareholders because stock prices are driven in large part by those profit margins.

The fundamental logic of capitalism: it is a remarkably powerful system for translating the wants and needs of consumers into signals that create the very products and services to satisfy those needs.

Large rewards accrue to managers and entrepreneurs, like those mentioned in this chapter, who are skilled at understanding customer needs, wants and preferences and in meeting them even when market research and the customers themselves initially react negatively to their innovations.

Action learning

Analyse a Product You Had to Have or Buy

Identify one product that you bought, because you felt you *simply had to have it*. Analyse *why* you HAD to have that product. Use what you have learned on your own organization's products. How can they be changed, improved or adapted to become 'have to have' products or services?

Readers are invited to view 'Pillars of Profit: Segment #8, Where is the Money? Markets, demand and customer intimacy', in the accompanying CD.

CASE STUDY 12.1

Rate Reduction or Investing in a Future Network at Nippon Telegraph and Telephone Corporation (NTT)?*

Case study discussion topics

1. How did NTT react to cost reduction with respect to deregulation in the telecom industry?
2. What was the magnitude of the price cuts in long-distance rates following increased competition?
3. Why cannot NTT expand its investment by incurring additional debt?
4. Where is NTT now in terms of its trade-off frontier?
5. Why is it necessary for NTT to match its competitors' rate reductions?
6. Why does the author believe that some investment funds should go towards network construction, rather than solely for funding rate reductions?

Nine years had passed since the deregulation of the telecommunications market and the privatization of NTT. More than 50 competitors had entered the market, with the emergence of three major players (DDI, TWJ and JT) in addition to NTT. Initially, when competition heated up, NTT had strong financial resources that allowed both a rate reduction

*This case study is a summary of the case authored by Norio Sakai.

Case study 12.1 continued

Case study 12.1 continued

(averaging $1 billion in lost revenues a year) and an investment in the network (averaging about $17 billion a year). The savings NTT reaped from improved efficiency and elimination of waste after being privatized had enabled it to reduce rates without reducing its investments. But continued fierce competition forced NTT to make further efforts to cut its prices and costs, posing a real trade-off dilemma.

In 1988, the big three New Common Carriers (NCC) entered the telecom market and within a span of 4 years their revenues soared to $4 billion. They enjoyed a share of little over 50 per cent in the main long-distance call market. To cope with the fierce 'rate reduction war' that developed between NTT and NCC, the former slashed its long-distance call rates, resulting in revenue losses of over $10 billion. Initially, when the industry was deregulated, the price elasticity of demand was greater than unity, which enabled NTT to cut its prices without losing revenues: price-sensitive demand caused consumers to make more long-distance calls and higher volume of calls more than offset the lower price per call. But subsequently stiff competition forced NTT to cut rates and suffer a big loss in net income. Long-distance rates had dropped dramatically, from 720 ¥ for a 3 minute call to only 180 ¥!

In an effort to cut costs, NTT had eliminated about 100,000 jobs since its privatization and reduced total count of its branches from 2,000 to 200. The downsizing finally reached the lower limit needed to sustain NTT's present scale of business and its net income started to decline beginning 1991. In 1995, it was close to recording a loss. Nevertheless, NTT continued to invest enormous amounts (over $17 billion a year) in its network, mainly by incurring huge debts ($30 billion).

NTT recognized that an investment of $6 billion in digital exchanges and optical fibre, and $10 billion in maintaining the existing network, would become the infrastructure of a multimedia network that would yield large profits for it in the future. But in its present position, NTT could neither expect an increase in revenues nor could it significantly reduce costs further. To survive fierce competition rate reduction was essential and if NTT could not survive the present competition investing in another network meant for the future seemed meaningless. This was NTT's trade-off dilemma. NTT was situated close to its full-efficiency trade-off frontier. Majority of NTT's board of directors favoured spending all possible funds on rate reduction in order to survive the present. But was this the best decision?

Trade-off analysis

In 1995, NCC announced a possible reduction in its long-distance call rate to 100 ¥ for a 3 minute call. Assuming this would be enforced, NTT

Case study 12.1 continued

Case study 12.1 continued

figured that they would lose $0.9 billion for each 10 ¥ rate reduction. Thus, NTT would need $9 billion for a 100 ¥ discount to compete with NCC. Simulating 15 years of rate reductions (1995 to 2010), with an average annual reduction rate of 4.6 per cent, the change in revenue for a 1 per cent drop in rates would be 0.75 per cent. NTT analysed that if it did not cut rates, NCC would not immediately slash its price to 100 ¥, but would instead maintain a 10 per cent differential between its prices and that of NTT. The total gain in net income to NTT was estimated at $35.32 billion for 15 years measured by discounted present value. The contribution of $35.32 billion to net income was calculated as [$35.32 billion × 2.47% = $869 million] where 2.47 per cent was the existing operating margin of NTT (net income as a percentage of sales revenues). The return on investment (ROI) for NTT if the rate reduction is enforced would be 9.6 per cent ($869 million divided by $9 billion).

A report released by the National Telecommunication Committee in 1994 forecast that digital multimedia would grow to be a $1,230 billion market by 2010, equal to 5.7 per cent of Japan's GDP. Building this market would require an investment of around $330 billion on infrastructure alone. Accordingly, NTT estimated that it would require investments of $60 billion a year to build the new network infrastructure. The last seven year financial statistics of NTT revealed that the company achieved a 7.2 per cent annual expansion in the market by investing $145 billion on its network, a contribution of 91 per cent of the industry's total investment. In order to continue this relationship and with an ongoing expenditure of around $6 billion a year on multimedia networks, NTT figured that it would gain $140 billion (present value) in net income over the years 1995 to 2010 and reap a ROI of 20.5 per cent.

The 9.6 per cent ROI and 20.5 per cent ROI represented the respective values of spending a dollar on cutting rates and building networks, respectively. As NTT lacked resources to do both, the ROIs represented the marginal opportunity cost of investing a dollar in an alternate employment. It was evident from these ROIs that a dollar invested in the network would bring over twice the return (20.5 / 9.6 = 2.15) earned by a dollar invested in rate reduction. The trade-off tool made it clear that the opinion voiced by NTT's board of directors, to spend all possible resources on rate reduction, was indeed not the optimal solution. The optimal point on the trade-off curve between rate reduction and network building involved allocating part of NTT's resources to rate reduction and a significant part to the network.

CASE STUDY 12.2

HDFC Bank—Creating Customer Intimacy

Established in 1994, HDFC Bank Limited today is one of India's leading private banks with total net revenues of Rs 24,293 million, i.e., about US $5.5 billion (financial year 2004–2005), a wide network of over 531 branches across 228 cities in the country and over a thousand networked ATMs.

The retail business of HDFC bank has been creating customer intimacy through its judicious choice of information technology. In order to deliver superior services and turnaround times to its customers, HDFC Bank has a system of centralized operations, which includes data processing. Centralized operations are fairly common in the banking industry and have been adopted by most Indian and foreign banks. However, centralized data processing has been the key differentiator for HDFC Bank vis-à-vis what other banks were doing. Most Indian banks including public sector banks have chosen branch-based automation by installing software in their individual branches.

While adopting new technology in the bank, the top management meticulously evaluates the business benefits that it would reap from such a move. The technology must help in one or more of the following: enable serving the customer better, reduce the bank's expenses or help perform straight-through processing and consequently cut down costs.

HDFC Bank outsources the management of its IT facilities, infrastructure, networks, etc. No bank staff is involved in managing its telecommunications infrastructure, IT hardware, etc., unlike in many other banks. Outsourcing these activities helps it to contain costs. Besides, specialist companies taking over such work are better equipped to handle the work on a nation-wide scale than HDFC Bank. Similarly, all software development at the bank is done through vendors, again for reasons of cost efficiency. If HDFC Bank were to do its software development in-house, it would have to hire people trained to do such work, and would have to continuously invest in educating them and updating their skills. In addition, it would have to work on finding ways of retaining them, which is a challenge, given the very bullish Indian IT industry. Through its policy of outsourcing its IT facilities and software development, HDFC Bank has been able to bring down its costs related to these activities significantly.

Case study 12.2 continued

Case study 12.2 continued

One of the tenets of HDFC Bank is to deliver superior customer experience. The organization aggressively addresses issues relating to customer service, service errors, turnaround time, etc. For instance, it started using imaging technologies over the last two years to speed up its customer-related processes. Since it has been growing at an annual compounded growth rate of 15 per cent, a phenomenal rate for a bank, it needs to keep pace with its growing customer base, offering new services and meeting new customer demands. It needs to ensure efficient processes and effective mechanisms to track problems. To fulfil this need, the bank has undertaken a lot of automation in many areas. Today, customers who fill up an account opening form want to know the exact status of their form, where exactly it is in the process and when exactly would they receive their welcome kit.

Apart from such 'point solutions', meaning solutions to particular problems, the bank has put in place processes for end-to-end solutions by adopting the Six Sigma methodology in all its processes that have customer linkage. For example, delivery of a welcome kit, delivering an e-mail to a customer, delivering the monthly account balance statement, delivering a credit card to a customer, etc., are subject to the discipline of Six Sigma methodology to minimize defects. Six Sigma puts the spotlight on the customer, focuses on areas that are important to customer experience and on how the bank should tailor its processes to make sure that the customer is at the top in terms of priority.

Several strategic initiatives implemented by HDFC Bank have had a large impact on the functioning and performance of the bank. One of the important initiatives has been the bank's investment in business intelligence and data warehousing technologies. By 2000, HDFC Bank had established all its direct channels—it had rolled out its mobile banking channel, Internet banking was in place and it had set up several ATMs. After implementing these direct channels, HDFC Bank realized that a wealth of data was being generated through all of these channels that could be used to make conscious decisions about who their profitable customers were, how well their customers were using the bank services and networks, what was the bank's profitability from particular customers, etc. The installation of a business intelligence system/data warehouse helped yield significant results to address these challenges.

The database that has all relevant details of its customers helps the bank to integrate the different relationships that a customer has with the bank. For instance, if a customer holds a HDFC Bank credit card, has a savings account with the bank and has a 'Demat' account (for buying and

Case study 12.2 continued

Case study 12.2 continued

selling shares) as well, then the data warehouse mechanism puts together all these account relationships that the customer has with the bank and consolidates this information. Using this and other available customer data, the bank is able to do a profiling of the customer. Based on the various accounts the customer holds with the bank and the characteristics of the customer's transactions, the bank is able to identify, for instance, a particular customer who is eligible for upgrade to a gold card or for a personal loan or any other suitable retail product. Once the customer profiling is done, it is available in the system and when the customer goes to any ATM or branch there could actually be a specific offer waiting for him while his transaction is being processed. Thus, the business intelligence mechanism enables the bank to pinpoint the potential customers for particular products and accordingly make suitable offers to them.

Retail banking products are liable to commoditization. It takes only 3 to 6 months for competition to catch up on any innovation that the bank comes up with. Thus, HDFC Bank has to constantly innovate, not only in terms of new products but in terms of reducing costs, thereby delivering more value to its customers. It continually seeks to come up with innovative processes and systems so that its various services can be better offered at a lesser cost to its customers. Hooking up all its direct channels on an online real-time basis is an example of such innovation. At the end of the day all this innovation is aimed at creating *customer intimacy*, while helping the bank to better understand its *markets* and *demand for its services* and also help it to create further *demand*. At the same time, the elaborate systems of HDFC Bank help its managers to answer the fundamental question, *where is the money?*, so that its decisions can help improve the bank's profitability, while providing 'customer intimacy.' HDFC Bank is always on the look out to see how it can empower its customers to conveniently perform all their transactions, while ensuring the bank's profitability.

Notes

1. S. Maital, *Executive Economics* (New York: Free Press, 1994).
2. Peter Drucker, www.brainyquote.com
3. Howard Moskowitz's research for Pepsi-Cola and Prego was recounted on a BBC World Service programme, Global Business, by Peter Day. The reader is referred to www.bbc.co.uk/worldservice/programmes/global_business.
4. For platform strategies, see Annabelle Gawer and Michael A. Cusumano, *Platform Leadership: How Intel, Microsoft and Cisco Drive Industry Innovation*. Harvard Business School Press, Boston, MA., 2002.

5. H. Leibenstein's classic article is 'Bandwagon, Snob, and Veblen Effects in the Theory of Consumers' Demand', *The Quarterly Journal of Economics*, May 1950.
6. The story of how Nicholas Hayek invented Swatch (Swiss + watch) is told in Harvard Business School case 9-504-096 'The Birth of the Swatch' (revised 2004).
7. For a fine article on empathic design, see Dorothy Leonard and Jeffrey Rayport, 'Spark Innovation Through Empathic Design', *Harvard Business Review*, November–December 1997.
8. The articles describing the profit-pool tool are: Orit Gadiesh and James L. Gilbert, 'Profit pools: A new look at strategy', and 'How to map your industry's profit pool', *Harvard Business Review*, May–June 1998; Data for Microsoft and IBM are taken from the 2005 Fortune 500 listings for the fiscal year 2004.

Chapter 13
Calculating risks: Decision-making in an uncertain world

Take calculated risks. That is quite different from being rash.
—General George S. Patton[1]

You can learn about yourself in the stock market—but it will be very expensive.
—Adam Smith, *The Money Game*[2]

LEARNING OBJECTIVES After you read this chapter, you should understand:

- **The difference between uncertainty and risk and how to transform uncertainty into risk**
- **How to define and measure expected value and use it in decision-making**
- **How to adapt the price–cost–value framework for risk**
- **How to measure, and use, net present value (discounted cash flow)**
- **How to build, and use, decision trees**
- **How to implement scenario planning**
- **The real-options approach to evaluating investment projects, how it differs from conventional net present value and when it is appropriate**
- **Why behaviour toward risk is non-rational, according to psychologists**

TOOL #9 The psychology of risk-taking

13.1 INTRODUCTION

This chapter has three central ideas. Engineers and managers who understand these ideas and integrate them in their daily decisions will gain immediate profit and avoid major loss.

Before stating these key ideas, let us first define the crucial difference between risk and uncertainty:

DEFINITIONS

- **Risk: The (quantitative) probability, or likelihood, that a given outcome or event will in fact occur.[3]**
- **Uncertainty: (qualitative) doubt about which of several outcomes will actually happen.**

The three key ideas:

- Uncertainty is pervasive. Making optimal decisions under uncertainty is unmanageable. *The only way to make good decisions is to transform uncertainty into risk* by measuring and quantifying it. This transforms decision-making under uncertainty into Patton's 'calculated risks'.
- Never *ever* think about capital markets as markets where various types of assets (e.g., stocks and bonds) are bought and sold. Never think about your *own* investment decisions as decisions about which asset to buy. It is *risk* that is bought and sold in capital markets. And it is the demand for and supply of risk in capital markets that determines the crucial *market price* of risk. You cannot buy or sell risk wisely unless you measure it.
- Human behaviour toward risk and odds is very, very odd (or 'non-rational', to be polite). Therefore, learn to become intimate with your own non-rational perceptions of risk, and those of other people before you take calculated risks.

A pervasive theme of this textbook is the vital importance of innovation in building profitable, high-growth business strategies. Innovation by definition is fraught with risk. For example, it is said that only one product out of 100 viable new-product ideas achieves marketplace success. A key aspect of innovation is how the innovation process is managed. Many of the tools and ideas presented in this chapter are essential for successful innovation management. *Innovation management* is simply a special case of *risk management*.

13.2 TURNING UNCERTAINTY INTO CALCULATED RISKS

This section shows how to transform uncertainty into risk for decisions that do not directly involve capital-market transactions.

We begin with a case study: the seemingly reckless behaviour of General George S. Patton Jr. in World War II.

Case study: Patton's Rash Dash

General George S. Patton Jr. was commander of the American Third Army in Europe during World War II. The German High Command believed General Patton was the Allies' 'best commander of armoured and infantry troops'. And they were right. Field Marshal Von Rundstedt called him the very 'best'. According to historians, 'George Patton's army liberated France, Belgium, Luxembourg, Germany, Bavaria, Austria and Czechoslovakia. It was George S. Patton's Third Army which travelled faster than the German blitzkrieg, captured or killed 1,000 Germans every day in combat, trapped 11 German divisions at Falaise, rescued the stranded Allies in Bastogne, finished off the Battle of the Bulge, surrounded and cut off 10 German divisions in the Hunsruck Mountains, crossed the Rhine with only 28 casualties, liberated the first concentration camp, and discovered the German gold reserve.'

On 4 June 1944, before the D-Day invasion in Normandy, Patton wrote to his son (who himself would become an army general): '*Take calculated risks. That is quite different from being rash*.'

Patton's dash with his Third Army from France all the way to Germany on dangerously low supplies of fuel and ammunition was regarded by some as rash or even irresponsible.

Yet Patton himself weighed the risks and the benefits calculated both and acted boldly. He felt the benefits—keeping the enemy off-balance and on the defensive—outweighed the risks. He clearly believed that the failure to take calculated risks was the riskiest alternative of all.

Following an incident in which he allegedly struck a hospitalized soldier, General Patton was removed from the command of Third Army in disgrace. His brilliance as a military strategist and leader of soldiers far exceeded his skill at diplomacy and internal High Command politics. He died in 1945 at the age of 60.

Source: The material on Patton was sourced from one of the George S. Patton Websites and from the film, *Patton*, starring George C. Scott.

13.3 RISK–BENEFIT ANALYSIS

The word 'risk' comes from an Italian word, *ricchiare*, meaning 'to dare', to have courage, guts or to gamble. But world-class decision-making under risk is the precise opposite. It is, as Patton said, calculating. But how?

Managerial decision-making under perfect certainty is as scarce as hounds' teeth, because few things in this world are known with absolute certainty. When they exist, such decisions are taken by answering three questions, corresponding to price, cost and value. These questions comprise what may be called *cost-benefit analysis*. In order of importance:

- Value: What is the value of the decision choice, option or outcome?
- Cost: What is its cost, both direct and indirect?
- Price: What will I receive for it, to capture its value?

Decision-making under risk retains this three-question price-cost-value framework, but expands the *value* question in a deceptively simple manner:

- Value: What is the value (payoff) of the decision choice, option or outcome and the likelihood, or probability, that it will in fact occur?

Under conditions of risk, the value of an option or outcome becomes 'expected value'—monetary value multiplied by its probability. When there are several, mutually exclusive outcomes, expected value is the sum of individual expected values. (Mutually exclusive events are either-or events [either it rains or it doesn't], hence those whose probabilities add up to one, or certainty, when all possible outcomes are included). This is why transforming uncertainty into risk is so crucial. Without knowing the odds, or at least estimating them, the price–cost–value framework cannot be applied.

DEFINITION

- **The expected value of a decision choice is the monetary value of an outcome, multiplied by its probability, summed up over all possible outcomes that arise from that choice.**

Case study: Why are they drilling for oil in an Ohio cemetery?

An oil rig pokes the sky, in the US state of Ohio. Nothing unusual about that except the site is a cemetery. As oil topped $58/bbl in 2005, the incentive to find oil spurs oil exploration, even in cemeteries.

Drilling for oil is a highly risky business. Chances of finding oil are only 10 per cent. The cost of drilling a well is $150,000 (technology has greatly reduced this cost). But if oil is found, even a minimal amount of 10 bbl/day is (at existing prices) worth $580/day or $211,700 per year. The net present value, or discounted cash flow, of $211,700 per annum for 30 years is over $3 million. Here is how to make the calculations for this calculated risk.

Source: Data on oil wells is taken from BBC World Service programme 'Global Business', April 2005.

> **DEFINITION**
>
> - **Net present value (discounted cash flow): The present value of a risky stream of future income or cash flow, taking into account the opportunity cost of the capital needed to secure that future income.**

The net present value (NPV), or discounted cash flow (DCF), of $211,700 a year, for 30 years, using a 5 per cent opportunity cost for capital, is:

$$\text{NPV} = \text{DCF} = \sum_{t=1}^{30} [211{,}700]/[1+0.05]^t$$

If we can invest our $150,000 in an equally risky asset or security and earn 5 per cent return, then the opportunity cost of our capital is 5 per cent. This is the risk-adjusted interest rate we should use in charging ourselves for the use of our own money. For instance, if we receive a cheque from Exxon-Mobil for $211,700 at the end of the first year, the value of that cheque today is

$$211{,}700 / (1 + 0.05) = \$201{,}619$$

since if we had the money now, we could have invested it at 5 per cent; $201,619 invested at 5 per cent for one year equals $201,619 (1.05), or $211,700.

A present value table, found in every finance textbook, shows that one dollar received at the end of every year, for 30 years, is worth $15.37 today for a 5 per cent opportunity-cost interest rate. Thus, we find that the NPV of 10 bbl/day for 30 years is:

$$\$211{,}700 \times 15.37 = \$3{,}253{,}829$$

Is it worth drilling for oil in the Ohio cemetery? The cost is $150,000. If oil is found, its value is $3,253,829. The probability of finding oil is 10 per cent. The expected value is thus:

$$\text{Probability} \times \text{Value} = 0.10 \times \$3{,}253{,}829 = \$325{,}383$$

Would you buy a 'lottery ticket' that costs $150,000, for a one-in-ten chance to earn over $3 million? The expected value is more than double the investment cost. If we drilled thousands of wells, we should have a payback more than double our investment. Yet few would take the risk. This is as it should be. Risky investments attract investors by offering them far higher returns than certain ones; when we stand a 90 per cent chance of losing, and $150,000 is every last cent we own in this world, a two-to-one payback ratio is still very unattractive. Because nine times in ten, if we drill the well, we will be paupers.

13.4 VISUALIZING EXPECTED VALUE–DECISION TREES

Two tools help visualize decision-making under risk: expected-value rectangles and decision trees.

Figure 13.1 shows how to graph and visualize expected value. On a graph, put 'probability' on the x-axis and 'value' on the y-axis. Expected value is the product of probability P and outcome value V. It is equal to the area of the rectangles in the figure (height times width).

The expected value of the risky choice with 10 per cent probability of success [e.g., the Ohio oil well] exceeds that of the certain outcome, by the area of the shaded rectangle, because investors who are averse to risk need to be compensated for taking that risk. This excess is the risk premium. (An accurate diagram would show a far bigger shaded rectangle.) It equals the amount of risk inherent in the risky project multiplied by the price of risk—the added compensation per unit of risk, a price set by the forces of demand and supply in capital markets.

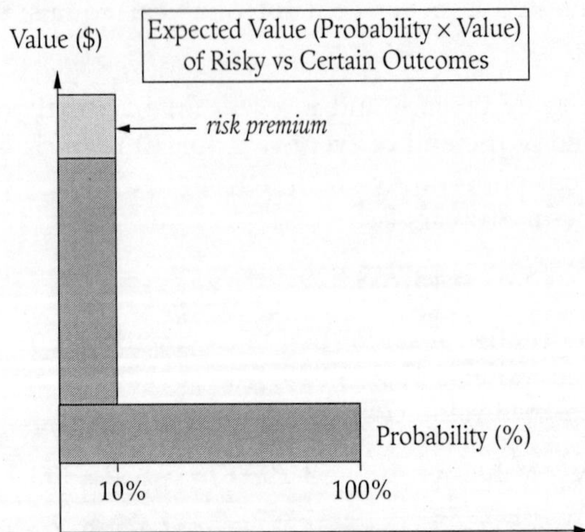

Figure 13.1
Graphic portrayal of expected value

Note: Expected value, the product of probability 'P' and value 'V', can be shown as a rectangle '$P \times V$'. Risky choices require larger rectangles, in order to persuade investors to accept the risk. The difference between *certain* expected value, and risky expected value can be regarded as a risk premium—the inducement to accept risk.

Figure 13.2 shows a decision tree for the oil well decision. We believe *every* important decision under risk should be visualized as a decision tree. Later, we will show how this can help avoid undervaluing risky investments.

The expected value of the oil well investment is:

–\$150,000 + [0.10 × (\$3,253,829) + (0.90) × (zero)]
= –150,000 + \$325,383 = \$175,383

The expected value (return) is very high; but so is the 90 per cent risk of failure. High risk requires high returns, to make the risk sufficiently worthwhile.

Case study 13.1, at the end of this chapter, provides a detailed example of how a decision tree enabled a national oil company to organize and optimize its decision on whether to lease or build locally, semi-submersible drilling rigs.

General Patton doubtless had a decision tree in his mind. The decision point, or 'node', was: Attack boldly or Be cautious (move slowly, and conservatively). Patton believed the outcome of attacking boldly would be low casualties with high probability, along with the possibility of running out of fuel and ammunition and being at the enemy's mercy; the outcome of avoiding risk and moving slowly would be high casualties with high probability. He took the calculated risk of attacking boldly because the payoff was worth the risk. In the end, he believed that what others felt was risky was in fact less so than the cautious alternative. This is often the nature of calculated risks.

Patton had two scenarios in his mind. He chose the boldest. Managers, too, can make effective use of scenarios in managing risk.

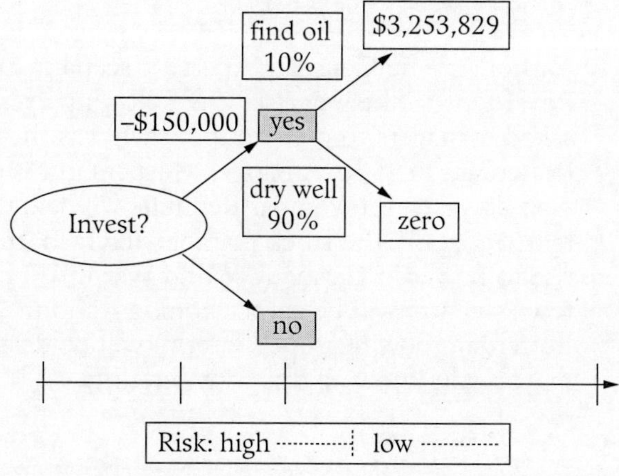

Figure 13.2
Decision tree for oil well decision

13.5 SCENARIO ANALYSIS

DEFINITION

- **Scenario: Sketch of the plot of a play; giving particulars of the scenes, situations, etc.**

Robert Johnson, legendary former head of foreign exchange trading for George Soros's Quantum Fund, once told an interviewer that even on weekends, beside the swimming pool with his family he constantly ponders: What could happen that might hurt me (i.e., cause financial losses to my forex [foreign exchange] position and strategy)? Johnson was implementing a powerful tool for converting uncertainty into risk, known as scenario analysis. Scenario analysis was invented by Rand Corporation futurist Herman Kahn, who got the world to 'think about the unthinkable' (such as nuclear war). This approach was successfully implemented at Royal Dutch/Shell. In 2004, the Dutch-based oil company had after-tax profits of $18.536 billion, second in the world only to Exxon-Mobil; at $221.5 billion, the market value of its shares made it the sixth largest firm in the world.[4]

Some management teams ask, 'what will happen to us?' This is forecasting. Other management teams ask, 'what will we do, if x, y or z happen?' This is contingency action planning based on *scenario analysis*. The problem with forecasting is that even if it is accurate, which is rare, it fails to prepare organizations to take action. The following action-learning exercise illustrates this dilemma.

Action learning

Clairvoyance has Dubious Value

Author Arie de Geus, an expert on scenario analysis at Royal Dutch/Shell, devised the following exercise: He asked managers to pretend that each was the mayor of Rotterdam in 1920. An angel whispers in his ear: In the next 25 years, the Weimar Republic will fall, there will be hyperinflation, the stock market will crash, the Nazis will rise to power in Germany, World War II will break out, the town's centre will be carpet-bombed, and in 1945 Rotterdam port (Europe's largest) will be destroyed. As mayor, you know all this with certainty.

Question: If you are the Mayor of Rotterdam in 1920, what should you do? What is your action plan? Write a short speech to your citizens. (*Note*: this is similar to the Action Learning exercise in Chapter 9, relating to IBM Chair John Akers' 'bad news' in 1990.)

Nearly all managers respond in the same way to this challenge: There is nothing the mayor can do. He would have neither the courage nor powers of persuasion to take drastic action required by clairvoyance.

The alternative to clairvoyance is the Boy Scout credo, Be Prepared. This is the approach taken by Royal Dutch/Shell.

Case study: Scenario planning at Royal Dutch/Shell

At Royal Dutch/Shell, where Herman Kahn's scenario analysis was implemented in a business context, it is assumed that the future is plural, not singular. Managers agree to abandon the presumption that there is only one possible future path. In 1968, a group in Shell began to study the year 2000. How soon will the world run out of oil? they asked. What happens to oil companies if it does? And, 'Is there life for Shell after oil?' The result: Shell diversified. Some of its new businesses did not work out. But a direct result of the Year 2000 project was to create a planning division, led by innovative managers such as Pierre Wack. They continually asked two questions: *How will we look as a company 20–30 years ahead? How can we get people to discuss together the 'unthinkable'?* Wack's scenario planners explored a wide variety of arenas: technology, politics, international finance, social values, consumption patterns, demography, life styles. Shell's scenario planners, according to Arie Geus, 'foresaw the energy crises of 1973 and 1979, ... and even the breakup of the Soviet Union .... Shell's management [made] decisions necessitated by these external changes.'

Source: Arie de Geus, *The Living Company* (Boston: Harvard Business School Press, 1977), pp. 44–54.

Identifying risks in scenarios is important. But it is equally important to find ways to measure those risks. This is our next challenge.

13.6 MEASURING AND MANAGING RISK AND RISK PREMIUMS

This section examines ways to measure and manage risk and risk premiums. Exaggerating risk or underestimating it can lead to equally bad management decisions.

Measuring risk

How is risk measured? This is the focus of a large sub-discipline of economics, the economics of finance. Managers of all kinds, not just Chief Financial Officers, need expertise in this complex area. In this chapter, it must suffice to describe two basic measures of risk.

- One measure is simply the *standard deviation* of the rate of return—the 'scatter' of the rate of return around its mean. A high standard deviation, or wide scatter, indicates high risk. A small standard deviation, or narrow scatter, indicates low risk. For instance, companies that can maintain steady growth in quarterly earnings per share (low standard deviation) are rewarded by high and rising share prices; companies whose per-share earnings fluctuate widely (high standard deviation) often find their share prices are punished by risk-averse analysts and investors.
- A second measure, known by the Greek letter Beta (not related to the learning-curve slope coefficient, also known as Beta), measures the extent to which assets are correlated with the level of market prices. A high correlation indicates high risk (your assets rise and fall with the market); a low correlation indicates your assets do not necessarily sink, like a ship with a hole in its bottom, when the capital market does, hence have lower risk. Assets that are 'out of sync' with the market (also known as counter-cyclical assets) are valuable, because they reduce the standard deviation (risk) of investment portfolios.

Visualizing expected value and the risk premium

Risk's quantitative fingerprint is often expressed as a 'risk premium'.

DEFINITION

- **Risk Premium: The extra return that investors demand for buying risky assets, compared to safe Treasury Bonds.**

Every asset has two 'fingerprints'—its rate of return, or profit and the risk associated with it. The higher the return, the higher the risk. For instance, US government treasury bonds may pay, say, a 5 per cent return annually and are almost risk free. Note that this is not entirely true however; the risk that the US Treasury may default on its debt, as the governments of Russia (in August 1998) or Argentina (in 2001) did, may be zero; but there is still substantial capital risk related to the rise and fall of the price of Treasury bonds in the marketplace. The fact is, there probably is no asset that is entirely risk-free. Junk bonds (high-risk corporate bonds), blue-chip stocks and high-risk stocks carry ever-higher risk premiums (Figure 13.3).

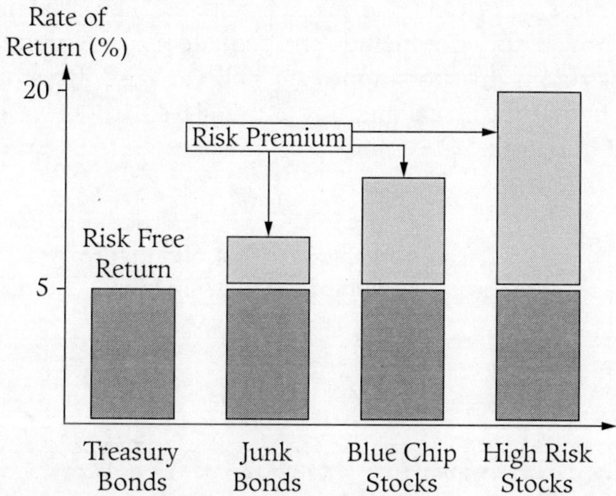

Figure 13.3
Risk premiums for various assets

When you buy or sell an asset, be certain you know its risk as well as its return. Many people who make their living selling capital-market assets do not provide adequate information about risk but rather stress the asset's high return. This is much like a used car salesman showing off a 1982 Chevy's glistening paint job and neglecting to mention that it badly needs a valve job.

The reason that you cannot wisely buy an asset without knowing both of its key risk-return fingerprints is simple. In capital markets, risk is bought and sold. The price of risk is determined by the forces of demand and supply. Capital market assets (stocks, bonds, options) each have a rate of return and a level of risk, comprising some point in the risk-return diagram. The price of each asset depends crucially on both its parameters. Wise buying and selling of assets requires that one knows each parameter.

In liquid competitive capital markets, each asset has two numbers attached to it, risk and return. This comprises a point in a two-dimensional risk-return diagram. These points are arrayed along a consistent trend line (see Figure 13.4). This line reveals the price of risk as set in the market. The price of risk is the inverse of the slope of the trend line that links assets of all types, or A/B—the added return paid for a unit of risk.

The 'smiley' shows an asset for which the risk premium *exceeds* that normally paid in the capital market, making this asset attractive. Even in highly sophisticated capital markets, there are such assets—wise investors detect that they are less risky than the market believes. The 'frowney' shows an asset whose return does not include an adequate risk premium. These assets are more risky than investors appear to believe. Wise investors make sure they know whether the assets they buy are 'smileys', 'frowneys' or are neutral on the trend line itself.

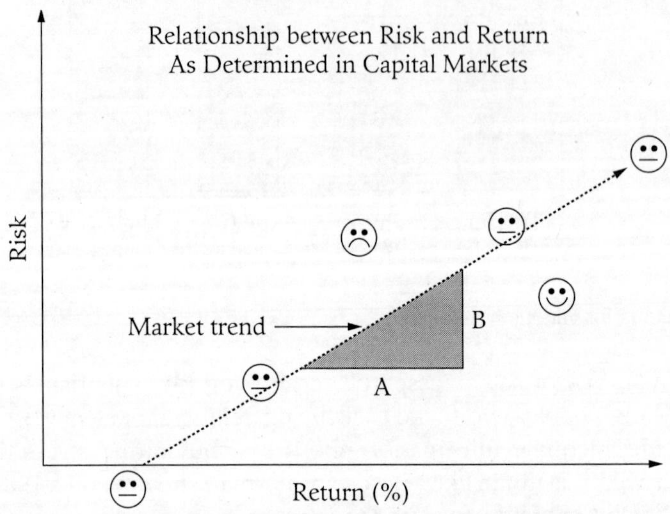

Figure 13.4
The link between risk and return, as determined in capital markets

Varieties of risk[5]

Inflation risk
The tendency of currency to lose value over time. The US dollar in 2005 can buy only one-fifth what it bought in 1970. Consider which asset preserves the value of your money best.

Event risk
For example, 9/11. A specific event can hurt the price of related assets; e.g., 9/11 shut down airlines for a time, led to a dramatic drop in air travel and affected disproportionately the stocks of airlines. The finding that a particularly profitable type of anti-pain drug known as cox-inhibitors increased the risk of heart attacks hurt the stock price of companies selling them and also hurt the pharmaceuticals industry in general.

Interest-rate risk
Bond prices move inversely to interest rates. As the US Federal Reserve raised rates in 2006, bond prices declined. So do shares in real estate investment trusts. This is because as the price of the bond rises, the 'yield' or interest rate falls. A $100 bond with 6 per cent coupon yields 7 per cent if the price falls to $85 [=(6 / 85) × 100].

Currency risk
If you invest abroad, to enjoy higher interest rates, for instance in Mexico or Brazil, a fall in the exchange rate of the local currency relative to the dollar [devaluation] can wipe out any gains accruing from higher interest rates in those countries. In January 2001, the value of Brazil's currency, 'real', relative to the dollar fell by over half, and earlier in December 1994 Mexico's 'peso' began a downward slide, falling from 3.50 pesos to the dollar to over 7.

Liquidity risk
A hedge fund known as Long Term Capital Management, founded in 1993, made enormous profits until the Russian debt default in August 1998 made it impossible for them to sell off assets anywhere, as liquidity disappeared everywhere. Their debts, estimated at one point at $1 trillion, almost led to a catastrophic collapse of world capital markets.[6]

Case study: Michael Milken and junk bonds

During his MBA studies, Michael Milken spotted a 'smiley'. He noticed that low-grade high-risk corporate bonds paid a very high return, or yield, to investors with a market risk premium higher than the true underlying, or inherent, risk. The reason: Companies rarely defaulted on paying principal and interest. To do so would have hurt chances to raise funds in the capital market in future. Milken created a new industry by leading his company, Drexel Burnham, to expand junk bond issues, sometimes to finance leveraged buyouts. He went to jail, and Drexel disappeared after Milken was tried for violating securities laws.

Action learning

Evaluate Your Portfolio: Smileys, Frowneys

Evaluate your own portfolio of investments, including your house or apartment, IRAs (independent retirement accounts), securities, etc.

Do you know the historical rate of return on each? Estimate it.

Now, try to evaluate the main risks attached to each asset (see 'Varieties of Risk'). Are your assets 'smileys' or 'frownies'? How do you know? What information do you need in order to answer this key question? Is this information readily available?

When you buy 100 newly-issued shares of a startup company, you gain the right to share in its equity capital and in its future profits (hence the name 'shares'), but accept the risk that there may never in fact be such profits and your money will go down the drain. Since you cannot buy or sell something successfully without measuring it—*always* estimate the risk inherent in investing in an asset before you act. If you cannot measure the risk, you are back in the stressful world of uncertainty where many many metaphorical shirts have been lost.

Case study: 'Fannie Mae' revisited

In Chapter 7, the case of Federal National Mortgage Co. (Fannie Mae) was presented, showing how it came to be one of Jim Collins' 11 (out of 1,400) truly great companies. The key reason: skill in measuring risk. When CEO David Maxwell took over in 1981, the company was losing

Case study continued

Case study continued

$1 million every business day. It was bleeding money. Maxwell transformed Fannie Mae in four short years into one of Wall Street's best firms. Fannie Mae, it may be recalled, sold mortgage-backed securities, profiting from the interest-rate spread between what it paid for borrowing and what it earned from mortgage assets. This spread fluctuates widely, as interest rates rise and fall. Maxwell, a Level 5 leader, realized Fannie Mae's path to greatness lay in measuring and managing risk. He led Fannie Mae managers to excellence in this area. Despite Fannie Mae's shaky profit-and-loss position, Maxwell pushed ahead with a very large initial investment in risk-management information technology that made Fannie Mae #1.

In 2004–05, Fannie Mae's Chairman and CEO Franklin Raines and CFO Tim Howard were compelled to resign when it was found that Fannie Mae's accounting practices improperly smoothed losses on financial trading related to risk management. Raines and Howard allegedly took the risk that reporting on Fannie Mae's risk-hedging transactions in ways that enhanced its profitability was wise. But in the end it was not; it undermined Fannie Mae's key asset and core competency—credibly managing, measuring *and reporting* risk, a competency on which David Maxwell had revived and built the company.

Why the opportunity cost of capital is often exaggerated

In pondering the 'cemetery oil well' case, sophisticated readers may well be asking—if oil exploration is highly risky, with 90 per cent failure rates, should not the risk-adjusted interest rate used in computing NPV or DCR be, say, 20 per cent, rather than 5 per cent? If we measure the standard deviation of the oil-well returns, it is very large indeed. [The formula for the standard deviation is $\sqrt{\Sigma(x_i - x)^2 p_i}$, or the square root of the sum of the squared deviations from the mean, weighted by probability, where x_i is the payoff or return (NPV) for outcome 'i', and x is the mean (average) pay off. The oil well has a high standard deviation, because 90 per cent of the time it is zero and the rest of the time it is huge (over $3 million)]. Surely the 5 per cent interest rate used in calculating NPV does not include a sufficient risk premium. This is an important question, revealing a key fallacious reason for under-investing in risky projects (such as R&D).

The reason why a low risk-free 5 per cent interest rate was used to compute net present value for a highly risky oil-well investment, rather than a more reasonable value of, say, 20 per cent, lies in understanding *when risk is high and when risk disappears.*

Return to Figure 13.2. Ask yourself: *when is the risk high, and when is it low for the oil-well investment?* Answer: the risk is high *only* when the oil well is being drilled—90 per cent chance of a dry well. But once the well is completed, and a depth of, say, 8,000 feet is reached, *all the uncertainty disappears.* Either you find oil, or you do not. The probability, after six months, is no longer 90 per cent / 10 per cent. It is 100 per cent—certainty that oil was found or certainty there is no oil. *If you do find oil, then you know with certainty you will get 10 bbls/day for 30 years.* This is no different than a US Treasury Bond, except you are clipping 'oil coupons' rather than bond coupons. The appropriate discount rate, or interest rate, then, is 5 per cent not 20 per cent. Using a 20 per cent discount rate when risk is zero is simply misguided.

By using a decision tree to understand the time profile of risk—when is risk high, when is it medium and when does it disappear altogether—managers can avoid the remarkably common fallacy of using excessively-high values for the opportunity cost of capital for the lifetime of a project, when in fact most of the project's risk is 'front-loaded' in its very early stages. For this reason, we recommend that the risk profile of every project over time be visualized.

Innovation risk is front-loaded

R&D investment in developing innovative products is not unlike the oil well case. Most of the uncertainty occurs in the early stages of the project. Once a prototype exists and is market-tested, managers largely know whether the product is a winner or a failure. *Using 20 per cent discount rates to compute lifetime benefits from the project greatly exaggerates the lifetime risk and undervalues the project.* This assumes permanently high risk and risk premiums—a false assumption. We believe such assumptions are made all the time. Drawing a decision tree and related risk profile over time can avoid this fallacy.

To understand this try the following action-learning problem.

Action learning

A Better Mousetrap

For an investment of $125,000 in Research and Development, a new improved mousetrap can be developed. It will take one year. At the end of that year, market tests will quickly show whether people will buy it or not. There is a 50 per cent chance the product will be successful. To build a factory to produce the new mousetrap will take another investment of $1 million; annual after-tax profits from the mousetrap are $250,000 for 30 years.

Would you, as CEO, invest the $125,000? What interest rate would you use in computing net present value? What is the risk profile over time—when is risk high and when is it zero? (To help you decide, draw a decision tree.)

Can you see the similarity between this project and the cemetery oil well?

In addition to helping us grasp the true time profile of risk, crucial for wise decision-making, decision trees are very helpful in spotting hidden benefits—'tree branches' that represent important but indirect gains from a project that are sometimes hard to see. Sometimes, such branches can turn what looks like an unattractive high-risk project into a valuable, winning one. This is the key message of what has become known as the 'real options' approach to project evaluation under risk.

Financial options and real options

A financial option is the right (not the obligation) to buy or sell an asset (stock, bond, foreign exchange or other security) at an agreed price, *on* a specified date or *by* a specified date. For example: One can buy an option to buy 100 shares of Intel common stock at $38 per share by 15 December 2006. This is called a 'call' (or buy) option. The right to sell shares is called a 'put' option.

Financial options have been known for well over a century. But the market for this so-called 'contingent asset'—contingent, because the transaction depends on a specific event, such as the stock price rising above $100—was very small, because those who bought and sold options did not know how to value them, or specifically, how to value the risk premium inherent in an options contract. And if you cannot measure something's value, it is hard to buy and sell it.

Then, in 1973, three scholars—Fisher Black, Myron Scholes and Robert Merton—discovered a formula, known today as the Black-Scholes equation, that expressed the price of an option contract in terms of five parameters: the exercise price of the option (i.e., the agreed price at which the asset is to be bought or sold in future), the current ('spot') price of the asset, the degree of volatility or uncertainty, the risk-free interest rate and the time period during which the option can be exercised. Once those five parameters are known, or are estimated, the value of the real option can be computed using the Black-Scholes formula. Scholes and Merton won the Nobel Prize on 14 October 1997; Fisher Black tragically died of cancer a few years earlier.

The Black-Scholes formula is the solution to a partial differential equation.[7] Like all theories, the formula is based on somewhat artificial assumptions. Yet because option traders today universally believe in and use this formula, the correlation between option prices and the theoretical formula is perfect—a case in which perception truly creates reality. Today, the market for 'derivatives'—contingent assets derived from demand and supply of securities in the spot market, such as options—is larger than the turnover of spot securities. It is doubtful that the huge market for derivatives would have developed *in the absence of* the Black-Scholes formula. With no objective pricing benchmark, option trading lacked a coherent standard of value that buyers and sellers could each accept and use.

It was first observed by Robert Pindyck and Avinash Dixit that investment in real assets, such as fabrication plants, is a kind of *call option*, in the sense that the plant can be built in stages.[8] Each stage comprises a call option to invest or not to invest; and the value of such 'real options' can be determined using the same Black-Scholes formula used widely to price financial options. Like a stock option, which gives the holder the right to purchase stock at a future date or at a set price, a real option provides managers with a series of flexible choices about what, when and how to invest that can be made as business conditions change. By using this approach, rather than standard 'net present value' (which ignores the option value of 'staging' real investment), one can show that many investment projects attain high return on invested capital (when the real option value is taken into account), while Net Present Value may be low or even negative. Moreover, 'real option' theory provides a strategic mindset for purposely organizing real investment in stages in order to maximize its option value.

We often explain the difference between 'real options' and Net Present Value, as the difference between a turnpike (toll express highway) with no exits from beginning to end (NPV), and a turnpike with many exits (real options). You may not use the exits but the fact they exist (in case you need food, gasoline, car repairs, or other exigencies) has high value. Exits are the staged options in an investment project.

Figure 13.5 shows an example of a decision tree that reveals the value of the flexible options approach. A manager faces a decision whether to develop new technology in-house or to acquire it. Acquiring it is an up-or-down (yes/no) decision. Developing the technology in-house has some flexibility. Depending on initial results, one can drop the project, spend a modest additional amount on it, or spend a large amount on it. These are all options.

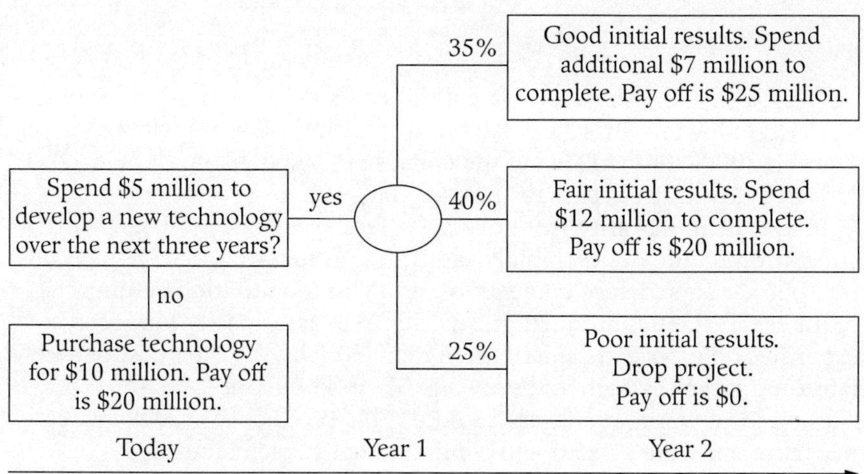

Figure 13.5
Example of a real-option decision tree

Source: Fabian d'Souza, 'Putting Real Options to Work to Improve Project Planning'. Harvard Business School Management Update, August 2002.

They can be evaluated using the Black–Scholes formula. As time passes, and more information is acquired, we can estimate the risks more accurately.

Pay special attention to the third branch labelled 'poor initial results, drop project'. Often, by building projects in stages, and adding a 'cancel the project' branch at each one, projects can ironically be made more attractive. The reason: just as with financial options, where the maximum loss is the price paid for the option (when the option expires without being exercised), so can the losses accruing from an unsuccessful project be truncated by cancelling it. These words—cancel the project—are easy to write. For managers who have had to kill projects, this is one of the most difficult decisions they ever encounter. But cancelling a losing project can save enormous resources, both time and money. And the option to cancel a losing project at every stage can have great value, by surgically amputating the potential for huge losses should the project prove unsuccessful.

Case study: Real option flexibility in volatile semiconductors: How to put exits on the turnpike when none exist

The semiconductor industry is one of the most cyclical and volatile of all industries. Since 1997, there have been three sharp downturns in the industry—the first in 1997, following the collapse of Thailand

Case study continued

Case study continued

(July 1997), Indonesia, Malaysia and other Asian countries; the second in 1998, following Russia's default and resulting crisis and slowdown; and again in 2000–2001, following the collapse of the dot.com bubble. A fourth downturn is perhaps not very far away.

Severe dilemmas arise from managing under volatile demand. With short product life cycles, rapidly capturing profits from new-generation microprocessors, before competition and commoditization set in, requires substantial production capacity. Yet that capacity may represent expensive, idle, wasted capital, when demand falls. And the cost of a new fabrication plant is high and growing: $3 to $5 billion.

In an ideal world, managers could double productive capacity when needed, then wave a wand and eliminate that capacity during a downturn. What innovative ideas could create such a wand? One possibility arises from real options. Here is an idea we heard from a senior manager.

Existing approach

A decision is carefully weighed whether or not to construct a fabrication plant ('fab'). Once the decision is taken, a finely-tuned process goes into action, whose ultimate goal is to construct the fab, populate it with machines and workers and put it into full production in a predefined time period (usually, 19–24 months or more). The decision is difficult because it requires among other things a forecast of (volatile) future demand. Under this approach, the project is like driving down a high-speed limited access highway with no exits. The only exit is the one at the destination when the car leaves the highway (the plant is completed and in full production). Here, the decision tree is simple: yes or no. After a 'yes', there is only a single long branch on the decision tree.

Proposed approach

Redefine facility construction, in order to maximize flexibility (call it 'FlexPlant') and enhance the real option value. Begin by constructing only the shell. When the shell is completed (a relatively small initial investment), if demand and market conditions warrant, proceed to populate it with machinery. If not leave the shell empty and waiting. When the machinery is in place, again, if demand and market conditions warrant, hire workers and begin trial runs. If not, leave the plant idle. By decomposing the project into stages, with decision nodes at each stage, losses can be truncated by avoiding investments when market conditions do not warrant them. This creates a multi-branch decision tree with many yes-no decision nodes.

Case study continued

Case study continued

This approach is not unlike a proposal to 'stage' equipment in various theatres around the world for advanced mobile armies in readiness. When needed, the 'option' can be exercised by sending personnel to the area—their equipment is already there and waiting. Soldiers can be transported faster and easier than tanks or artillery or ammunition or fuel.

The real option approach to risky investment has caught on very slowly. Managers continue to use the old Net Present Value/Discounted Cash Flow approaches. It is a case of how the way you *measure* something drives the way you *manage* it. Once the real options idea is understood, projects are structured in ways to maximize flexibility and option value. The gains are substantial.[9]

The next section explores findings by psychologists showing many ways in which our behaviour toward risk is non-rational, in sharp contrast to the assumption that economics is based entirely on rational behaviour.

13.7 ODD BEHAVIOUR TOWARD ODDS

It is important to be aware of non-rationality in behaviour toward risk, both introspectively, within ourselves and on the part of those with whom we work and deal. These non-rationalities are double-edged swords—they create enormous business opportunities for those who understand them and huge business risks for those who do not.

Pioneers in exploring the psychology of behaviour toward risk are the late Professor Amos Tversky, Stanford University, and Professor Daniel Kahneman, Princeton University, Nobel Laureate in Economics. An article in *Psychological Science* states that the research programme initiated by Kahneman and Tversky (now known as Prospect Theory) is considered psychology's 'leading intellectual export to the wider academic world'. This section briefly describes some of their findings.

Buy Insurance? Gamble? both?

Why do people seem to pay dearly to take risk and pay dearly to avoid it at one and the same time?

If a million persons each pay $10 to buy one lottery ticket, with a single winning prize of $5 million, the expected value of a single ticket is 1/1,000,000 (the probability of winning) times $5 million (the prize), or $5.

In terms of risk-benefit, this seems like a losing deal. How many of us would pay $10 for something that is worth only $5? How many of us would buy a $5 dollar bill if the going price was $10? Yet gambling is one of the world's biggest industries. Why? Since casinos or state lotteries all make a profit, generally a large one, it is *prima facie* true that the cost of gambling or buying a lottery ticket (what you pay) far exceeds the expected value of winnings (what you get back). Why then do you think people persist in this behaviour?

The simplest answer: People enjoy gambling. They enjoy risk and pay to experience it. But why, in other contexts, do people appear to *hate* risk? And why then is insurance—purchase of risk borne by individuals and its transfer (for a fee) to insurance companies—America's (and many other countries') largest industry? Those who buy insurance—nearly everyone does—pay insurance companies high fees in order to avoid risk, well above the expected value of the risky outcomes; otherwise, how else would insurance companies show high economic value added? Economists and psychologists have struggled to explain this phenomenon.

Case study: The world's biggest industries: Gambling and Insurance

Two of the largest industries in the world are insurance and gambling. The first industry is built on dislike of risk; the second, on love of risk. What is puzzling is that the consumers of both industries are to a large extent the same persons.

America's largest industry, arguably, is insurance. Total revenues of life, property and casualty, and health insurance companies (both joint stock and mutual) totalled $768 billion in 2004, some $44 billion more than revenues of American oil companies (the 2nd largest industry), despite the high prices of oil and gasoline.

Americans buy a great deal of insurance. This suggests that the buyers of insurance—nearly the entire population—are averse to risk. The aggregate after-tax profits of the insurance industry totalled $64 billion. This implies that Americans pay significant excess sums to insurance companies in return for shifting risk to life, limb, health and property to them.

Americans also gamble a lot. Numbers here are harder to acquire, because a great deal of gambling is unofficial sports betting. However, for example, the three largest Las Vegas casinos (Harrah's, Caesars, MGM

Case study continued

Case study continued

Mirage) alone earned revenues of $13.9 billion, and after-tax profits of over $1 billion.

One estimate shows that half of all Americans gamble in some manner.[10] Those who gamble are ostensibly risk-lovers. They pay significant excess sums to casinos, bookies and others for the right to bear risk.

What is interesting is that many of the same people who purchase large amounts of insurance are also those who engage in gambling. *They are apparently both risk haters and risk lovers at one and the same time.*

This is only one of many interesting anomalies that show how behaviour toward risk is non-rational.

Action learning

Expected Value of the Last Lottery Ticket you bought

Readers who purchase lottery tickets or who gamble or bet on sports games are invited to explore their reasoning and motivation. Take your most recent bet or gamble or lottery ticket.

- What did the bet or ticket *cost* you?
- What was its estimated expected value? (i.e., the likelihood of winning multiplied by the sum you get if you win).
- If the bet cost you more than it was worth why did you choose to take it?

Case study: Mr and Mrs Yeh

Case Study 13.2 at the end of this chapter focuses on a private banker who with the wisdom of King Solomon managed to resolve a prickly conflict. Mrs Yeh disliked risk. Mr Yeh loved it. How can one tailor an investment portfolio that satisfies both of them and preserved marital harmony? Answer: build a portfolio with both risk-taking and risk-avoiding elements, by cautiously investing the principal (insuring the value of the Yeh's capital) and 'riskily' investing the interest.

Psychology and risk-taking

Researching the psychology of risk is deceptively simple. Offer people (surgeons, statisticians, psychologists, ordinary people) a series of pair choices, such as:

Would you prefer:

A. 50 per cent chance to win a three-week one-weektour of England, France, and Italy	OR	B. (100 per cent certain) tour of England
C. 5 per cent chance to win a three-week tour of England, France Italy	OR	D. 10 per cent chance to win a one-week tour of and England

Observe their behaviour carefully and generalize.

Rational choice requires consistency. If you pick A, then you should also pick C, because the C versus D choice is the same as A versus B, except the odds for C an D are 1/10 those for A and B. *Yet Kahneman and Tversky*[11] *found that a large majority of subjects pick B and then pick C.* The reason: B is a sure thing—a 'bird in the hand'. With C and D, both choices are risky, so why not go for the larger prize? This led to the finding that:

- People overweigh outcomes that are certain, relative to outcomes that are merely probable.[12]

This is perhaps why a company's promise that products are free of defects is far more powerful than the statement that 99.99 per cent of the time there will be no defects in the products. A very small probability of disaster means, to people, that *it could happen* and that they are in the world of risk, rather than certainty.

Case study: Intel's Pentium

Intel's early Pentium microprocessor had a small bug that once in 28,000 years could cause a mathematical error. Despite the miniscule chance of error, Intel had to spend $300 million to recall the defective chips and replace them. Once buyers lost the certainty that the chip was error-free, the chip lost most of its value. Intel had learned about 'overweighting' of certainty the hard, expensive way.

- '[People have] undue confidence in early trends,[13, 14] e.g., the data of the first few subjects'. As the feeling of uncertainty is uncomfortable, we may try to dispel it by deciding quickly, too quickly. General Patton addressed this issue through a dose of pragmatic advice. When uncertain, he said, ask questions; when *certain*, ask many *more* questions. He practised his own advice.

- 'We normally reinforce others when their behaviour is good and punish them when their behaviour is bad. [But behaviour is characterized by 'regression toward the mean'—unusually great performances, or bad ones, are usually random and are followed by a return to the average.] By regression alone, therefore, they are most likely to improve after being punished and most likely to deteriorate after being rewarded. Consequently, we are exposed to a lifetime schedule in which *we are most often rewarded for punishing others and punished for rewarding.*'[15]

Case study: Reward pilots? Or punish them?

As colleagues at the Hebrew University of Jerusalem in 1968, Tversky and Kahneman taught Israeli Air Force flight instructors. They were fascinated by how the instructors used rewards and punishments to motivate their pilot-trainees. The instructors refuted psychologists' stock-in-trade, that reward is far more powerful than punishment. They claimed the policy led to bad results because in their experience '... good execution of complex manoeuvres (reinforced by reward) typically results in a decrement of performance on the next try'. How would a psychologist respond? The answer to the riddle lies in the concept of 'regression toward the mean'. Regression is inevitable in flight manoeuvres, Kahneman and Tversky observe, because performance is not perfectly reliable and progress between successive manoeuvres is slow. Hence it was likely that pilots who did well on one trial deteriorated on the next. Flight instructors wrongly attributed this 'regression' to the detrimental effect of their positive reinforcement.

This particular instance of non-rationality reflects in part our dislike of randomness, and our desire to understand the world entirely in terms of certain cause-and-effect. If poorer performance *follows* reward, then we believe it must be true that the *cause* of that deterioration was the reward. Wise managers avoid the trap of 'post hoc ergo propter hoc' ('happening after' means 'caused by').

- 'Subjects predict outstandingly high achievement with very high confidence and they have more confidence in the prediction of utter failure than of mediocre performance ... factors which enhance confidence [consistency, extremity] are often negatively correlated with predictive accuracy.'[16]

- 'The same decision can be framed in several different ways; different frames can lead to different decisions'; 'alternate descriptions of a decision problem give rise to different preferences'.[17]

For example, surgeons who tell us we have a 5 per cent chance of dying during an operation usually find unwilling patients but saying we have a 95 per cent of survival gets many more assenting signatures. The advertising industry is built almost entirely on framing.

'... valuation of single risky prospects neglect the possibilities of pooling risks and are therefore overly timid'.[18] Ten different stocks together are less risky than a single one. This is sometimes ignored.

'... it is [considered] acceptable for a firm to raise prices when profits are threatened ... but ... unfair to exploit shifts in demand by raising prices'. This is one of many examples of 'asymmetry' in our behaviour and reasoning.

'most people have a risk-seeking preference for the gamble over the sure loss', 'losses have greater impact on preferences than gains'.[19]

This explains in part why investors hold on to assets whose prices collapse longer than they should. The mounting losses encourage risk-taking, hoping the price will rise in future. It rarely does. It also explains why investors tend to sell an asset too quickly, when its price rises, to capture profits. We are risk averse when winning, risk affine when losing.

- 'low probabilities are commonly overweighted'.[20] This explains in part the massive purchase of lottery tickets. The odds of one in 10 million are perceived as higher than they really are; and the tempting huge prizes ($10 million to $100 million) swamp the miniscule chance we will actually win them.
- 'there is a case for paternalistic interventions' ... 'it is plausible that the state knows more about an individual's future tastes than the individual knows presently'.[21] In the face of non-rational anomalous behaviour, it may well be that there is a case for state regulation in stark contrast to the economic principle that individual freedom for choice is almost always optimal.

Kahneman has wise words on the conflict between the 'rational' economic theory of behaviour toward risk and the 'non-rational' psychological findings. In 1994, he wrote, 'the time has perhaps come to set aside the overly general question of whether or not people are rational, ... allowing research to be focused on more specific and more promising issues.' In other words: let us *observe* how people really behave toward risk, rather than assume it. This is not only good science, it is also the basis of strong management.

13.8 CONCLUSION

The growing pervasiveness and magnitude of uncertainty compels every manager to acquire a toolbox that turns uncertainty into quantitative risk and then helps manage that risk.

This chapter has provided some of these tools. They are deceptively simple. As with all tools, the key lies not in understanding them conceptually but in practising them daily and adapting them to changing circumstances and needs.

Readers are invited to view 'Pillars of Profit: Segment #9, Calculating Risks: Decision-making in an uncertain World', in the accompanying CD.

CASE STUDY 13.1

Putting your Money where your Stakeholders' Heart is*

Case study discussion topics

1. What are the two broad drilling options appropriate for different depths of water?
2. What are the three options for drilling in deep water?
3. What decision did the National Oil Company actually make? Why?
4. Using hindsight: What is the case author's recommendation?
5. Why does the case author believe that 'flexibility' is a major advantage of leasing semi-submersible rigs?

National Oil Co. (NOC) (note: name changed to protect the identity of the company), belonging to a large developing country, engaged in the exploration, drilling and production of oil. In 1998, NOC had to make a choice to either switch over to an advanced technology or continue using the current low-cost technology for its oil exploration and drilling purpose. The stakes were high. Changing to the new technology implied

*This case study is a summary of the case authored by Max P. Michaels.

Case study 13.1 continued

Case study 13.1 continued

writing off around $1.5 billion and investing over $3 billion over the next 5 years. Over 80 per cent of the total revenues of NOC was from operations on the high seas. Offshore drilling was a critical NOC activity and hence the strategic importance of the drilling technology deployed. In 1988, NOC owned 30 offshore drilling rigs and leased 10. Rigs are classified into four types based on the drilling technologies used—Submersible rigs (SR), Drillships (DS), jack-up rigs (JUR) and Semi-submersible rigs (SSR). The portfolio of offshore drilling rigs NOC deployed is summarized in Table 13.1.1.

Table 13.1.1
Portfolio of offshore drilling rigs deployed by NOC

Drill type	*Nos. owned and leased*	
DS	Own: 2	Lease: 1
SSR	Own: 1	Lease: 9
SR	Own: 2	Lease: 0
JUR	Own: 25	Lease: 0

NOC had four choices—(*a*) continue drilling in shallow waters with jack-up technology by primarily relying on JURs owned by the company for offshore operations in the short term. Doing so would involve no new investments and therefore, costs would be minimal. However, NOC would be constrained to drill in less prospective shallow waters, where the probability of finding oil was only, p = 0.1, vis-à-vis, p = 0.2 in deep waters (*b*) drill in deep waters with semi-submersible technology by replacing JURs incrementally with SSRs leased in the international market. This would be extremely expensive in the long run as the lease rate of each SSR was 70 per cent more than the amortized cost of an owned SSR. However, this choice would give NOC the strategic flexibility to decrease its offshore activities when oil prices would go down (*c*) acquire SSRs incrementally from international shipyards (US, Norway, Korea, Japan). The international cost of construction was around $100 million and the average technology life of SSR was 10 years (*d*) acquire SSRs incrementally from indigenous shipyards. The cost of indigenous acquisition was 10 per cent higher than that of international acquisition due to lower economies of scale (fewer than 10 rigs/year). These strategic trade-offs and attendant risks were summarized as shown in the Decision Tree (Figure 13.1.1).

NOC chose to go with the last option i.e., acquiring SSRs incrementally from indigenous shipyards. It decided to put its money where its

Case study 13.1 continued

Case study 13.1 continued

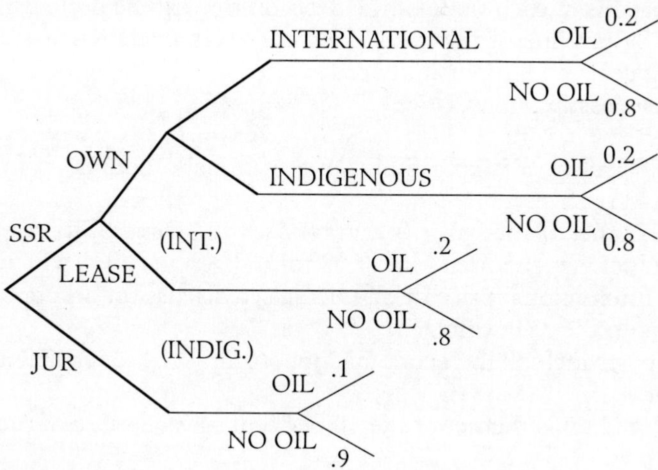

Figure 13.1.1
Decision Tree for NOC

stakeholders heart was! The decision was intuitive and the top management at NOC had this to say:

> The objective of NOC is indeed long-term profit maximization. However, being a public sector enterprise, the interest of the residual stakeholders (the citizens of the country) needs to be incorporated in the decision. If we were to continue to lease the SSR from international markets, it would mean lost opportunity for the country to develop the technology within the country, utilize its shipyards, employ its people and save scarce foreign exchange resources. Moreover, the lease-rates are exorbitantly high compared to the cost of operating owned rigs.

NOC's choice made several key stakeholders happy—the government, the shipyards, the press and the politicians. However, there were many unhappy ones too—the drill site engineers, the operating managers, the acquisition department. However, everyone seemed to be happy that NOC decided to switch over to an advanced technology.

Application of microeconomic tools

An economic analysis of the situation gives further insights into the decision. The quality of decision analysis can be improved by applying microeconomics tools—trade-offs and expected value. The calculation of

Case study 13.1 continued

Case study 13.1 continued

the net payoffs at each node of the decision tree can be done using the concepts of revenues, sunk costs, fixed costs, variable costs, average costs, switching costs and opportunity costs.

Some basic assumptions:

- 5M barrels/year is an estimate of the annual production of each of the 40 rigs.
- Probability of success is 0.1 and 0.2 for JURs and SSRs respectively.
- \$20 includes the premium of \$2 for indigenous oil production over the international price of oil (please see discussion on opportunity costs in the following).
- All costs include the economic opportunity cost of capital at 10 per cent.
- \$50 million is the net of the 10 per cent salvage value of the JURs.

NOC produced 0.5 million barrels a day and on an average each drilling rig produced about 5 million barrels/year. Therefore the actual average revenue per rig is,

5 million barrels per year × \$20 per barrel = \$100 million/year

When the revenues from the wells drilled by JURs and SSRs are broken down, the contribution of each SSR is seen to be double that of each JUR. In the context of the current portfolio of rigs deployed, the total yearly oil production can be calculated. Weighted average of 25 JURs and 10 SSRs gives the oil production of each JUR and SSR to be 3.5 million and 7 million barrels per year, respectively. It is important to note that the rate of production and the potential revenues for JUR and SSR are the same at \$700 million. However, their expected values depend on their probabilities of success (please see the discussion on the 'Operationalization of the Decision Tree'.)

1. Sunk costs are those costs that are irrevocably committed to a particular use and cannot be recovered if NOC switches from JUR to SSR. In the case of NOC, the average sunk cost on each JUR owned by the company was over \$50 million.
2. Variable costs are costs that vary with the output. In this case the variable cost of operating JUR depends on the metres drilled. Therefore, the yearly variable cost of each JUR =

   Cost/Metre × Metres drilled per year = \$500 × 10,000 = \$5 million.

Case study 13.1 continued

Case study 13.1 continued

Table 13.1.2 provides a comparison of variable costs. It is interesting to note that adoption of SSR increases the variable costs. Thus, the motive for the adoption of new technology is not economies of scale but increased quality of operations (higher success ratios).

3. Average cost is the cost per unit of output. It takes into account both fixed and variable costs. In this case,

   yearly average cost of the SSR = Acquisition Cost/year + Variable Cost of drilling/year.

The total acquisition costs include the $5 million in switching costs, the one-time costs of changing over from JUR to SSR technology. The acquisition costs can be calculated by dividing the total acquisition costs by the technology life cycle of SSR (10 years). Similarly, the variable cost of drilling is the cost of drilling per metre multiplied by the total depth drilled per year.

Therefore total average cost (TAC) of international production = $100 M/10 + $400 × 10,000 = $14 million.

For indigenous construction, TAC = $110 M/10

4. Social opportunity cost is the amount that could have been earned by the residual stakeholders by committing the resource to its best alternative use. In this case, the shareholders are the citizens of the country. Hence, their social opportunity costs should be foremost in the investment decisions of NOC. As the country is not self-sufficient in oil, any further reduction in the production of oil would include opportunity costs of the country due to the depletion of foreign exchange and the reduction in employment opportunities in the oil sector. This figure would be higher than the opportunity cost to the company itself, the foregone profits. NOC could incorporate this opportunity cost by adding a premium of $2 per barrel to its revenues. This premium would increase the propensity of the company choosing the most appropriate technology to maximize its revenues.

The same logic applies to deciding the source of acquisition of the technology. NOC needs to explicitly consider the opportunity costs to the residual stakeholders of buying SSR from abroad. The three shipyards in the country currently constructing the JURs would be

Case study 13.1 continued

Case study 13.1 continued

underutilized if they got no contracts for SSRs. The social opportunity costs would include the amortized fixed expenses on the shipyards, the lost employment opportunities in ship construction industry and the loss of foreign exchange to the country. The total fixed costs in the three shipyards that built 2 JURs each is above $500 million. Another $250 million may be added to account for other opportunity costs to the country over a five year period. Hence, at least $5 million may be attributed to each SSR each year.

Operationalization of the decision tree

The raw data used in operationalizing the above economic concepts are given in Table 13.1.2:

Table 13.1.2
Data used to operationalize NOC's decision-making

DS	Own: $60,000/day (2)	Lease: $80,000/day (1) $600/meter	Variable Cost (VC):
SSR	Own: $30,000/day (1)	Lease: $50,000/day (9)	VC: $400/metre
SR	Own: $20,000/day (2)	Lease: $25,000/day (0)	VC: $500/metre
JUR	Own: $25,000/day	Lease: $30,000/day (0)	VC: $300/metre

The operationalized values can be used to calculate the net payoffs for each branch of the decision tree and the expected values of the net payoffs at each node. Figure 13.1.2 presents the expected values for a public sector enterprise like NOC with social opportunity costs. NOC

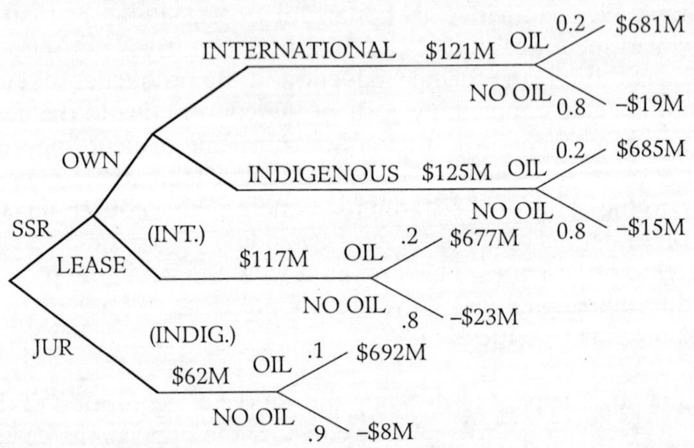

Strategic trade-offs and payoffs in new technology adoption (with social opportunity costs)

Figure 13.1.2
Decision tree for a public sector enterprise

Case study 13.1 continued

Case study 13.1 continued

has an expected saving of $160 million by acquiring SSRs from indigenous sources over an investment horizon of five years.

Net Payoffs and Trade-offs:
Net payoff = (Potential Revenue) – (Total Costs)
Potential Revenue = Estimated Value/Barrel ($20)* Potential Number of Barrels/Rig

SSR-International: Total Costs = Average Costs + Social Opportunity Costs
NP (SSR, Own, International, Oil) = (700M) – (14 + 5) = $681M
NP (SSR, Own, International, No Oil) = (0M) – (14 + 5) = –$19M

SSR-Indigenous: Total Costs = Average Costs
NP (SSR, Own, Indigenous, Oil) = (700M) – (15) = $685M
NP (SSR, Own, Indigenous, No Oil) = (0M) – (15) = –$15M
SSR-Lease: Total Costs = Yearly Lease Cost + Social Opportunity Costs
NP (SSR, Lease, Oil) = (700M)–(18 + 5) = $677M
NP (SSR, Lease, No Oil) = (0) – (18 + 5) = –$23M

JUR-Old: Total Costs = Variable Cost + Social Opportunity Costs
NP (JUR, Oil) = (700M) – (3M + 5M) = $692M
NP (JUR, No Oil) = (0M) – (3M + 5M) = –$8M

For NOC, investments in SSR can preserve flexibility by preventing lockout from a high technology and hence from oil exploration in deep waters. However, irrevocable investments in SSR could lead to complete dependence on this technology, leaving no options for revision. This could happen if the company decides to replace all JURs with newly acquired SSRs. Revisions in plans would be necessary if any of the assumptions change. For instance, if future geophysical surveys show that onshore sedimentary basins and coastal regions are more promising in terms of prognosticated oil reserves, NOC would be better off not drilling in deep waters using SSR. Also, if world oil prices plummet to below $12 per barrel, the country would be better off buying oil in international markets, rather than producing it offshore at a cost of above $12. NOC may choose to preserve its reserves rather than exploit it. In all these scenarios preserving the flexibility would certainly be valuable even if it costs a premium. Leasing SSRs from international contractors certainly provides such flexibility by enabling NOC to terminate the yearly lease contracts when circumstances change. This is

Case study 13.1 continued

Case study 13.1 continued

in line with the theories of dynamic strategic planning and system dynamics, which advocate building-in flexibility in planning models.

One may ask what is an acceptable 'premium for flexibility'? System dynamics suggests that flexibility can be 'improved' by incremental decision-making. The discipline, though, is silent on how much profits can be foregone (or 'premium paid') while opting for cautious stage-wise decisions instead of an all-out strategic commitment to any given course of action. More managerial tools are required to solve these complex issues.

In the example of NOC, the profit objective was focused upon, and the technology and social objectives were incorporated into the model as constraints. But when the criteria changes the decisions change. For instance, if NOC were a private sector enterprise, the social opportunity costs would not have been very close to the heart of the decision-makers of NOC and the most economically-viable decision would be to acquire semi-submersible rigs from international shipyards. A company needs to know where its stakeholders' heart really is. Economic tools help determine the price paid for the fulfilment of stakeholders' desires.

CASE STUDY 13.2

Investment Strategy: A Case Study of Private Banking*

Case study discussion topics

1. How did Mr and Mrs Yeh differ in their attitude towards investment?
2. How did Mr Yeh justify investments that lost money 9 times out of 10?
3. How did the author manage to satisfy both with a single portfolio?

Mr Yeh was an important private banking client of Bank X (name changed to preserve confidentiality), an American Bank. For more than 3 years now, Mr Yeh held a deposit of an average of $14 million with Bank X. He also maintained an account with three other international banks. The Yeh family was one of the leading furniture manufacturers in Taiwan.

*This case study is a summary of the case authored by Holly Li-Chen Yeh Liu.

Case study 13.2 continued

Case study 13.2 continued

Mr Yeh was confident of his very reliable furniture business and unafraid to take great risks in his personal investments. He had some knowledge about financial markets, foreign exchange markets and risky derivative products. Owing in part to his unsophisticated knowledge and high-risk tolerance, Mr Yeh had lost $3 million in the foreign exchange market a couple of years ago. As a result, he had now decided to return to the foreign exchange market to recover his loss. Unlike her husband, Mrs Yeh was conservative, risk averse and disapproved of her husband's speculative activities in the foreign exchange market. She preferred keeping the deposit as a 'nest egg' to support her children's education and the factories' future expansion (Figure 13.2.1 gives the difference in risk tolerances of Mr and Mrs Yeh). One fine morning, Mrs Yeh came to Bank X to close the Yeh account and put an end to Mr Yeh's speculative activities.

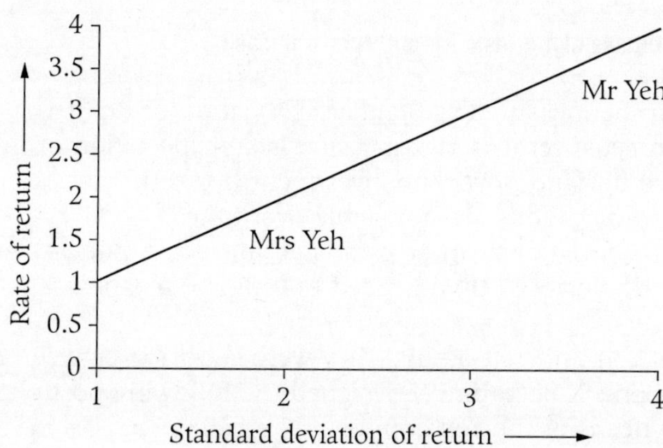

Figure 13.2.1
The difference in risk tolerance of Mr and Mrs Yeh

While banks reap substantial profits from the 'foreign exchange speculation' product (sometimes called 'Margin Trading Accounts'), fewer than 10 per cent of clients/investors profit from this product that is subject to a highly volatile market. However, in the interest of Bank X's business, an optimal investment strategy had to be created for Mr Yeh by using economic tools to optimize his deposit with the bank. Bank X had to identify the level of risk that would encourage investors like Mr Yeh move up to an efficient portfolio with an expected return. It is to be noted that greater risk aversion moves the solution closer to the minimum risk

Case study 13.2 continued

Case study 13.2 continued

portfolio and less risk aversion moves the solution farther out to the 'Wing' of the frontier. Figure 13.2.2 presents this trade-off.

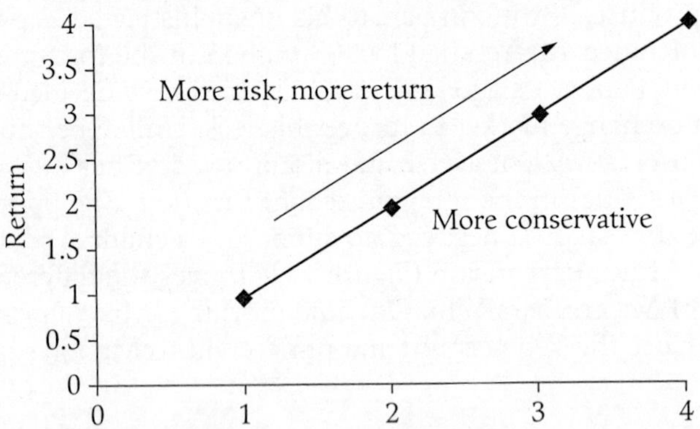

Figure 13.2.2
Higher return entails higher risk: Mr and Mrs Yeh clash

- Risk can be measured as Standard Deviation of Return.
- Like expected returns, risk measure is an expectation of the standard deviation over the investment horizon.
- Standard deviations are not stable over time.
- Standard deviations can be estimated more accurately with a shorter time period elapsed than needed to estimate means.

Mr and Mrs Yeh understood that they were choosing between risk and return and Bank X accordingly designed the following portfolio that included all needs of the Yeh couple.

- Use one year Time Deposit Rate as the scale of measurement (say 6 per cent per annum for US Dollars Time Deposit).
- Use the 6 per cent interest earnings to invest in a high risk/high return vehicle (for example, Margin Trading, Small Stock IPO and so on). Investing only this sum would ensure zero capital loss, thus protecting Mrs Yeh's 'nest egg'. For example, \$100 becomes \$106 at the end of the year. A high risk investment of \$6 leaves the original capital of \$100 secure even if all \$6 is lost (an unlikely result).

The Yeh couple was satisfied with the above arrangement as a means to protect their capital. With the expectation of earning more profit, they determined to distribute their deposit as—(*a*) use US Dollars as base currency, but as a lot of the Yeh business was with Japan, most of the

Case study 13.2 continued

Case study 13.2 continued

income would be valued in Japanese Yen, (*b*) keep 47 per cent of the deposit in non-US Government Bonds, and 47 per cent in Treasury Bills, and (*c*) use one year as the investment time horizon. The expected return in percentage is as shown in Table 13.2.1. Thus, Mr Yeh got his high-risk speculation, Mrs Yeh got her risk-free nest egg and Bank X successfully retained the Yeh account.

Table 13.2.1
Expected return in percentage

	Expected return (in per cent)	*Standard deviation (in per cent)*
Treasury Bill	7.5	2.6
Non-US Government Bond	11.9	13.9

Expected return = Arithmetic mean return for 1970–91
Standard deviation = Standard deviation of annual return for 1970–91

CASE STUDY 13.3

Sundram Fasteners Ltd.–Turning Uncertainty into Calculated Risks

With turnover of over $160 million, Sundram Fasteners Ltd. (SFL) is one of India's leading auto components manufacturer. A part of the TVS group, which has around 51 per cent stake in the company, SFL manufactures high-tensile fasteners, automotive components, automotive and other miscellaneous cold formed/extruded parts, powder metal parts, iron powders, radiator caps, gear shifters and tyre carriers. Being India's largest manufacturer of high-tensile fasteners, which find application primarily in the automobile sector, 70 per cent of SFL's production caters to the demand from this sector.

Driven by the mission of becoming a vibrant, dynamic, customer-oriented global company through technology and quality initiatives, SFL was looking for new avenues of growth in 1992. Although, having tripled its turnover every 5 years and having achieved a phenomenal annual compounded growth rate of 14 per cent, SFL aspired to grow at a faster rate. With the Indian market growing at only 5–6 per cent, the top management at SFL resolved that they needed to have a game plan or

Case study 13.3 continued

Case study 13.3 continued

strategy that would propel the achievement of the company's aspirational growth targets. The company was always at the forefront to pick up new technology and manufacturing excellence was one of SFL's key strengths, which it decided to leverage.

General Motors, the US auto giant, manufactured among many automobile components, radiator caps used in cars. As part of a process of consolidating its business around a set of core activities, GM was eager to get out of the radiator caps business and wanted its manufacturing plant (which manufactured 5 million caps per annum) to be bought by a company that could manufacture radiator caps for and supply them to GM, giving GM significant cost savings. SFL won the bid and agreed to supply GM its entire requirement of radiator caps. It also took on the risk of entering a business that was completely unknown to it. Taking on the radiator caps business involved several financial, customer, process and people-related challenges that SFL had to cope with.

Financial risks

- GM being the only foreign customer of SFL, a collapse in GM's business would have a direct impact on SFL's radiator caps business.
- Financing the whole deal was a major issue.
- Committing a lion's share of its financial resources to the radiator caps project, SFL was unsure of the impact it would have on its ability to fund other projects.
- SFL had to think of ways to meet the cost reduction commitment it had made to GM as part of the condition to get the contract.
- SFL was unsure if the 5 million per year volume was enough to run the business profitably.

Challenges on the customer front

- SFL had to come up with solutions to reduce cost of the radiator caps.
- SFL had to ensure continued supply of radiator caps from its proposed factory to ensure that GM's production line was kept running at all times (any disruption of radiator caps supply from SFL's India plant to GM's car manufacturing facilities could bring the GM plant to a grinding halt, as the cars cannot be released into the market without radiator caps!).
- SFL had to explore whether there were possibilities of selling the radiator caps to customers other than GM and would have to

Case study 13.3 continued

Case study 13.3 continued

determine carefully if GM would have any objection to such a possibility.

- SFL had to prepare itself for the possibility of the radiator caps technology becoming redundant a few years down the road.
- India had no presence in world markets in precision manufacturing of any kind, let alone for meeting the highly-stringent demands of the global auto industry. This project would be the 'flag bearer' for Indian precision manufacturing industry into the world markets. Customer mindsets on Indian products had to be changed.

Challenges on the processes front

- SFL had to determine if it had the capability of manufacturing 5 million radiator caps annually to meet the stringent norms of GM.
- SFL had to ensure it met the quality requirements of the product, had to figure out the supplying logistics, raw material sourcing logistics from global sources and find ways of making the product (radiator caps) supplies to GM just in time (JIT) as GM was not interested in holding this item in its inventories.

Challenges on the people front

- People working at SFL had no knowledge of radiator caps, nor knew the basics of how to manufacture it. The business had no synergy with what SFL was doing at that time.

Despite the several challenges and uncertainties of entering the radiator caps business, SFL's top management felt that the strategic fit of the deal was perfect. SFL saw an opportunity to enter a large market space with high-growth potential and hence opted to take the plunge. In other words, SFL took the 'irrational route'. It signed an agreement with GM to supply its entire requirement of radiator caps and undertook several key initiatives to meet the demands of the agreement, innovating every step of the way. In retrospect, the company took *calculated risks and made the right decisions in an uncertain world.*

Notes

1. The Patton quote, and story, is drawn from S. Maital, *Minds, Markets & Money* (New York: Basic Books, 1982), p. 202.
2. Adam Smith, *The Money Game* (New York: Alfred Knopf, 1976).

3. The definition of risk is from Susan Lee, *ABZ's of money and finance: From annuities to zero coupon bonds* (New York: Poseidon Press, 1988), p. 180.
4. Data on Royal Dutch/Shell are from the *Forbes Global 2000* (special issue, 18 April 2005). The story of Royal Dutch/Shell's scenario analysis is found in *The Living Company*, pp. 50–54.
5. The 'Varieties of Risk' section is based on an article in *Business Week Online*, 5 May 2005, by Standard & Poor's Beth Piskora.
6. The story of Long Term Capital Management is fascinatingly told in a Public Broadcasting Service 'Nova' programme, The Trillion Dollar Bet, available from www.pbs.org.
7. The seminal Black-Scholes formula article is Fisher Black and Myron Scholes, 'The pricing of options and corporate liabilities', *Journal of Political Economy*, 81, May–June 1973, pp. 637–54.
8. The first thorough statement of the idea that projects involving risk are similar to real options is: Robert Pindyck and Avinash Dixit, *Investment Under Uncertainty* (Princeton NJ: Princeton University Press, 1994).
9. Analyzing projects as real options is explained by Timothy Luehhrman, 'Investment Opportunities as Real Options: Getting Started on the Numbers', *Harvard Business Review*, July–August 1998.
10. Data on insurance and gambling are taken from the Fortune 1,000 database (*Fortune*, 18 April 2005, pp. F-56, F57–58).
11. The pair choice used as an example of psychological research on risk taking is based on D. Kahneman and A. Tversky, 'Prospect Theory', *Econometrica*, 1979, p. 267.
12. The 'overweighing of certain outcomes' is described in Kahneman and Tversky (1979), p. 265.
13. The 'early trend' finding is described in Tversky and Kahneman (1971) (p.109).
14. For a critical review of Kahneman's and Tversky's research and a comprehensive bibliography, see S. Maital, 'Daniel Kahneman: On Redefining Rationality', *Journal of Socio-economics*, 33 (2004), pp. 1–14.
15. The belief that punishing failure is more effective than rewarding success, against clear evidence, is explained in Kahneman and Tversky, *Psychological Review*, 1973, p. 251.
16. The link between confidence and high performance is found in Kahneman and Tversky (1994), p. 249.
17. 'Framing' is discussed in Kahneman and Tversky (1982), p. 139.
18. Ignoring risk reduction through risk pooling is descibed in Kahneman, Knetsch and Thaler, *Journal of Business* (1986), p. 128.
19. Risk affinity toward loss, risk aversion toward gain, is described in Kahneman and Tversky (1982), p. 13; and Tversky and Kahneman (1991), p. 143.
20. Overweighing of low probabilities is discussed in Kahneman and Tversky (1982), p.138; also Kahneman and Tversky (1979).
21. The case for 'paternalism' is in Kahneman (1994), pp. 758, 760.

Chapter 14
Competing by collaborating

Each organic being is striving to increase at a geometrical ratio; ... each generation ... has to struggle for life, and to suffer great destruction ... death is generally prompt, ... and the vigorous, the healthy and the happy survive and multiply.

—Charles Darwin[1]

I am a firm believer in both an individual and a team effort ... I could have done little without the support of colleagues. We have worked together as a strong and motivated team as indeed we did on Mount Everest.

—Sir Edmund Hillary[2]

LEARNING OBJECTIVES After you read this chapter, you should understand:

- **Why collaboration is a new stage in globalization**
- **How to analyse conflict with a 2×2 strategy matrix**
- **How to understand critical-mass markets and market 'tornados'**
- **How to strategize price wars**
- **How convergence of technologies creates new industries and demands collaborative skills**
- **How to implement product platforms and platform leadership**
- **How to collaborate with customers by identifying promoters and detractors, and learning why they exist**
- **How to build excellence in teamwork within organizations as winning sports teams do**

TOOL #10
The 2×2 Strategy matrix

14.1 INTRODUCTION

In this concluding chapter, we explore the complex interaction between competing and collaborating. The chapter's core message is paradoxical:

> In order to compete successfully, managers need to collaborate—with other managers, with their suppliers, with their colleagues and workers, with their customers, and at times, within legal limits, even with their competitors. Skill in teamwork and cooperative effort is an essential ingredient in every successful competitive strategy.

In other words, competing successfully in global markets will increasingly require the kind of high-level collaboration mindset that made Edmund Hillary the first to reach the summit of Everest at 11:30 A.M. on 29 May 1953, along with Tenzing Norgay. Indian entrepreneur Narayana Murthy, founder of the global software giant Infosys, puts it as follows:

> The development of a product or service might typically be split among countries, with experts in America defining the customer requirements; the British defining the product attributes; the Australians defining the technology architecture; the Indians doing the software development; the Germans or the Japanese doing the manufacturing; and the Taiwanese doing the packaging. *This new business model will distribute high-quality jobs around the world and deepen international collaboration.*[3]

Increasingly managers will be asked to cultivate an Eastern yin-yang philosophy of performing an action and its opposite at one and the same time. In Darwin's language: Collaboration is an adaptive attribute that makes organizations more competitive, hence fit to survive. Increasingly, it will be those most skilled at cooperative teamwork who will compete best and grow geometrically.

Chapter 8 focused on the central organizing principle of societies all around the world—the economic theory of market-based competition. There, we noted that 'on November 9, 1989, the Berlin Wall fell. This was the signal that the entire world had embraced the economic notion of "survival of the fittest" (free and open competition in free markets) as its organizing principle.'

Globally, a growing number of markets and industries are characterized by what may be called *hyper-competition*—fierce competition characterized by falling prices, commoditization, cost reduction, abrupt erosion of profit margins and rapid exit and entry of firms. This chapter will show why survival in such markets requires a managerial mindset that blends *hard-nosed competitive energy* with *sensitive collaborative skills*. The primary tool employed will be a once-esoteric branch of mathematics known as game theory, invented just over 60 years ago, which has emerged from obscure scholarly journals to become one of the most insightful and practical frameworks in economics for exploring strategic relationships among people, groups, companies, industries and countries and specifically, for successfully resolving the paradoxical tension between the urge to win and the need to help others win.

The title of the 1994 version of this chapter, in *Executive Economics*, was 'Competing by *Cooperating*'. The title of this chapter is 'Competing by *Collaborating*'. The difference is subtle but important.

'Collaborate' comes from two Latin words, '*com*', together with, and '*laborare*', to work or labour. 'Cooperate' comes from '*com*' and '*operari*', to *do work*, derived in turn from the noun '*opus*', a work. Collaborating has, we believe, a connotation of *high-level* cooperation, focused on the *process* of working together rather than the result or output. As with many management issues, attaining an optimal product through collaboration depends vitally on the somewhat counterintuitive notion of furthering the interests of others in order to achieve our own goals.

Globalization, release 4.0

According to *New York Times* columnist Tom Friedman, there were three stages or versions, of globalization.[4]

Globalization 1.0 (1492 to 1800) shrank the world from a size large to a size medium and the dynamic force in that era was countries globalizing for resources and imperial conquest. Globalization 2.0 (1800 to 2000) shrank the world from a size medium to a size small, and it was spearheaded by companies globalizing for markets and labour. Globalization 3.0 (which started around 2000) is shrinking the world from a size small to a size tiny and flattening the playing field at the same time. The dynamic force in Globalization 3.0 is individuals and small groups globalizing.

Each stage had a different focus. We believe we are embarking on a fourth stage. To summarize:

Globalization 1.0

The focus was the *world*—opening trade and communications. Political scientist Robert Gilpin notes that under the British Empire, globalization was perhaps more advanced even than today:

> As the 21st century opens, the world is not as well integrated as it was ... prior to World War I. Under the gold standard and the influential doctrine of laissez-faire, for example, the decades prior to World War I were an era when markets were truly supreme and governments had little power over economic affairs.[5]

Globalization 2.0

The focus was *countries*—some countries joined global markets, and some were left out. China, India, Korea, Taiwan, Singapore—all benefited by focusing country-level strategies aimed at leveraging competencies for global advantage, growth and exports. Much of Africa was sidelined.

Globalization 3.0

The focus was *individuals*. Digital technology plus white-collar professional outsourcing, for instance, meant that Boston's Massachusetts General Hospital could outsource its radiology to Indian radiologists, whose salary was a fourth that of American doctors, simply by e-mailing digitized X-rays and receiving in return the diagnosis. The message: If your job can be digitized, then you face fierce new competition from professionals halfway around the world. MIT Professor Paul Samuelson has even argued that the United States may be a net *loser* from globalization, because low-wage skilled labour abroad competes with US white collar professionals and permanently reduces their incomes.[6] Can you export heart surgery? Apparently, yes. Americans can travel to India to get triple bypass surgery done by a US-trained Indian surgeon at one-fourth the cost. It is not difficult to understand the impact on American heart surgeons' incomes. This example may be replicated across a large proportion of white-collar professional skills.

Continuing Friedman's argument, we believe that we are today deep into Globalization 4.0.

Globalization 4.0

The focus is *teamwork*, networking and collaboration. In this phase, competing successfully involves global deployment, seamlessly integrating skills, people, capital, and knowledge around the world in collaborative efforts whose metaphor is a smooth well-oiled machine—a machine whose gears mesh quietly and powerfully to drive the business and delight customers.

A recent survey of nearly 200 senior global executives by *The Economist* and Agilent revealed that Globalization 4.0 and Infosys' Narayana Murthy's vision has become best-practice in R&D. Globalized R&D teams are now a core competency of innovation-driven global companies. The study reports: 'From Bangalore to Beijing, R&D organizations are splitting up research and design work, distributing it around the globe and re-assembling the results. Around half of the survey group manage R&D multinationally, either through global teams that work on pieces of the same problem or via regional R&D resources that support several national markets.'[7]

DEFINITION

- **Collaboration: The act of working together, with the success of *others* as well as your own as a central goal ('win-win').**

The fundamental logic of Globalization 4.0 is simple to state and extremely difficult to implement. It is this. Strategy games in business are not played only one time. They are usually played repeatedly by engineers and managers. If so, then:

- If I win and you win ('win-win'), we are both happy and the result is relatively stable.
- If I win, and you lose ('win-lose'), I may be happy now. But you will probably find a way to shift the situation to lose-lose, by taking revenge (e.g., by slashing your prices) in future rounds of the game. This situation, too, is relatively stable, but we are both unhappy. And lose-lose is wasteful and inefficient.

This chapter has four sections. The first is about how to collaborate with your *competitors*. The second is about collaboration with your *industry*—with your fellow workers, suppliers and those who form part of your value chain. The third is about collaborating with your *customers*. And the last section deals with teamwork—collaborating with your *colleagues*, which, surprisingly, managers sometimes find the most challenging of all.

14.2 COLLABORATING WITH COMPETITORS

Anti-trust and anti-cartel laws in the US and Europe forbid companies from colluding to fix prices or limit competition. But within these legal limits, there are many tacit and overt ways that companies can join together to enlarge and grow their industry for mutual gain rather than slice and dice a constant pool of revenue and profit at others' expense. This is a 'win-win' solution. Many who use this phrase may not know that its origins lie in an obscure branch of mathematics known as game theory.

Game theory: Collaborating with competitors

There is nothing more powerful than good theory, it has been said. There are two approaches to knowing whether a theory is good. One is academic, classroom-based: Does the data fit the theory's predictions? Another is practical, field-based: Does the theory, when implemented, generate good results?

Game theory is a good example of a theory originally understood by a small handful of mathematicians that ultimately moved from the classroom to the boardroom and changed the world. As J.M. Keynes once said in his 1936 book, *General Theory*, 'It is ideas, not vested interests, that are forces for good or evil.' The enormous impact of game theory is a strong case study.

Game theory originated in the brilliant mind of Hungarian-born mathematician John von Neumann who specialized in solving unsolvable problems. Emigrating to the Institute for Advanced Study, in Princeton, NJ, in the early 1930s, von Neumann teamed with former Austrian economist Oskar Morgenstern to write *Theory of Games and Economic Behavior* in 1944. In games of strategy, Morgenstern wrote retrospectively, 'each participant is striving for his greatest advantage in situations where the outcome depends not only on his actions alone, nor solely on those of nature, but also on those of other participants whose interests are sometimes opposed, sometimes parallel, to his own.'[8] Since the actions of others are not known with certainty, Morgenstern observed, each player faces uncertainty.

If what I do depends on what my opponent does, and if I have no clue as to what my opponent will do, nor does he or she know what I will do clearly, the result must be utterly unknowable, correct?

Surprisingly no, not correct. Von Neumann and Morgenstern found remarkable ways to solve this problem, to learn when we can indeed predict behaviour in game situations and how to define optimal or rational strategy.

A decade later, it was again at Princeton University that another brilliant flash of insight forever changed the way we think about business and management.

A beautiful mind

John Nash won a Nobel Prize in Economics mainly for two scholarly papers, written when he was a Princeton University graduate student in mathematics, that not only changed forever the way economists think but also changed the lives of ordinary people. In the film *A Beautiful Mind*, about Nash, a scene, apparently apocryphal, shows Nash in a bar with his friends and some attractive female students. In a flash of insight, Nash sees the fatal flaw in conventional economics.[9]

According to Adam Smith's model, individuals selfishly striving to do the best they can for themselves will optimize the market result. Smith's famous quote from *Wealth of Nations* (1776) stresses this: 'It is not from the benevolence of the butcher, the brewer, or the baker, that we expect our dinner, but from their regard to their own interest.' Our daily bread apparently comes from the baker's avarice, not his altruism, and from the fruits of competitive selfishness.

But this, Nash saw, is not the case! Why? Suppose all of us compete for the blonde! We're all trying to do the best we can for ourselves. But if we all mob the blonde, she will leave and none of us will gain her friendship. This result is far from optimal. The reason: *None of us took into account the strategic effects of what others are likely to do in addition to thinking about our own behaviour.* In other words: we competed so fiercely, we ruined things for everyone. It is lose-lose. In this case, single-minded 'survival of the fittest' leaves no-one fit to survive. And it happens all the time.

Nash went on to write two seminal papers that applied the then-novel tool of game theory to strategic behaviour. In his papers, he explores the result when players take into account how others will respond to their own strategies. The result revolutionized the way economists think about markets, market behaviour and competition.

Soon after he wrote his seminal papers, Nash was afflicted with paranoid schizophrenia. Never again was he able to do significant research. Yet those two graduate papers were so original and revolutionary they completely changed the direction of economic research.

Game theory has become a powerful applied tool for managers in devising their competitive strategies. A simple 2×2 game matrix (two players, two strategies) can yield surprising insights into the dynamics of market behaviour. Rapoport has shown that 78 different strategic games can emerge from this exceptionally simple 2×2 model!

Here is a brief description of this 2×2 framework. Before presenting this tool, we begin with a case study: The first author's own decision to abandon a beloved old MAC SE30 and buy a PC, narrated in first person.

Case study: MAC vs PC

I bought an Apple MacIntosh (MAC) SE-30 in 1985 and used it for 10 years. It was by far the best computer I ever owned, before or since. After I bought the MAC, I took it out of the box, switched it on and it was ready to go to work for me in 30 seconds. Using simple easy-to-use software, I could produce clear graphs with one click. The desktop operating system precursor to Windows was marvellous and infallible. In 1995, with deep regret, I bought a PC not because I had fallen out of love with the MAC, or because the SE30 didn't work (it still did) but because nearly everyone else by now was using PCs and more important, nearly everyone was writing software applications for PCs, not for MACs and it was highly inconvenient to be out-of-step. Out of sentiment, I kept the MAC for years after it had been mothballed.

Here is a tool that helps us understand this MAC versus PC game, and many other strategic games—the strategy matrix.

The 2×2 strategy matrix

'Simplify as much as possible', Albert Einstein said, 'but not more so'. Suppose that a competitive situation can be simplified, so that each of two players (perhaps, 'me' and 'others') has to choose between one of two strategies (for instance, 'buy a MAC' and 'buy a PC'). There are thus four possible outcomes to this game.

While this 2×2 framework is highly simplified, it is capable of capturing key elements of strategic dilemmas. Which of the four outcomes will be the eventual result? Is there a win-win outcome? Is there a stable outcome? Which of the two strategies is best for me? for my counterpart? Is there a strategy that is best for me, whatever my counterpart does? To answer these questions, carry out the following steps.

1. If each of two players chooses between two strategies, there are four possible outcomes. Draw a matrix with four cells corresponding to the four outcomes (Figure 14.1). There are two rows, one for each strategy chosen by my counterpart 'others' (Row Player). There are two columns, one for each strategy chosen by myself (Column Player).
2. For each of the four cells, or outcomes, calculate its payoff value twice: once, from the point of view of 'me' (the player who chooses the 'column') and once, from the point of view of 'others' (the player who chooses the row). [Note: this in itself is a powerful insight of game theory—to succeed, you must be as sensitive to, and knowledgeable about, your adversary or counterpart, as you are about your own.]

others \ me	BUY PC	BUY MAC
BUY PC	4, *4*	3, *1*
BUY MAC	1, *3*	2, *2*

Figure 14.1
2×2 Strategy matrix

3. In each cell, write one of four numbers: 1, 2, 3 or 4, where '1' indicates a low value or payoff or score, and '4' indicates a high value or payoff or score. The first number is the payoff for the row player 'others'; the second number in each cell is the payoff for the column player 'me'. Alternately, if you can, use real payoff values (net profit, for instance).
4. Now, analyse the resulting matrix. Ask:
   (*i*) Is there a dominant strategy for me (i.e., one of the two columns is always best for me, no matter what my counterpart does)?
   (*ii*) Is there a dominant strategy for my counterpart (i.e., one of the two rows is always best for him or her, no matter what I do)?
   (*iii*) Is there a 'Nash equilibrium'—an outcome, such that neither player, my adversary or I have any incentive to change the strategy?

DEFINITION

- **Nash equilibrium: In his seminal papers, John Nash defined what is now known as a Nash equilibrium: an outcome (in the 2×2 matrix, one of the four cells), such that no individual player has any incentive to unilaterally alter his or her strategy.**

The first number in each cell indicates the payoff for the player ('others') who chooses the row. The numbers represent the size of payoffs, not ranks of outcome. So '4' is the best, while '1' is the worst. The second number in each cell is the payoff for the player who chooses the column (in this case, 'me').

Studying this matrix reveals that it portrays a very common market situation known as 'critical mass'. Its logic is as follows:

- If I buy a MAC, and so does everyone, we all attain our next-to-worst outcome '2', because MAC's closed architecture leads to a paucity of software for everyone.
- If I stick to the MAC while everyone else buys a PC, I am worst off ('1'), while others are 'next-to-best-off' ('3') and vice versa when I buy a PC, and others buy a MAC I am 'next-to-best-off' ('3') and the others are worst off ('1'). But if very few buy a PC, I have no incentive to buy one myself.
- If everyone buys a PC, everyone is best off, since the broad market lowers prices of PC clones and generates large amounts of software.
- To shift the market from MAC (2,2) [a Nash equilibrium] to PC (4,4) [also a Nash equilibrium], a *critical mass* of PC buyers is needed. Once that critical mass is attained, the market 'tips' and very quickly shifts

from MACs to PCs. The critical mass can be 80 per cent of computer buyers—or it can be as little as 1–2 per cent, provided the latter are opinion leaders (for instance, renowned surgeons who endorse a new surgical instrument).

Author Malcolm Gladwell describes this phenomenon brilliantly in his book *The Tipping Point.*[10] His basic idea is 'ideas spread like plagues'. So do winning products. Very large groups of people can be brought to change their behaviour, e.g., to buy a new product, like the iPod, very quickly, when a critical mass forms, almost the way epidemics of contagious diseases spread from one person to another.

Those who bring to market innovative products face the marketing challenge of generating a critical mass or a tornado.[11] Sometimes, it can be done by giving the product away for free. Once there is a large enough installed base, profits can be made indirectly. Netscape gave away its Internet browser, created a large customer base and then used it to sell expensive networking software.

Note that the (2,2) outcome in Figure 14.1 is a Nash equilibrium. I will not alone buy a PC if no one else does, nor will anyone else, alone. So 'Buy MAC' for all players is a stable, Nash equilibrium. But if a sufficient coalition of people buy PCs, more than N*, then suddenly, the market 'tips' and everyone buys PCs. So the (4,4) outcome, 'Buy PC', is *also* a stable Nash equilibrium. This can be what Geoffrey Moore calls a 'tornado'—a storm of buyers or a period of mass-market adoption, when the general market switches over from the old product to the new one, often at blinding speed. In the age of Internet, cell phones and instant communications, such 'tornados' happen often.

Figure 14.2 shows another way of portraying this 'tipping model'. Let the 'perceived value from the computer for a typical user' vary with 'the proportion using PCs', for MACs and PCs. There are two such curves: one for PCs, one for MACs. If everyone uses MACs, MACs create superior perceived value. But as more persons use PCs, and hence more PC software is available, the utility of PCs rises and that of MACs declines (Figure 14.2). This process was strengthened by Apple's decision to close the MAC architecture, i.e., try to prevent outside software providers from taking away what they saw as Apple's business, by not revealing the software code of the MAC operating system, while PC architecture was open, to both PC producers who made 'clones' and to software developers.

The 'tipping point' is N*. Until N* people buy PCs, the MAC utility is still superior. In principle, if less than N* people buy PCs, their disappointment will ultimately lead everyone to shift back to MACs. But once MORE than N* people buy PCs, ultimately EVERYONE will buy them.

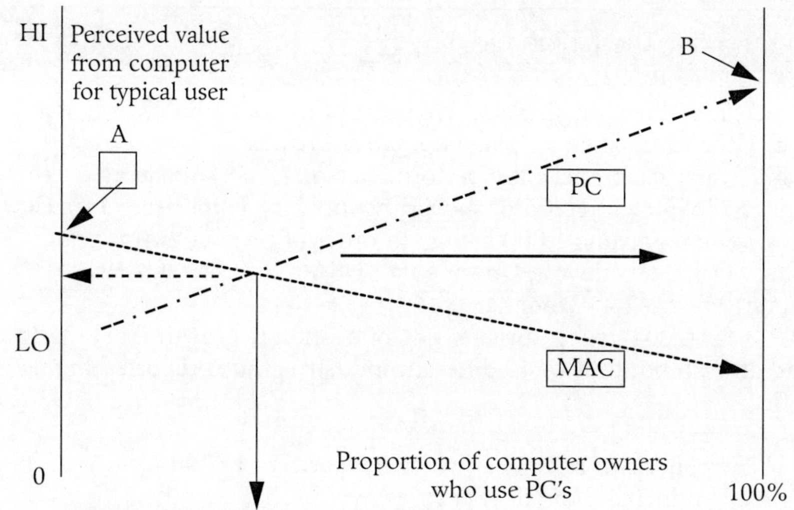

Figure 14.2
'Tipping model' for PC vs MAC

The higher the perceived value of a MAC or PC, the more people use each. Once N* per cent of computer users buy PCs, everyone follows suit, leading the market to point B; but if less than N* per cent buy PCs, then everyone eventually buys MACs. The market is won by the product that can generate 'tornado' effects (superior perceived value, leading to more people buying it, which in turn itself creates higher value and so on) and can achieve the *tipping* value N*.

Action learning

Analysing Conflict and Strategy with a 2×2 Strategy Matrix

Consider a business, or personal, conflict in which you are at present involved. Define two alternate strategies, for yourself and for your counterpart. Built the 2×2 strategy matrix. Fill in each cell with outcomes for yourself and your counterpart. Is there a way to move both of you to a better outcome? How?

you

counterpart	strategy 1	strategy 2

Case study: The airline industry

We have a recurring nightmare. We dream that we are in charge of a major US airline. Then we wake up in a cold sweat.

Fortune magazine tracks the performance of 47 US industries. Here is the incredible track record of the airline industry, comprising 11 airlines in the annual Fortune 1,000 listing, in order of revenues: American, United, Delta, Northwest, Continental, USAir, Southwest, Alaska, America West, ATA, Expressjet.

In a year (2004) when 'a rising tide of economic growth lifted many a Boat' and 'all but four of 42 different industry groups reported higher profits':

- US airlines saw revenues rise by 9.9 per cent in 2004 (close to the median increase for all industries), yet in that year their losses tripled; from 1999–2004, profits declined by approximately 20 per cent yearly, the worst of all industries.
- Airlines lost 7.6 per cent on every revenue dollar, next-to-worst of any industry, in 2004.
- Airlines lost 6 per cent on every dollar of assets in 2004, and had negative return on shareholders' equity.

In total return to shareholders (which measures stock and dividend performance), the airlines were 47th out of 47 industries in 2004, and in the period 1999–2004 and in the entire *decade* 1994–2004. If you bought a basket of shares of the 11 airlines in 1994, they are worth far less today.

Why has this industry done so badly? (There is a major exception: Southwest Airlines, the only one of the top 10 US airlines to be profitable in 2004). In 2005, only two of the ten largest airlines (Southwest and Skywest) were profitable.

There were external factors—jet fuel costs, which rose 40 per cent in 2004, 9/11 and the resulting decline in air travel, deregulation and entry of new low-cost airlines.

But there was also an internal factor—incessant, fierce, bitter price wars that occur regularly. Travellers benefit in the short run. But in the long run they too will suffer if airlines disappear and flight frequencies shrink.

What insights can the 2×2 strategy matrix yield?

Source: Data on US Airlines: 'Fortune 1000' issue, *Fortune*, 18 April 2005.

Figure 14.3 applies the 2×2 strategy framework. There are two competitors, say, American Airlines and United Airlines and two decisions: keep fares stable or lower them. United reasons as follows:

United \ American	Lower prices	Stable prices
Lower prices	2, 2	4, 1
Stable prices	1, 4	3, 3

Figure 14.3
Prisoner's dilemma

> If we keep our prices stable, and American lowers theirs, we lose (we get '1', the worst; they get '4', the best), because they grab all the customers in this highly price-sensitive industry. But if we lower our fares and they keep theirs stable, we get '4'. The worst that can happen is that we both end up with '2'. So, United lowers their prices, both to try to exploit American and to protect themselves against being exploited.

Since the matrix is symmetric, the same reasoning applies to American. Lowering prices is a dominant strategy for both. The (2,2) outcome is a 'Nash equilibrium'. Once there, neither airline has any reason to raise its prices. And they both lose heavily.

Persistent price wars break out in air fares, and the result is that all the airlines lose out; the (2,2) outcome is stable (neither player will raise prices unilaterally).

This type of conflict is known as Prisoner's Dilemma. It was first presented by Princeton University mathematician Abraham Tucker. The name Prisoner's Dilemma comes from the following story.

> Two prisoners rob a bank and are caught. The police lack evidence. They interrogate each robber separately. Each is told, cooperate, 'squeal' (slang for 'give evidence') and the Judge may go easy on you. The dominant

strategy for each is to 'squeal'. The result is a long sentence for each; if each had remained silent, they may have both been acquitted.

This is quickly recognized as a version of the Price War, where 'cutting prices' is equivalent to 'squeal'. What is rather unique about this conflict, is that the dominant strategy for each player (slash prices, or 'squeal') leads to an inferior outcome (lose-lose) for both. (Just ask the airlines.) The question arises—is there some way to collaborate in this situation? An answer is provided by political scientist Robert Axelrod.

The evolution of cooperation

Political scientist Robert Axelrod once organized a clever tournament. Fourteen computer programmes, or algorithms, played a 2×2 'compete or cooperate' Prisoner's Dilemma game against each other.[12] Each contest went on for 200 'rounds', where a round was a decision by each programme. The payoff matrix (in points) was:

	Compete	Cooperate
Compete	1,1	5,0
Cooperate	0,5	3,3

The winning algorithm was also the simplest: 'Tit for Tat', i.e., start by playing 'cooperate' and thereafter copy what the opponent does. The top-scoring algorithms all had the following properties: they were

a) *'nice'* (i.e., they tried to achieve 3,3); many were also
b) *forgiving* (switched to 'cooperate' if the opponent did, without exacting revenge), and
c) *clear* (it was clear to the opponent what the reaction would be).

There are subtle reasons for the individual pragmatist to be *nice, forgiving and optimistic*, Axelrod concluded.

In business conflicts, too, these three characteristics together can achieve win-win outcomes even when rational behaviour seemingly dictates highly egoistic competitive strategies. As Adam Brandenburger and Barry Nalebuff observe, in their book *Coopetition*, 'Business is simultaneous war and peace ... you have to compete and cooperate at the same time .... You can compete without having to kill the opposition. If fighting to the death destroys the pie, there'll be nothing left to capture. In business your success doesn't require others to fail—there can be multiple winners.'[13]

Collaboration to create and build an industry is a strong example.

14.3 COLLABORATING WITH THE INDUSTRY

One reason why collaborative teamwork dominates Globalization 4.0 is that increasingly, innovative products comprise portfolios of diverse technologies, each requiring a different kind of expertise. Few organizations can command world-class expertise in every technology. When technologies converge into innovative products, collaboration is vital for survival.

Technology portfolios in innovative products are hardly novel. In the 1930s, the DC-3, one of the world's most durable, profitable and long-lived aircraft, combined over a dozen innovative technologies. But today, convergence is the rule rather than the exception. Here are two case studies.

Case study: MIT media centre

MIT Computer Science Professor Nicholas Negroponte used Figure 14.4 to make the case for founding the MIT Media Lab. In the 1970s, he argued that convergence of three once-separate industries—broadcasting, printing and publishing and computing—would require collaboration, since incumbents in one industry lacked the skills prevalent in the other two, for survival and success. The MIT Media Lab explores such innovative collaborations.

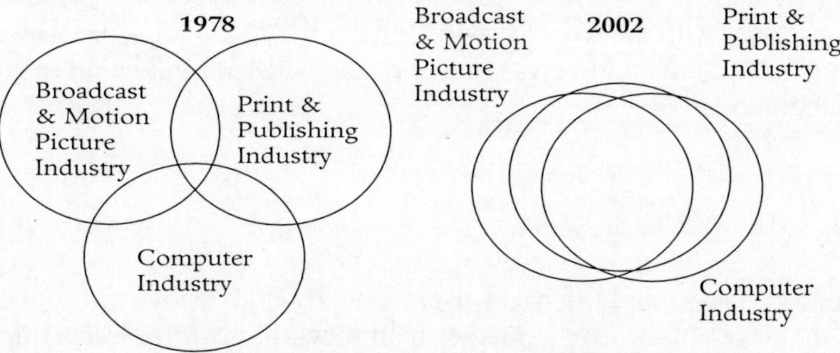

Figure 14.4
Converging industries

In the 1980s, entertainment, publishing and computers converged to create a wide array of innovative services and products. A wave of mergers resulted, as companies sought to achieve technical competence in all three technologies.

Case study: NBIC and digital convergence

The tidal wave of technological innovation that began in 1970 and ended in the 'techno-bubble' of March 2000 was led by four key technologies: materials science, microprocessors, computer software and biotechnology.

The next wave of technological innovation is now taking shape. It will be led by two types of converging technologies.

One is 'NBIC'—nanotechnology, biotechnology, information technology and cognitive science. NBIC will generate innovative new products that combine two or more of these technologies. Each of these technologies is highly complex. Success in 'NBIC' will require high-level collaboration.

The second type of convergence is 'digital convergence'—the emergence of appliances and devices that merge the functions of several existing technologies (e.g., cell phone, computer, PDA) through digital technology, i.e., conversion of voice, text and image data into digital (0,1) bits and bytes.

Each of these two convergences will generate large industries, and millions of jobs, for nations that gain competitive advantage in them. Competitive advantage, in turn, will rest crucially on the ability to weave partnerships among those with the required skills and knowledge. Companies who thrive in the fierce competition prevailing in those industries will be those good at collaboration.

Platform leadership

Annabelle Gawer and Michael Cusumano have built a powerful concept for collaborative competitive strategy which they call platform leadership:[14]

> Platform leadership is the ability of a firm to drive innovation around its particular platform at the broad industry level. The platform is located functionally at the heart of a variety of other products. Platform leaders operate within an ecosystem of firms, and set in motion a rapid pace of

innovation not only on their own product, but on the array of complementary products that function in conjunction with their own, resulting in virtuous cycle of interactions.

Case study: Intel Architecture Lab: Build an Ecosystem

Intel produces microprocessors (see Chapter 7 case study, 'Pentium M-Centrino'). This product is the brains of personal computers. In order for Intel's sales to grow more rapidly, demand for products that use Intel's microprocessors must grow. Intel can either sit and wait for this to happen or it can pursue 'platform leadership' and take pro-active measures to stimulate innovation of such products. The head of the Intel Architecture Lab, Craig Kinnie describes his mission is to '... grow the innovation which is occurring in the ecosystem that's creating opportunity for all the actors in the ecosystems in which Intel can participate'.[15]

Both technological convergence and platform leadership often require implementing a strategy of acquiring, or merging with, other firms with complementary technologies and skills. Such collaboration, within an existing old industry or with a burgeoning new one, demands skill in integrating the people, resources, skills and knowledge of two firms.

Build, Buy, Ally

A key management decision relates to build, buy, ally: Whether to *build* new capabilities (as for example, in the US Postal Service's decision to enter third-party logistics), to *buy* such capabilities from other organizations or to *ally* and collaborate to create them. As Jeff Weiss and Jonathan Hughes note, there are difficult trade-offs among the three options, related to the required time frame (buying and allying is faster than building), internal resources, complexity, control and integration.[16]

Case study: Third party logistics

This case shows how the US Postal Service deploys in order to respond to rapidly changing customer expectations of what a delivery service company must provide to win and keep their business. Since the 1990s, value added means offering third-party logistics services—logistics support, order fulfilment, inventory management, return merchandize

Case study continued

Case study continued

processing and limited merchandise assembly and repair. The decision the Postal Service faced was whether to develop the capability in-house, buy it or do it in partnership. Case 14.1 towards the end of this chapter presents the critical thinking in the organization to make a decision to collaborate—to seek a third party ally whose core business is third-party logistics. (See Case 14.1, 'US Postal Service, Strategic Alliance' for further details.)

Why collaborative joint ventures frequently fail

Business mergers are increasingly the principal way competitors collaborate. From the mid-1990s, there was a remarkable surge in merger activity in the US that later spread worldwide. One cause was the soaring stock market, that enabled companies to be acquired cheaply without cash and without overvalued shares.

The enormous popularity of merger strategies clashes directly with the bleak success record of such mergers. There is a fundamental paradox in the growth strategies of many technology-intensive global companies. In addition to organic growth—building labour, capital and productive capacity internally—growth by acquisition (merger & acquisition, 'M&A') is often a key part of collaborative competitive strategy. Yet it is now widely understood by senior managers that the post-merger performance of companies has generally (though not always) been poor. Most mergers do not achieve their objectives and the stock market performance of merged companies has been much poorer than the market average. A study by Deloitte, Touche Worldwide of 540 companies, mainly US, with sales revenues totalling $500 billion revealed that only about a third of the CEOs of acquiring companies were satisfied with the results. The subjective probability that a merger will be considered successful was only 9 per cent.

A study by Bridgewater Associates reveals[17]

> the 20 companies with the greatest merger-and-acquisition activity over the past four years, a group that includes Cisco Systems, AT&T and General Electric, are now being punished by Wall Street. Through 4 February 2002, their stocks were down an average 15 per cent since the beginning of 2002, compared with a decline of 5 per cent for the companies in the Standard & Poor's 500-stock index. Of the most acquisitive companies,

those who took on the heaviest debt loads to support their acquisitions were down more than 20 per cent through February 4.

Consider America OnLine (AOL). It rose to #271 (by sales revenue) in the Fortune 500 list for year 2000, with sales of $6.886 billion (up 44 per cent from 1999) and net profits of $1.232 billion. By having the largest number of subscribers, it positioned itself strongly to dominate the Internet Service Provider (ISP) market, not only in the US but also abroad, where its growth has been even stronger. After America On Line merged with Time Warner, AOL-Time Warner in 2001 posted the largest corporate loss in history, $54 billion, due to write-downs of merger-related assets. The merged firm continues to struggle.

Case study: M&A à la Cisco

On the opposite pole, consider Cisco Systems, the San Jose, California, company, specializing in networking hardware and software. Cisco and its CEO John Chambers are studied intensively by scholars and managers alike, because of their remarkable M&A growth strategy. Cisco's growth and profitability record during the 1990s were universally admired. In year 2000, Cisco had sales of $19 billion up 55.7 per cent from 1999, and earned $2.688 billion in profits, up 28 per cent from 1999. For the decade 1990–2000 earnings per share rose at a remarkable annual rate of 59 per cent, and total return to investors (capital gains and dividends) averaged 73.4 per cent yearly. Cisco achieved this rapid growth with consummate skill in acquiring companies whose knowledge and human resources it needed.

At the peak of its acquisition activity, Cisco acquired some 30 companies every year, one every 10 days. Cisco has a systematic well-defined approach for integrating a newly acquired firm into Cisco's business strategy and cultures. One key aspect of this approach was in 'pairing' a Cisco manager with a counterpart in the acquired company and ensuring that Cisco manager integrated the new employee in every possible way. Many companies sought to imitate Cisco's strategy of 'growth by acquisition' but lacked the model, skills and focus such strategy requires.

Why have mergers proven difficult and strategically disappointing? One reason is that a substantial proportion of M&As involve cross-border deals. The Economic Report of the President, 2002, notes: 'In 2001, 29 per cent of all announced mergers and acquisitions in which a US-headquartered firm was a party also involved either a foreign buyer or a foreign seller. This was a ... markedly higher percentage than was common during much of the 1970s and 1980s.' This adds more issues to the already formidable task of merging two companies—issues of communication, culture and management style across countries. Often M&A deals are led principally by the financial side of management and enormous effort is invested in the deal's financial structuring—valuation, deal structure, compensation for employees who leave or who remain, etc. But in many ways, finance is the easy part. Ultimately it is *people*, not money, who merge, bond, ally and work together; and it is on *them* that successful cross-border M&A integration and collaboration should focus.

And, of course, it is *people* whom our products and services are meant to serve. Above all, it is our customers with whom collaboration is most vital.

14.4 COLLABORATING WITH CUSTOMERS

Competition is *not* the heart of capitalism, though many believe it is. *Collaboration* is its heart—principally, collaboration with customers. Businesses whose products find their way to customers' hearts, literally, endure and prevail. Collaborating with customers is the heart of successful competitive strategy. This is a truth often forgotten. It is only when the butcher, baker and candlestick maker reveal their benevolence by truly understanding their customers' needs, and meeting them, that free markets work well, and they themselves survive and grow wealthy. Egoistic managers unable to 'read' the needs of others rarely survive.

Reading customer satisfaction

Most CEOs know that it costs on average 11 times more to acquire a *new* customer, than to retain the loyalty and business of an *existing* one. Why then do so many companies spend endless millions of dollars trying to acquire their *competitor*'s customers, rather *than truly satisfy their own*?

Customers acquired by advertising, gimmicks, price cuts or deals are like desert tumbleweed. These customers lack roots and will roll on to anyone who offers a better deal. Ask the cell phone companies.

Great global companies know how to do three things: *create* customer loyalty, *measure* it continually, and *act* to *retain* it. They understand the simple rule stated by Andy Taylor, CEO of Enterprise Rent-a-Car:

The only way to grow a business is to get customers to come back for more and tell their friends. This is the ultimate collaboration.

Customer loyalty builds *top-line* (revenue) growth, because happy customers tell other people. And it builds *bottom-line* (net profit) growth, because, as noted, it is far cheaper in the long run to keep clients than to lure new ones. The cheapest and most effective advertising is word-of-mouth—when the word is positive. When it is negative, as Malcolm Gladwell shows in *The Tipping Point,* you can lose your customers faster than you can swallow an aspirin.

> Once, Bain & Co. Director Frederick Reichheld attended a day-long benchmarking workshop led by Taylor and attended by other CEOs. Everyone in the room knew that customer satisfaction surveys were long, expensive and unsatisfactory but indispensable. [We have one such survey in our hand; it is four pages long, with 53 questions, and must have caused many customers to die of boredom. We doubt any useful information ever emerged.] And worse than that—a Bain & Co. study showed *zero correlation* between conventionally measured customer satisfaction and annual sales growth.

Taylor and his team had a solution. They had invented the impossible: An impossibly brief customer satisfaction survey that truly worked. It could be used in all 5,000 branches every day, and the results translated into immediate action. The questions simply asked about the quality of the rental experience, and *the likelihood they would rent again from Enterprise*, on a scale of one to ten.

Taylor focused solely on the 9s and 10s. Why? He wanted to zero in not on *satisfied* customers, but on what Babson College Professor Anirudh Dhebar calls *delighted* customers—those who tell their friends. He wanted to know the *drivers of delight*. '*Delight*, not satisfaction, builds loyalty. *Delight* is the ultimate goal of true collaboration with our customers.'

Reichheld refined Taylor's method into what has now become a widely-embraced method, known as NPS-Net Promoters Score. As Reichheld observes: 'You might be surprised that the average company in America, the median, has only 11 per cent positive net promoter scores (NPS). These are the same companies that are seeing their market research results give satisfaction scores ranging from 85 per cent to 90 per cent. Those average satisfaction scores are the same thing as 11 per cent net promoter scores. We've found that the one number you need to grow is not satisfaction; it is *the number of promoters that you have in excess of the number of detractors [see Action Learning below]*. By measuring net promoters, you'll be looking at the one number you need to grow.'[18]

Here is how NPS works. We suggest you try it on a random sample of your own customers.

Action learning

Calculate Your Net Promoters' Score

1. Select randomly a statistically valid sample of customers.
2. Ask each: 'How likely is it that you would recommend our company (or product) to a friend or colleague?' Answer on a scale of 1 to 10, where 1 is 'not likely at all', 10 is 'highly likely'.
3. Group your customers into '*Promoters*' (9 or 10), 'passively satisfied' (7–8) and '*detractors*' (6 or less). Subtract the percentage of detractors from the percentage of promoters. This is your Net Promoters' Score (NPS).

For benchmarking: some best-practice NPS Scores are: Harley-Davidson, 81 per cent; Amazon, 73 per cent; eBay, 71 per cent; Cisco, 56 per cent; FedEx, 56 per cent; Dell, 50 per cent.

How to use the NPS

1. Track NPS regularly and compare it across branches, products or regions (an example of within-firm benchmarking).
2. Use NPS to send a clear message to both managers and employees, about the crucial importance of promoters and the disastrous potential of detractors.
3. Interview selected promoters to find out the key drivers of their loyalty. (You may be surprised!) Interview selected detractors, to find out why they dislike your product. Strengthen the drivers, fix the problems quickly. CEOs themselves should conduct at least some of these interviews.

In 1995, when Taylor first began using his two-question method, Enterprise's corporate NPS average was only 68 per cent, while the lowest-scoring branch was 55 per cent. By 2003, the corporate average was 78 per cent and the lowest branch was 75 per cent. This means that the standard deviation of service quality had dropped almost to zero and the number of detractors had plummeted.

14.5 COLLABORATING WITH COLLEAGUES

Michael Porter, Harvard Business School Professor who invented the new discipline of competitive strategy with his 1980 best-selling book of the same name, defines the concept of value chain.

> **DEFINITION**
>
> - **Value Chain—The series of steps and processes through which a product passes, from start to finish, in order to create value for customers.**

There is an industry value chain and a separate value chain for an individual firm. According to Porter, the firm's value chain consists of the following:

- *Inbound logistics*: storing, inventory, shipping
- *Operations*: machining, packaging, maintenance, testing
- *Outbound logistics*: order fulfilment, transportation, distribution
- *Marketing and Sales*: channels, advertisement, promotion, pricing, selling
- *Service*: customer support, repair, installation, training
- *Procurement*: raw materials, parts, buildings
- *Technology Development*: R&D, innovation, design, redesign, process, automation
- *Human Resources Management*: recruitment, development, compensation, retention
- *Firm Infrastructure*: general management, legal, finance, accounting, public affairs, quality assurance
- *Business Intelligence: Strategy*
- *Customer Intimacy*

Each of these value chain steps demands high-level collaboration with the whole organization. And linking them smoothly one to another similarly requires first-rate teamwork. If any one of them is flawed, it will seriously detract from the ability of the product to create superior value and customer delight.

Another way to understand intra-firm collaboration is by noting the three disciplines in which, according to Tracy and Wiersma,[19] all competitive businesses must excel: (*i*) product leadership and innovation; (*ii*) operational excellence; and (*iii*) customer intimacy. Each of these three depends crucially on teamwork.

- Innovation management requires seamlessly integrating 'ideation' (coming up with workable creative ideas) with processes that get those ideas to market in a suitable rapid manner;
- Operational excellence seamlessly links all parts of the firm's internal value chain;
- Customer intimacy involves close cooperation in transmitting key information from those who deal with customers to whose who rarely see them, to understand and meet customer needs.

Businesses as teams

In many ways, a business that has excellent teamwork (a key part of operational excellence) is like a winning sports team. Here are two case studies that show why and how this is true.

Case study: Blue-collar teamwork vs white-collar stars

Few experts gave the Pistons much of a chance. The Detroit Pistons faced the Los Angeles Lakers in the 2004 US National Basketball Association final. LA had superstars Shaquille O'Neal and Kobe Bryant and had won many NBA crowns. Detroit had what sports commentators called a 'blue collar team'—players who worked hard, helped each other and never quit. Detroit had last won the NBA title in 1990.

This time, blue collar beat white collar. And collaboration defeated individual 'star' competition. Detroit won the best-of-seven series four games to one. In the final game, which they won, 100-87, Detroit led at one point by 25 points. It almost seemed as if LA had given up.

The victory made sports history. Piston owner William Davidson's Palace Sports & Entertainment company owns four sports teams. Three of those teams won national championships in 2004—Detroit Pistons (NBA), Detroit Shock (WNBA, the women's NBA) and Tampa Bay Lightning (National Hockey League, Stanley Cup winners).

Here are the collaborative management principles that Davidson and his company apply to achieve success.

Teamwork trumps stars

Davidson hired former star Joe Dumars as Pistons' President. Dumars was one of the few players to be named Most Valuable Player in an NBA

Case study continued

Case study continued

final (in 1990) without ever having been chosen for an NBA All-Star team. Dumars was a blue-collar hard-working player who gave 120 per cent to every game. He hired only players he knew would do the same.

Mutual support

Piston's Coach Larry Brown realized the only way he would succeed with the Pistons would be to (*a*) get them to *believe* they could win the championship, and (*b*) build a strategy based on team play. It baffled LA. When LA star Kobe Bryant evaded the Piston player guarding him, more often than not he encountered *another* Piston who quickly came over to help. 'We never stopped believing we could win,' said the NBA series Most Valuable Player Chauncey Billups. Journeyman player Billups had played and failed, with five teams—Boston, Toronto, Denver, Orlando and Minnesota—before he came to the Pistons. And like Dumars, Billups was chosen Most Valuable Player without ever having been an All-Star.

Case study: Lance Armstrong and the Tour de France

Legendary American cyclist Lance Armstrong won the Tour de France race a record six times in a row, overcoming life-threatening cancer while doing so. What motivated him to endure the endless days and months of training, to win the fifth and six races? Money? Fame? Glory? He had all of those already.

Says Armstrong: 'I did not want to let my team down.' He knew he owed everything to his superb supporting team of near-anonymous cyclists whose sole job it is to protect and position him—and he felt he had to win for their sake. In high-performance R&D teams, as in team cycling, *the goal of peer esteem* becomes far more important than monetary reward.

As Katzenbach and Smith note in their 2003 book *The Wisdom of Teams*: 'What is perhaps less well appreciated is how the opportunity (for teamwork) to meet clearly stated customer and financial needs *enriches jobs and leads to personal growth*.'[19] When global teamwork 'clicks', when it is working well and in top gear, team members love it. And happy workers are more productive and less likely to quit. And, they might add, in your organization, be sure to remember to celebrate team successes, as sports teams do. *Celebrated* success breeds more success.

Action learning

The Wisdom of Teams

The next time you are in a meeting, ask the participants to estimate the height of one of the group (chosen at random). Ask each to write down their guess on a piece of paper. Measure the person's height. Calculate the average of all the participants' guesses. Chances are, that average is very close to the correct height and probably closer to the correct height than more than half of the individual guesses!

Teams are wiser than individuals. Hence, in good teamwork, when team members speak, other members truly listen.

How does your teamwork rate?

There are seven characteristics of effective teamwork. Score a team in which you are a member (company, sports, or family) for each. Where are your strengths and weaknesses? And which of the seven are in urgent need of improvement?

Great teams have:

1. Clear common goals, with each team member committed to them;
2. Clear decision-making process;
3. Full commitment of all team members to close-knit cooperation;
4. Clear roles assigned to each team member;
5. Clear understanding by all about constraints, deadlines and resources;
6. Individual egos put into cold storage for the duration;
7. Clear measurable outputs, on which success or failure is defined.

14.6 CONCLUSION: HELLO, STRANGER

Two thinkers have written major books suggesting that the intimate collaboration that once characterized human society, enriched our lives and enabled it to survive and thrive is being destroyed by technology and ideology.

In *Bowling Alone*, author Robert Putnam argues that modern society is becoming increasingly impersonal; social contacts, community networks, even friendships, continue to diminish.[20] Increasingly, we even go bowling—a sport inherently team-oriented—by ourselves.

In *Company of Strangers*, Paul Seabright asks whether the great 5,000-year-old experiment—collaborative society, where small and large groups join to find win-win outcomes and improve human well-being—is coming to an end?[21]

There is evidence that the love of friends and family is a more important component of our happiness and well-being than even our material wealth and income. It would be truly ironic if a fundamental misunderstanding, that the heart of capitalism is *competition* rather than *collaboration*, weakened the system that has such enormous potential for building individual happiness and freedom.

Readers are invited to view 'Pillars of Profit: Segment #10, Competing by Collaborating', in the accompanying CD.

CASE STUDY 14.1

The US Postal Service, Strategic Alliance*

Case study discussion topics

1. Why did US Postal Service want to enter the third-party logistics market?
2. What were the three options available for entering this market? What were the advantages and disadvantages of each?
3. How does the author use the 'competency curve' to help guide the final decision?
4. How did the Postal Service go about finding an appropriate partner?
5. What financial analysis was carried out to compare the three options?

The US Postal Services no longer enjoyed a meaningful protection in its postal monopoly in the delivery of small packages. UPS, Federal Express (FedEx) and Roadway Package Express together enjoyed an

*This case study is a summary of the case authored by Rod DeVar.

Case study 14.1 continued

Case study 14.1 continued

85 per cent share (UPS holding two-thirds) of the $25 billion small-package delivery market. The three companies offered a superior array of value-added features that included parcel tracking, guaranteed delivery on specific days or time of day, electronic manifesting and discounted pricing for large volume customers. Their focus was on business-to-business opportunities (67 per cent of the market growing at 6 per cent annually) where delivery densities were high (lowest variable costs are achieved). US Postal Services had invested little into its package delivery service lines. Business correspondence and advertising mail had grown 3 per cent and 7 per cent annually for two decades and there was little incentive to protect share erosion. In the late 1980s electronic communications had arrived and was beginning to slow the growth of first-class mail. The only bright spot in the next century seemed to be the growth opportunities in small-package delivery. This was particularly true for home deliveries where UPS had a 47 per cent share (home deliveries comprised 31 per cent of the total market volume and was growing at 9 per cent annually). US Postal Service did not have the same depth in value-added services as its competitors, but it did have significant economies of scale. This had enabled it to price its services 20–30 per cent below UPS's published rates.

Aggressive downsizing that began in the late 1980s caused many companies in the postal services sector to look at outsourcing non-core functions, primarily the product-distribution activity. The result was a boom in the third-party logistics industry. In keeping with diverse customer needs, third-party logistics providers started to perform activities such as product assembly, inbound telemarketing, inventory purchasing, picking and packing, electronic data interchange (EDI) for order acceptance, return merchandise acceptance and refurbishing, receivables management and the like. UPS and FedEx saw these activities as a threat to their business. However, the phenomenal annual growth rate of most big third-party players (15–30 per cent) and the projections that the logistics industry would grow from a base of $6 billion annual sales to $50 billion by the end of the century, created interests in UPS and FedEx to create their own subsidiary units in logistics. Regardless of whether either of these companies made money through their new venture, US Postal Service believed it needed to respond to competitor activities by engaging in third-party logistics services, else it ran the risk of further eroding an already tenuous position.

While US Postal Service had multiple options to pursue a service solution, it concluded that the chosen solution had to meet the following criteria:

Case study 14.1 continued

Case study 14.1 continued

- There should be a positive cash flow within 24 months of the investment.
- The offer would have to be equal or superior to the competitions' offer.
- It would have to be approved by the Executive Committee (the senior management team that ran the Postal Service).

US Postal Service arrived at three options worthy of consideration:

- Build option—create third-party capabilities from within the Postal Service and make it a new line of service offering, similar to that of UPS and FedEx.
- Buy option—seek a Third-Party Logistics company with the right profile and purchase an equity position.
- Partner option—pursue strategy (2), but rather than purchasing a position in the company, establish a strategic alliance.

Understanding the trade-offs (scaling the walls of Pain and Gain)
The 'build' and 'buy' options would detract heavily from management's attention to its core product lines. These options would involve heavy dollar capital and legal/political capital. The 'build' and 'buy' options scaled and exceeded the wall of pain threshold on all three counts. However, using the same three measures, the 'partnering' option seemed to cause very little pain. Management would have virtually no involvement from the headquarters (HQ) on down to field operating units with the partner's business. A small amount of expense money for marketing efforts would be required and because the partner would be providing the third-party services US Postal Service would not be subjected to any legal or political controversy instigated by competitors. The 'build' and 'buy' strategies produced some gains in the area of unique competitive positioning, increased profits and greater service depth but not to the same degree to which the 'partnering' strategy was judged to produce.

Hidden costs
US Postal Service did a traditional cost analysis to determine the investment required to execute the 'build' and 'partner' options. The 'buy' option could not be fully assessed as a suitable company could not be identified. Further, a positive cash flow from the 'build' strategy could not be attained until the new venture was well into the third year of its

Case study 14.1 continued

Case study 14.1 continued

operations. The Marketing Department at US Postal Service felt that positive cash flow had to happen within two years of a new service venture. US Postal Service concluded that the only way to reduce costs of the 'build' option was to set up logistics support in fewer locations, but this would cause US Postal Service to lose the very points of value differentiation felt necessary to attract new business i.e., total distribution flexibility for the customer. This meant that if the customer had the densities of merchandise distribution, they could locate products in multiple warehouses around the country and use lower cost delivery options to attain next day or two day deliveries. The competitors' operations were in single sites or at most a few. The 'partner' option had very low start-up costs limited to marketing and some administration. Although through the 'partner' option, US Postal Service would be sacrificing possible eventual profits from its third-party logistics activities, it would begin showing positive cash contribution against costs from new package delivery sales early in year two.

The competency curve

Before outsourcing its distribution activities, US Postal Service had to first learn to trust the logistics service provider and that the latter would efficiently run this activity for it. For US Postal Service to be successful, it needed to demonstrate a high level of competency from the first sales call itself. Rather than racing down the learning curve, US Postal Service needed to climb a competency curve quickly if it hoped to establish a foothold in the third-party business. Clearly, competency would grow more gradually if US Postal Service chose the 'build' strategy. Customers would initially be sceptical and there would be difficulties as the company learned the business. The 'buy' strategy would give US Postal Service an instant offer. However, the negotiation for the deal would be long and public. In the interim, US Postal Service could begin teaming with the company to sell but it would be ad hoc and full marketing commitment would not be made. With the 'partnering' strategy, US Postal Service could produce an agreement quickly, train the sales force to identify leads, which could be turned over to the partner for further development and closing the sales.

Scale? scope? or both?

Providing third-party logistics support to customers would add the needed scope to US Postal Service's service line and equip the organization to better meet customers' emerging needs and stay

Case study 14.1 continued

Case study 14.1 continued

competitive. The questions before each strategy option were: 'Does the option bring about scope economies, scale economies, or both?' According to US Postal Services, the 'build' strategy allowed it almost no economies of scope. The proposition would perhaps facilitate shared marketing expenses through the use of existing sales force but did not provide for operational economies. Further, there would be losses in the third-party portion of the business with modest profits from increased package volumes. The scope and scale economy benefiting from the execution of a 'buy' strategy could only be speculated upon. It was likely that the package delivery profits would increase, but at the same time it was unlikely that US Postal Service would realize profits from its third-party investment for the first three years of operations. The 'partner' strategy would provide US Postal Services no profits (or losses) from the third-party logistics part of the business. All those gains would accrue to the partner. However, over the three years it was projected there would be significant scale gains from an increase in the package delivery business. Adopting the 'partner' solution meant adding scope without adding scope to gain scale.

US Postal Service eventually chose the 'partner' strategy. The partner selection process involved floating a detailed letter of intent to twenty of the largest third-party logistics firms in the business; five companies that seemed to best match US Postal Services' needs were selected; onsite visits and in-depth interviews by a team of professionals from US Postal Service were carried out; and after five months of assessments and deliberations a partner was selected. US Postal Services was confident that its new logistics service would give it a sustainable competitive advantage for quite some time.

CASE STUDY 14.2

i-flex Solutions—Collaborating with the Industry*

i-flex Solutions Ltd provides information technology solutions exclusively to the financial services industry. The company services 625 customers spread over 120 countries. With a penchant for entering the insurance vertical, i-flex acquired Castek, a Toronto-based company that

*Material from Websites in the public domain.

Case study 14.2 continued

Case study 14.2 continued

provided IT solutions for Property and casualty (P&C) insurance, in the year 2005.

In order to meet technology needs for policy requirements, insurance companies could either opt to buy large software suites, or could procure best-of-breed applications and then put great efforts in integrating them with existing legacy systems. There was a need to provide the insurance industry a component-based IT solution that was capable of improving response time in operational priorities such as supporting customer-centred business models as well as flexible product management and deployment. Recognizing the need for such a flexible, yet comprehensive solution, i-flex came up with an innovative solution that was capable of providing best-of-breed applications, with built-in integration. Very soon, Tokio Marine Management (TMM), New York, showed keen interest in incorporating i-flex's innovative insurance solution within its organization.

TMM is the manager for the insurance operations of Tokio Marine and Nichido Fire Insurance Co. Ltd. (Japan) in North America. TMM had two compelling reasons to replace its existing legacy system—deteriorating performance of the system, which had resulted in increased maintenance costs and the need to keep pace with market demands by rolling out new insurance products and by making changes to the existing products quickly and cost-effectively. With the incoming software required to fulfil these objectives, TMM floated a contract to replace its 'commercial lines policy-processing platform' with i-flex's insurance solution proposition that was centred on Castek's Insure3 policy administration platform and included 'best-of-breed' components from five other partners. After several months of intense interaction and demonstration of capabilities by multiple vendors, TMM zeroed in on three vendors (Hartford-based Insurity, California-based ePolicy Solutions and India-based i-flex solutions) to create the desired next generation solution.

The unique solution crafted by i-flex was set to revolutionize the technology platform of the insurance industry, and was being developed by collaborating with six other partners, each a leading player in its respective field. Each of the participating companies had to execute assigned tasks and responsibilities, to enable the development of the solution.

- i-flex was responsible for:

  —creating the consortium,
  —management of the group involved in the development and

Case study 14.2 continued

Case study 14.2 continued

'selling' the new system,
—system integration, and
—programme management.

- Appix (Richmond, VA) was to provide vital inputs on the subject matter along with P&C project management.
- Castek Software (Toronto, Canada) was to provide the Insure3 policy administration platform around which all other products would be integrated.
- CCH Insurance Services was to deliver industry-standard forms.
- Document Sciences was to provide the printing requirements through its Xpression tool set.
- ISO (Jersey City, NJ) was to provide rating services, statutory codes and custom-rating configuration.
- Systems Task Group International was to provide agency and direct billing functionality through its Renaissance billing tool set.

The above consortium enabled TMM to derive unparalleled technology efficiencies. Each of the products that formed part of the insurance solution was complete in itself, capable of accommodating the business needs of a specific business process. The i-flex solution roped in 'best-of-breed' products and provided an extensive suite of sophisticated products to TMM with the benefit of a single provider. It demonstrated the power of innovating through *Competing by Collaborating*.

Notes

1. Charles Darwin, *On The Origin of Species*, 1859, pp. 78–79.
2. The quote by Sir Edmund Hillary, first person to climb Mount Everest, is from the Foreword to *Peak Performance: Inspirational Business Lessons from the World's Top Sports Organizations*, by Clive Gilson, Mike Pratt, Kevin Roberts and Ed Weymes (New York: Texere, 2000), p. 7.
3. The quote by Murthy is from the article, 'Globalcorp, 2005', *The Economist*: The World in 2005 (available at www.economist.com).
4. Thomas Friedman's article in the New York Times is: 'It's a Flat World after All', *NYT*, 3 April 2005.
5. The quote by Robert Gilpin is from R. Gilpin, *Global Political Economy: Understanding the International Economic Order* (Princeton, NJ: Princeton University Press, 2001), p. 364.
6. The argument by Paul Samuelson that the US loses from globalization is found in 'Where Ricardo and Mill rebut and confirm arguments of mainstream economists supporting globalization'. *Journal of Economic Perspectives*. Summer 2004, pp. 135–46.

7. The Economist study on Global Innovation is: 'Harnessing Innovation: R&D in a Global Growth Economy'. *The Economist*, 2004 (available at www.economist.com).
8. The quote by Oskar Morgenstern is from: 'Game Theory', *Int. Encyclopedia of the Social Sciences, vol. 6,* David Sills, ed. (New York: Macmillan Co. and The Free Press, 1968), p. 62. See also Shlomo Maital and Sharone L. Maital, *Economic Games People Play* (New York: Basic Books, 1984).
9. The film *A Beautiful Mind*, starring Russell Crowe, is based on the biography of Nash by Sylvia Nassar.
10. Malcolm Gladwell, *The Tipping Point: How Little Things Can Make a Big Difference* (New York: Little, Brown, 2000).
11. For 'Tornados', see Geoffrey A. Moore, *Inside the Tornado: Marketing Strategies from Silicon Valley's Cutting Edge* (New York: Harper Business, 1995).
12. Robert Axelrod, *The Evolution of Cooperation*, Basic Books: New York, 1984; see also R. Axelrod, 'Effective choice in the Prisoner's Dilemma', *Journal of Conflict Resolution*, 24, 1980, pp. 3–26.
13. Adam Brandenburger and Barry Nalebuff, *Coopetition* (Boston, MA: Harvard Business School Press, 1997).
14. Annabelle Gawer and Michael A. Cusumano. 'What does it take to be a Platform Leader: Some recent lessons from Palm and NTT DoCoMo?' working paper, 2004, p. 1. See also: Annabelle Gawer and Michael A. Cusumano, *Platform Leadership: How Intel, Microsoft and Cisco Drive Industry Innovation* (Cambridge, MA: Harvard Business School Press, 2002).
15. Craig Kinnie's quote is from *Platform Leadership*, p. 111.
16. Build, buy, ally: see Jeff Weiss and Jonathan Hughes, 'Want Collaboration? Accept-and actively manage-conflict'. *Harvard Business Review*, March 2005, pp. 93–101.
17. Source for the Bridgewater study on Mergers and Acquisitions: *Business Week*, 25 February 2002, p. 33.
18. Frederick Reichheld. 'The One Number You Need to Grow', *Harvard Business Review*, December 2003.
19. The three disciplines of excellence are noted in Tracy and Wiersma. The Discipline of Market Leaders. Jon R. Katzenbach, Douglas K. Smith. *The Wisdom of Teams: Creating the High-Performance Organization* (New York: Harper Business, 2003).
20. Robert D. Putnam. *Bowling Alone: The Collapse and Revival of American Community* (New York: Simon and Schuster, 2000).
21. Paul Seabright, *The Company of Strangers: A Natural History of Economic Life* (Princeton, NJ: Princeton University Press, 2005).

Epilogue

TEN ESSENTIAL TOOLS

Before they take-off, pilots methodically prepare their aircraft for flight by running down a checklist.

We hope this book helps *you* launch your organization toward growth and profit, through winning strategy and focused innovation, based on powerful microeconomic concepts. Before take-off, we recommend that you ask yourself the questions on the following checklist, based on the 10 essential tools described in the preceding chapters of the book.

Tool #1: Price–cost–value

Q Have you invested the same creative energy in your business design [how you price your product, how you manage the cost of making and selling it, and how you create value for your customers] as you have in inventing the product itself? Have you visually benchmarked your price–cost–value dimensions against competitors?

Tool #2: The hidden costs of lost opportunities, the hidden benefits of intangible assets

Q Have you audited your operations, to detect hidden costs [especially, the cost of your shareholders' equity capital] and made them more visible or eliminated them? Have you made sure every dollar of cost, hidden or visible, has a person directly responsible for them? When you evaluate project proposals, do you take into account hidden benefits [including option value] and try to quantify them?

Tool #3: Managing tradeoffs: Even swaps

Q Have you identified the major trade-offs facing your organization? Have you captured all the gains that accrue to eliminating waste and inefficiency, *without* trade-offs? Does your trade-off decision process systematically compare costs and benefits of alternative choices, perhaps by using the 'even swap' approach?

Tool #4: Cost functions

Q Do you know how your costs change as your output and sales rise? Do you know the cost of producing one more unit of your good or service (i.e., marginal cost), as well as the average, or unit, cost? Can you split your costs into production (variable) and overhead (fixed) cost components, and accurately allocate fixed costs to each product? And do you know which of your products are most profitable?

Tool #5: Free lunch productivity

Q Do you know how productive your labour, capital, materials and knowledge are, relative to their cost, and do you track this regularly? Is the 'mix' of labour and capital optimal in the light of new technologies? Do you know how the gains in productivity of your workers divide between 'expensive' ones, driven by investment, and 'free lunch' ones, driven by working smarter.

Tool #6: Creating and measuring economies of scale and economies of scope

Q Can you lower costs by achieving higher volumes of production (scale)? Or by broadening the range of products and services your organization provides (scope)? Or perhaps by both? How can you best scale up your organization, and grow it?

Tool #7: Building and measuring learning curves

Q Is your organization good at learning, and quick to learn? Is this skill revealed in constantly declining costs as experience builds and cumulative production rises? Are errors freely admitted and truth told to enable steep learning curves? Is your organization's learning curve steeper than those of your competitors? Does your organization know what it knows?

Table E1
The 10 innovation tools

Tool #1	:	Price–Cost–Value
Tool #2	:	The Hidden Costs of Lost Opportunities, The Hidden Benefits of Intangible Assets
Tool #3	:	Managing Trade-offs: Even Swaps
Tool #4	:	Cost Functions
Tool #5	:	Free Lunch Productivity
Tool #6	:	Creating and Measuring Economies of Scale and Economies of Scope
Tool # 7	:	Building and Measuring Learning Curves
Tool # 8	:	Price and Income Sensitivity; Profit Pools
Tool # 9	:	The Psychology of Risk Taking
Tool # 10	:	The 2 × 2 Strategy Matrix

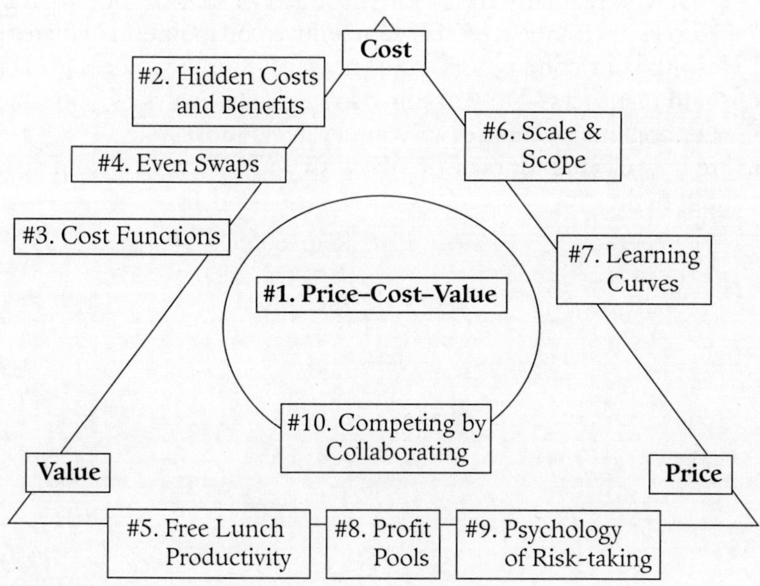

Figure E1
The 10 innovation tools on the price-cost-value tripod

Tool #8: Price and income sensitivity; profit pools

Q Do you know the price sensitivity of demand and income sensitivity of demand for your products and do you track them carefully? Does your strategy seek to reduce price sensitivity and avoid 'commoditization'? Do you know where the money is today in your industry? Do you know where the money *will be* in five years and are you positioning your organization and its products to be there?

Tool #9: The psychology of risk taking

Q Do you evaluate risks appropriately and accurately weigh risks and benefits? Do you avoid the many pitfalls associated with psychological biases and fallacies related to our odd behaviour toward odds? Do you know your own personal affinity for, or aversion to, risk?

Tool #10: The 2 × 2 Strategy matrix

Q Do you regularly seek win-win strategies? Does your organization excel in all four types of 'competitive collaboration': collaborating with your competitors, your industry, your customers, your fellow workers and managers? Do you think strategically, analysing your counterparts' or opponents' responses to your strategic moves?

You are now cleared for take-off. We wish you a successful, and above all, interesting, flight.

Index

About the Authors

Shlomo Maital is Academic Director of Technion Institute of Management (TIM), Israel's leading executive leadership development institute and a pioneer in action-learning methods, and Senior Researcher, S. Neaman Institute for Advanced Studies in Science and Technology, Technion. He was summer Visiting Professor for 20 years in MIT Sloan School of Management's Management of Technology M.Sc. programme, teaching over 1,000 R&D engineers from 40 countries. He is the author, co-author or editor of eight books including *Executive Economics* (The Free Press), translated into seven languages, and the recent *Managing New Product Development & Innovation*. He is co-editor of a new journal, *International Journal of Technology & Innovation Management Education*. He was a pioneer in behavioural economics and co-founder of SABE-Society for Advancement of Behavioural Economics, an academic society based in the USA and Canada. He has published over 80 scholarly articles in refereed journals. He has written guest editorials for *Barron's*, and writes regular col-umns for *Globes* (Israel's business daily) and *Jerusalem Report* (fortnightly). He served as Director of the National & Economic Planning Authority, Economics Ministry, Government of Israel. He initiated *USAToday*'s annual survey of total factor productivity growth among Fortune 100 companies. He has taught managers from 200 Israeli companies and consulted with such leading ones as Intel and Bank HaPoalim. His research currently focuses on profit-driven innovation—how to combine creativity and discipline to achieve marketplace success. He is a senior researcher at the S. Neaman Institute, Technion.

D.V.R. Seshadri is Visiting Faculty in the Marketing area at the Indian Institute of Management (IIM), Bangalore. His areas of interest are: Strategy, Business-to-business Marketing including Value-based Marketing, Corporate Entrepreneurship and Innovation. He holds a B. Tech. (Mechanical Engineering) from IIT, Madras (1978), M.S. (Engineering Sciences) from University of California, San Diego and a Fellow title (Doctorate) from IIM Ahmedabad. His specialization area during the doctoral programme at IIM Ahmedabad was in Production and Quantitative Methods.

Seshadri has over 15 years of industrial experience. This includes a five-year stint at Madras Refineries Limited in the computer control and refinery optimization areas and a three-year stint with a Chennai-based drugs and pharmaceuticals group, where he was involved in setting up from grass-roots level, several medium-sized bulk drug and pharmaceuticals projects. Prior to joining the Institute, he spent seven years as the Managing Director of a world-class compact disc manufacturing facility, where he was responsible for implementation and subsequent operation of the unit. This company had extensive technical collaboration with a major Japanese company. Concurrently, he was also the Managing Director of a software company, involved in multimedia, animation and application software.

During his academic career over the last six years, he has developed a number of case studies and research papers in his areas of interest. He teaches extensively in various executive education programmes of the institute. He offers the 'Business Marketing Strategies' course to second-year participants in the institute's two-year post-graduate programme in management (PGP) and to three-year post-graduate programme for software managers (PGSEM). He teaches 'Reinventing Government' in the institute's PGPP (one-year post-graduate programme on public policy for civil services officers) programme and 'Venturing through Entrepreneurial/Intrapreneurial Leadership' to PGSEM participants at IIM Bangalore. He also teaches 'Strategy Formulation and Implementation' to second-year PGP students and courses on B2B Marketing and Intrapreneurship in the one-year executive MBA (PGPX) programme at IIM Ahmedabad. He works closely with several companies in India and provides training/consulting services to them in India in his areas of expertise.